早稲田大学学術叢書 42
Waseda University Academic Series

An Automodular View of Ellipsis

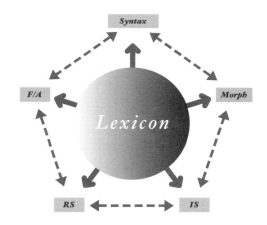

Yoshio Ueno

早稲田大学出版部
Waseda University Press

An Automodular View of Ellipsis

Yoshio Ueno is professor of linguistics at the Center for English Language Education in Science and Engineering, Waseda University and was visiting scholar at the Department of Linguistics, the University of Chicago in the academic year of 2012/13.

First published in 2015 by
Waseda University Press Co., Ltd.
1-9-12 Nishiwaseda
Shinjuku-ku, Tokyo 169-0051
www.waseda-up.co.jp

© 2015 by Yoshio Ueno

All rights reserved. Except for short extracts used for academic purposes or book reviews, no part of this publication may be reproduced, stored in a retrieval system or transmitted in any form whatsoever—electronic, mechanical, photocopying or otherwise—without the prior and written permission of the publisher.

ISBN978-4-657-15706-5

Printed in Japan

Contents

Preface

Introduction 1
    About this book   1

1 Automodular Grammar Overview 5
    1.1   Syntax Overview   5
    1.2   Function Argument Structure Overview   14
    1.3   Event Role Structure Overview   24
    1.4   Information Structure Overview   31
    1.5   Lexical Items and Lexical Entries   32
    1.6   Brief Discussion on Raising   34
        1.6.1   Subject raising   34
        1.6.2   Object raising   39
    1.7   Brief Discussion on Unique Control Verbs   44
    1.8   Brief Discussion on Passivization   47
        1.8.1   Agentless passives of transitive verbs   47
        1.8.2   Passivization of object raising and object control verbs   51
        1.8.3   Passivization of VP idioms   52
    1.9   Brief Discussion on Unbounded Dependencies   54

2 Inferential Interpretation 61
    2.1   Inferential Nature of Utterance Interpretation and Relevance Theory   61
    2.2   Preliminary Considerations on Inferential Interpretation of Fragments   70
    2.3   Review of SA and LA Superstructures   78
    2.4   Inferential Nature of Illocutionary Force Identification   86
    2.5   Indirect Speech Acts and Implicatures   89

3 An Automodular View of Fragments 93
    3.1   Preliminary Description of Fragments   93
    3.2   Explaining Fragment Interpretation   95

	3.3	Properties of Fragments		109
		3.3.1	Fragments with parentheticals	109
		3.3.2	Ban on complementizer deletion	111
		3.3.3	Apparent c-selection	113
		3.3.4	Fragments as focus	113
		3.3.5	Controlled VPs as fragments	114
		3.3.6	Three types of inferred syntax	117
		3.3.7	Quantifier fragments	120
		3.3.8	Bound variables in fragments	121
		3.3.9	Fragments and pronouns	122
		3.3.10	Island insensitivity of fragments	125
	3.4	Access to Lexical Entries		128
	3.5	Language Acquisition and Preposition (Non)Stranding		133
		3.5.1	Fragments and acquisition of syntax	134
		3.5.2	Acquisition of preposition stranding	134
4	An Automodular View of Sluicing			141
	4.1	Preliminary Description of Sluicing		141
	4.2	Syntax of *Wh*-Fragments		145
	4.3	Interpreting *Wh*-Fragments		147
	4.4	*Wh*-Fragments and Inference		149
	4.5	Need for Syntactic Structures Inferred by Direct Reference		153
	4.6	Multiple *Wh*-Fragments		157
	4.7	*The Hell*		159
	4.8	Access to Lexical Entries		161
	4.9	Island Insensitivity		166
	4.10	Close Examination of *Wh*-Fragment Island Insensitivity		169
		4.10.1	Relative clause island	169
		4.10.2	Conjunct Constraint	171
		4.10.3	Element Constraint	173
		4.10.4	Derived position islands	175
		4.10.5	Adjunct Island and Sentential Subject Constraint	178
		4.10.6	COMP-trace effects	179
		4.10.7	Weak islands	180
		4.10.8	Left Branch Constraint	183
	4.11	A'-traces Under Sluicing		193

5 An Automodular View of VP Ellipsis 195
- 5.1 VP Gap Analysis of VP Ellipsis — 195
- 5.2 Pro-VP Form Analysis of VP Ellipsis — 197
- 5.3 Similarities and Differences Between Pro-VP Forms and Pronouns — 216
- 5.4 Lexical Entries for Pro-VP Forms — 224
- 5.5 Missing Antecedent Phenomenon — 234
- 5.6 Syntactic Status of Inferred VP — 238
- 5.7 Antecedent Contained Deletion — 243
- 5.8 Ambiguity in Pro-VP Form Interpretations — 252
- 5.9 Strict and Sloppy Identity Interpretations — 255
- 5.10 Restrictions on VP Ellipsis — 257
  - 5.10.1 VP ellipsis in *tough* construction — 257
  - 5.10.2 Disappearance and reappearance of sloppy identity interpretation — 262

6 An Automodular View of Gapping 265
- 6.1 Preliminary Description of Gapping — 265
- 6.2 Gapping and Inference — 271
- 6.3 Gapping as Construction — 279
- 6.4 Speaker's Intention in Gapping — 297
- 6.5 Interpreting Gapped Conjuncts — 300
- 6.6 Gapping and Speech Acts — 317
- 6.7 Operator Sharing in Gapping — 319
- 6.8 Stripping — 327

7 An Automodular View of Right Node Raising 341
- 7.1 Preliminary Description of Right Node Raising — 341
- 7.2 RNR as a Construction — 351
- 7.3 Inferentially Interpreting the RNR Construction — 361

8 Conclusion 371
- 8.1 Summary of Chapter 1 — 371
- 8.2 Summary of Chapter 2 — 373
- 8.3 Summary of Chapter 3 — 376
- 8.4 Summary of Chapter 4 — 381

8.5	Summary of Chapter 5	383
8.6	Summary of Chapter 6	387
8.7	Summary of Chapter 7	392
8.8	Epilogue	396

Appendix: Definitions, Rules, and Principles 399
References 419
Index 425

Preface

An Automodular View of Ellipsis investigates major types of ellipsis in English, namely, fragments, sluicing, VP ellipsis, gapping, and Right Node Raising and analyzes them using a multi-modular approach known as Automodular Grammar (AMG), the latest version of which is presented in Jerrold M. Sadock (2012) *The Modular Architecture of Grammar*, Cambridge University Press, and is further explored in my previous book, Ueno (2014) *An Automodular View of English Grammar*, Waseda University Press.

As was the case with my previous book, while writing this book, I always had in mind two pieces of advice that the late Jim McCawley gave me as a student at the University of Chicago. The first was to learn not just one but several approaches and try to see the advantages and disadvantages of each, and the second was that once you have decided which approach to take for your linguistic analysis, you must apply it thoroughly and consistently to as large a set of data as possible. As for his first piece of advice, this book is greatly influenced in many ways by various approaches to ellipsis including not only Jerry Sadock (1974, 2012) and Jim McCawley (1993b, 1998) but also Culicover and Jackendoff (2005), Kuno (1976), Merchant (2001, 2004), and relevance-based approaches such as Sperber and Wilson (1995), Carston (2002), and Wilson and Sperber (2012). As for his second piece of advice, I tried to explore the full potential of Jerry's latest formulation of AMG, presented in Sadock (2012), and show that the essential design feature of AMG, the multi-modularity of grammar, has interesting advantages over other approaches to ellipsis comprehension, when combined with an inferential model of human communication such as Relevance Theory.

I am well aware that the AMG view of ellipsis comprehension presented in this book is only one of the many possible alternative multi-modular views. I believe that the worth of publishing this work lies in promoting research on similar approaches to the grammars of natural languages in general and on ellipsis comprehension in particular.

The first draft was completed in 2012 while I was at the University of Chicago as a visiting scholar. I cannot thank Jerry enough for reading not only the first draft of my previous book but also that of the current book and giving me a lot of suggestions and comments. Without his support, it would have been impossible to publish these two books. I would also like to express my gratitude to Amy Dahlstrom, my LFG teacher, who was kind enough to be my sponsor at Chicago, and to Jason Merchant, chair of the linguistics department, who kindly gave me useful information about recent literature on ellipsis. I am extremely grateful to three anonymous reviewers for their comments and suggestions, which were very helpful and informative. For comments and encouragement I received at various stages of this book project, I would like to thank Hisano Nakamoto, Saeko Reynolds, Yoko Sugioka, Etsuyo Yuasa, and Ichiro Yuhara. On this very occasion, I would also like to extend my sincere gratitude to Ray Jackendoff and my teachers here in Japan, Shuji Chiba, Masaru Kajita, Heizo Nakajima, and Ken-ichi Takami for their comments and encouragement I received when I published my previous book. Finally, I would like to thank Atsushi Kanamaru and Naomasa Tanabe, Waseda University Press, for their painstaking editorial work. The publication of this book and that of my previous book were made possible by publishing grants from Waseda University, for which I am most grateful.

Introduction

About this book

This book concerns some of the elliptic phenomena in English, namely, fragments, sluicing, VP ellipsis, gapping, and Right Node Raising, and analyzes them from a multi-modular view of English grammar, according to which English, or for that matter, any natural language, is precisely described and adequately explained as a result of interactions between several autonomous modules.

The multi-modular view of English grammar that is assumed in this book is a version of Automodular Grammar (AMG) as presented in Sadock (2012) and extended in Ueno (2014). AMG is a non-derivational approach and hence does not employ "transformations" (movements, insertions, or deletions). Each of the autonomous modules is generative in its own way and formulated in context-free phrase structure grammar (CFPSG). Each module only performs its own work with its own primitives and rules. All modules are connected by the interface including intermodular default correspondences. Because of this architecture, lexical entries and lexical rules are stated module by module, which forms the basis of the interface.

It is agreed across all theoretical persuasions that lexical entries, at least, consist of syntactic information, semantic information, and phonological information. This is a standard and traditional view. Consider that each type of information can be diachronically affected independently of the other types of information and that each type of information for a lexical item can be learned separately from the other types of information in language acquisition. AMG is a natural extension of this view in that there is a set of generative rules behind each type of lexical information.

This book is organized as follows. Chapter 1 Automodular Grammar Overview provides an overview of and a rapid introduction to the version of AMG assumed in this book and presents a brief sketch of the modules that are needed in later chapters, namely, Syntax, Function Argument (F/A) Structure, Event Role (E/R) Structure, and Information Structure (IS). In addition, we will briefly review how such phenomena as raising, control, passivization, and unbounded dependencies are dealt with in this version of AMG. The content of this chapter is based on Sadock (2012) and Ueno (2014) with some minor revisions. Readers can find the details of each topic briefly covered in Chapter 1 in these works. In Chapter 2 Inferential Interpretation, we will discuss the inferential nature of utterance comprehension in general and ellipsis comprehension in particular. We will also introduce such basic notions as relevance, explicatures, and implicatures on the basis of the inferential model of communication explored in Relevance Theory (Sperber and Wilson 1995, Carston 2002, Wilson and Sperber 2012, and Clark 2013). We will also revisit speech act aspects of utterance meaning, which were discussed in Chapter 7 of Ueno (2014), and examine the inferential nature of speech act comprehension. We will argue that the ability to use fragments (e.g., one-word utterances) is acquired very early in children's language acquisition, enabled by human inferential ability and that the learning of other forms of ellipsis such as sluicing, VP ellipsis, and gapping comes later. Therefore, we will reason that it would be surprising if humans, when comprehending other types of ellipsis, did not use their inferential ability, which has been at their disposal from birth. We will conclude that it is quite reasonable to assume that when these elliptic forms are interpreted, the same type of inference that is involved in fragment interpretation is also involved. In Chapter 3 An Automodular View of Fragments, we will discuss various kinds of fragments in discourse and show how inference plays an important role in fragment interpretation. Fragments provide a strong motivation to assume extra-grammatical pragmatic inference processes, without which they cannot be accounted for adequately. Fragments are peculiar in two ways: that children learn to use them very early before the acquisition of syntax; and that non-demonstrative inference plays a bigger role in fragment interpretation than in the interpretation of any other ellipsis type. We will formulate the procedure of fragment utterance interpretation based on the procedure of sentential utterance interpretation. The former will be applied to other ellipsis types discussed in later chapters. In Chapter 4 An Automodular View of Sluicing, we will discuss various properties of sluicing including its island insensitivity and explain them from our AMG and Relevance Theoretic perspectives. We will call sluiced *wh*-phrases "*wh*-fragments" and treat them identically to the fragments discussed in Chapter 3. In Chapter 5 An Automodular View of VP ellipsis, we will discuss various phenomena related to what has been called "VP ellipsis" and claim that these are best explained by categorizing VP ellipses as auxiliary verbs used as pro-VP forms. That is, each auxiliary verb "left behind after VP deletion" will be treated as an anaphoric device (AD). In Chapter 6 An Automodular View of Gapping, we will examine various properties of gapping and claim that gapping is best explained by formulating it as a construction that involves a coordinate structure. This approach to gapping can be easily extended to stripping. In Chapter 7 An Automodular View of Right Node Raising, we will examine various properties of Right Node Raising (RNR) and analyze them from our multi-modular perspectives. We will extend a constructional analysis to RNR. In Chapter 8 Conclusion, we will summarize each chapter and add some remarks.

In each chapter, we will present basic data on these phenomena and describe their properties: where they can occur in syntactic structures (e.g., whether or not restricted to coordinate structures), how they interact with each other in discourse, and how they are interpreted. Through close examination of these elliptic phenomena, we would like to (i) show that pragmatic (non-demonstrative) inference plays a crucial role in determining the explicatures and implicatures (intended interpretations) of ellipses, and (ii) propose an AMG analysis of these phenomena by taking into consideration the observation that ellipsis comprehension is inferential. This approach will offer a simpler account of ellipsis than purely syntactic approaches such as those that have been pursued in Mainstream Generative Grammar (MGG). In other words, we would like to strike a proper balance between grammar and inferential pragmatics in the domain of ellipsis comprehension.

Ellipsis has often been explained by the "deletion transformation" that is applied to syntactic structures. However, because AMG's syntax module is monostratal (i.e., there is no derivation in syntax and hence no distinction between D-structure and S-structure), "deletion transformation" does not exist as such in AMG.

Through close examination of the comprehension process of fragments, sluicing, VP ellipsis, gapping, and RNR, the following picture of language comprehension (Chapter 3 (5b)) will emerge.

elliptic utterance U → Language Module → decoded four-tuple of U → Inferential Comprehension Module → inferred four-tuple of U → developed four-tuple of U → explicatures and implicatures of U (in Mentalese)

The Language Module (LM) consists of several autonomous submodules including syntax, F/A, E/R, and IS, which are each purely representational and static in that the LM only computes the representation of an utterance in each submodule.

By contrast, the Inferential Comprehension Module (ICM) is fully derivational and dynamic in that it constructs the explicatures and implicatures of an utterance that maximize their relevance.

Ellipsis comprehension processes proceed as follows. First, the LM computes the decoded four-tuple (syntax, F/A, E/R, IS) of an elliptic utterance U. Second, the ICM inferentially constructs its inferred four-tuple on the basis of its decoded four-tuple and the accessible contextual assumptions at the time of comprehension. Finally, the ICM inferentially constructs the explicatures and implicatures of U on the basis of the inferred four-tuple of U. The construction of the inferred four-tuple of U and its explicatures and implicatures is all guided by the Relevance-guided comprehension heuristic (Chapter 2 (8)).

Because the ICM is very powerful, readers might wonder if this ellipsis comprehension process accepts too many utterances (i.e., a danger of overgeneration) including those that have been excluded as ungrammatical in the previous literature. However, we will show in each subsequent chapter that most of those utterances that have been excluded as ungrammatical are excluded as such by reducing them to the ungrammaticality of their decoded or inferred four-tuple representations. Therefore, this approach will correctly predict that there are utterances in real verbal communication that are ill-formed in terms of grammar but have clear intended meanings (i.e., explicatures and implicatures). In our terms, some utterances have ill-formed decoded/inferred four-tuple representations but the ICM still constructs their explicatures and implicatures.

Chapter 1
Automodular Grammar Overview

> The aim of this chapter is to provide an overview of and a rapid introduction to the version of AMG assumed in this book by presenting a brief sketch of the modules that are needed in later chapters, namely, Syntax, Function Argument (F/A) Structure, Event Role (E/R) Structure, and Information Structure (IS). In addition, we will briefly review how such phenomena as raising, control, passivization, and unbounded dependencies are dealt with in this version of AMG. The content of this chapter is based on Sadock (2012) and Ueno (2014) with some minor revisions. For the details of each topic briefly covered in this chapter, readers are referred to those works.

1.1 Syntax Overview

We adopt the phrase structure grammar (PSG) (1) for the syntax module of English. All the PS rules in (1) only show constituent structures without specifying the linear order between sisters. The underlying assumption here is that the linear order between sisters is specified separately from the specification of constituent structures along the lines of GPSG's ID/LP format. See (59).

The PS rules such as [$_{VP}$ V, NP], [$_{PP}$ P, NP], or [$_{CP}$ C, S] that introduce the lexical head (indicated by the symbol H[0], a head (H) with <BAR, 0>) of a headed phrase and its complements are not listed in (1), because they constitute lexical information and are included in the syntactic field of each lexical entry. Therefore, except (1a, b), the PS rules in (1) are all adjunction rules for modification.

(1) PS rules for syntax module (cf. Ueno 2014: 15)
    a. [$_S$ NP, VP]   b. [$_{NP[DET]}$ NP[POS], NP]   c. [$_{NP}$ {A | RRC}, NP]

d. [$_{HP}$ {PP | ADVP}, HP], where H ∈ {A, V, P}
e. [$_{HS}$ {PP | ADVP}, HS], where H ∈ {A, V, P} (See (2).)

In (1b), NP[DET] is an NP with a determiner (DET), which includes a possessive NP (NP[POS]). For example, the internal syntax of *the boring book* is [$_{NP[DET]}$ [$_{DET}$ *the*] [$_{NP}$ [$_A$ *boring*] [$_N$ *book*]]] and that of *Mary's boring book* is [$_{NP[DET]}$ [$_{NP[POS]}$ [$_{NP}$ *Mary*] *'s*] [$_{NP}$ *boring book*]]. The POS and DET features are unary features. That is, if an NP appears with a determiner, its category is NP[DET], whereas if it appears without a determiner, its category is NP. Therefore, although, strictly speaking, we need to use NP[(DET)] to refer to both an NP with a determiner and an NP without, we will use NP for brevity, if it is clear that it is intended as NP[(DET)]. Note that [$_{NP[DET]}$ DET, NP] is not included in (1), because this constitutes lexical information and belongs to the syntactic field of the lexical entry for each determiner.

In (1c), RRC stands for restrictive relative clause, which includes what McCawley (1998: 393) called a reduced relative clause such as *any person proud of himself*, *the little house on the prairie*, and *a child taking a nap*.

We will use the terms subject and object (in syntax) only for descriptive purposes and not as theoretical primitives to respectively refer to the NP in (1a), namely, the NP that is directly dominated by an S and is a sister of a VP and the NP that is directly dominated by a VP and is a sister of a V.

All syntactic categories are sets of feature-value pairs. The part-of-speech (POSP) feature takes as its value N, V, A, P, ADV, DET, PRT (particle), PN (pronoun), CNJ (coordinating conjunction), etc. The BAR feature, following McCawley (1998), distinguishes between words (<BAR, 0>) and phrases (<BAR, 1>). The defining characteristic of a headed phrase is that a lexical head (<BAR, 0>) takes its complement(s), if any, and forms a phrase (<BAR, 1>). For example, a noun is {<POSP, N>, <BAR, 0>} and a noun phrase is {<POSP, N>, <BAR, 1>}. A verb is {<POSP, V>, <BAR, 0>} and a verb phrase is {<POSP, V>, <BAR, 1>}.

Following GPSG and HPSG, we take the V of a clause S (i.e., [$_S$ NP, VP]) as the syntactic head of S. We will use S to refer to categories of clausal level (<BAR, 2>). An ordinary S is a clause headed by a verb, and hence it is denoted as VS (= {<POSP, V>, <BAR, 2>}). A clause headed by an adjective such as *Is* [$_{AS}$ *Mary* [$_{AP}$ *afraid of dogs*]]? is denoted as AS (= {<POSP, A>, <BAR, 2>}). A clause headed by a preposition such as *Is* [$_{PS}$ *Mary* [$_{PP}$ *in the room*]]? is denoted as PS (= {<POSP, P>, <BAR, 2>}). A clause headed by a noun such as *Is* [$_{NS}$ *Mary* [$_{NP[DET]}$ *a student of mathematics*]]? is denoted as NS (= {<POSP, N>, <BAR, 2>}). In this respect, we treat CP, a phrase whose head is a complementizer (C) as clausal (<BAR, 2>). That is, CP = {<POSP, C>, <BAR, 2>}. The situations described so far are summarized in (2).

(2) BAR values in syntax (cf. Ueno 2014: 15)

category	N	V	A	P	ADV	C
<BAR, 0>	N	V	A	P	ADV	C
<BAR, 1>	NP	VP	AP	PP	ADVP	
<BAR, 2>	NS	VS(=S)	AS	PS		CP

We assume a very loose version of the Head Feature Convention (HFC) for default cases, which can be overridden by specific requirements (cf. Gazdar et al. 1985: 94ff.) such as lexical information.

(3) Head Feature Convention (HFC) (Ueno 2014: 16)
In each headed local tree, the mother and its head daughter must meet conditions (i) and (ii), unless otherwise specified.
  (i) The set of head features on the mother is identical to that on its head daughter.
  (ii) For each head feature in (i), its value on the mother is identical to that on the head daughter.

(4) list of head features (Ueno 2014: 16)
BAR, form features (NFORM, PFORM, VFORM, and CFORM),
POSP (part of speech), AUX, INV,
AGR (agreement), which subsumes PER (person), NUM (number), and GEN (gender)

(5) list of VFORM values (Ueno 2014: 17)
BSE (base form), PRP (present participle form), PSP (past participle form), PAS (passive participle form), *to*,
FIN (finite), which subsumes PRES (present tense) and PAST (past tense)

Here are examples of various clause structures. In (6), the verb *want* takes an S[*to*] complement, which is a clause headed by *to*, whose lexical entry is given in (12c).

(6) a. John wants Mary to stay home.
    b. [$_{S[PRES]}$ John [$_{VP[PRES]}$ [$_{V[PRES]}$ wants] [$_{S[to]}$ Mary [$_{VP[to]}$ [$_{V[to]}$ to] [$_{VP[BSE]}$ stay home]]]]].

In (7), the verb *arrange* takes a CP[*for*] complement, a complementizer phrase (CP) headed by the complementizer (C) *for*, whose lexical entry is given in (12e).

(7) a. John arranged for Mary to stay home.
   b. [$_{S[PAST]}$ John [$_{VP[PAST]}$ arranged [$_{CP[for]}$ [$_{C[for]}$ for] [$_{S[to]}$ Mary [$_{VP[to]}$ to stay home]]]]].

In (8), the verb *count* takes a PP[*on*] complement, a prepositional phrase headed by the preposition *on*. The preposition *on*, in turn, takes an S[PRP] complement, a clause headed by a verb in the present participle form (V[PRP]).

(8) a. John counted on Mary staying home.
   b. [$_{S[PAST]}$ John [$_{VP[PAST]}$ counted [$_{PP[on]}$ [$_{P[on]}$ on] [$_{S[PRP]}$ Mary [$_{VP[PRP]}$ staying home]]]]].

In (9), the verb *seem* takes a VP[*to*] complement. This is an example of subject raising.

(9) a. John seems to like Mary.
   b. [$_{S[PRES]}$ John [$_{VP[PRES]}$ seems [$_{VP[to]}$ to [$_{VP[BSE]}$ like Mary]]]].

In (10), the verb *persuade* takes two complements, NP and VP[*to*]. This is an example of object control.

(10) a. John persuaded Mary to stay home.
    b. [$_{S[PAST]}$ John [$_{VP[PAST]}$ persuaded [$_{NP}$ Mary] [$_{VP[to]}$ to [$_{VP[BSE]}$ stay home]]]].

The subject-verb agreement is achieved in syntax through the PS rule (11), which is an elaboration of (1a).

(11) subject-verb agreement (Ueno 2014: 18)
    [$_{S[FIN, AGR[3SGN]]}$ NP[AGR[α, β]], VP[FIN, AGR[α, β]]],
    where α is a PER value with α ∈ {1, 2, 3}, and β is a NUM value with β ∈ {SG, PL}.

The AGR feature is one of the head features listed in (4) and consists of three features: PER with its values 1, 2, and 3, NUM with its values SG and PL, and GEN with its values M, F, and N. In English subject-verb agreement, only PER and NUM are relevant. (11) says that the AGR values are shared in a finite clause between its subject NP and finite VP. The AGR value on the mother node S[FIN] is specified as third person singular neuter (<PER, 3>, <NUM, SG>, <GEN, N>). Because AGR is a head feature, the AGR value on VP and that on its head V must be shared, due to the HFC (3). However, because the AGR value is already specified on the mother S (= V[2]) node in (11), the HFC (3) does not force the VP's AGR value AGR[α, β] onto the mother S[FIN, AGR[3SGN]].

For ease of future reference, we will give sample lexical entries in (12), including lexical information about the semantic modules F/A and E/R, which will be reviewed in 1.2 and 1.3. Some lexical items are defective in that they lack their representation in one or more modules, which is indicated as *nil* in (12c, d, e). As for the syntactic field of a lexical entry, we adopt the convention that we omit the phrasal category of the subcategorization frame in question: for example, "V in [__ , NP]" in place of "V in [$_{VP}$ __ , NP]," because the categorical information of a phrasal node is predictable from the categorical information of the head by the HFC.

(12) sample lexical entries with annotations (Ueno 2014: 19–20)
    a. *sneeze*
        syntax: V (syntactic category: verb) in [__] (subcategorization frame: [$_{VP}$ __])
        F/A: Fa (a functor that takes one argument and returns a proposition: [$_{PROP}$ Fa, ARG])
        E/R: [$_{TYPE}$ "sneeze"] in [$_{EV}$ __ AG] (a verb that denotes an event (EV) that takes one participant role, namely, agent (AG))
        morph: V[0] (morphological category: verb stem)
        mphon: [$_{V[0]}$ /sni:z/] (the other forms are supplied by the morphophonological rules for regular verbs (Ueno 2014: 10))

    b. *take*
        syntax: V in [__ , NP]
        F/A: Faa (a functor that takes one argument and returns an Fa: [$_{Fa}$ Faa, ARG])
        E/R: [$_{TYPE}$ "take"] in [$_{EV}$ __ AG PT] (a verb that denotes an event (EV) that takes two participant roles, namely, agent (AG) and patient (PT))
        morph: V[0]

mphon: [$_{V[0]}$ /teɪk/], [$_{V[1, PAST]}$ /tʊk/], [$_{V[1, PSP]}$ /teɪkən/] (the other forms are supplied by the morphophonological rules for regular verbs (Ueno 2014: 10))

c. *to*
syntax: V[AUX, *to*] in [__, VP[BSE]] (a non-finite auxiliary verb (AUX) with <VFORM, *to*> that takes a VP[BSE] complement, which is a VP headed by a verb in the base form (V[BSE]))
F/A: nil (no representation in F/A)
E/R: nil (no representation in E/R)
morph: W (word, a morphological category {<BAR, 1>}, which means no inflection or derivation.)
mphon: [$_W$ /tə/]

d. complementizer *that*
syntax: C[*that*] in [__, {S[FIN] | S[BSE]}]
(C with <CFORM, *that*>, which takes as its complement an S[FIN] or S[BSE])
F/A: nil
E/R: nil
morph: W
mphon: [$_W$ /ðæt/]

e. complementizer *for*
syntax: C[*for*] in [__, S[*to*]] (C with <CFORM, *for*>, which takes S[*to*] as its complement)
F/A: nil
E/R: nil
morph: W
mphon: [$_W$ /fɚ/]

In (12c), the infinitival *to* is treated as a semantically null non-finite auxiliary verb V[AUX, *to*] (a verb with the feature AUX and the VFORM value *to*), which is supported by the similarities between *to* and auxiliary verbs: (i) VP ellipsis (… *but I don't think I <u>can</u>.* vs. … *but I don't want <u>to</u>.*), (ii) VP preposing (… *and buy a new car I really <u>should</u>.* vs. … *and buy a new car I really want <u>to</u>.*), (iii) *to* occupies the Modal position in the auxiliary verb sequence: Modal + Have(-*en*) + Be(-*ing*) (*John <u>may</u> have been at home last night* vs. *John seems <u>to</u> have been at* *home last night.*), (iv) no inflection for modal auxiliaries and *to*, and (v) modal auxiliaries and *to* take a VP[BSE] complement. Note that *to* cannot undergo inversion (14) because it is not a finite auxiliary verb. See (13) and (14).

In (12d), the complementizer C[*that*] takes two kinds of complement, S[FIN] or S[BSE]. Verbs such as *think* and *say* take a CP[*that*] complement with an S[FIN] daughter (*John said [that Mary stayed home]*), whereas verbs such as *propose* and *demand* take a CP[*that*] complement with an S[BSE] daughter (*John proposed [that Mary stay home]* and *I demand [that John not be here]*). The choice in a CP[*that*] of its complement type between S[FIN] and S[BSE] is not syntactic but semantic and pragmatic, which is illustrated by *John demanded something. It was that Mary stay home* and *What is the Case Filter? It is that an NP be assigned Case.*

Here is a brief review of inversion in AMG. Because there is no "movement rule" in AMG, there is no "head movement" that "moves" a finite auxiliary verb to the clause-initial position. In Ueno (2014), subject-auxiliary verb inversion was achieved in a GPSG manner by the feature co-occurrence restriction (FCR) (13) and the Inversion Lexical Rule (14). The underlying assumption here is that all the inverted auxiliary verbs (V[INV]) are registered in the lexicon: for example, *aren't* for first person singular, *won't* with a phonological irregularity, and the lack of *mayn't*. For full discussion on this point, see Ueno (2014: 47).

FCR (13) says that whenever the INV feature appears on a category, AUX, <VFORM, FIN>, and <POSP, V> also appear on that category. This means that INV only appears on a finite auxiliary verb (V[FIN, AUX]). The Inversion Lexical Rule (14) says that for every finite auxiliary verb that takes a VP complement with the VFORM value α (VP[α]), there exists a corresponding auxiliary verb with the INV feature that takes an S[α] complement, which is an S headed by a verb with the same VFORM value α.

(13) FCR for INV (Ueno 2014: 48)
INV → {AUX, <VFORM, FIN>, <POSP, V>}

(14) Inversion Lexical Rule (Ueno 2014: 48)
input lexical entry
syntax: V[AUX, FIN] in [$_{VP}$ __, VP[α]] → V[INV] in [$_S$ __, S[α]],
output lexical entry
where [$_S$ V[INV] ≤ NP...]

In the output of (14), V[INV] precedes S[α], which is due to the default word order rule between sisters (59a) and also due to English being a head-initial language (60).

A lexical rule is a rule that captures relationships between two sets of lexical entries in the lexicon. More specifically, it is a rule that guarantees the existence in the lexicon of a lexical entry that meets the output conditions of the lexical rule if there is a lexical entry in the lexicon that meets the input conditions.

For example, the auxiliary *can* (V[AUX, PRES]) takes a VP[BSE] complement and therefore (14) guarantees the existence in the lexicon of a lexical entry for the corresponding V[INV, PRES] that takes an S[BSE] complement (15).

(15) lexical entry for *can* → output
    syntax: V[AUX, PRES]   syntax: V[INV, AUX, PRES] in [$_S$ __, S[BSE]]
    in [__, VP[BSE]]   where [$_S$ V[INV] ⩽ NP...]
    F/A: [$_{Fp}$ PRES]∘[$_{Fp}$ CAN]   F/A: [$_{Fp}$ PRES]∘[$_{Fp}$ CAN]
    E/R: [$_{TYPE}$ "can"] in   E/R: [$_{TYPE}$ "can"] in
    [$_{EV}$ __ [$_{TH}$ EV]]   [$_{EV}$ __ [$_{TH}$ EV]]

(16) is an example of an inverted clause. Recall that INV, AUX, PRES, and BSE, of which the latter two are VFORM values, are head features and therefore obey the HFC (3). Recall also that the head of S is a V.

(16) syntax of *Can John fix the car?*

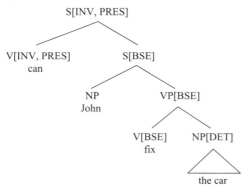

In the remainder of this section, we will give the definitions of dominate, c-command, S-mates, and well-formedness of syntactic structures.

(17) definition of *directly dominate* (Ueno 2014: 21)
    For two nodes X and Y in a given tree, X <u>directly dominates</u> Y iff there is a branch in the tree that connects X and Y with X immediately above Y.

(18) definition of *dominate* (Ueno 2014: 21)
For two nodes X and Y in a given tree, X <u>dominates</u> Y iff there is a series of nodes in the tree X = X_1, ..., X_n = Y, such that for each pair of X_i and X_{i+1}, X_i directly dominates X_{i+1}.

The notion of c-command is a member of the command family. Each family member x-command shares the same basic definition and is parameterized by the set of bounding nodes φ(x) (McCawley 1984, 1998: 352–353).

(19) definition of *x-command* (Ueno 2014: 21)
For two nodes X and Y in a given tree, X <u>x-commands</u> Y iff (i) the first (lowest) non-adjoined node that dominates X and is a member of φ(x), the set of bounding nodes for x, also dominates Y, and (ii) X does not dominate Y.

(20) definition of *non-adjoined node* (Ueno 2014: 21)
The <u>non-adjoined node</u> in an adjunction structure is the node that dominates all the adjoined nodes.

For example, in a syntactic structure [$_S$ NP [$_{VP}$ [$_{VP}$ [$_{VP}$ VP PP] PP] PP]], where three PPs are adjoined to the VP, the highest VP node (underlined) is the non-adjoined node.

(21) definition of *c-command* (Ueno 2014: 21)
For two nodes X and Y in a given syntactic structure, X <u>c-commands</u> Y iff X x-commands Y, where φ(x) = {all nodes in the syntactic structure}.

(22) definition of *asymmetric c-command* (Ueno 2014: 22)
For two nodes X and Y in a given syntactic structure, X <u>asymmetrically c-commands</u> Y iff X c-commands Y and Y does not c-command X.

(23) definition of *S-command* (Ueno 2014: 22)
For two nodes X and Y in a given syntactic structure, X <u>S-commands</u> Y iff X x-commands Y, where φ(x) = {S}.

(24) definition of *S-mates* (Ueno 2014: 22)
For two nodes X and Y in a given syntactic structure, X and Y are <u>S-mates</u> iff X and Y S-command each other.

(25) is the definition of a well-formed syntactic structure.

(25) definition of *well-formed syntactic structure* (Ueno 2014: 22)
   a. A local syntactic structure is well formed iff it is either (ia) an instantiation of one of the syntactic PS rules admitted by the language in question (i.e., (1) for English) or (ib) an instantiation of the syntactic field (i.e., subcategorization frame) of one of the lexical entries of the language in question, and (ii) it also meets all the relevant syntactic constraints on syntactic structures (e.g., the HFC (3) and subject-verb agreement (11)).
   b. A syntactic structure is well formed iff all the local syntactic structures that it contains are well formed.

1.2 Function Argument Structure Overview

Function Argument (F/A) structures are representations of logical structures (semantic forms) of sentences and consist of such semantic categories as proposition (PROP), argument (ARG), and various types of functor (Fφ). They are order-free phrase structures that are binary branching except for cases of coordination. An infinite set of such F/A structures is generated by the PSG (26). In (26a), *a* and *p* refer to ARG and PROP, respectively.

(26) PS rules for F/A module (Ueno 2014: 23)
   a. [$_{F\varphi}$ Fxφ, x], where x is either *a* or *p*, and φ is a finite string of *a*'s and *p*'s, and Fe = PROP for the empty string e. (Sadock 2012: 16 (4))
   b. [$_\alpha$ Mα, α], where Mα is a modifier of an F/A category α. (Sadock 2012: 17–18)

(27) provides examples of F/A structures generated by (26a).

(27) (Ueno 2014: 23)
   a. [$_{PROP}$ Fa, ARG], where Fa is an intransitive functor such as *dance*.
   b. [$_{Fa}$ Faa, ARG], where Faa is a transitive functor such as *kick*.
   c. [$_{Faa}$ Faaa, ARG], where Faaa is a ditransitive functor such as *give*.
   d. [$_{PROP}$ Fp, PROP], where Fp is a *seem*-type functor, which includes TENSE (PRES and PAST), NOT, and auxiliary verbs.
   e. [$_{Fa}$ Fpa, PROP], where Fpa is a functor such as *know* that takes an internal PROP and the subject ARG.
   f. [$_{Faa}$ Fpaa, PROP], where Fpaa is a functor such as *tell* that takes an internal PROP, the object ARG, and the subject ARG.

1.2 FUNCTION ARGUMENT STRUCTURE OVERVIEW

We will use the terms subject ARG and object ARG (in F/A) for descriptive purposes and not as theoretical primitives. The subject ARG refers to the ARG in (27a), namely, the ARG that is directly dominated by a PROP and is a sister of the Fa, whereas the object ARG refers to the ARG in (27b), namely, the ARG that is directly dominated by an Fa and is a sister of the Faa.

In (26b), a modifier of the F/A category Mα is adjoined to the F/A category α and returns a more complex member of the same category α. (28a–c) are examples of F/A structures generated by (26b).

(28) common types of modifier (Ueno 2014: 24)
 a. [$_{PROP}$ Mp, PROP], where Mp is a propositional modifier, e.g., *probably*
 b. [$_{Fa}$ M$_{Fa}$, Fa], where M$_{Fa}$ is a predicate modifier, e.g., *intentionally*
 c. [$_{ARG}$ Ma, ARG], where Ma is an argument modifier, e.g., an attributive adjective or a restrictive relative clause

Although most adjectives can be used predicatively and attributively, some adjectives are only used attributively and some others only predicatively. The attributive use of an adjective is Ma in F/A whereas its predicative use is Fa, Faa, or Fpa, depending on the semantic type of the adjective. (29a–c) are lexical entries of the adjectives *drunken*, *drunk*, and *careful*.

(29) a. lexical entry for *drunken* (attributive use only)
  syntax: A
  F/A: Ma
 b. lexical entry for *drunk* (predicative use only)
  syntax: A in [__]
  F/A: Fa
 c. lexical entry for *careful* (attributive and predicative)
  syntax: A   syntax: A in [__, PP[*of*]]
  F/A: Ma   F/A: Faa

The attributive adjective *drunken* is only specified as A in syntax without its subcategorization frame, meaning that it does not constitute its own AP. This adjective can only appear in syntax through the PS rule (1c) [$_{NP}$ A, NP]. The predicative *drunk* is specified in syntax as A in [__], meaning that it constitutes its own AP, and as such it appears where an AP can appear in syntax. An adjective such as *careful* in (29c), which is used attributively and predicatively, has two types of lexical entry: one for the attributive adjective use and the other for the predicative adjective use.

(30) is the definition of a well-formed F/A structure.

(30) definition of *well-formed F/A structure* (Ueno 2014: 24)
   a. A local F/A structure is well formed iff it is an instantiation of (26a) or (26b), and its terminal nodes, if any, are instantiations of the F/A field of one of the lexical entries of the language in question.
   b. An F/A structure is well formed iff all the local F/A structures that it contains are well formed.

(31) is an example of a well-formed F/A structure of a sentence.

(31) (Ueno 2014: 24)
   a. John knows that Mary met a tall boy yesterday.
   b. F/A structure of (31a)

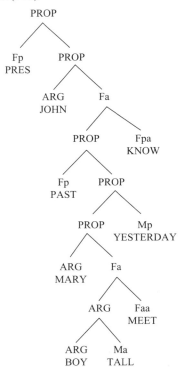

Note that each local F/A structure in (31b) is well formed by (30a) and therefore the whole F/A structure is well formed by (30b). We capitalize each word in (31b) to represent the F/A aspects of its meaning (i.e., the F/A field of its lexical entry).

Coreference relations between two NPs are primarily a semantic notion and are represented in F/A. However, this information is accessible to the other modules (e.g., syntax, E/R, and Information Structure) through an extended interpretation of Feature Osmosis (Sadock 2012: 154 (19)), which says that in unmarked situations, there are correspondences of features between modules. To indicate coreference between ARGs, we use the IND (index) feature, which consists of ref (referential index) and AGR with PER, NUM, and GEN.

(32) feature structure of IND (Ueno 2014: 25)

$$\text{IND} \begin{pmatrix} \text{ref} & i \\ \text{AGR} \begin{pmatrix} \text{PER} & \{1 \mid 2 \mid 3\} \\ \text{NUM} & \{SG \mid PL\} \\ \text{GEN} & \{M \mid F \mid N\} \end{pmatrix} \end{pmatrix}$$

For example, if in *John loves her*, *John*'s referential index is i and that of *her* is j, their respective ARGs in F/A are [$_{\text{ARG[IND[i, 3SGM]]}}$ JOHN] and ARG[IND[j, 3SGF]]. That is, each ARG has its own IND value. In fact, the AGR value (i.e., the set of PER, NUM, and GEN values) is a function of the referential index (IND[j, AGR(j)]) in the sense that once the referential index is determined (that is, the referent is determined), the AGR value is determined as a result. We will treat non-reflexive pronouns as consisting only of the INDEX feature (i.e., their referential index and AGR value). We define coreference as follows. Two ARGs are coreferential if and only if they have the same referential index. From this definition, it follows that when two ARGs are coreferential, they have the same AGR value, because AGR is a function of the referential index.

TENSE (PRES and PAST) and auxiliary verbs (V[AUX]) are treated as Fp. For example, the non-finite perfect auxiliary *have* is [$_{Fp}$ PAST] in F/A (McCawley 1998: 221, Sadock 2012: 161–162). In (33), mismatches arise between syntax and F/A, which are represented as crossings of association lines. They are all innocuous mismatches of subject-raising type. (See 1.6.1.)

These mismatches are unavoidable, because TENSE and other Fp functors, although taking scope over their sister PROP, are all realized within the VP in syntax. Therefore, Fp functors c-command the subject ARG in F/A, whereas this c-command relation is not maintained in syntax. See (45) for the definition of c-command in F/A.

(33) innocuous mismatches between syntax and F/A (Ueno 2014: 26)
  a. [$_{S[PAST]}$ John [$_{VP[PAST]}$ [$_{V[PAST]}$ kicked] the dog]].

  [$_{Fp}$ PAST]([$_{ARG}$ JOHN]([$_{Faa}$ KICK]([$_{ARG}$ DOG])))

  b. [$_{S[PRES]}$ John [$_{VP[PRES]}$ [$_{V[PRES]}$ has] [$_{VP[PSP]}$ kicked the dog]]].

  PRES(PAST(JOHN(KICK(DOG))))

  c. [$_{S[PRES]}$ John [$_{VP[PRES]}$ has [$_{V[PSP]}$ been [$_{VP[PRP]}$ kicking] the dog]]]].

  PRES(PAST(PROG(JOHN(KICK(DOG)))))

  d. [$_{S[PRES]}$ John [$_{VP[PRES]}$ may [$_{VP[BSE]}$ have [$_{VP[PSP]}$ been [$_{VP[PRP]}$ kicking] the dog]]]]].

  PRES(MAY(PAST(PROG(JOHN(KICK(DOG))))))

Note that in (33b, c), the perfect auxiliary verb in the present tense *has* corresponds to PRES and PAST, the latter being within the scope of the former. Note also that in (33c, d), the verb in the present participle form (V[PRP]) *kicking* in syntax corresponds to [$_{Fp}$ PROG] and [$_{Faa}$ KICK]. This is due to the fact that a V[PRP] can express its progressive/imperfective aspect (PROG) in its own right when it is used as a fragment. See (35) and its discussion in Chapter 3. This means that the *be* verb in the past participle form (V[PSP]) *been* in (33c, d) is meaningless, that is, an instance of the empty *be* verb (Sadock 2012: 29, Ueno 2014: 54) that takes a VP[PRP] complement. The empty *be* verb is pressed

1.2 FUNCTION ARGUMENT STRUCTURE OVERVIEW

into service here because of the perfective *have*, which requires a VP[PSP] complement.

(34a) is an example in which a common noun is used as a predicate and its F/A and E/R are given in (34b). (E/R, the module that represents events and their participant roles, will be reviewed in the next section.) In (34b), the predicative BABY, which is the second argument of the Faa functor =, carries the INDEX value IND[3SG] without a referential index, because it is not referentially used. See (42) for the lexical entry for the Faa functor =.

(34) (Ueno 2014: 27)
  a. John is a baby.
  b. F/A and E/R of (34a)

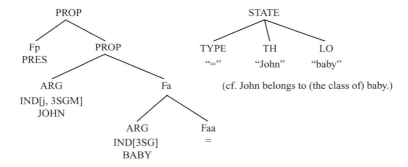

The common noun *baby* has the following lexical entry, in which the referential index (ref) is optional. It is present when used referentially but absent when used non-referentially. Note that a common noun, whether used predicatively or as an argument, is treated as ARG in F/A.

(35) lexical entry for common noun *baby* (Ueno 2014: 27)
  syntax: N in [$_{NP}$ __]
  F/A: [$_{ARG[IND[(ref), 3SGN]]}$ BABY]
  E/R: ROLE

When a common noun is used as a predicate, as in (34a), it serves as the lower ARG of the Faa type-identity functor = and forms an Fa, as in (34b). (See (42) for the lexical entry for the type-identity Faa =.) "α = β" means that α is equal to β in type or α is an instance of type β. (See Jackendoff 1983: 78ff. and Lyons 1977: 13ff. for type-token distinction.) We assume that a predicate NP, when representing a type as the second argument of the type-identity functor =, lacks its referential index, as in (34b). The verb *is* and the indefinite article *a* in (34a) are meaningless and lack their F/A and E/R representations (except, of course, the tense PRES and agreement information carried by *is*) (Sadock 2012: 29). In *Mary considers John a baby*, the meaning of the type-identity functor = is evident, although there is no *be* verb. Therefore, we claim that the source of the meaning "=" in (34a) is not the verb *be* and that *be* in (34a) is meaningless.

An NP in syntax corresponds to an ARG in F/A in default cases, according to (57a). When a noun is modified in syntax by an adjective, as in (*a*) [$_{NP}$ *cute baby*], BABY in F/A is an ARG and CUTE is an Ma (modifier of an argument). Therefore, the F/A of the NP is [$_{ARG}$ [$_{Ma}$ CUTE], [$_{ARG}$ BABY]] and when the NP is used predicatively, its F/A is [$_{Fa}$ [$_{Faa}$ =][$_{ARG}$ [$_{Ma}$ CUTE], [$_{ARG}$ BABY]]].

The F/A module is the place where quantifiers and their scopes are represented. (36) is a set of well-formedness conditions that a quantifier phrase (QP) must satisfy. In (36), a QP that quantifies a variable x is denoted by QP$_x$ with the subscript x.

(36) well-formedness conditions on QPs (Ueno 2014: 30)
    a. [$_{PROP}$ QP$_x$, PROP], where the matrix PROP must contain x.
    b. [$_{QPx}$ Q, PROP], where the domain expression PROP must contain x.
    c. All the instances of the variable x must be either dominated or c-commanded by a single QP$_x$.

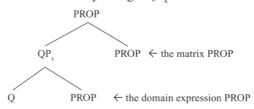

(37a) below has a quantified NP (QNP) *every baby* as its subject. The lexical entry for *every* is given in (38). The syntax of (37a) is (37c) and its F/A structure that meets the well-formedness conditions (36) is (37b).

1.2 FUNCTION ARGUMENT STRUCTURE OVERVIEW

(37) (Ueno 2014: 31)
   a. Every baby sleeps.
   b.

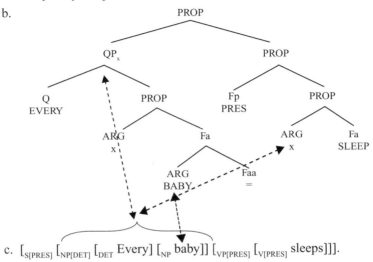

   c. [$_{S[PRES]}$ [$_{NP[DET]}$ [$_{DET}$ Every] [$_{NP}$ baby]] [$_{VP[PRES]}$ [$_{V[PRES]}$ sleeps]]].

(38) lexical entry for *every* (Ueno 2014: 31)
   syntax: DET in [$_{NP[DET]}$ ___, NP[3SG]]
   F/A: [$_Q$ EVERY]
   E/R: nil
   morph: {<BAR, 1>} (i.e., a morphological word)

In (37b, c) above, the QNP *every baby* in syntax corresponds to the QP$_x$ and one of the variables [$_{ARG}$ x] in the matrix PROP. (In (37b), there happens to be only one variable in the matrix PROP.) This is because a QP in F/A is required to be outside the matrix PROP by (36a), whereas in syntax, a QNP is required to occupy an ordinary NP position. In addition, the NP *baby* of the QNP corresponds to the second ARG of the type-identity Faa functor = in the domain expression PROP. The type-identity Faa functor = in (37b) indicates that x is equal to BABY in type (that is, x is an instance of the type BABY).

1 AUTOMODULAR GRAMMAR OVERVIEW

(39a) is a sentence with two QNPs. Its syntax is shown in (39b). As is well known, it has two interpretations: (i) *every student* has wide scope or (ii) *a professor* has wide scope. Interpretations (i) and (ii) correspond to F/A structures (39c) and (39d), respectively. Note that although (39a) has one syntactic structure, namely (39b), and one E/R (to be reviewed in 1.3), namely (39d), it has two well-formed F/A structures, namely (39b, c), due to the autonomy of the F/A module, because (39a) contains two quantifiers *every* and *a*.

(39) (Ueno 2014: 32)
  a. Every student admires a professor.
  b. [$_{S[PRES]}$ [$_{NP[DET]}$ Every student] [$_{VP[PRES]}$ admires [$_{NP[DET]}$ a professor]]].
  c. [[$_{QPx}$ EVERY x = STUDENT] [[$_{QPy}$ A y = PROFESSOR] (PRES [x ADMIRE y])]]
  d. [[$_{QPy}$ A y = PROFESSOR] [[$_{QPx}$ EVERY x = STUDENT] (PRES [x ADMIRE y])]]
  e. [$_{EV}$ [$_{TYPE}$ "admire"] [$_{AG}$ "student"] [$_{PT}$ "professor"]]

The detailed F/A structure of (39c) is given in (40), in which QP_x asymmetrically c-commands QP_y, representing the fact that QP_x has scope over QP_y.

(40) F/A of *Every student admires a professor* with interpretation (i)

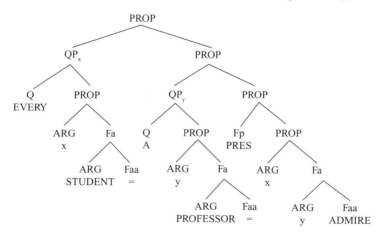

In (39) and (40), the indefinite article is treated as a kind of existential quantifier. The lexical entry for this use of the indefinite article is given in (41). (42) is the lexical entry for the type-identity Faa functor =.

1.2 FUNCTION ARGUMENT STRUCTURE OVERVIEW 23

(41) lexical entry for indefinite article
    a (as existential quantifier)
    (Ueno 2014: 32)
    syntax: DET in [$_{\text{NP[DET]}}$ ___, NP[3SG]]
    F/A: [$_Q$ A]
    E/R: nil
    morph: W (= {<BAR, 1>})
    mphon: [$_W$ /ən/] in the phonological
        environment of ___ ⩽ V
    [$_W$ /ə/] elsewhere

(42) lexical entry for type-identity
    Faa functor = (cf. (34b))
    (Ueno 2014: 32)
    syntax: nil
    F/A: [$_{\text{Faa}}$ =]
    E/R: [$_{\text{TYPE}}$ "="] in [$_{\text{STATE}}$ ___
    [$_{\text{TH}}$ *token*] [$_{\text{LO}}$ *type*]]
    morph: nil
    mphon: nil

In the E/R field of (42), which will be reviewed in the next section, the type-identity functor takes a theme role (TH) representing a token, and a locative role (LO) representing a type. Note that TH outranks LO in the Role Hierarchy (55) and therefore TH corresponds to the subject ARG in F/A and LO to the lower ARG under the default geometric correspondences (57b). Note also that in the E/R of (42), the label STATE is used instead of EVENT (EV). See the Event Hierarchy (50). Later we will also need another Faa functor ∈ in (43), to deal with set membership. This functor takes an individual as the theme role (TH) and a set as the locative role (LO) in the sense that an individual belongs to a set. Along with the indefinite article in (41), we will be treating the definite article *the* (44) as a kind of existential quantifier (McCawley 1993a: 205).

(43) lexical entry for set-membership
    Faa functor ∈
    syntax: nil
    F/A: [$_{\text{Faa}}$ ∈]
    E/R: [$_{\text{TYPE}}$ "∈"] in [$_{\text{STATE}}$ ___
    [$_{\text{TH}}$ *individual*] [$_{\text{LO}}$ *set*]]
    morph: nil
    mphon: nil

(44) lexical entry for definite article
    the (as existential quantifier)
    syntax: DET in [$_{\text{NP[DET]}}$ ___, NP[3]]
    F/A: [$_Q$ THE]
    E/R: nil
    morph: W
    mphon: [$_W$ /ðɪ/] in the phonological
        environment of ___ ⩽ V
    [$_W$ /ðə/] elsewhere

The quantifier-like property of *the* is evident in *Every man admires the woman who raised him* (McCawley 1993a: 205), where the definite noun phrase *the woman who raised him* is in the scope of *every man*.

In the discussion on the F/A structure (40), we used the notion of c-command. This notion is defined easily in F/A structures, in exactly the same way we defined it in syntactic structures. The definitions of *directly dominate*, *dominate*, *x-command*, and *non-adjoined node* are the same as (17), (18), (19), and (20).

(45) definition of *c-command* in F/A
For two nodes X and Y in a given F/A structure, <u>X c-commands Y</u> iff X x-commands Y, where ϕ(x) = {all nodes in the F/A structure}.

Going back to the F/A structure (40), we claimed that QP_x asymmetrically c-commands QP_y. Note that QP_y does not c-command QP_x in (40), because the two QPs are not adjoined to the matrix PROP. For one thing, their F/A category is not Mp (i.e., a modifier of PROP as in [$_{PROP}$ Mp, PROP]), and for another, QP is obligatory in the sense that if we omitted QP_x or QP_y from the well-formed F/A in (40), it would violate (36c) and would be ill formed.

1.3 Event Role Structure Overview

The Event Role (E/R) module, which was called Role Structure (RS) module in Sadock (2012) and Ueno (2014), represents the cognitive content of an event and the cognitive status of the participant roles in it. (46) provides examples of E/R. In (46c), the event (EV) consists of its event type (TYPE) "explain" and the roles that are required in this event. They are agent (AG), patient (PT), and goal (GO). In the E/R on the right, the patient role dominates another event whose event type is "die." Note that we will use double quotation marks to indicate the E/R aspects of meaning.

(46) a. [$_{NP}$ John] explained [$_{NP[DET]}$ the fact] [$_{PP[to]}$ to Mary].
b. [$_{NP}$ John] explained [$_{PP[to]}$ to Mary] [$_{CP[that]}$ that Sam died].
c. E/R of (46a, b) (Ueno 2014: 34)

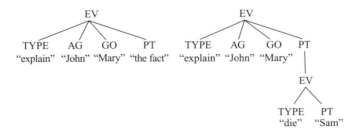

To generate this kind of event structure, we need the following PS rules for the E/R module.

(47) PS rules for E/R module (cf. Ueno 2014: 34)
    a. [$_{EV}$ TYPE ROLE^m MOD^n]   b. [$_{ROLE}$ EV]   c. [$_{MOD}$ EV]

(47a) generates a local E/R structure that dominates a certain number of roles (ROLE) and a certain number of modifiers (MOD) including zero. (47b) generates a local E/R structure in which a role dominates an EV and (47c) generates a local E/R structure in which a modifier (MOD) dominates an EV. Note that (47b) and (47a), if n = 0, are part of the E/R field of a lexical entry.

(48) definition of *well-formed E/R structure* (cf. Ueno 2014: 35)
    a. A local E/R structure is well formed if and only if it is an instantiation of (47a), (47b), or (47c), and is matched by the E/R field of one of the lexical entries of the language in question.
    b. An E/R structure is well formed if and only if all the local E/R structures that it contains are well formed.

The MOD in (47a, c) subsumes its subcategories: time modifier (TIME), place modifier (PLACE), manner modifier (MANNER), etc.
  (49) provides partial lexical entries for *explain* in (46a, b).

(49) partial lexical entries for *explain*
    syntax: V in [__, NP, PP[*to*]]   syntax: V in [__, PP[*to*], CP[*that*]]
    F/A: Faaa   F/A: Fpaa
    E/R: [$_{TYPE}$ "explain"] in   E/R: [$_{TYPE}$ "explain"] in
      [__ AG PT GO]   [__ AG GO [$_{PT}$ EV]]

Regarding the distinction between events, states, actions, and so on, the Event Hierarchy (50) was proposed in Ueno (2014). It introduces various kinds of events, including state, action, and volitional action. The term *event* (EV) has been and will be used as a cover term for these kinds of events.

(50) Event Hierarchy (Ueno 2014: 183)

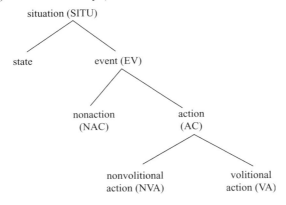

Regarding participant roles in E/R structures, two-tiered roles were first proposed in Jackendoff (1990: 126–127) and adopted in Ueno (2014: 35), according to which, a participant role is a combination of two roles: one from the action tier consisting of AG and PT and the other from the thematic tier consisting of source (SO), goal (GO), theme (TH), and locative (LO). For example, in (46a) [$_{AG}$ *John*] *explained* [$_{PT}$ *the fact*] *to* [$_{GO}$ *Mary*], *John* is not only the agent who did the explaining, but also the source (SO) (of information), because *the fact* was conveyed from *John* to *Mary*. We represent the role carried by *John* as [AG, SO], which combines AG (from the action tier) and SO (from the thematic tier). The object NP *the fact* is of course a patient (PT) of the event, because *the fact* changed its possessor from *John* to *Mary* by it being explained to *Mary*, and in this sense, *the fact* was affected by the explaining (*the fact* known to *John* became known to *Mary*), but it is also a theme (TH), because *the fact* was "moved" (i.e., *conveyed*) from *John* to *Mary*. We represent the role carried by *the fact* as [PT, TH], which is a combination of PT (from the action tier) and TH (from the thematic tier). Sometimes, a role may lack its action tier specification (i.e., specification of AG or PT) or thematic tier specification (i.e., specification of SO, GO, TH, or LO). For example, the role carried by *Mary* in *John explained the fact to Mary* is GO on the thematic tier but lacks its action tier specification. That is, *Mary* is not AG or PT in this example. These two-tiered roles are represented in (51), in which VA and NAC stand for volitional action and nonaction, respectively (cf. (50)).

(51) two-tiered roles

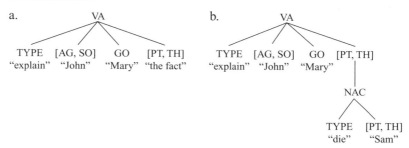

Based on the discussion so far, we propose the following revised and complete lexical entries for *explain* (52).

(52) lexical entries for *explain* (revised)
    syntax: V in [__, NP, PP[*to*]]   syntax: V in [__, PP[*to*], CP[*that*]]
    F/A: Faaa   F/A: Fapa
    E/R: [$_{TYPE}$ "explain"] in [$_{VA}$ __   E/R: [$_{TYPE}$ "explain"] in [$_{VA}$ __
    [AG, SO] [PT,TH] GO]   [AG, SO] [$_{[PT,TH]}$ EV] GO]
    morph: V[0] (i.e., verb stem)   morph: V[0]
    mphon: [$_{V[0]}$ /ɪksplaɪn/]   mphon: [$_{V[0]}$ /ɪksplaɪn/]

Let us consider another set of examples, two uses of the verb *give*. In *John gave a book to Mary*, *John* carries the role of [AG, SO], which is AG on the action tier and simultaneously SO on the thematic tier, *a book* carries the role of [PT, TH], which is PT on the action tier and TH on the thematic tier, and *Mary* carries GO, which is GO on the thematic tier with no specification for the action tier. By contrast, in the ditransitive use of *give*, as in *John gave Mary a book*, *Mary* assumes the role of [PT, GO] (i.e., recipient) and *a book* carries the role TH with no action tier specification. Therefore, these two uses of *give* differ in which role the speaker conceptualizes as the patient (PT) of the *giving* event, theme (TH), or goal (GO). In other words, there are two ways the speaker can conceptualize a *giving* event. (53) and (54) provide lexical entries for the two kinds of *give*.

(53) lexical entry for *give* (transitive with *to*) (Ueno 2014: 36)
syntax: V in [__, NP, PP[*to*]]
F/A: Faaa
E/R: [$_{\text{TYPE}}$ "give"] in [$_{\text{EV}}$ __
[AG, SO] [PT, TH] GO]
morph: V[0]
mphon: [$_{\text{V[0]}}$ /gɪv/], [$_{\text{V[1, PAST]}}$ /geɪv/], [$_{\text{V[1, PSP]}}$ /gɪvn̩/]

(54) lexical entry for *give* (ditransitive) (Ueno 2014: 36)
syntax: V in [__, NP, NP]
F/A: Faaa
E/R: [$_{\text{TYPE}}$ "give"] in [$_{\text{EV}}$ __
[AG, SO] [PT, GO] TH]
morph: V[0]
mphon: [$_{\text{V[0]}}$ /gɪv/], [$_{\text{V[1, PAST]}}$ /geɪv/], [$_{\text{V[1, PSP]}}$ /gɪvn̩/]

In syntax and F/A, the structural relation *c-command* was defined quite naturally ((17) for syntax and (45) for F/A) as a useful way of measuring the prominence of each NP or ARG, but since E/R structures are flat, *c-command* cannot be defined in E/R in a similar fashion. Instead, the relation *outrank* (56) is defined on the basis of the Role Hierarchy (55) to compare the prominence of roles.

(55) Role Hierarchy (Ueno 2014: 37)
action tier: AG > PT > ø
thematic tier: SO > GO > TH > LO > MOD

The Role Hierarchy (55) says that on the action tier, AG outranks PT, which in turn outranks a role that lacks its action tier specification (i.e., a role that has a specification for the thematic tier alone), whereas on the thematic tier, the outrank relations are indicated in (55). MOD is outranked by any other role.

We define the general notion of outrank as (56i), based on the tier-specific notion of outrank in (55). (56i) says that any role with AG outranks any role with PT, which in turn outranks any role that is not specified for the action tier. If roles are not specified for the action tier, SO outranks GO, GO outranks TH, TH outranks LO, and LO outranks MOD. For example, the roles were listed in the outrank order in lexical entries (52), (53), and (54). (56iii) says that outrank is a transitive relation: if A > B and B > C, then A > C.

(56) definition of *outrank* (Ueno 2014: 37)
  i. Outrank (" > ") is determined by the action tier specifications of roles. Otherwise, it is determined by their thematic tier specifications.
  ii. If A outranks B and B dominates C in E/R, then A outranks C.
  iii. If A outranks B and B outranks C, then A outranks C. (transitive relation)

1.3 EVENT ROLE STRUCTURE OVERVIEW

The default correspondences between syntax, F/A, and E/R are given in (57).

(57) default correspondences (Ueno 2014: 37–8)
    a. default categorial correspondences (Sadock 2012: 78 (8))
        syntax   F/A   E/R
        S   <---------->   PROP   <---------->   EV
        NP   <---------->   ARG   <---------->   ROLE
        VP   <---------->   Fa
    b. default geometrical correspondences (Sadock 2012: 35 (24))
       i. Dominance relations should be preserved between corresponding nodes in each module.
       ii. C-command relations should be preserved between corresponding nodes in syntax and F/A.
       iii. C-command relations in syntax and F/A and outrank relations in E/R should be harmonic.

(57biii) says that c-command relations in syntax and F/A translate into outrank relations in E/R and vice versa in default cases.

Because of (57), we have the following default correspondences between the syntax, F/A, and E/R of a transitive sentence. In (58), NP_1 corresponds to ARG_1 and $ROLE_1$ and NP_2 corresponds to ARG_2 and $ROLE_2$ (Sadock 2012: 81 (14)).

(58) default correspondences of transitive sentence (Ueno 2014: 38)

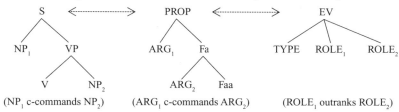

These default correspondences between the syntax and F/A of a transitive sentence hold between NPs in syntax and ARGs in F/A and not between NPs and QPs. In (39), we briefly discussed the scope ambiguity of *Every student admires a professor*, whose approximate F/A is [QP [QP [$_{PROP}$ [$_{ARG}$ x] [$_{Faa}$ ADMIRE] [$_{ARG}$ y]]]] (39c, d). The default geometrical correspondences (57bii)) only claims that the c-command relations between the two NPs in syntax, *every student* and *a professor*, and between the two ARGs in F/A, [$_{ARG}$ x] and [$_{ARG}$ y], should be preserved. This means that there is no violation of (57bii) in (39d), in which *a professor* has wide scope, and therefore the two interpretations (39c, d) are equally accessible.

The following default linear order rules were proposed in Ueno (2014). They account for the default linear order between sisters in syntax.

(59) default linear order between sisters based on complexity (Ueno 2014: 39)
A less complex sister precedes a more complex sister by default.
  a. pronoun $\prec$ word (<BAR, 0>) $\prec$ phrase (<BAR, 1>) $\prec$ clause (<BAR, 2>)
  b. NP $\prec$ PP
  c. syntactic correspondent of ARG $\prec$ syntactic correspondent of Fa or PROP

In (59), the notation A $\prec$ B means A precedes B. Because a pronoun (PN) is less complex than a full word in terms of syntactic, semantic/informational, and phonological complexity, pronoun $\prec$ word in (59a) is predicted. Note that although the set of words includes the set of pronouns, this rule (pronoun $\prec$ word) cannot linearly order two pronouns properly, and the only available interpretation of this rule is that a pronoun precedes a non-pronoun word. In (59b), we claimed, following Sadock (2012: 115), that a PP is more complex syntactically than an NP, because a PP consists of NP and the head P: [$_{PP}$ P, NP]. (59c) is a syntactic reflection of semantic (F/A) complexity. PROP is more complex than ARG because PROP consists of ARG and Fa: [$_{PROP}$ ARG, Fa]. Fa is also more complex than ARG because Fa consists of ARG and Faa: [$_{Fa}$ ARG, Faa]. Note that the syntactic correspondent of ARG is usually NP or PP whereas the syntactic correspondent of Fa or PROP is usually VP, AP, S, or CP. Because {NP | PP}$\prec${S | CP} is already covered by (59a), the net effect of (59c) is {NP | PP}$\prec${AP | VP | PP}, where the latter PP corresponds to an Fa in F/A. For example, in a VP such as [$_{VP}$ *think* [$_{PP}$ *of John*] [$_{PP}$ *as clever*]], the first PP is an ARG and the second PP is an Fa; therefore the former precedes the latter by (59c). Because (59) only deals with default orders between sisters in general, we need a separate, more specific, statement (60) about where the head comes in head-complement structures (i.e., the head parameter).

(60) (Ueno 2014: 40)
English is a head-initial language. That is, in head-complement structures, where a lexical head (H[0]) takes one or more complements within its phrase (H[1]), the head must precede all the complements.

(60) is more specific than (59a) in that the former only applies to head-complement structures. Therefore, the application of (60) preempts that of (59a) by the Elsewhere Principle (Ueno 2014: 11). See Ueno (2014: 40–1) for examples of how (59) and (60) determine English default word orders.

1.4 Information Structure Overview

The Information Structure (IS) module was proposed in Ueno (2014: 42) to deal with the following points. First, IS represents the familiarity status (old vs. new) of information with respect to discourse or addressee (Huddleston and Pullum 2002: 1368ff.). Old information tends to precede new information. For example, the topic (TOP) of an utterance (U), which expresses what the utterance is about and is discourse-old, precedes the rest of the utterance. This is stated in (61a).

(61) a. $[_U \text{TOP} \prec \textit{rest}]$ b. $[_U \textit{rest} \prec \{\text{FOC} \mid \text{HEAVY}\}]$

The subject NP of a clause appears clause-initially and tends to be a default topic (cf. (62) and (63)). On the other hand, the focus (FOC) of an utterance bears the strongest stress and carries addressee-new information, whereas the rest of the utterance carries addressee-old information. Therefore, the focus tends to occur at the utterance-final position (cf. (62) and (63)). For example, in the locative inversion construction (Ueno 2005, 2014: 88), the locative PP comes first as the topic of the clause and the theme NP comes last as (presentational) focus. In the predicate inversion construction (Ueno 2014: 154), the discourse-old or discourse-linked predicate phrase comes first and the subject NP or CP comes last as focus. Furthermore, in the Heavy Constituent Shift (Ueno 2014: 170), a phonologically heavy sister phrase or clause of the verb in a VP occurs at the clause-final position. This is captured in (61b). Note that there is an intrinsic connection between phonological heaviness and informational focus: a phrase or clause that is phonologically heavy in terms of number of syllables tends to express complex information, which in turn tends to be discourse-new.

Second, IS also represents a more general distinction between foreground information (FI) and background information (BI). FI is the part of an utterance that the speaker intends to convey to the addressee. This includes new information, focus, and assertion. The rest of the utterance represents BI, the information the speaker takes for granted. This includes old information, topic, and presupposition. For example, a factive verb takes a CP[*that*] that carries BI (Ueno 2014: 301). In the case of manner-of-speaking verbs such as *mumble*, the meaning component of the manner of speaking 'mumblingly' is FI (Ueno 2014: 303). The PP (underlined) that modifies a "performative clause" in <u>*In case you haven't heard,*</u> *Bob and Frieda have decided to get married* carries BI and the main clause FI (Ueno 2014: 379).

Finally, linear order requirements in IS are stronger than and override those in syntax, which is illustrated by, for example, the locative inversion construction and the predicate inversion construction.

1.5 Lexical Items and Lexical Entries

In Sadock (2012) and Ueno (2014), we gave module-by-module lexical entries for lexical items, as we have done so far in this chapter. Lexical items are units that are stored in the mental lexicon, the long-term memory repository of lexical items in the brain. They include not only words (lexemes) but also morphemes, idioms (including clichés and fixed expressions), collocations, constructions, and texts (Jackendoff 2002: 152). Note that the adjective *lexical* in *lexical entry* and *lexical item* does not mean 'of lexemes (<BAR, 0> syntactic entities)' but 'of or in the lexicon.' From this perspective, phrase structure rules themselves are viewed as lexical items stored in the lexicon (Sadock 1996, Jackendoff 2002: 154, Jackendoff 2010: 17–20).

Lexical entries for lexical items, whether they are entries for morphemes, words, idioms, constructions, or phrase structure rules, are all constraints on the linguistic forms in which they are instantiated in the sense that lexical entries (as well as other constraints such as the Head Feature Convention) impose constraints on linguistic forms and guarantee their well-formedness (Pollard and Sag 1987: 44, Jackendoff 2002: 48). Because lexical entries are given module by module, they provide the basis of the interface that connects various autonomous modules (Sadock 1991: 36, 2012: 25, Jackendoff 2002: 131, 425, Marantz 1984: 53).

For example, the default transitive and ditransitive clauses are registered in the lexicon as (62) and (63) without any phonological information. The Information Structure (IS) field in (62) and (63) says that the topic (TOP) and focus (FOC) appear utterance-initially and utterance-finally, respectively, in default cases.

(62) lexical entry for default transitive construction (Ueno 2014: 44)

syntax: [$_S$ NP [$_{VP}$ V NP]] (as in *The girl kicked a boy*)

F/A: [$_{PROP}$ ARG [$_{Fa}$ Faa, ARG]]

E/R: [$_{EV}$ TYPE AG PT]

IS: [$_U$ TOP ≺ *rest* ≺ FOC]

(63) lexical entry for default ditransitive construction (Ueno 2014: 44)

syntax: [$_S$ NP [$_{VP}$ V NP NP]] (as in *She gave the boy a book*)

F/A: [$_{PROP}$ ARG [$_{Fa}$ ARG [$_{Faa}$ ARG, Faaa]]]

E/R: [$_{EV}$ TYPE [AG, SO] [PT, GO] TH]

IS: [$_U$ TOP ≺ *rest* ≺ FOC]

Because the intermodular correspondences in (62) and (63) are default, much of the information they contain is predictable and hence redundant. However, the advantage of registering redundant information in (62) and (63) is to help facilitate the process of language acquisition in such a way that when a baby hears a transitive or ditransitive clause with an unknown verb, they can still guess the basic semantic and discourse information from (62) or (63), which would help them learn the unknown verb. Alternatively, when a baby wants to express a message that has transitive or ditransitive semantics, they can guess its syntactic structure from (62) and (63).

Wide-scale redundancy of function exists between the modules (Sadock 1983). In addition, lexical items are often redundantly specified for various properties (Sadock 1984). Recall that there is no reason to think that the brain stores information non-redundantly (McCawley 1998: 8–9, Jackendoff 2002: 153).

Redundancy in the lexicon and in the grammatical modules is important and useful in language acquisition and verbal communication (Sadock 1991: 14). It not only facilitates language acquisition, as stated in the previous paragraph, but also allows for language to work under less than ideal circumstances (Sadock 2012: 227). For example, a learner who only knows *wow* as an interjection of excitement or surprise and first hears an utterance such as "Mark Zuckerberg wowed an audience at Beijing by doing this" (*NBC Nightly News*, October 23, 2014) has no difficulty understanding it, because the learner can apply the default correspondences (62) and correctly guess that the utterance has a transitive semantics with *Mark Zuckerberg* as agent and *an audience* as patient, something along the lines of 'Mark Zuckerberg did something that led the audience to say "wow".'

Therefore, redundancy is NOT something that is pernicious and should be purged from the lexicon and grammar. Rather, it is a fundamental feature of language design, which helps facilitate language acquisition and verbal communication (Sadock 2012: 225, Sadock 1991: 14–15). We took this view very seriously in Ueno 2014 and continue to do so in this book.

1.6 Brief Discussion on Raising

In the following sections, we will briefly review raising, control, passivization, and unbounded dependencies. For the details of each topic, see Sadock 2012 and Ueno 2014.

1.6.1 Subject raising

The subject raising construction (subject raising for short) is illustrated in (64b). Subject raising occurs with verbs such as *seem*, *appear*, and *happen* and adjectives such as *likely* and *certain*. Semantically, these subject raising predicates take only one role (i.e., [$_{TH}$ EV]) that corresponds to a proposition), which is expressed in syntax as a CP[*that*] or S[FIN]. This is shown in (64a), in which the matrix subject NP position is filled by the dummy *it*, because the VP *seems that John likes Mary* is semantically saturated and there is no role that the matrix subject can bear.

(64) (Ueno 2014: 141)
    a. It seems [$_{CP[that]}$ that John likes Mary].
    b. John seems [$_{VP[to]}$ to like Mary].
    c. [$_{NP}$] seems [$_{S[to]}$ [$_{NP}$ John] [$_{VP[to]}$ to like Mary]].

The other way of expressing the meaning of (64a) is the subject raising construction (64b), in which the subject raising predicate *seem* takes a VP[*to*] complement and the subject *John* of the embedded clause appears as the matrix subject.

Subject raising occurs, first and foremost, when an Fp in F/A (a functor that takes a proposition and returns a proposition: [$_{PROP}$ Fp, PROP]) is morphologically or phonologically realized in a verb in the case of TENSE (McCawley 1973: 259, 1998: 223), or when its syntactic correspondent takes a VP complement in the case of auxiliary verbs. For example, in (65), the present tense [$_{Fp}$ PRES] and the transitive functor [$_{Faa}$ LOVE] in F/A correspond to the finite verb [$_{V[PRES]}$ loves] in syntax. This correspondence involves a mismatch between syntax and F/A in that *John* c-commands the present-tense verb *loves* in syntax, whereas JOHN is c-commanded by PRES in F/A.

(65) (Ueno 2014: 142)

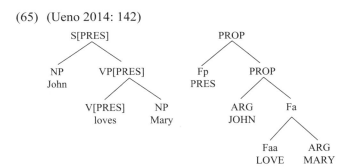

This mismatch is displayed in bracket notation in (66), in which the mismatch shows up as a crossing of association lines. (67) is the lexical entry for the present tense.

(66) (Ueno 2014: 143)

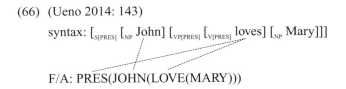

(67) lexical entry for present tense (Ueno 2014: 143)
syntax: PRES in V[__] (a value of the VFORM feature)
F/A: [$_{Fp}$ PRES]

E/R: nil
morph: PRES in V[1, __] (a value of the VFORM feature)
mphon: [$_{V[1, PRES, AGR]}$ V[0] [$_{AF}$ {Z}]], when AGR=3SG
         [$_{V[1, PRES, AGR]}$ V[0]], elsewhere

This type of mismatch is unavoidable in English, and for that matter, in any language in which the tense is morphologically realized in the verb, because TENSE is an Fp in F/A that asymmetrically c-commands the subject ARG, as in [$_{PROP}$ [$_{Fp}$ TENSE], [$_{PROP}$ ARG, Fa]], whereas the syntactic correspondent of TENSE is morphologically realized in the finite V. This is an innocuous mismatch between syntax and F/A, and as such occurs in a clause more than once without any loss of acceptability. (68a) is a sentence with the finite auxiliary verb *may*, which corresponds to [$_{Fp}$ PRES]∘[$_{Fp}$ MAY] in F/A, the composition of two Fp functors.

(68) (Ueno 2014: 144)
    a. John may like Mary.
    b. syntax: [$_{S[PRES]}$ John [$_{VP[PRES]}$ may [$_{VP[BSE]}$ like Mary]]]

        F/A: PRES(MAY(JOHN(LIKE(MARY))))
              composite Fp

    c. John may have been seeing Mary.
    d. syntax: [$_{S[PRES]}$ John [$_{VP[PRES]}$ may [$_{VP[BSE]}$ have [$_{VP[PSP]}$ been [$_{VP[PRP]}$ seeing Mary]]]]]

        F/A: PRES(MAY(PAST(PROG(JOHN(SEE(MARY))))))
              composite Fp

In (68b), the syntactic correspondent of the F/A subject [$_{ARG}$ JOHN], namely, [$_{NP}$ John], and that of its associate predicate [$_{Fa}$ LIKE(MARY)], namely, [$_{VP[BSE]}$ like Mary], are separated by *may*, the syntactic correspondent of the composite Fp [$_{Fp}$ PRES]∘[$_{Fp}$ MAY]. (68c) is a sentence with a series of auxiliary verbs. Again, the correspondences between its syntax and F/A are the same. That is, the syntactic correspondent of the F/A subject [_ARG JOHN] and that of its associate predicate [_Fa SEE(MARY)] are separated by the string *may have been*, which is the syntactic correspondent of the composite Fp [_Fp PRES]∘[_Fp MAY]∘[_Fp PAST]∘[_Fp PROG]. There are two association line crossings in (68b) and four in (68d), each due to the innocuous subject raising mismatch.

The innocuous mismatches in subject raising that we have been considering so far are characterized by (69), in which (i) the outermost subject NP and the innermost VP in syntax correspond respectively to the ARG and Fa of the innermost PROP in F/A, and (ii) the two are separated in syntax by a string of verbs that corresponds to a string of Fp functors in F/A, namely, the composite Fp.

(69) innocuous mismatches in subject raising (Ueno 2014: 145)
      syntax: [_S[FIN] NP [_VP[FIN] V[FIN] [_VP V ...[_VP V VP]...]]]

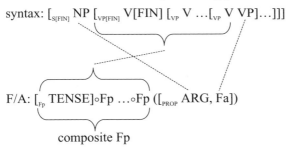

      F/A: [_Fp TENSE]∘Fp ...∘Fp ([_PROP ARG, Fa])
           composite Fp

In (68d), the functor [_Fp PAST] that occurs in a non-finite environment corresponds to the perfect auxiliary verb *have* in syntax (McCawley 1973: 259–260). The lexical entry for this perfect auxiliary verb is given in (70).

(70) lexical entry for perfect auxiliary *have* (Ueno 2014: 145)
      syntax: V[AUX] in [__, VP[PSP]]
      F/A: [_Fp PAST]
      E/R: nil
      morph: V[0]
      mphon: [_V[0] /hæv/], [_V[1, PRES, 3SG] /hæz/], [_V[1, PAST] /hæd/]

Note that the three forms [_V[1, BSE] /hæv/], [_V[1, PRES] /hæv/], and [_V[1, PRP] /hævɪŋ/] that are not listed in the morphophonological (mphon) field of (70) are to be supplied by the morphophonological rules for regular verbs (Ueno 2014: 10) and that the F/A of V[PRES, AUX] *have* and *has* and that of V[PAST, AUX] *had* are [$_{Fp}$ PRES]∘[$_{Fp}$ PAST] and [$_{Fp}$ PAST]∘[$_{Fp}$ PAST], respectively.

(71) provides examples of the subject raising verb *seem*, whose F/A category is Fp. This verb works in exactly the same way as tenses and auxiliary verbs. The mismatches represented by the association line crossings between the syntax and F/A in (71) are all innocuous subject raising mismatches characterized by (69). The lexical entry for *seem* is given in (72), whose syntactic field contains three subcategorization frames.

(71) (Ueno 2014: 146)
   a. John seems to like Mary. (= (64b))
   b. syntax: [$_{S[PRES]}$ John [$_{VP[PRES]}$ seems [$_{VP[to]}$ to [$_{VP[BSE]}$ like Mary]]]]

   F/A: PRES(SEEM(JOHN(LIKE(MARY))))

   composite Fp

   c. John seems to have been seeing Mary.
   d. syntax: [$_{S[PRES]}$ John [$_{VP[PRES]}$ seems [$_{VP[to]}$ to have [$_{VP[PSP]}$ been [$_{VP[PRP]}$ seeing Mary]]]]]

   F/A: PRES(SEEM(PAST(PROG(JOHN(SEE(MARY))))))

   composite Fp

   e. John may seem to have been seeing Mary.
   f. syntax: [$_{S[PRES]}$ John [$_{VP[PRES]}$ may [$_{VP[BSE]}$ seem [$_{VP[to]}$ to have [$_{VP[PSP]}$ been [$_{VP[PRP]}$ seeing Mary]]]]]]

   F/A: PRES(MAY(SEEM(PAST(PROG(JOHN(SEE(MARY)))))))

   composite Fp

(72) lexical entry for *seem* (Ueno 2014: 146)
   syntax: V in [__, VP[*to*]], [__, CP[*that*]], [__, S[FIN]]
   F/A: [$_{Fp}$ SEEM]
   E/R: [$_{TYPE}$ "seem"] in [$_{EV}$ __ [$_{TH}$ EV]]
   morph: V[0]
   mphon: [$_{V[0]}$ /siːm/]

1.6.2 Object raising

In the object raising construction (object raising for short) such as (73b), the verb takes an object NP and a complement VP[*to*], which are interpreted as forming an embedded proposition. Object raising occurs with verbs such as *believe* and *think*. Semantically, these verbs take two arguments, as in (73a): a person who holds a belief or thought, which is expressed as the subject NP, and the content of the belief or thought, which is expressed as a CP[*that*] complement. Verbs of this class express the meaning of (73a) in another way, namely, as the object raising construction (73b).

In transformational grammars, object raising was explained either (i) by a rule that "moves" the subject NP of the complement clause to the matrix object NP position, as in (73c), or (ii) by Exceptional Case Marking (ECM), an "exceptional" way of assigning accusative Case to the subject NP of the embedded nonfinite clause, as in (73d). The ECM analysis of object raising (73d) assumes the binary-branching VP structure [$_{VP}$ V S[*to*]], which was argued against on the basis of a series of empirical data in Ueno (2014: 168–81).

(73) (Ueno 2014: 161)
    a. John believes that Mary likes music.
    b. John believes Mary to like music.
    c. John believes [$_{NP}$] [$_{S[to]}$ [$_{NP}$ Mary] to like music].
    d. John believes [$_{S[to]}$ [$_{NP}$ Mary] to like music].
                                accusative Case

Note that French and German verbs of the same semantic class lack this construction (i.e., [$_{VP}$ V NP[ACC] VP[–FIN]]), although both languages allow the small clause construction for this class of verb, just like English, as in *Je te trouve amusant* and *Ich finde dich witzig*. However, French and German allow the subject control use of these verbs. For example, the French verb *croire* and the German verb *glauben* take not only a CP[*that*] complement (CP[*dass*] in German and CP[*que*] in French) but also a nonfinite VP complement: *Je crois* [$_{VP[BSE]}$ *pouvoir l'aider*] and *Ich glaube* [$_{VP[zu]}$ *ihm helfen zu können*].

In AMG terms, object raising verbs take two complements in syntax, an NP object and a VP[*to*] complement, and their F/A category is Fpa. The default

40   1 AUTOMODULAR GRAMMAR OVERVIEW

correspondence rules (57) establish the correspondences between the three modules shown in (74): $NP_① \leftrightarrow ARG_① \leftrightarrow [AG, LO]_①$ and $NP_② \leftrightarrow ARG_② \leftrightarrow ROLE_②$. There is no constituent in syntax that corresponds to the PROP and EV enclosed in a rectangle. The ternary-branching VP structure in the object-raising construction was defended in Ueno (2014: 168–81).

(74) syntax, F/A, and E/R of *I believe John to be fond of Mary* (Ueno 2014: 162)

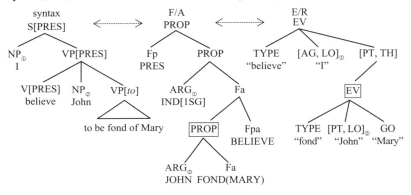

(75) (Ueno 2014: 162)
syntax: [$_{S[PRES]}$ I [$_{VP[PRES]}$ believe [$_{NP}$ John] [$_{VP[to]}$ to be fond of Mary]]]

F/A: PRES(I(BELIEVE(JOHN(FOND(MARY)))))

There is a mismatch between syntax and semantics (F/A and E/R) in (74) and (75) such that the object NP of the matrix clause in syntax corresponds to the subject of the complement clause in semantics. This mismatch is forced by the fact that there is no CP or S in syntax that corresponds to the embedded PROP in F/A and the embedded EV in E/R. Mismatches of this type must be innocuous in English, though not in French and German since they lack this construction. (76) is the lexical entry for object raising verbs.

(76) lexical entry for object raising verbs in English (Ueno 2014: 162)
syntax: V in [__ NP[ACC] VP[*to*]]
F/A: Fpa
E/R: TYPE in [$_{EV}$ __ [AG, LO] [$_{[PT, TH]}$ EV]]

1.6 BRIEF DISCUSSION ON RAISING 41

(77a) is an example of object raising in which the complement PROP has its own Fp functors (TENSE and ASPECT). This is a nonfinite counterpart of *I believe that John has been seeing Mary (for a year now)*, in which the present perfect progressive ($[_{Fp}$ PRES]∘$[_{Fp}$ PAST]∘$[_{Fp}$ PROG] in F/A) corresponds to the string of *to have been*. Even the sentence *I believe John to be fond of Mary* in (74), repeated here as (77b), is interpreted as a nonfinite counterpart of *I believe that John is fond of Mary*. Note that the PRES in the embedded PROP in (77a, b) is another defective lexical item (78), which has only the F/A value PRES and nil in all the other fields.

(77) (Ueno 2014: 163)
    a. I believe John to have been seeing Mary (for a year now).
       syntax: $[_{S[PRES]}$ I $[_{VP[PRES]}$ believe $[_{NP}$ John] $[_{VP[to]}$ to have been seeing Mary]]]

       F/A: PRES(I(BELIEVE($[_{PROP}$ PRES(PAST(PROG(JOHN(SEE(MARY))))))])))

                       composite Fp

    b. I believe John to be fond of Mary. (= (74))
       syntax: $[_{S[PRES]}$ I $[_{VP[PRES]}$ believe $[_{NP}$ John] $[_{VP[to]}$ to be fond of Mary]]]

       F/A: PRES(I(BELIEVE($[_{PROP}$ PRES(JOHN(FOND(MARY)))])))
                        Fp

(78) lexical entry for nonfinite PRES (Ueno 2014: 163)
    syntax: nil
    F/A: $[_{Fp}$ PRES]
       with its mother PROP corresponding to a nonfinite S or VP in syntax
    E/R: nil
    morph: nil
    mphon: nil

The presence of (78) in a nonfinite PROP in F/A accounts for the contrast found in *I believe John to be sick in bed {today | *yesterday}* and in *John seems to be sick in bed {today | *yesterday}*. This is another coerced material that is available freely to guarantee the well-formedness of F/A structures. See Ueno (2014: 201) for coercion.

The hallmark of object raising is that there is no syntactic constituent S or CP that corresponds to the complement PROP (the PROP enclosed in a rectangle in (74)) of the Fpa functor of an object raising verb. This is in exact parallel with subject raising, in which there is no syntactic constituent S or CP that corresponds to the complement PROP of the Fp functor of a subject raising verb such as *seem*. Therefore, the subject ARG of these complement PROPs must find its expression somewhere in syntax, and it corresponds to the matrix object NP in the case of object raising and to the matrix subject NP in the case of subject raising. Note that these NPs do not carry any role of the matrix raising verb.

The matrix object NP of an object raising verb does not carry any of the verb's participant roles, since the theme role ($[_{\text{PT, TH}}$ EV]) of an object raising verb is borne by the embedded PROP in F/A that corresponds to two non-constituent phrases in syntax, the matrix object NP and the complement VP[*to*]. This is again in exact parallel with subject raising, in which the matrix subject NP of a subject raising verb does not carry any of the verb's participant roles. The theme role ($[_{\text{PT, TH}}$ EV]) of a subject raising verb is borne by the embedded PROP in F/A that corresponds to two non-constituent phrases in syntax, the matrix subject NP and the complement VP[*to*].

Based on these exact parallels between object raising and subject raising and the characterization of innocuous mistakes in subject raising (69), the following characterization of innocuous mismatches in object raising was proposed in Ueno (2014: 164).

(79) innocuous mismatches in object raising (Ueno 2014: 146)
    (i) The subject ARG of the complement PROP of an object raising verb (V_{OR}) is allowed to correspond to the matrix object NP in syntax.
    (ii) syntax: $[_{\text{VP}}$ V_{OR} NP $[_{\text{VP}[to]}$ V ...$[_{\text{VP}}$ V VP]...]]]

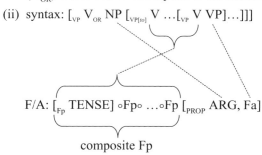

F/A: $[_{\text{Fp}}$ TENSE] ∘Fp∘ ...∘Fp $[_{\text{PROP}}$ ARG, Fa]

composite Fp

(79i), which is a language particular property that French and German do not share, captures the correspondences in (74) between the matrix object NP and the subject ARG of the complement PROP of an object raising verb. On the other hand, (79ii) captures the type of innocuous mismatches countenanced by object raising verbs, which are exactly the same as the type of innocuous mismatches permitted by subject raising verbs (69).

The semantic characteristics of raising verbs are (i) that these verbs express how the speaker conceives the content of the complement proposition (the speaker's epistemic attitude toward the content of the proposition), for example, how plausible the speaker takes it to be, or how she comes to know it, and (ii) that these verbs assert the content of the proposition, that is, it is not a presupposed background part but an asserted foreground part of the sentence meaning. (The subject raising verb *happen* is an implicative verb, but (i) and (ii) still hold.) Because factive verbs express that the speaker takes the content of the complement proposition for granted, their complement proposition is not an asserted part. Therefore, subject and object raising verbs are not factive verbs (Kiparsky and Kiparsky 1971: 346, 348). Factivity also explains why subject raising verbs cannot have a clausal subject (*CP[*that*] *seems/ appears/happens*). A clausal subject is interpreted as factive, that is, presupposed (background) information (Sadock 2012: 36, Kiparsky and Kiparsky 1971: 366), which contradicts the non-factive characteristic of subject raising verbs.

(69) and (79) are conflated into (80), which guarantees innocuous mismatches between the syntax and F/A of raising predicates.

(80) Raising Principle (Ueno 2014: 168)
 i. The subject ARG of the complement PROP of a raising predicate X_R (X = V or A) is allowed to correspond to a matrix NP position in syntax.
 ii. syntax: NP, X_R, [$_{VP[-FIN]}$ V …[$_{VP}$ V VP[–FIN]]…]

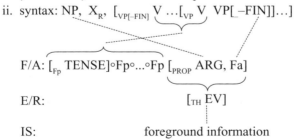

F/A: [$_{Fp}$ TENSE]∘Fp∘…∘Fp [$_{PROP}$ ARG, Fa]

E/R: [$_{TH}$ EV]

IS: foreground information

In (80i), the matrix NP position can be either the subject NP or the object NP. (80ii) says that the matrix NP and its non-finite associate VP can be separated in syntax by a string of verbs if the string corresponds to a composite Fp in F/A.

1.7 Brief Discussion on Unique Control Verbs

The verb *order* is said to be an object-control verb, because the semantic subject of its VP[*to*] complement is coreferential with the verb's object NP. That is, the controller of an object-control verb is its object NP. By contrast, the verb *promise* is said to be a subject-control verb, because the semantic subject of its VP[*to*] complement is coreferential with the verb's subject NP. That is, the controller of a subject-control verb is its subject NP. These verbs are called unique control verbs in the sense that their controller is uniquely specified in their lexical entries. The controller of a unique control verb is determined by its lexical semantics. Therefore, the semantic information in the lexical entry for a unique control verb must contain the specification of its controller. In AMG, this is done by stating the coreference requirement between the controller and controllee in the E/R field of the lexical entry for a unique control verb. (81) and (82) are lexical entries for *order* and *promise*.

(81) lexical entry for *order*
(cf. Ueno 2014: 187)
syntax: V in [__, NP, VP[*to*]]
F/A: Fpaa
E/R: [$_{TYPE}$ "order"] in [$_{VA}$__ [AG, SO]
[PT, GO] [$_{TH}$ [$_{EV}$ HAR …]]]

(82) lexical entry for *promise*
(cf. Ueno 2014: 188)
syntax: V in [__, NP, VP[*to*]]
F/A: Fpaa
E/R: [$_{TYPE}$ "promise"] in [$_{VA}$ __
[AG, SO] [PT, GO] [$_{TH}$ [$_{EV}$ HAR …]]]

The dotted lines in the E/R fields of (81) and (82) indicate the coreference requirement between the controller role and the controllee role. The controllee in both cases is the highest associable role (HAR) of the subordinate event. Recall that the roles listed on the E/R field of a lexical entry are ordered by the outrank relation defined by (55) and (56). A role is associable if it corresponds to an NP in syntax and an ARG in F/A by (57a). Otherwise, it is called unassociable. As reviewed in the next section, when a transitive verb is passivized (88), its highest associable role (HAR) becomes unassociable and the second highest role becomes the highest associable role (HAR). The dotted lines in (81) and (82) indicate that the controllee role is the HAR of the subordinate event, which covers cases like *Try to be respected by your coworkers* (Sadock 2012: 236, note 8). This coreference

1.7 BRIEF DISCUSSION ON UNIQUE CONTROL VERBS

requirement forces the two ARGs (the ARG that corresponds to the controller role and the subject ARG that corresponds to the controllee role of the subordinate event) to share the same IND value (cf. (32)).

When we consider how a child learns which argument is the controller of a unique control verb, no matter how we linguists may theorize the mechanism of predicting the controller, the undeniable fact remains that a child must learn the lexical meaning of a unique control verb before it can determine the controller of the verb in question, and that learning the meaning of each lexical item is an integral part of language acquisition. Two factors were pointed out in Ueno (2014: 189) that facilitate the learning of the lexical properties of unique control verbs. First, interpreting [$_S$ NP V NP VP[*to*]] as object control, which is predicted by the Minimal Distance Principle (Rosenbaum's (1967: 6) Erasure Principle), is a default case and might be used in language acquisition. That is, unless there are conflicting data available, the controller of the verb in the syntactic structure [$_S$ NP V NP VP[*to*]] is assumed by default to be the object NP. In fact, among the verbs with their subcategorization frame [$_{VP}$ V NP VP[*to*]], object-control verbs far outnumber subject-control verbs. Second, learning in real life what exactly the acts of order and promise are is an essential prerequisite for learning what the verbs *order* and *promise* mean. As for the object-control verb *order*, children must learn in real life what an act of order (or more generally, an act of directive) is before they learn the lexical item *order*. That is, at least a rough definition of an act of order (e.g., an act of order is the speaker's attempt to make the addressee perform a certain act) must be learned before the lexical item *order* can be learned. This definition must include the pragmatic knowledge that it is the person who is ordered (i.e., the addressee in this case) who is responsible for performing the act. By contrast, as for the subject-control verb *promise*, children must learn in real life what an act of promise (or more generally, an act of commissive) is before they learn the lexical item *promise*. That is, at least a rough definition of an act of promise (e.g., an act of promise is the speaker's commitment to perform a certain act) must be learned before the lexical item *promise* can be learned. This definition must include the pragmatic knowledge that it is someone who does the promising (i.e., the speaker in this case) who is responsible for performing the act.

The following discussion is only necessary when we consider free control (Ueno 2014: 194–195) and not needed for unique control verbs. The semantic subject of a freely controlled VP is not represented in syntax but is represented semantically in F/A and E/R. We adopt Sadock's (2012: 47) treatment of the controlled subject as a defective lexical item that is called RHO.

(83) lexical entry for RHO (Ueno 2014: 190)
   syntax: nil
   F/A: ARG[IND[j, AGR(j)]]
   E/R: ROLE
   morph: nil
   mphon: nil

RHO is in effect a zero pronoun that is not represented in syntax. It bears a certain participant role in E/R and serves in F/A as an ARG that carries a certain INDEX value (cf. (32)). In the following, we will be treating RHO as if it were a lexical item in F/A that occupies an ARG, but this is just for ease of exposition. As shown in (83), the real substance of RHO is the value of its INDEX feature.

The distribution of a freely controlled RHO is restricted in English to the semantic subject of a nonfinite VP, that is, the subject ARG of the PROP headed by a functor that corresponds to a nonfinite verb (V[–FIN]) in syntax. A controlled nonfinite VP appears without its syntactic subject. In such a case, an innocuously mismatched correspondence (84) is allowed between a nonfinite VP in syntax and its correspondent PROP in F/A, because there is nothing in syntax that corresponds to the RHO in F/A.

(84) intermodular correspondences of nonfinite VP without syntactic subject (Ueno 2014: 192)

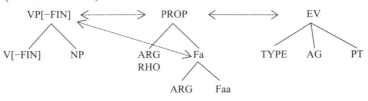

In (84), the VP[–FIN] in syntax corresponds to the Fa in F/A by the default correspondence (57), and at the same time, it corresponds to the PROP that directly dominates the Fa, because the subject ARG (i.e., RHO) is not represented in syntax.

We need something special for such languages as English that only allow RHO to appear as the semantic subject of a nonfinite VP. To restrict the distribution of RHO in these languages, we will incorporate (84) into the lexical entry for RHO (83).

(85) lexical entry for RHO (revised)
　　　syntax: nil
　　　F/A: ARG[IND[j, AGR(j)]] in [$_{PROP}$ __, Fa], where the PROP corresponds to a VP[–FIN] in syntax.
　　　E/R: ROLE
　　　morph: nil
　　　mphon: nil

1.8 Brief Discussion on Passivization

1.8.1 Agentless passives of transitive verbs

The syntax, F/A, and E/R of a transitive active sentence such as (86a) and those of its agentless passive counterpart such as (86b) are given below. The intermodular correspondences between syntax, F/A, and E/R in (86a) and those in (86b), which are indicated by circled numbers, are established by the default correspondence rules (57).

(86) (Ueno 2014: 95)
　　　a. The boy kicked the dog.

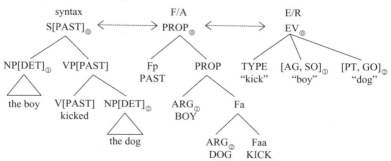

b. The dog was kicked.

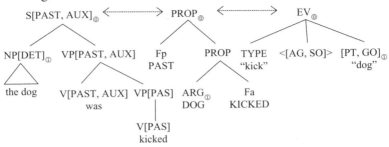

In the active (86a), the subject $NP_①$ in syntax corresponds to the subject $ARG_①$ in F/A and the agent $[AG, SO]_①$ in E/R, whereas the object $NP_②$ in syntax corresponds to the object $ARG_②$ in F/A and the patient $[PT, GO]_②$ in E/R. Note that $NP_①$ c-commands $NP_②$ in syntax, $ARG_①$ c-commands $ARG_②$ in F/A, and $[AG, SO]_①$ outranks $[PT, GO]_②$ in E/R. (86b) is an agentless passive sentence. The subject $NP_①$ in syntax corresponds to the subject $ARG_①$ in F/A and the patient $[PT, GO]_①$ in E/R. The empty verb *be* (Ueno 2014: 54) is used either (i) to carry the tense, because the passive participle (V[PAS] in syntax) is morphologically a full-fledged word (V[1,PSP] in morphology) and hence cannot inflect for tense, or (ii) to satisfy the subcategorization requirement of a lexical item that takes a VP complement. For example, in *The dog seemed* [$_{VP[to]}$ *to* [$_{VP[BSE]}$ *(be) kicked*]], *to* takes a VP[BSE] complement (12c), but cannot take a VP[PAS] complement. The empty *be* is pressed into service to satisfy this requirement. Except for the presence of the empty verb *be*, (86b) is an intransitive sentence, which is evident in its F/A: the functor Fa takes an ARG to form a PROP.

When a role appears in an E/R structure with angled brackets (<ROLE>), it represents an unassociable role: that is, one that counts as a full-fledged role in E/R and is interpreted as such but does not correspond to anything in syntax or in F/A (Sadock 2012: 82). For example, <[AG, SO]> in the E/R structure of (86b) is an unassociable agent role, which does not correspond to anything in syntax or in F/A. In this respect, an unassociable role is special, because an associable role (without angled brackets) corresponds to an NP in syntax and to an ARG in F/A under default correspondences (57a). There is no such thing as a lexical entry for an unassociable role. Where it can occur is specified in the lexical entry for a relevant word, for example, in the lexical entry for the passive participle V[PAS] of a transitive verb.

The unassociable agent (<AG>) in the agentless passive can be interpreted in various ways: it can be singular or plural (87a), specific (87d) or nonspecific (87b), and in some cases almost nonexistent (87c). (87e) can be interpreted as 'I want someone or some people to leave me alone,' where the referent of 'someone or some people' is determined pragmatically in discourse, or can be interpreted as a universally quantified proposition 'I want everyone to leave me alone.' These examples show that the semantic range of <AG> goes far beyond simply assuming *someone* (human and singular) as the hidden/underlying agent for agentless passives (McCawley 1998: 91).

(87) (McCawley 1998: 91)
 a. We have been outvoted.
 b. The Earth was formed 4 billion years ago.
 c. My brother was drowned in a boating accident.
 d. Chomsky's *Syntactic Structures* was written in 1956.
 e. I want to be left alone.

The relationships between active transitive clauses, such as (86a), and their agentless passive counterparts, such as (86b), cannot be explained by "NP-movement" in AMG, because there is no such thing as a "movement" rule in AMG. Instead, they are stated in the lexicon by the Passive Lexical Rule (88) (Sadock 2012: 83). A lexical rule is a statement that captures regular relationships between two sets of lexical entries in the lexicon. More specifically, a lexical rule says that if there is a lexical entry in the lexicon that meets its input conditions, there is another lexical entry in the lexicon that meets its output conditions. For example, the Inversion Lexical Rule (14) captures the regular relationships between the set of lexical entries for finite auxiliary verbs (V[AUX, FIN]) and the set of lexical entries for inverted auxiliary verbs (V[INV]). The Passive Lexical Rule captures the regular relationships between the set of lexical entries for active transitive verbs and the set of lexical entries for passive participles (V[PAS]).

(88) Passive Lexical Rule for transitive verbs (Ueno 2014: 165–6)
 input (active)   output (passive)
 syntax: V in [__, NP, ψ]   → V[PAS] in [__, ψ]
 F/A: Fφa   → Fφ

E/R: TYPE in [$_{EV}$ __ AG PT χ]   →   TYPE in [$_{EV}$ __ <AG> PT χ]
morph: V[0]   →   V[1, PSP]

An advantage of this formulation is that (88) is applicable not only to transitive verbs (Faa in F/A), object control verbs (Fpaa in F/A), and ditransitive verbs (Faaa in F/A) but also to object raising verbs (Fpa in F/A).

The specifications of the four modules in (88) are not independent of each other but closely related: in the output lexical entry, an NP object is lost in syntax, the highest ARG is lost in F/A, and AG is made unassociable in E/R. This output lexical entry, together with the default correspondences (57), predicts that in the passive clause, the subject NP in syntax must correspond to the subject ARG in F/A, which in turn must correspond to the highest associable role (HAR), namely, PT in E/R (Sadock 2012: 82). These correspondences are shown in (86b).

The defining property of the Passive Lexical Rule (88) is its specification <AG> in the E/R field of the output lexical entry, which forces the passive participle in syntax and the corresponding functor in F/A to reduce its valance by one. The net result is that if we compare an active transitive clause and its passive counterpart side by side, a transitive verb corresponds to an intransitive verb (i.e., passive participle) in syntax, and the object ARG of the input transitive functor corresponds to the subject ARG of the output intransitive functor in F/A. This creates an *illusion* of the object NP in the active clause moving in syntax to the subject NP position of the passive clause ("NP-movement") under passivization. Note that the V[PAS] in the syntax of the output lexical entry is the passive participle, which is the past participle (V[1, PSP]) in morphology. (89) illustrates how the Passive Lexical Rule (88) applies to the lexical entry for the transitive verb *kick*.

(89) (Ueno 2014: 99)
   lexical entry for *kick*   lexical entry for passive participle
                                         kicked
   syntax: V in [__, NP]   →   V[PAS] in [__]
   F/A: Faa   →   Fa
   E/R: [$_{TYPE}$ "kick"] in   →   [$_{TYPE}$ "kick"] in
        [$_{EV}$ __ [AG, SO]   [$_{EV}$ __ <[AG, SO]>
        [PT, GO]]   [PT, GO]]
   morph: V[0]   →   V[1, PSP]

1.8 BRIEF DISCUSSION ON PASSIVIZATION 51

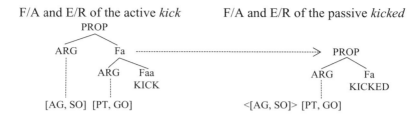

Lexical entries for passive participles (V[PAS]) are needed independently of whether the corresponding active lexical entries exist or not. There are a handful of verbs that are used only in the passive voice (Huddleston and Pullum 2002: 1435 and Quirk et al. 1985: 162). *Rumor* is such an example: *It is rumored that John failed the test* and *John is rumored to have failed the test* but **They rumored that John failed the test*. *Say* has a subject-raising use in the passive (*John is said to have failed the test*) without its corresponding object-raising use in the active (**People say John to have failed the test*). Furthermore, there are VP idioms that only exist in the passive: *be taken aback, be caught short,* and *be written/carved/engraved/set in stone*.

Passive participles have an unassociable agent (<AG>) in the E/R field of their lexical entry. Therefore, they can support intentional modifiers, such as *purposely* or *in order to …* (Sadock 2012: 81). On the other hand, the E/R of an unaccusative verb such as *fall* is [$_{EV}$ [$_{TYPE}$ "fall"] [PT, TH]], which lacks an agent, and cannot support intentional modifiers. This is illustrated in (90).

(90) (Ueno 2014: 100)
 a. The tree was purposely felled. (Sadock 2012: 81)
 a'. The windows were broken in order to enter the house.
 b. *The tree purposely fell. (Sadock 2012: 80)
 b'. *The windows broke in order to enter the house.

1.8.2 Passivization of object raising and object control verbs

When an object raising verb such as *believe* (76) is passivized, it becomes a subject raising verb. This is illustrated in (91).

(91) a. John believes Mary to be a genius.
 b. Mary is believed to be a genius.
 c. Mary seems to be a genius.

In fact, if we apply the Passive Lexical Rule (88) to the lexical entry for *believe*, as in (92), its output is a lexical entry for a subject raising verb. Compare this output with the lexical entry for *seem* (72).

(92) (Ueno 2014: 165)
   lexical entry for *believe* (76)   lexical entry for the passive
                                                participle *believed*
   syntax: V in [__, NP, VP[*to*]]   →   V[PAS] in [__, VP[*to*]]
   F/A: Fpa   →   Fp
   E/R: [$_{TYPE}$ "believe"] in   →   [$_{TYPE}$ "believe"] in
      [$_{EV}$ __ [AG, LO] [$_{[PT, TH]}$ EV]]   [$_{EV}$ __ <[AG, LO]> [$_{[PT, TH]}$ EV]]
   morph: V[0]   →   V[1, PSP]

By contrast, when an object control verb such as *order* (81) is passivized, it becomes a subject control verb. This is shown in (93).

(93) a. Mary ordered John to stay home.
     b. John was ordered to stay home.
     c. John promised to stay home.

In fact, if we apply the Passive Lexical Rule (88) to the lexical entry for *order*, as in (94), its output is a lexical entry for a subject control verb. Compare this output with the lexical entry for *promise* (82). In the passive lexical entry, the controller role ([PT, GO]) corresponds to the (highest) ARG in F/A, which in turn corresponds to the subject NP in syntax. Note also that the coreference requirement between the patient and the agent of the volitional action (VA) is kept intact in the passive lexical entry.

(94) (Ueno 2014: 196)
   lexical entry for *order* (81)   lexical entry for passive participle
                                                ordered
   syntax: V in [__, NP, VP[*to*]]   →   V[PAS] in [__, VP[*to*]]
   F/A: Fpaa   →   Fpa
   E/R: [$_{TYPE}$ "order"] in   →   [$_{TYPE}$ "order"] in
      [$_{EV}$ __ [AG, SO] [PT, GO]   [$_{EV}$ __ <[AG, SO]> [PT, GO]
      [$_{TH]}$ [$_{VA}$ AG ...]]   [$_{TH]}$ [$_{VA}$ AG ...]]
   morph: V[0]   →   V[1, PSP]

1.8.3 Passivization of VP idioms

Those VP idioms with meanings that are construed as having transitive semantics (i.e., Faa in F/A and TYPE with AG and PT in E/R) can passivize (Sadock

2012: 98). Their meaning is distributed over their parts in a harmonious way. For example, the VP idiom [_VP_ [_V_ *pull*] [_NP_ *strings*]] means 'exploit personal connections' and this meaning is distributed over the idiom in such a way that the verb *pull* carries the meaning 'exploit' when it takes *strings* as its object and the NP *strings* carries the meaning 'personal connections' when it occurs as the object of the verb *pull*. Idioms of this type are called idiomatically combining expressions (ICE) (Nunberg et al. 1994: 496).

We adopt bipartite lexical entries such as (95) for these ICE VP idioms. The first part gives the entry for the idiom as a whole and serves for record keeping. The second part gives the entry for the transitive verb in the idiom. The Passive Lexical Rule (88) is applicable to the second part, as in (96), whereas the first part is kept intact. Note that the default correspondence rules (57) establish from the first part the intermodular correspondences in the idiom: [$_{NP[3PL]}$ strings] ↔ [$_{ARG}$ PERSONAL.CONNECTIONS] ↔ [$_{PT}$ "personal connections"] and [$_V$ pull] ↔ [$_{Faa}$ EXPLOIT] ↔ [$_{TYPE}$ "exploit"].

(95) bi-partite lexical entry for ICE *pull strings* (Ueno 2014: 127)
syntax: [$_{VP}$ [$_V$ pull] [$_{NP[3PL]}$ strings]]   syntax: V in [__, NP]
F/A: [$_{Fa}$ [$_{Faa}$ EXPLOIT], [$_{ARG}$ F/A: Faa
    PERSONAL.CONNECTIONS]]   E/R: TYPE in [$_{EV}$ __ AG PT]
E/R: [$_{EV}$ [$_{TYPE}$ "exploit"] AG   morph: V[0]
    [$_{PT}$ "personal connections"]]

(96) passive lexical entry for ICE *pull strings* (Ueno 2014: 127)
syntax: [$_{VP}$ [$_V$ pull] [$_{NP[3PL]}$ strings]]   syntax: V[PAS] in [__]
F/A: [$_{Fa}$ [$_{Faa}$ EXPLOIT], [$_{ARG}$ F/A: Fa
    PERSONAL.CONNECTIONS]]   E/R: TYPE in [$_{EV}$ __ <AG> PT]
E/R: [$_{EV}$ [$_{TYPE}$ "exploit"] AG   morph: V[1, PSP]
    [$_{PT}$ "personal connections"]]

In the passive lexical entry (96), we can tell from the second part that the patient (PT) corresponds to the sole ARG in F/A and the subject NP in syntax. From the first part of the passive lexical entry, we can tell further that this patient corresponds to the NP [$_{NP[3PL]}$ strings] in syntax.

In fact, because the NP object of this idiom carries a specific meaning ('personal connections') as part of the idiom, its syntactic behavior is expected to be just like a regular NP. This expectation is borne out. The object NP can be modified

54   1 AUTOMODULAR GRAMMAR OVERVIEW

(97b, g), can be quantified (97a, e, f, g), can be topicalized (97d), can be raised (97g), can be referred to by anaphoric devices (pronouns) (97e, f), can appear in the *tough* construction (97f), and can be relativized (97c).

(97) (Ueno 2014: 127–8)
  a. What strings were pulled to give the heretofore heartless Cheney a new heart? (from the web)
  b. Pat pulled the strings that got Chris the job. (Nunberg et al. 1994: 510)
  c. The strings that Pat pulled got Chris the job. (Nunberg et al. 1994: 510)
  d. Those strings, he wouldn't pull for you. (Nunberg et al. 1994: 501)
  e. Kim's family pulled some strings on her behalf, but they weren't enough to get her the job. (Nunberg et al. 1994: 502)
  f. Some strings are harder to pull than others. (Nunberg et al. 1994: 517)
  g. All the right strings seem to have been pulled in securing the proper state-of-the-art support staff. (from the web)

For more details of VP idioms, see Ueno (2014: 126–130).

1.9 Brief Discussion on Unbounded Dependencies

In this section, we briefly review direct *wh*-questions. For full discussions on unbounded dependencies exhibited by *wh*-questions and relative clauses from an AMG perspective, see Chapter 6 in Ueno 2014.

(99a) is an example of a direct *wh*-question. A direct *wh*-question is syntactically the local tree (98), in which the clause CP with the WH[Q] feature dominates two daughters, a *wh*-phrase of the category XP (i.e., XP[WH[Q]]) and an inverted clause (S[INV]) and the former precedes the latter, due to the default word order rule between sisters (59a). Note that the *wh*-phrase of a *wh*-question is generated at the clause-initial position in syntax and hence there is no "*wh*-movement" in AMG.

(98) syntax of *wh*-question (Ueno 2014: 256)
  [$_{CP[WH[Q]]}$ XP[WH[Q]], S[INV]]

The internal syntax of CP[WH[Q]] in (98) is an exocentric construction, that is, the CP lacks its own head C. However, the HFC (3) is not violated, because there is no head that the mother CP[WH[Q]] must share head features with. (99b) shows the syntax, F/A, and E/R of (99a).

(99) (Ueno 2014: 256–7)
   a. Which medicine did Mary take?
   b. syntax, F/A, and E/R of (99a)

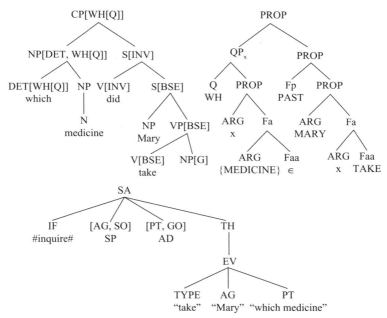

   c. syntactic dominance path (from top CP[WH[Q]] to bottom NP[G]) of (99a)
   CP[WH[Q]] S[INV] S[BSE] VP[BSE] NP[G]
   d. F/A dominance path (from top PROP to bottom variable [$_{ARG}$ x]) of (99a)
   PROP PROP PROP Fa [$_{ARG}$ x]

In (99b), the clause-initial *wh*-phrase and the NP gap (NP[G]) in syntax correspond to the QP$_x$ and the variable [$_{ARG}$ x] in F/A, respectively. In the F/A structure, because of the interrogative determiner *which*, the variable x is interpreted as belonging to a definite set (43) that is contextually evoked in the discourse. The E/R shows that a direct *wh*-question in syntax corresponds to a speech act (SA) in E/R with the illocutionary force (IF) #inquire#, in which the speaker (SP) asks the addressee (AD) a question. (The details of SA were discussed in Chapter 7 of Ueno 2014 and will be reviewed in Chapter 2.) In the case of a direct *wh*-question, the CP[WH[Q]] in syntax corresponds to the SA with the #inquire# illocutionary force, which requires of the *wh*-question that its daughter be an inverted clause (S[INV]). Furthermore, the PT role of the verb *take* is borne by *which medicine*, because the ARG that corresponds to the PT role is the variable x, which belongs to a contextually salient set of MEDICINE in the domain expression for the quantifier [$_Q$ WH]. In other words, as far as the E/R of a *wh*-question is concerned, the clause-initial *wh*-phrase is interpreted *in situ* as one of the roles in E/R, as if there was no "movement."

(99c) shows that the relationship between the top CP[WH[Q]] node and the bottom NP[G] node is captured by a dominance path, which represents the dominance relations of the nodes in the syntactic structure in (99b) from the top CP[WH[Q]] to the bottom NP[G]. (99d) shows that the relationship between the top PROP node and the bottom variable [$_{ARG}$ x] is captured by a dominance path that represents the dominance relations of the nodes in the F/A structure in (99b) from the top PROP to the bottom [$_{ARG}$ x]. For every *wh*-question (CP[WH[Q]] in syntax), there are always syntactic and F/A dominance paths from the top node to the bottom node.

The unbounded dependencies in *wh*-questions are specified by the dominance path conditions, which are encoded in the lexical entry (100) for a clause-initial *wh*-phrase.

(100) lexical entry for clause-initial interrogative *wh*-phrase XP[WH[Q], α]
   (Ueno 2014: 287)
   syntax: XP[WH[Q], α] in [$_{CP[WH[Q]]}$ ___ S[{FIN|INV}]], where α is a PFORM value if X = P
   - syntactic dominance path conditions
      a. subject gap: CP[WH[Q]] $\mathcal{A}$* S[FIN] NP[G]
      b. non-subject gap: CP[WH[Q]] $\mathcal{A}$* VP $\mathcal{B}$* XP[G, α], where $\mathcal{A}$={S, VP, AP, CP[{*that* | *for*}]} and $\mathcal{B}$={NP, PP}
   - F/A dominance path condition
      PROP {PROP, Fa, Faa, Fpa}* {ARG, POS}* [$_{ARG}$ x]

Two remarks are in order about (100). First, (100) does not apply to an *in situ wh*-phrase. Therefore, the dominance path conditions are irrelevant to *in situ wh*-phrases such as those in multiple *wh*-questions and quiz questions. The implication is that only the clause-initial *wh*-phrase exhibits island phenomena. Second, the Kleene star * is used in (100). For any set A, A* refers to the set of all the strings of elements of A of any length (including zero) in any order. For example, the subject gap dominance path condition (100a) means that the dominance path of a *wh*-question starts with CP[WH[Q]] and ends with the string S[FIN] NP[G] (i.e., a subject NP gap), and there may be between the two any number, including zero, of S, VP, CP[*that*], or CP[*for*] in any order. The correct order will be determined separately by the relevant PS rules and lexical entries.

The dominance path conditions in (100) capture the fact that *wh*-questions exhibit unbounded dependencies: that is, however deeply the bottom gap XP[G] may be embedded, it is associated with the clause-initial topmost *wh*-phrase XP[WH[Q]]. This is illustrated in (101).

(101) (Borsley 1999: 188–189)
    a. Who [$_{S[INV]}$ do [$_{S[BSE]}$ you think [$_{S[PAST]}$ Hobbs saw __]]]?
        dominance path: CP[WH[Q]] S[INV] S[BSE] VP[BSE] S[PAST] VP[PAST] NP[G]
    b. Who [$_{S[INV]}$ do [$_{S[BSE]}$ you think [$_{S[PAST]}$ Hobbs said [$_{S[PAST]}$ he saw __]]]]?
        dominance path: CP[WH[Q]] S[INV] S[BSE] VP[BSE] S[PAST] VP[PAST] S[PAST] VP[PAST] NP[G]
    c. Who [$_{S[INV]}$ do [$_{S[BSE]}$ you think [$_{S[PAST]}$ Hobbs said [$_{S[PAST]}$ he imagined [$_{S[PAST]}$ he saw __]]]]]?
        dominance path: CP[WH[Q]] S[INV] S[BSE] VP[BSE] S[PAST] VP[PAST] S[PAST] VP[PAST] S[PAST] VP[PAST] NP[G]

Since every *wh*-question comes with its syntactic and F/A dominance paths from the top (CP[WH[Q]] in syntax and PROP in F/A) to the bottom (XP[G] in syntax and [$_{ARG}$ x] in F/A), we can think of the unbounded dependency of a *wh*-question as consisting of three parts: the top, the middle, and the bottom of its dominance path. The top is always CP[WH[Q]] and PROP, and the bottom is always XP[G] and [$_{ARG}$ x]. Capturing the unbounded dependencies in *wh*-questions boils down to how we can specify the infinite set of the middle parts of licit dominance paths. We did this in (100) and in Ueno (2014: 262–275) by borrowing from LFG a similar idea called outside-in functional uncertainty and using the Kleene star operator * on the set of syntactic and F/A categories that allow "*wh*-movement" out of them.

The dominance path conditions encoded in (100) account for many well-known islands, which was shown in Ueno (2014: 262–275). For example, every time "*wh*-movement" violates the Complex NP Constraint (CNPC), there will always be a string of NP (NP) (CP) S somewhere in the middle of its syntactic dominance path and a string of ARG Ma PROP somewhere in the middle of its F/A dominance path. However, these strings are excluded from the syntactic and F/A dominance path conditions in (100). (102) is an example of CNPC violation. See Ueno (2014) for accounts of other islands.

(102) CNPC violation
    a. *What topics does Mary like to read books that are about?
       cf. What topics does Mary like to read books about?
    b. syntactic dominance path
       CP[WH[Q]] S[INV] S[BSE] VP[BSE] VP[*to*] VP[BSE]
       <u>NP CP[*that*]</u> S[FIN] VP[FIN] PP[*about*] NP[G]
       (offending node underlined)
    c. F/A dominance path
       PROP PROP PROP Fa PROP Fa <u>ARG Ma</u> PROP Fa [$_{ARG}$ x]
       (offending nodes underlined)

The dominance path conditions in (100) are *positive* specifications of infinite licit "*wh*-movement" paths. This is quite different from *negative* specifications of islands, which list illicit paths of "*wh*-movement" (i.e., syntactic environments out of which "*wh*-movement" is impossible). What children need to learn from their primary data is not a list of islands per se but the *positive* specifications of licit "*wh*-movement" paths (i.e., environments where "*wh*-movement" is *possible*). The islands that happen to have been discovered so far in the history of Generative Grammar since Ross (1967) are a very small subset of the complement set of licit dominance paths. That is, the following relations hold.

(103) (Ueno 2014: 271)
    {islands discovered so far} ⊂ {all dominance paths licit or illicit}
    −{dominance paths captured by the dominance path conditions}

The essential part that characterizes unbounded dependencies in terms of the dominance path conditions (100a, b) is $\mathcal{A}$ = {S, VP, AP, CP[{*that* | *for*}]}. Children need to learn the set $\mathcal{A}$ by finding what syntactic categories are generators of $\mathcal{A}$*.

1.9 BRIEF DISCUSSION ON UNBOUNDED DEPENDENCIES

For the sake of concreteness, let us assume that children can learn that a syntactic category X is a generator of $\mathcal{A}^*$ if and only if they are exposed to *wh*-questions in which X appears at least twice in the middle part of the dominance paths. If so, the set $\mathcal{A}$ can be learned from a very simple set of data. For example, a simple, short-distance *wh*-question like (104a) contains in its dominance path two occurrences of S, namely, S[PAST, INV] and S[BSE], and shows a learner that S is a member of $\mathcal{A}$. A *wh*-question like (104b) contains in its dominance path two occurrences of VP, namely, VP[PRES] and VP[PSP], and tells a learner that VP is a member of $\mathcal{A}$. A *wh*-question like (104c) is enough for a learner to learn that CP[*that*] is a member of $\mathcal{A}$. Such an example as (104d) is sufficient to learn that both S and VP are members of $\mathcal{A}$.

(104) (Ueno 2014: 271–2)
  a. What did you eat?
     What [$_{\text{S[PAST, INV]}}$ did [$_{\text{S[BSE]}}$ you [$_{\text{VP[BSE]}}$ eat NP[G]]]]?
  b. I don't know what you have eaten.
     I don't know what [$_{\text{S[PRES]}}$ you [$_{\text{VP[PRES]}}$ have [$_{\text{VP[PSP]}}$ eaten NP[G]]]].
  c. What did you say that Mary told you that John ate?
     What [$_{\text{S[PAST, INV]}}$ did [$_{\text{S[BSE]}}$ you [$_{\text{VP[BSE]}}$ say [$_{\text{CP[}that\text{]}}$ that [$_{\text{S[PAST]}}$ Mary [$_{\text{VP[PAST]}}$ told you [$_{\text{CP[}that\text{]}}$ that [$_{\text{S[PAST]}}$ John [$_{\text{VP[PAST]}}$ ate NP[G]]]]]]]]]?
  d. What did you say John ate?
     What [$_{\text{S[PAST, INV]}}$ did [$_{\text{S[BSE]}}$ you [$_{\text{VP[BSE]}}$ say [$_{\text{S[PAST]}}$ John [$_{\text{VP[PAST]}}$ ate NP[G]]]]]]?

Furthermore, there seem to be clear implication relations between the members of $\mathcal{A}$: if CP[*that*] is a member of $\mathcal{A}$, so is S, and if S is a member of $\mathcal{A}$, so is VP.

Chapter 2
Inferential Interpretation

> In this chapter, we will discuss the inferential nature of utterance comprehension, in general, and fragment comprehension, in particular, by introducing basic Relevance Theoretic notions. We will argue that the ability to use fragments is acquired very early in children's language acquisition, which is supported by human inferential ability. We will conclude that when various elliptic forms are interpreted, the same type of inference that is involved in fragment interpretation is also involved. We will also revisit the notions of speech act and indirect speech act.

2.1 Inferential Nature of Utterance Interpretation and Relevance Theory

The hearer/interpreter's process of utterance interpretation is largely inferential (Sperber and Wilson 1995: 13, Wilson and Sperber 2012: 3, 332). An utterance produced by the speaker and directed to the hearer provides only a piece of "evidence" of her intended meaning (what the speaker intended to communicate) in the sense that the meaning linguistically decoded by the hearer from an utterance vastly underdetermines its explicit content (i.e., explicatures) and implicit content (i.e., implicatures). The hearer, therefore, needs to infer the speaker's intended meaning on the basis of the evidence (i.e., the utterance) provided to him, the linguistic and non-linguistic context in which it is uttered, and the set of assumptions the hearer can access at that time by developing the decoded meaning as defined in (9).

(1) is an exchange to illustrate this point. It takes place when Lisa drops by her neighbor Alan one evening as he and his family are sitting down to supper.

(1) (Wilson and Sperber 2012: 11)
   Alan: Do you want to join us for supper?
   Lisa: No, thanks. I've eaten.

Lisa inferentially interprets Alan's interrogative sentence not as a request for information about whether she desires to join them for supper but as an invitation to supper, probably based on a script that a family invites to supper a friend of theirs who happens to visit them at supper time. Lisa replies "No, thanks" based on this invitation interpretation. Alan inferentially interprets Lisa's "I've eaten" as 'Lisa has <u>already</u> eaten <u>supper this evening</u>.' Note the inferential enrichments indicated by the underlines. Enrichment of this type is usually performed automatically and unconsciously during the on-line processing of utterances. Furthermore, Alan inferentially interprets this as Lisa's providing a reason for declining his invitation, probably based on the following encyclopedic information about the concept of supper.

(2) (Wilson and Sperber 2012: 14)
   a. People don't normally want to eat supper twice in one evening.
   b. The fact that one has already eaten supper on a given evening is a good reason for refusing an invitation to supper that evening.

As far as the human inferential ability is concerned, humans are extremely good at inferring another person's feelings, thoughts, and intentions ("theory of mind" or "mind-reading") (Anzai 2011: 17–18, Hakoda et al. 2010: 337, 348, Michimata et al. 2011: 25, 269, 275, Carston 2002: 43). This inferential ability seems to have antedated the linguistic ability both phylogenetically (Sperber and Wilson 1995: 176, Wilson and Sperber 2012: 338) and ontogenetically (Bloom 2002: 10, 55, 261, Anzai 2011: 60, 62). For one thing, not only humans but also other primates possess inferential ability (Michimata et al. 2011: 25, 240, Hakoda et al. 2010: 337–338, 348, Katori et al. 2011: 45, 291–292, Sperber and Wilson 1995: 173, 174). Wilson and Sperber (2012: 338) wrote: "From a pragmatic perspective, it is quite clear that the language faculty and human languages, with their richness and flaws, are only adaptive in a species that is already capable of naive psychology (the ability to represent the mental states of others) and (non-verbal) inferential communication" (parentheses added by YU). For another, very young children can infer what is in another person's mind (intention-reading) even before learning their first language (Tomasello 2003: 21, Gray 2011: 414–415, 445–446, Wilson and Sperber 2012: 234). Wilson and Sperber (2012: 266) also wrote: "Yet preverbal infants already appear to be heavily involved in inferential communication." In fact, this is what occurs among children at the one-word stage of language acquisition. They communicate with their parents and other children by uttering one-word utterances (i.e., fragments). The communication at this stage is largely based on inference. Human inferential ability seems to come with a substantial innate endowment, just as does human linguistic ability (Wilson and Sperber 2004: 280). Therefore, we follow Wilson and Sperber (2004: 280, 2012: 262–278) and assume the existence of the Inferential Comprehension Module (ICM), a dedicated module for inferential comprehension, in addition to the Language Module (LM).

As was described in the preceding paragraph, learning how to use fragments (e.g., one-word utterances) is achieved very early in language acquisition and is enabled by human inferential ability. Learning to use other forms of ellipsis such as sluicing, VP ellipsis, gapping, and Right Node Raising comes later. It would be surprising if humans, when comprehending other types of ellipsis, did not use their inferential ability, which must be already at their disposal and must have been so ever since they were born. Therefore, it is quite natural to assume that when these elliptic forms are interpreted, the same type of inference is performed as in fragment interpretation.

In order to better explain utterance interpretation, we assume that the Language Module (LM) is an input system (Sperber and Wilson 1995: 73, 177) that automatically and unconsciously decodes every utterance U. We further assume that the LM contains a version of Automodular Grammar (AMG) such as the one proposed in Sadock (2012) and Ueno (2014) and briefly reviewed in Chapter 1. The LM computes the decoded four-tuple representations (syntax, F/A, E/R, IS) of U on the basis of the information from the lexical items in U, the phrase structure rules in each module (syntax, F/A, and E/R) of AMG, and the default correspondences between the syntax, F/A, and E/R modules. This decoding computation is carried out automatically, spontaneously, and subconsciously. The decoded four-tuple representations (syntax, F/A, E/R, IS) of U, namely the output of the LM, are then sent to the Inferential Comprehension Module (ICM).

The ICM integrates information coming from various input systems, including the LM, vision, smell, and memory, performs non-demonstrative inference (Sperber and Wilson 1995: 71), and constructs interpretative hypotheses of U. The ICM is assumed to be a submodule of the mind-reading (or theory-of-mind) module (Wilson and Sperber 2012: 262, 267, 271, 278), and is dedicated to constructing interpretive hypotheses by non-demonstrative inference. The non-demonstrative inference carried out in the ICM is guided by the Relevance-guided comprehension heuristic (defined in (8)). The output of the ICM is the explicatures and implicatures of U (defined in (12) and (13)) expressed in Mentalese. This whole process is shown in (3).

(3) Utterance comprehension process
utterance (U) → LM → decoded four-tuple of U → ICM →
development of decoded four-tuple of U → explicatures and implicatures of U

In short, (3) shows that utterances are interpreted by decoding and inference, namely, that the LM decodes an utterance U and computes the decoded four-tuple representations of U and that the ICM develops them (as defined in (9)) and constructs the explicatures and implicatures of U by non-demonstrative inference.

The human ICM is said to employ "non-demonstrative inference" (Sperber and Wilson 2004: 249, 263, Wilson and Sperber 2012: 262), also known as "non-deductive inference" (Clark 2013: 131). Deductive inference is a type of "safe" and "reliable" inference process in which true premises guarantee true conclusions. By contrast, non-demonstrative inference is a type of evidence-based inference process we use unconsciously and spontaneously that leads to "plausible" conclusions that are not guaranteed to be true (i.e., that can occasionally lead from true premises to false conclusions). Non-demonstrative inference includes abductive (inference to the best explanation), inductive, probabilistic, and statistical reasoning (Clark 2013: 132). Non-demonstrative inference consists of hypothesis formation and hypothesis confirmation/disconfirmation (Sperber and Wilson 1995: 68–69, Carston 2002: 378). It is said to be a global process that can freely access all information in the memory (Sperber and Wilson 1995: 65) and to use only logical rules that are spontaneously accessible to the human mind (Sperber and Wilson 1995: 69), namely, elimination rules but not introduction rules (Sperber and Wilson 1995: 97).

Here, we give a series of definitions of the key terms from relevance theory that we need for later discussion. For details of relevance theory, see Sperber and Wilson (1995), Carston (2002), Wilson and Sperber (2012), and Clark (2013).

(4) definition of *relevance* (Wilson and Sperber 2012: 6, 63)
   a. Relevance is a property of inputs to cognitive processes which makes them worth processing (whether external stimuli, which can be perceived and attended to, or internal representations, which can be stored, recalled, or used as premises in inference).

b. An input is relevant to an individual when it connects with available contextual assumptions to yield *positive cognitive effects*: for example, true contextual implications, or warranted strengthenings or revisions of existing assumptions.
c. Everything else being equal, the greater the positive cognitive effects achieved, and the smaller the mental effort required (to represent the input, access a context and derive these cognitive effects), the greater the relevance of the input to the individual at that time.

(5) Cognitive Principle of Relevance (Wilson and Sperber 2012: 6, 38, 64, 103, 272)
Human cognition tends to be geared to the maximization of relevance.

(6) Communicative Principle of Relevance (Wilson and Sperber 2012: 6, 38, 65, 104, 275)
Every act of ostensive-inferential communication (i.e., every utterance) by the speaker conveys to the hearer a presumption of its own optimal relevance.

(7) definition of *presumption of optimal relevance* (cf. Wilson and Sperber 2012: 7, 65, 276)
a. The hearer presumes that the utterance directed to him is so relevant to him that he expects it to be worth processing.
b. The hearer presumes that the utterance directed to him is the most relevant one compatible with the speaker's abilities and preferences.

(8) Relevance-guided comprehension heuristic (Wilson and Sperber 2012: 7, 276)
a. The hearer follows a path of least effort (in order of accessibility) in constructing interpretative hypotheses about the utterance (and in particular in resolving ambiguities and referential indeterminacies, in going beyond linguistic meaning, in supplying contextual assumptions, constructing implicatures, etc.).
b. The hearer stops constructing interpretive hypotheses when his expectations of relevance are satisfied.

(9) definition of *development of decoded four-tuple representations of utterance* (cf. Sperber and Wilson 1995: 181, Wilson and Sperber 2012: 12)

The development of the decoded four-tuple representations (syntax, F/A, E/R, IS) of an utterance U is a process of constructing a semantically complete, truth-evaluable (i.e., fully propositional) interpretive hypothesis from the syntactically and semantically incomplete decoded four-tuple representations of U on the basis of the contextual assumptions, the information assessable from memory, the background knowledge shared by the speaker and hearer, etc., through such inferential tasks as disambiguation, reference assignment, enrichment, and assumption schema embedding.

(10) definition of *explicitness* (cf. Sperber and Wilson 1995: 182)
An interpretive hypothesis constructed by the hearer from an utterance U is explicit if and only if it is a development of the decoded four-tuple representations (syntax, F/A, E/R, IS) of U.

(11) definition of *implicitness* (cf. Sperber and Wilson 1995: 182)
An interpretive hypothesis constructed by the hearer from an utterance U is implicit if and only if it is not explicit.

(12) definition of *explicature* (cf. Sperber and Wilson 1995: 182, Wilson and Sperber 2012: 12)
An explicature of an utterance U is a fully propositional interpretive hypothesis (expressed in Mentalese) that is explicit.

(13) definition of *implicature* (cf. Sperber and Wilson 1995: 182; Wilson and Sperber 2012: 12)
An implicature of an utterance U is a fully propositional interpretive hypothesis (expressed in Mentalese) that is implicit.

Both explicatures and implicatures are constructed inferentially (Wilson and Sperber 2012: 5, 12, 13) by the hearer from the speaker's utterance, which is the best clue to the speaker's intended meaning. The human Inferential Comprehension Module (ICM) constructs the explicatures and implicatures of every utterance spontaneously, automatically, and unconsciously. The smaller the relative contribution of the development process (9), the more explicit the explicatures will be (Sperber and Wilson 1995: 182).

An utterance typically has two types of explicature, basic explicatures and higher-level explicatures.

(14) definitions of *basic* and *higher-level explicatures*
(cf. Carston 2002: 119, Wilson and Sperber 2012: 23, 153)
a. The basic explicature of an utterance U is the explicature of U that determines the explicit truth-conditional content of U. It is also called the proposition expressed.
b. The higher-level explicatures of U are those explicatures that the hearer constructs by embedding the basic explicature P into higher-level descriptions such as *X* (= the speaker of U) *says that P* and *X asks whether P* (speech-act descriptions), and *X believes that P, X regrets that P,* and *X is surprised that P* (propositional-attitude descriptions).

There are two types of implicature: implicated premises and implicated conclusions (Sperber and Wilson 1995: 195), which are illustrated below.

(15) a. John: Do you like sushi?
   Mary: I like all kinds of Japanese food.
b. implicated premise of Mary's utterance
   'Sushi is a Japanese food.'
c. implicated conclusion of Mary's utterance
   'Mary likes sushi.'

In exchange (15a), John constructed the implicated premise (15b) by accessing his encyclopedic knowledge. By contrast, John constructed the implicated conclusion (15c) from the explicature of Mary's utterance and the implicated premise (15b).

In utterance interpretation, there is a huge gap between the information recovered by the linguistic decoding of an utterance U (i.e., the decoded four-tuple representations of U) and the semantically complete explicatures of U. This gap is filled by a development process defined in (9) (Sperber and Wilson 1995: 179–180, 188–189, Wilson and Sperber 2012: 331–332).

Here is an example of inferentially constructing explicatures of an utterance of sentence (16a), whose syntax, F/A, E/R, and IS are shown in (16b). In the case of a sentential utterance U, the output of the LM is the decoded four-tuple representations (syntax, F/A, E/R, IS) of U, in which the E/R of U contains the SA superstructure (to be reviewed in 2.3), as in the E/R of (16b), with the default illocutionary force (IF), #assert# for a declarative sentence, #inquire# for an interrogative sentence, and #order# for an imperative sentence (cf. (36)). When the decoded four-tuple representations are sent to the ICM and combined

68 2 INFERENTIAL INTERPRETATION

with the contextual assumptions, the default IF may be readjusted to a more contextually appropriate IF.

(16) a. (utterance) "He left a straw there." (cf. Sperber and Wilson 1995: 186 (16))
b. decoded four-tuple representations of (16a)

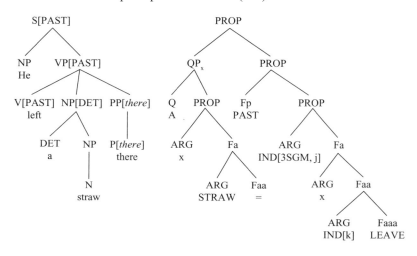

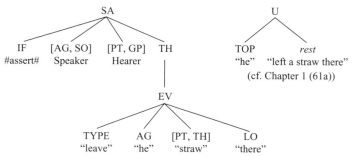

c. (basic explicature) 'The boy in a blue shirt left a drinking straw in the glass that he drank orange juice out of,' in which
[reference assignment] *He* refers to *the boy in a blue shirt* and
[reference assignment] *there* refers to *in the glass that he drank orange juice out of* and
[disambiguation] *a straw* is *a drinking straw*.

d. (higher-level explicature) [assumption schema embedding] 'The speaker has asserted that the boy in a blue shirt left a drinking straw in the glass that he drank orange juice out of.'
e. (higher-level explicature) [assumption schema embedding] 'The speaker believes that the boy in a blue shirt left a drinking straw in the glass that he drank orange juice out of.'

To obtain the semantically complete explicatures of utterance (16a), the hearer will perform at least three types of development: reference assignment, disambiguation, and assumption schema embedding. First, the hearer has to determine the referents of the proforms *he* and *there*. For example, *he* refers to the most accessible referent, let's say, *the boy in a blue shirt* in the context at hand and *there* refers to the most accessible referent in this context *in the glass he drank orange juice out of*. Second, the hearer has to remove the ambiguity of the noun *straw*. For example, the *straw* in this utterance probably means a 'drinking tube' and not a 'cereal stalk' because a child drinking from a glass with a *straw* is a stereotypical event, which is stored in the long-term memory as a script (also known as a schema or frame) and is highly accessible as a single chunk (Sperber and Wilson 1995: 88, 186, Eysenck and Keane 2010: 401, Anderson 2010: 138, Gray 2011: 338, Michimata et al. 2011: 155, Hakoda et al. 2010: 198). Finally, the assumption so obtained, the basic explicature (16c) of (16a), is embedded into assumption schemas such as *The speaker has said that P*, which produces higher-level explicatures (16d, e). The construction of basic and higher-level explicatures does not proceed sequentially but in parallel (Wilson and Sperber 2012: 13, 312).

Here is another example of the inferential construction of explicatures and implicatures.

(17) a. (utterance) "It will get cold." (cf. Sperber and Wilson 1995: 187 (18))
b. (basic explicature) 'The soup on the table will get cold very soon,' in which
[reference assignment] *It* refers to *the soup on the table* and
[disambiguation] *cold* is used in a cold-inducing sense and
[enrichment] the future *will* refers to immediate future 'will very soon.'
c. (higher-level explicature) [assumption schema embedding] 'The speaker has said that the soup on the table will get cold very soon.'

d. (higher-level explicature) [assumption schema embedding] 'The speaker believes that the soup on the table will get cold very soon.'
e. (implicature) 'The speaker tells the hearer to come and eat the soup on the table before it gets cold very soon.'

To obtain semantically complete explicatures of utterance (17a), the hearer will perform at least four types of development: reference assignment, disambiguation, enrichment, and assumption schema embedding. First, the hearer has to determine the referent of the pronoun *it*. For example, *it* refers to *the soup on the table*, the most accessible referent in the context at hand. Second, once the referent of the pronoun is determined, the ambiguity of *cold* is removed. This means not a cold-feeling sense (as in *I am cold*) but a cold-inducing sense (as in *The ice is cold*). Third, the hearer has to narrow the vagueness of the future *will* to a more contextually specific sense, for example, the prediction of immediate future such as *will very soon* (Sperber and Wilson 1995: 179). Finally, the hearer embeds the basic explicature into assumption schemas such as *The speaker believes that P*. In this way, the basic explicature (17b) of (17a) and its higher-level explicatures (17c, d) are constructed.

An utterance has not only explicatures but also implicatures. One possible implicature of (17a) is (17e), which is constructed inferentially on the basis of, among other things, its explicatures, the non-linguistic context at hand, and the script or real world knowledge that food served hot should be eaten before it gets cold.

2.2 Preliminary Considerations on Inferential Interpretation of Fragments

Subsentential fragments uttered in discourse, which will be discussed in Chapter 3, are treated in the same way as sentential utterances in terms of the construction of explicatures and implicatures. First of all, we need to consider why the utterance of a fragment is not simply ignored as ungrammatical or gibberish by the hearer. When a fragment utterance U is directed by the speaker to the hearer, because it is uttered as part of ostensive-inferential communication, U conveys to the hearer a presumption of its own optimal relevance (by the Communicative Principle of Relevance (6)) and therefore the hearer expects that it must be relevant enough to be worth processing (by (7a)). This triggers an inferential comprehension process

2.2 PRELIMINARY CONSIDERATIONS ON INFERENTIAL INTERPRETATION

that includes supplying the fragment with missing elements based on their accessibility (due to the Relevance-guided comprehension heuristic (8)).

Here is an example of an NP fragment.

(18) (context: The following exchange takes place in a cafeteria, where Mary has almost finished eating breakfast when John comes in and talks to her.)
John: What did you have?
Mary [happily]: A steak.

When Mary interprets John's *wh*-question, she needs to construct its explicatures and implicatures by disambiguating the verb *have*, which means 'eat' in the *wh*-question, and enriching the interpretation with 'for breakfast' and 'this morning' as in (19).

(19) John: What did you have?
　　　Mary's interpretation
　　　　basic explicature: 'What did Mary eat for breakfast this morning?'
　　　　higher-level explicatures: 'John asks Mary what she ate for breakfast this morning.'
　　　　　'John does not know what Mary ate for breakfast this morning.'
　　　　　'John wants to know what Mary ate for breakfast this morning.'
　　　Mary [happily]: A steak.
　　　John's interpretation
　　　　basic explicature: 'Mary ate a steak for breakfast this morning.'
　　　　higher-level explicature: 'Mary is happy that she ate a steak for breakfast this morning.'
　　　　implicatures: 'Mary is full.'
　　　　　'Mary was so hungry as to be able to eat a steak for breakfast.' etc.

The whole interpretive process of Mary's NP fragment "A steak" in (18) is shown in (20) in view of (3), the interpretive process of a sentential utterance.

(20) interpretive process of Mary's NP fragment "A steak" in (18)
　　　STEP 1: The Language Module (LM) computes the decoded four-tuple representations of utterance "A steak" from the lexical entries for *a* and *steak*, from the default correspondences between syntax, F/A, and E/R: NP ↔ ARG ↔ ROLE, and from the fact that the NP fragment

72   2 INFERENTIAL INTERPRETATION

>>is intended as an answer to the *wh*-question (i.e., FOC in IS): ($[_{NP[DET]}$ $[_{DET}$ a] $[_{NP}$ steak]], $[_{ARG}$ STEAK], ROLE, $[_U$ $[_{FOC}$ "a steak"]]).
STEP 2: The LM sends the decoded four-tuple representations to the Inferential Comprehension Module (ICM).
STEP 3: The ICM, following the Relevance-guided comprehension heuristic (8), accesses the most accessible information, namely, the decoded four-tuple representations of the preceding *wh*-question and its explicatures and implicatures.
STEP 4: The ICM constructs as the most relevant interpretive hypothesis the inferred four-tuple representations of "I had a steak" and its basic explicature 'Mary ate a steak for breakfast this morning' and higher-level explicature 'Mary is happy that she ate a steak for breakfast this morning' and implicatures (e.g., 'Mary is full') by referring to the explicatures and implicatures of the *wh*-question and by developing the four-tuple representations of *I had a steak*.

When an NP fragment is uttered, its decoded four-tuple representations are computed automatically by the default categorial correspondences (NP ↔ ARG ↔ ROLE ↔ FOC). These correspondences show that an NP, which must be part of an S, corresponds to an ARG in F/A that must be an argument of some proposition (PROP), to a ROLE in E/R that must be a participant role of some event (EV), and to a focus (FOC) in IS that carries new information against the phonologically unrealized old information (i.e., background information (BI) as in $[_U$ FOC BI]). This in turn induces the default modular correspondences S ↔ PROP ↔ EV ↔ U. Therefore, every time an NP fragment is directed to the hearer, his LM computes skeletal four-tuple representations ($[_S$ ... NP ...], $[_{PROP}$ ... ARG ...], $[_{EV}$ ... ROLE ...], $[_U$ ... FOC ...]). This triggers an inferential comprehension process that leads to identifying the S, PROP, and EV in which the NP, ARG, and ROLE are properly located, respectively.

Here is an example of a temporal PP fragment.

(21) John: What time did you have breakfast?
>>Mary's interpretation
>>>basic explicature: 'What time did Mary eat breakfast this morning?'
higher-level explicature: 'John asks Mary what time she ate breakfast this morning.'
'John does not know what time Mary ate breakfast this morning.'
'John wants to know what time Mary ate breakfast this morning.'

2.2 PRELIMINARY CONSIDERATIONS ON INFERENTIAL INTERPRETATION 73

    Mary: Before dawn.
       John's interpretation
          basic explicature: 'Mary ate breakfast before dawn this morning.'
          higher-level explicature: 'Mary claims that she ate breakfast before dawn this morning.'
          implicature: 'Mary is already hungry.'

(22) interpretive process of Mary's PP fragment "Before dawn" in (21)
    STEP 1: The LM computes the decoded four-tuple representations of utterance "Before dawn" from the lexical entries for *before* and *dawn*, from the default correspondences between syntax, F/A, and E/R: PP ↔ Mp ↔ TIME-MOD (cf. Chapter 1 (47)), and from the fact that the PP fragment is intended as an answer to the *wh*-question (i.e., FOC in IS): ($[_{PP}$ $[_{P}$ before] $[_{NP}$ dawn]], $[_{Mp}$ BEFORE.DAWN], TIME-MOD, $[_{U}$ $[_{FOC}$ "before dawn"]])
    STEP 2: The LM sends the decoded four-tuple representations to the ICM.
    STEP 3: The ICM, following the Relevance-guided comprehension heuristic, accesses the most accessible information, namely, the four-tuple representations of the preceding *wh*-question and its explicatures and implicatures.
    STEP 4: The ICM constructs as the most relevant interpretive hypothesis the inferred four-tuple representations of "I had breakfast before dawn" and its explicatures (e.g., 'Mary claims that she ate breakfast before dawn this morning') and implicatures (e.g., 'Mary is already hungry') by referring to the explicatures and implicatures of the *wh*-question and by developing the inferred four-tuple representations of *I had breakfast before dawn*.

When a temporal PP fragment is uttered, its decoded four-tuple representations are computed automatically by the default categorial correspondences (temporal PP ↔ Mp ↔ TIME-MOD ↔ FOC), which shows that the Mp is a modifier of some PROP and the TIME-MOD is a temporal modifier of some event. This in turn leads to skeletal four-tuple representations ($[_{S}$ ... PP ...], $[_{PROP}$ ... Mp ...], $[_{EV}$ ... TIME-MOD ...], $[_{U}$ ... FOC ...]).

(23) is an example of a locative PP fragment. In (23a), the speaker only utters a locative PP fragment without an overt topic, which is a theme NP. The missing topic of the utterance is inferentially supplied from the context, as in (23b).

(23) (Carston 2002: 17)
a. (context: The speaker realizes that the hearer is making breakfast and looking for butter.) "On the top shelf."
b. (basic explicature) 'The butter the hearer is looking for is on the top shelf of the kitchen the hearer is in.'
[enrichment] The zero topic refers to *the butter the hearer is looking for*.
[reference assignment] *The top shelf* refers to *the top shelf of the kitchen the hearer is in now*.
c. (higher-level explicatures) 'The speaker has informed the hearer that the butter he is looking for is on the top shelf of the kitchen he is in.'
'The speaker believes that the butter the hearer is looking for is on the top shelf of the kitchen he is in.'
d. (implicatures) 'The butter the hearer is looking for is not on the bottom shelf.'
'The speaker has returned the butter the hearer is looking for to its proper place.'
'The speaker is not trying to hide the butter the hearer is looking for.' etc.

(24) is an example of a *wh*-fragment.

(24) (context: John and Mary are talking about their cat, which went missing a few days ago.)
John: I saw it in the morning.
  Mary's interpretation
    basic explicature: 'John saw the cat this morning.'
    higher-level explicature: 'John claims that he saw the cat this morning.'
Mary [in a surprised voice]: Where?
  John's interpretation
    basic explicature: 'Where did John see their cat this morning?'
    higher-level explicatures: 'Mary wants to know where John saw the cat this morning.'
    'Mary is surprised to know that John saw the cat somewhere this morning.'

The utterance of a *wh*-fragment leads to skeletal four-tuple representations ($[_{CP[WH[Q]]}$ XP[WH[Q]] ...], $[_{PROP}$ QP ...], $[_{EV}$ ... {ROLE | PLACE-MOD} ...],

2.2 PRELIMINARY CONSIDERATIONS ON INFERENTIAL INTERPRETATION 75

[$_U$ ... FOC ...]), which trigger an inferential process, due to the lexical entry for the *wh*-phrase (clause-initial interrogative) (Chapter (100)) and the lexical entry for the *wh*-word *where*. This inference will lead to the identification of the contextually appropriate CP[WH[Q]], PROP, and EV in which the XP[WH[Q]], the QP, and the ROLE are properly located, respectively.

Here is another example of a fragment. In this example, the fragment is an adverb.

(25) (context: John and Mary are teachers and have been teaching the same group of students, who all have to pass today's test. If students fail the test, they have to take it again and again until they pass.)
John: They will pass.
    Mary's interpretation
        basic explicature: 'The students Mary and John have been teaching will definitely pass the test Mary and John are giving them today.'
        They refers to *the students John and Mary have been teaching* and the phonologically null object refers to *the test Mary and John are giving them today* and *will* expresses strong prediction.
Mary: Absolutely.
    John's interpretation
        higher-level explicature: 'Mary has agreed strongly with John's prediction that the students will pass the test.'
        implicatures: 'Mary believes firmly that no one will fail the test.' 'Mary expects that she and John will not have to give another test.' etc.

(26) is an example of an idiom chunk fragment. The idiom used in this example is *pull someone's leg*, whose lexical entry is given in (29).

(26) John: Whose leg was pulled at the party?
Mary [smiling and in a happy voice]: Bill's.
    John's interpretation
      basic explicature: 'Bill was teased at the party.'
      higher-level explicatures: 'Mary knows that Bill was teased at the party.'
        'Mary is happy that Bill was teased at the party.'
      implicature: 'Mary has wanted someone to tease Bill.'

Note that the interpretive process of *Bill's* in (26) is almost the same as (3).

(27) interpretive process of *Bill's* in (26)
STEP 1: The LM computes the four-tuple representations of the utterance "Bill's" from the lexical entries for *Bill* and the possessive clitic, from the default correspondences between syntax, F/A, and E/R: NP ↔ ARG ↔ ROLE, and from the fact that the NP fragment is intended as an answer to the *wh*-question (i.e., FOC in IS): ([$_{NP[POS]}$ Bill's], [$_{ARG}$ BILL], ROLE, [$_U$ [$_{FOC}$ "Bill's"]])
STEP 2: The LM sends the decoded four-tuple representations to the ICM.
STEP 3: The ICM, following the Relevance-guided comprehension heuristic (8), accesses the most accessible information, namely, the four-tuple representations of the preceding *wh*-question and its explicatures and implicatures.
STEP 4: The ICM constructs as the most relevant interpretive hypothesis the four-tuple representations of "Bill's leg was pulled at the party" and its explicatures (e.g., 'Mary is happy that Bill was teased at the party') and implicatures by referring to the passive lexical entry for the idiom *pull X's leg* (28) and to the four-tuple representations, explicatures, and implicatures of the *wh*-question, and by developing the four-tuple representations of "Bill's leg was pulled at the party."

Recall from 1.8.3 that an idiom is registered in the lexicon in the form of a bi-partite lexical entry. (29) is the lexical entry for this idiom and (28) is its passive counterpart. These two lexical entries are related by the Passive Lexical Rule (Chapter 1 (88)).

(28) passive lexical entry for *pull X's leg* (bi-partite lexical entry as ICE) (Ueno 2014: 129)
syntax: [$_{VP}$ [$_V$ pull] [$_{NP[DET, 3SG]}$ NP[POS]], [$_{NP[3SG]}$ leg]]]
(cf. Chapter 1 (1b))
F/A: [$_{Fa}$ [$_{Faa}$ TEASE], ARG]
E/R: [$_{EV}$ [$_{TYPE}$ "tease"] AG PT]

syntax: V[PAS] in [__]
F/A: Fa
E/R: TYPE in [$_{EV}$ __ <AG> PT]
morph: V[1, PSP]

(29) active lexical entry for *pull X's leg* (bi-partite lexical entry as ICE) (Ueno 2014: 129)
syntax: [$_{VP}$ [$_V$ pull] [$_{NP[DET, 3SG]}$ NP[POS]], [$_{NP[3SG]}$ leg]]] (cf. Chapter 1 (1b))

syntax: V in [__ , NP]
F/A: Faa

2.2 PRELIMINARY CONSIDERATIONS ON INFERENTIAL INTERPRETATION 77

F/A: [$_{Fa}$ [$_{Faa}$ TEASE], ARG] E/R: TYPE in [$_{EV}$ __ AG PT]
E/R: [$_{EV}$ [$_{TYPE}$ "tease"] AG PT] morph: V[0]

(30) and (31) are examples of gapping and stripping, respectively. The second conjunct of these constructions acquires its interpretation (explicatures and implicatures) from the first conjunct, which is the most accessible information when interpretive hypotheses of the second conjunct are being constructed.

(30) a. (context: Mary invited her friends to her house. They are all busy talking to each other.)
Mary: "The food will get cold and the beer warm." (gapping)
b. (basic explicature) 'The food on the table will become cold very soon and the beer on the table will become warm very soon.'
[reference assignment] *The food* refers to *the food on the table in the room* and *the beer* refers to *the beer on the same table.*
[disambiguation] *Get* means 'become' and *cold* has a cold-inducing sense (as in *The beer is cold*) but not a cold-feeling sense (as in *I'm cold*).
Warm has a warm-inducing sense.
[enrichment] the future *will* means immediate future 'will very soon.'
c. (higher-level explicature) 'Mary believes that the food on the table will become cold very soon and the beer on the table will become warm very soon.'
d. (implicature) [as advice] 'Mary tells the guests to eat the food before it gets cold and drink the beer before it gets warm.'

(31) a. (in the same context as (30a))
Mary: "The food will get cold, and the soup too." (stripping)
b. (basic explicature) 'The food on the table will get cold very soon and the soup on the table will get cold very soon too.'
[reference assignment] *The food* refers to *the food on the table in the room* and *the soup* refers to *the soup on the same table.*
[disambiguation] *Get* means 'become' and *cold* means a cold-inducing sense (as in *The beer is cold*).
[enrichment] The future *will* means immediate future 'will very soon.'

78   2 INFERENTIAL INTERPRETATION

  c. (higher-level explicature) 'Mary believes that the food on the table will get cold very soon and the soup on the table will get cold very soon too.'

  d. (implicature) [as advice] 'Mary tells the guests to have the food and soup before they get cold very soon.'

So far, we have shown that there are at least two sources that trigger the inferential interpretation process of a fragment: one is the combined effect of the Communicative Principle of Relevance (6) and the Relevance-guided comprehension heuristic (8) and the other is the multi-modular architecture of AMG. As for the first source, when a fragment utterance U is directed by the speaker to the hearer, because it is uttered as part of ostensive-inferential communication, U conveys to the hearer a presumption of its own optimal relevance and therefore the hearer expects that it must be relevant enough to be worth processing, due to (7a). This triggers an inferential comprehension process that includes supplying the fragment with the most accessible missing elements based on their accessibility. As for the second source, because AMG is organized in a multi-modular fashion, default correspondences between the modules often create a situation in which a fragment leads to skeletal four-tuple representations such as ($[_S$ … NP …], $[_{PROP}$ … ARG …], $[_{EV}$ … ROLE …], $[_U$ … FOC …]) for an NP fragment in (20), ($[_S$ … PP …], $[_{PROP}$ … Mp …], $[_{EV}$ … TIME-MOD …], $[_U$ … FOC …]) for a temporal PP in (22), and ($[_{CP[WH[Q]]}$ XP[WH[Q]] …], $[_{PROP}$ QP …], $[_{EV}$ … ROLE …], $[_U$ … FOC …]) for a *wh*-fragment in (24). These skeletal four-tuple representations trigger an inferential comprehension process that leads to identify the contextually appropriate S, PROP, and EV in which the fragment is properly located.

2.3 Review of SA and LA Superstructures

Generally speaking, demonstrative *that* can refer to a proposition (PROP) in F/A and/or the event (EV) in E/R that the PROP corresponds to. In (32a), for example, *that* refers to the PROP and/or the EV that A has just asserted. In (32b), *that* refers to the PROP and/or the EV expressed by the CP[*that*] *I took the money*. Note that *that* cannot refer to the whole PROP or the whole EV of *I confess that I took the money*, the utterance of which contains a performative verb (PV) that is used performatively: *promise* in the instantaneous present tense (i-PRES in (39)).

Hence the whole PROP or the whole EV does not qualify to be described as true or false (non-truth-conditional) (Cruse 2011: 367). On the other hand, if A had said "I confessed that I took the money," B's utterance would have been ambiguous in that *that* could have referred to *I took the money* or *I confessed that I took the money*.

(32) a. (McCawley 1993a: 290)
    A: The moon is owned by General Motors.
    B: That's false.
   b. (Cruse 2011: 367)
    A: I [$_{PV}$ confess] that I took the money.
    B: That's not true.

By contrast, the demonstrative *that* in (33) does not refer to the PROP or the STATE expressed by the declarative sentence but rather refers to the speech act (SA) of assertion that A has just performed.

(33) (McCawley 1993a: 290)
    A: Your father is a retired pimp.
    B: That's pretty damn cheeky of you.

To capture such speech-act aspects of an utterance meaning, Ueno (2014: 353) proposed positing a speech act (SA) superstructure on top of an event structure in E/R. As shown in (34a), an SA superstructure consists of its illocutionary force (IF), the speaker (SP) with the [AG, SO] role, the addressee/audience (AD) with the [PT, GO] role, and the theme (TH) role that dominates the event (EV) that corresponds to the PROP in F/A and the S in syntax of the utterance in question. ([AG, SO] and [PT, GO] are two-tiered roles, reviewed in 1.3.) The intermodular correspondences in (34a) between the E/R with an SA of assertion and the syntactic and F/A structures of a declarative clause are a default case, which can be overridden by various factors both linguistic and nonlinguistic. For example, *You will close the door* is ambiguous in its illocutionary force (Sadock 1974: 15): it can be produced/interpreted either as an assertion or as an order. If it is produced/interpreted as an assertion, the intermodular correspondences are given in (35a). On the other hand, if it is produced/interpreted as an order, the correspondences are given in (35b).

(34) (Ueno 2014: 354)

a.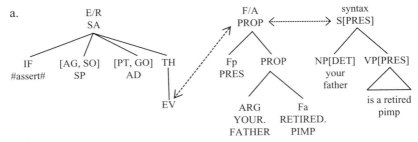

b. lexical entry for SA superstructure
   syntax: nil
   F/A: nil
   E/R: [$_{SA}$ IF [$_{[AG, SO]}$ SP] [$_{[PT, GO]}$ AD] [$_{TH}$ EV]]
   phonology: nil

(35) (Ueno 2014: 355)
   a. default case (direct speech act)
      declarative S   <--->   PROP   <--->   SA with the #assert#
      in syntax   in F/A   illocutionary force in E/R
   b. non-default case (indirect speech act)
      declarative S   <--->   PROP   <--->   SA with the #order#
      in syntax   in F/A   illocutionary force in E/R

The SA superstructure in (34a) only exists in the E/R module and does not correspond to anything in the other modules, which is guaranteed by the defective lexical entry (34b). This part of E/R is an unassociable structure and is inaccessible to the other modules, just like unassociable roles (1.8.1, Ueno 2014: 102) and coerced materials (Ueno 2014: 201). This predicts that there is no direct interaction between the SA superstructure in E/R and the syntax and F/A of the sentence whose corresponding EV in E/R is dominated by the SA superstructure in question. In particular, an SA superstructure does not directly interact with QPs or Fp functors such as NOT. The F/A structure of a sentence captures its propositional content (including truth conditions), whereas the SA superstructure in E/R of an utterance captures the speech act/pragmatic aspects of its meaning.

An SA superstructure is not an obligatory part of E/R but is optional in the sense that it is present only when its presence is required. For example, embedded clauses lack their SA superstructures. Again, this is a default case and can be overridden. Cases were discussed in Ueno (2014: 364) in which a performative verb that is used performatively appears in an embedded clause. An SA superstructure is a freely available E/R material and is similar to freely available coerced materials such as causative coercion discussed in Ueno (2014: 202).

If a sentence is an explicit performative with an overt performative verb as in *I order you to stay here* and is uttered/interpreted performatively as an expression of the illocutionary force named by the performative verb in question (i.e., as an order, in this case), the IF #order# of the SA superstructure and the TYPE "order" of the EV coincide, as in [$_{SA}$ [$_{IF}$ #order#] SP AD [$_{EV}$ [$_{TYPE}$ "order"] AG PT [$_{TH}$ EV]]]. In such a case, the explicit SA superstructure might not be necessary, because it is predictable from the TYPE "order" and the instantaneous present tense Fp (i-PRES) in the corresponding F/A structure (cf. (39)). However, when an explicit performative sentence is uttered as an expression of an illocutionary force that is different from the illocutionary force of the performative verb contained in it, the SA superstructure is needed to represent this discrepancy: for example, the utterance "I order you to go ahead and shoot me" can be produced/interpreted as an ironical order (i.e., as a challenge in this case). The following are the default lexical entries for declaratives (36a), interrogatives (36b), and imperatives (36c).

(36) (Ueno 2014: 356)
    a.   default lexical entry for declaratives (as a construction)

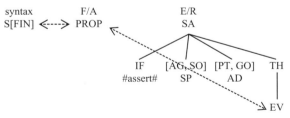

        phonology: falling intonation
    a'. AD takes the IF of an utterance U by SP as #assert# if AD holds the following higher-level explicatures, where P is the basic explicature of U:
          SP believes that P and
          SP believes that AD wants to know that P.

b. default lexical entry for yes/no interrogatives with inversion (as a construction)

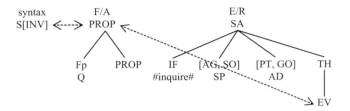

phonology: rising intonation

b'. AD takes the IF of an utterance U by SP as #inquire# if AD holds the following higher-level explicatures, where P is the basic explicature of U:
SP does not know whether P and
SP wants to know whether P.

c. default lexical entry for imperatives (as a construction)

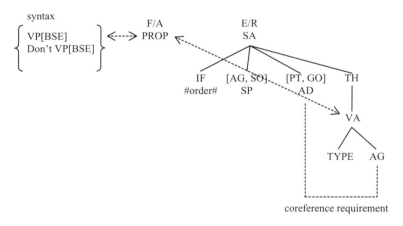

phonology: falling intonation

c'. AD takes the IF of an utterance U by SP as #order# if AD holds the following higher-level explicatures, where P is the basic explicature of U:
SP believes that AD can do the act of P and
SP wants AD to do the act of P.

As for (36a), the utterance of a declarative sentence in syntax corresponds by default to an SA of assertion, but it can also correspond to an SA with some other illocutionary force if the sentence in question is an explicit performative with an IF other than #assert# (e.g., #promise# in *I promise to help you* uttered to make a promise).

As for (36b), the utterance of an interrogative sentence (S[INV]) in syntax corresponds by default to a question, but it can also correspond to a request (*Can you close the door?*), to an exclamative (*Boy, am I ticked off!*) with falling intonation, to an assertion (*May I tell you that the square root of a quarter is a half?* (Levinson 1983: 266)), or to a queclarative, an interrogative sentence used with the force of assertion of opposite polarity (*Does anyone study Aristotle anymore?* (Sadock 1974: 79)).

As for (36c), the utterance of an imperative sentence in syntax corresponds by default to a command, but it can also correspond to a wish (*Have a nice day!* or *Don't catch a cold!*), to an offer (*Have another drink!* (Levinson 1983: 275)), to a curse or swearing (*Shut up!* (Levinson 1983: 275)), or to a welcoming (*Come in!* (Levinson 1983: 275)). The coreference requirement in the E/R of (36c) between the addressee (AD) and the agent (AG) of the volitional action (VA) is required not grammatically but pragmatically. It comes from the definition of the act of command, or more generally from the definition of directive, which is not part of grammatical knowledge but properly belongs to pragmatic knowledge. According to Searle (1969: 66 and 1979: 13), a speech act is a directive if it counts as an attempt by the speaker to get the addressee to do something.

It was also proposed in Ueno (2014: 358), following McCawley (1985, 1993a: 584 note 3), to posit a locutionary act (LA) superstructure on top of SA superstructure. As shown in (37b, d), an LA consists of the TYPE #direct#, the SP with [AG, SO] role, the AD with [PT, GO] role, and the TH that dominates an SA, and represents the pragmatic meaning that the SP directs this SA to the AD. Note that the SP and AD in an LA superstructure are the same as those in the SA superstructure that the LA dominates.

(37) (Ueno 2014: 359)
    a. Tom, you wash the dishes, and Lucy, you empty the garbage. (McCawley 1993a: 295)
    a'. [pointing to different addressees] You wash the dishes, and you empty the garbage.

b.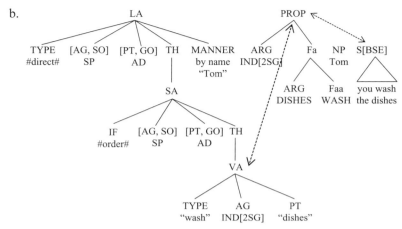

c. I order you to shine these shoes, and I warn you that if you don't obey that order immediately, you'll be court-martialed. (McCawley 1993a: 295)

d. lexical entry for LA superstructure
syntax: nil
F/A: nil
E/R: [$_{LA}$ [$_{TYPE}$ #direct#] [$_{[AG, SO]}$ SP] [$_{[PT, GO]}$ AD] [$_{TH}$ SA] (MANNER)]
phonology: nil

For example, the utterance of a sentence can express two locutionary acts, each with its own illocutionary force. This is illustrated in (37a), where the first LA is directed to Tom and the second to Lucy, and the IF of each SA is #order#. Therefore, the whole modular representation of (37a) is that in which two Ss are coordinated in syntax, two PROPs are coordinated in F/A, and two LAs are coordinated in E/R. Each LA dominates an SA whose illocutionary force is #order#. The correspondences between the syntax, F/A, and E/R of the first conjunct S are given in (37b).

According to McCawley (1985: 51, 1993a: 585 note 3, 1998: 752), an LA is the level of E/R where vocative expressions are represented. For example, the vocative expression *Tom* in the first conjunct of (37a) is represented as MANNER under the LA node in (37b). Note that in the syntax of (37b), the vocative NP and the S[BSE] do not form a syntactic constituent. (In other words, the two pairs of vocative NPs and their following Ss in (37a) are mere juxtapositions without forming a single S, instances of parataxis in syntax (McCawley 1998: 302).)

A vocative is only used for attention getting and there is no SYNTACTIC evidence that it and the following sentence form a single SYNTACTIC constituent.

There is no tense in the imperative F/A of (37b), because the verb is in the base form (V[BSE]) when it is used in the imperative, as in *Everybody stand up*. (37c) is an example of a sentence in which two explicit performatives are coordinated and whose utterance is a single LA that dominates two SAs, the first being an SA of ordering and the second an SA of warning. In the syntax of (37c), two explicit performative Ss are coordinated. In its F/A, two PROPs are coordinated. In its E/R, assuming that their SA superstructures are represented, the TH node of the LA dominates two coordinated SA nodes, each with its own IF: $[_{LA} [_{TYPE}$ #direct#] SP AD $[_{SA} [_{SA} [_{IF}$ #order#] SP AD VA] $[_{SA} [_{IF}$ #warn#] SP AD EV]]].

As discussed in Ueno (2014: 360), there are two kinds of present tense: habitual present (h-PRES) and instantaneous present (i-PRES). Habitual present is used to report the usual state of affairs (McCawley 1993a: 294), whereas instantaneous present is used to express what the speaker is doing (the speaker's verbal or nonverbal act) at the moment of utterance. Instantaneous present is used in demonstrations (38a, b) and play-by-play commentaries (38c).

(38) (Ueno 2014: 360)
    a. Magician: I display the inside of the box. I roll up my sleeves to show that they are empty. I reach into the box with my right hand... (McCawley 1993a: 294)
    b. I now beat the eggs till fluffy. (said in demonstration as a report of a concurrent action; Levinson 1983: 232)
    c. Jones passes and Raul kicks the ball into the net.

In explicit performatives such as (37c) and *I bet you sixpence it will rain tomorrow* (Austin 1975: 5), the instantaneous present is used to express the speaker's verbal act at the moment of utterance (Austin 1975: 56, Searle 1989: 556). The distinction between habitual present (h-PRES) and instantaneous present (i-PRES) must be represented in F/A as part of the propositional meaning, because this difference leads to another difference in what kind of time adverbial (Mp in F/A) can modify the proposition: for example, *every day* for h-PRES and *now* for i-PRES. Time adverbials are part of the propositional content. Still another difference between h-PRES and i-PRES is that the latter is non-truth-conditional, as was pointed out in relation to (32b).

86   2 INFERENTIAL INTERPRETATION

As an example of intermodular correspondence, when the utterance *I promise VP[to]* is used to make a promise (i.e., used performatively), its E/R and F/A representations look as follows.

(39)

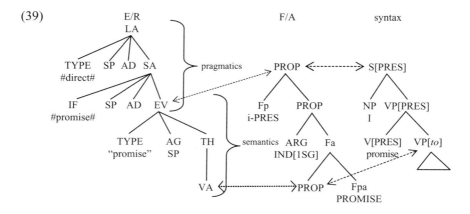

In the above representations, #promise# represents the IF (pragmatic notion) in E/R of the performative verb *promise*, and "promise" represents the event type (cognitive semantic notion) in E/R, which captures the E/R aspects of the meaning of *promise*, and PROMISE represents the functor (propositional semantic notion) in F/A, which captures the F/A aspects of the meaning of *promise*.

2.4 Inferential Nature of Illocutionary Force Identification

Determining what illocutionary force an utterance U has (i.e., what type of speech act the speaker has performed by uttering U) is an important part of the inferential interpretation of what the speaker has intended to convey (i.e., the explicatures and implicatures of U). The hearer's identification of the exact type of speech act performed by U is an inferential task, because utterance interpretation itself is an inferential task, as shown in 2.1. This point is further illustrated below.

Wilson and Sperber (2012: 210ff.) and Carston (2002: 120ff.) proposed that mood and illocutionary force are distinct in that the former is a semantic category and grammatically encoded in each sentence type (declarative, interrogative, imperative, exclamative, etc.), whereas the latter is a pragmatic category whose exact type is determined inferentially by the linguistic and nonlinguistic context and the semantic mood encoded in the utterance in question.

2.4 INFERENTIAL NATURE OF ILLOCUTIONARY FORCE IDENTIFICATION

On the basis of the AMG analysis of declarative, interrogative, and imperative sentences in (36), these sentence types are registered (as constructions) in the lexicon. The E/R field of the lexical entry for each sentence type contains the SA superstructure whose default illocutionary force (IF) is specified as #assert# for declaratives, #inquire" for interrogatives, and #order# for imperatives. This means that the decoded four-tuple of the utterance in question (the output of the Language Module (LM) and the input to the Inferential Comprehension Module (ICM) in (3)) contains the default IF, which will be readjusted by taking account of contextual information including the speaker's intention. For example, the identification of the IF of an utterance as #assert#, #inquire#, or #order# involves such inferential tasks as (36a', b', c'). Because of this readjustment in the ICM of the default IF, some declaratives are interpreted not as assertions but as performatives, some imperatives not as orders but as advice, permission, threats, or good wishes, and some interrogatives not as requests for information but as rhetorical questions, exam questions, guess questions, surprise questions, expository questions, or speculative questions.

The performative verb *promise* in the present tense with the first person singular subject can be used non-performatively, as illustrated in (40). The present tense of the verb *promise* is interpreted not as i-PRES (instantaneous present) but as h-PRES (habitual present).

(40) (Ueno 2014: 356)
   a. A: How do you get me to throw all these parties?
      B: I promise to come. (as an answer to the question; ellipsis of *I get you to do so by promising to come*) (Levinson 1983: 233)
   b. Whenever I see you on Tuesday I always do the same thing: I promise to come and see you on Wednesday. (habitual practice) (Searle 1989: 538)
   c. A: What do you do when you leave?
      B: I promise you to come back. (habitual present as an answer to the question)

For these utterances to be interpreted correctly as non-performative, the hearer must recognize that *promise* in (40) is not used performatively, which requires a non-demonstrative inference that takes account of contextual information.

The examples of *I promise* in (41) are used performatively, not to make a promise but to perform some other speech act. *I promise* in (41a) is used as a warning or threat, (41b) as an emphatic assertion, and (41c, d) as an apology. In these cases, although the event type (EV) of each E/R is "promise," its IF # promise#

in the respective SA superstructure is readjusted to #warn# or #threaten# in (41a), #assert# in (41b), and #apologize# in (41c, d). Again, this identification of the exact type of speech act is achieved by non-demonstrative inference.

(41) (Ueno 2014: 356)
    a. If you don't hand in your paper on time, I promise you I will give you a failing grade in the course. (as a warning or threat) (Searle 1969: 58)
    b. A: You stole that money, didn't you?
        B: No, I didn't. I promise you I didn't. (as an emphatic assertion) (Searle 1969: 58–59)
    c. I promise there won't be a next time. (as an apology)
    d. I promise this won't happen again. (as an apology)

Searle (1969: 58) remarked about (41a, b) that *I promise (you)* and *I hereby promise (you)* are among the strongest illocutionary force indicating devices for *commitment* provided by the English language. Therefore, speakers can use them either to emphasize the degree of their commitment to their intention to perform the speech act that is damaging to the addressee in (41a) or to emphasize the degree of their commitment to the truth of their statement in (41b).

Constative sentences (non-performative sentences such as *The cat is on the mat* or *Birds fly*) by default have an SA superstructure with IF #assert# or a much weaker generic IF #say# (Sperber and Wilson 1995: 247). In (42) and (43), A has uttered a constative sentence and performed a speech act of assertion or a much weaker speech act of saying. However, B's echoic utterance (Sperber and Wilson 1995: 238, Carston 2002: 159) (repeating what A has just said) is not an assertion. By repeating what A has just said, B expresses her attitude of disbelief, rejection, or dissociation toward what A said (cf. Sperber and Wilson 1995: 239–240). A and the other audience members need to understand by non-demonstrative inference what attitude B wants to express.

(42) (cf. Sperber and Wilson 1995: 239)
    A: It's a lovely day for a picnic.
    [It suddenly starts raining.]
    B [sarcastically]: It's a lovely day for a picnic, indeed.
    explicatures: 'A says that it's a lovely day for a picnic.'
                  'B believes that it is not appropriate that A says that it's a lovely day for a picnic.'

possible implicatures: 'B believes that it is impossible to go out for a picnic today.'

(43) (cf. (32a))
A [self-assuredly]: The moon is owned by General Motors.
[Everyone laughs.]
B [jokingly]: The moon is owned by General Motors, indeed.
explicatures: 'A claims that the moon is owned by General Motors.'
'B believes that it is not appropriate that A claims that the moon is owned by General Motors.'
possible implicature: 'B is asking A to stop talking non-sense.'

In (42) and (43), one of B's explicatures is a repetition of A's basic explicature that is embedded in an appropriate higher-order propositional attitude description such as 'B believes that it is not appropriate that A says that' (cf. Wilson and Sperber 2004: 274).

2.5 Indirect Speech Acts and Implicatures

A speech act is said to be direct or literal if its "default" illocutionary force is realized ("default" in a broad sense), namely, (i) if the utterance in question satisfies one of the default correspondences between syntax, F/A, and E/R specified in (36), that is, a declarative sentence uttered to make an assertion (36a), an interrogative sentence uttered to ask a question (36b), or an imperative sentence uttered to give an order (36c) or (ii) if the utterance in question is a declarative sentence and, simultaneously, an explicit performative with the illocutionary force named by the performative verb in the matrix clause (e.g., *I promise to be honest* is uttered to make a promise) (cf. Levinson 1983: 263–264). In (ii), the default IF #assert# is readjusted to the IF of the performative verb, as discussed in 2.4. By contrast, a speech act is said to be indirect or non-literal if its default illocutionary force is not realized, namely, a speech act about which neither (i) nor (ii) above holds. For example, when the interrogative (44a) *Can you pass me the salt?* is uttered not to ask a question (default illocutionary force) but to make a request (non-default illocutionary force), its illocutionary force is not the default #inquire# but the non-default #request# (i.e., *Please pass me the salt*).

From an inferential point of view, the distinction between direct and indirect speech acts can be reduced to the distinction between explicatures (literal meanings expressed as F/A and E/R after development (9)) and implicatures of the utterance in question. The interpretation of, say, (44a) as a direct speech act is a question about the addressee's physical ability, which is recovered through its F/A and E/R. However, the context tells the addressee that this interpretation is not appropriate and hence is not the speaker's intended meaning. At the same time, non-demonstrative inference leads to a contextually more appropriate request interpretation through inferential tasks such as something along the lines of (36c'). In other words, the interpretation of an utterance as an indirect speech act is constructed as an implicature (13) that the speaker intended to convey.

Indirect speech acts form a continuum from the least indirect (i.e., the most direct) to the most indirect, depending on how much their interpretation as indirect speech act (indirect interpretation) deviates from their interpretation as direct speech act (literal interpretation). (In other words, implicatures form a continuum from the least implicit (the most explicit) to the most implicit (the least explicit). See the definitions of *explicitness* (10) and *implicitness* (11).)

(44) (Ueno 2014: 362)
    a. Can you pass me the salt? (as a request)
    b. Can you reach the salt? (as a request) (Searle 1979: 30)
    c. I wish you wouldn't do that. (as a request) (Searle 1969: 68)
    d. Sir, you are standing on my foot. (as a request) (Searle 1979: viii)
    e. Gosh, I'm cold. (as a request) (Jerry Sadock (p.c.))

Recall first of all that determining contextually appropriate explicatures, implicatures, and speech act types of utterances are all inferential tasks.

As for (44a), its indirect interpretation is a speech act of making a request 'Please pass me the salt.' (Because of this request interpretation, *please* can be added to this interrogative utterance, as in *Can you please pass me the salt?* and a negative interrogative is possible as in *Can you (please) not smoke here?*, which is a request to refrain from smoking here.) Although the speaker (SP) intentionally utters it as an indirect speech act with the #request# illocutionary force (IF), it can still be understood either literally as a question about the addressee (AD)'s physical ability or indirectly as a request to AD. However, if this question is asked at a dinner table where AD is sitting within easy reach of the salt, AD can reject the literal interpretation and choose the indirect interpretation (i.e., the implicature of the utterance), because the answer to the question, if interpreted literally, is predictably "yes," which is obvious to both SP and AD.

Note that this indirect request interpretation is obtained by non-demonstrative inference as an implicature, if we assume the implicated premise 'If you can pass me the salt, pass me the salt' (i.e., more generally, 'If you have the ability to do the act A, do A'). By asking "Can you pass me the salt?" both SP and AD expect that the answer is "yes," that is, 'You can pass me the salt' from SP's point of view. This assumption together with the implicated premise leads to the implicated conclusion 'Pass me the salt' (cf. (15)).

As for (44b), its intended interpretation is not 'Please reach the salt' but 'Please pass me the salt.' AD can again reject the literal interpretation, which is irrelevant in this discourse context, and can recover the intended indirect interpretation based on non-demonstrative inference, if we assume the conjunction of two implicated premises 'If you can reach the salt, then reach the salt and if you reach the salt, then pass it to me,' in which being able to reach the salt is a prerequisite for passing the salt to someone. This conjunction of implicated premises clearly shows that (44b) is more indirect than (44a) as a request.

In (44a) and (44b), a request is made by asking AD's ability (*Can you ...?*). Searle (1969: 66 and 1979: 45) claimed that AD's ability to perform an act A (that is, AD is able to do A) is a preparatory condition for SP's requesting AD to do A, and that asking the preparatory condition conventionally satisfies the essential condition for requesting AD to do A, that is, conventionally counts as an attempt by SP to get AD to do A. From our perspective, what is conventionalized is the implicated premise 'If both SP and AD know that AD can perform an act A and SP asks if AD can do A, then SP requests AD to do A.' Note that *Can you ...?* is conventionalized as a requesting form, because *Are you able to ...?*, although it has the same literal meaning as *Can you ... ?*, is far more difficult to understand as a requesting form.

As for (44c), AD interprets it literally as an expression of SP's wish and in addition interprets it indirectly as a request. The literal interpretation is not rejected, as opposed to (44a, b), which is shown by the fact that "What else do you wish?" is an odd-sounding but possible response to (44c). In fact, the literal interpretation acts as a conduit leading to the intended request interpretation. A request is made in (44c) by SP's stating her wish, just as a request for money is made by saying "I want money." Again, Searle (1969, 1979) claimed that 'SP wants AD to do A' is a sincerity condition for requesting AD to do A, and that stating the sincerity condition conventionally satisfies the essential condition for requesting

AD to do A, that is, it conventionally counts as an attempt by SP to get AD to do A. From our perspective, what is conventionalized is the implicated premise 'If SP believes that AD can do an act A and SP says that she wants AD to do A, then SP requests AD to do A.'

As for (44d), AD interprets it literally as a statement of fact and in addition indirectly as a request through non-demonstrative inference (if someone is standing on your foot, you want that person to move it because no one likes to be stepped on). The literal interpretation is not rejected here, either, which is shown by the fact that "So, what?" is a possible response to (44d).

As for (44e), AD interprets it literally as a statement of fact and might in addition interpret it indirectly as an assertion that 'today is the coldest day this winter.' Or it might be indirectly interpreted as a request whose content depends on the context in which (44e) is uttered (e.g., 'Please close the window' or 'Please turn on the heater'). If this is said by a general to a private, it might be indirectly interpreted as an order. It might also be indirectly interpreted as a wish ('I want something to put on' or 'I want something hot to drink') or even as a proposal at the end of the workday to a colleague that they stop in at a warm tavern on their way home. All sorts of indirect interpretations of (44e) are available, depending on the discourse context in which it is uttered. The literal interpretation is not rejected here, either, which is shown by the fact that "Really? Is it so cold?" or "Me, too" is a possible response to (44e). The indirect interpretations of (44d, e) are quite different from their literal interpretations and hence must be recovered by means of non-demonstrative inference on the part of AD. In this respect, these indirect interpretations are implicatures.

Chapter 3

An Automodular View of Fragments

> In this chapter, we will discuss various kinds of fragments in discourse and show how inference plays an important role in their interpretation. Fragments provide a strong motivation to assume extra-grammatical pragmatic inference processes, without which they cannot be accounted for adequately. They are peculiar in two ways: that children learn to use them very early before the acquisition of syntax and that inference plays a bigger role in fragment interpretation than in the interpretation of any other ellipsis type. We will formulate the procedure for fragment comprehension (5c), which will be applied in a similar formulation to other ellipsis types discussed in later chapters.

3.1 Preliminary Description of Fragments

Fragments are subsentential phrases uttered by the speaker to perform a speech act (making a statement, asking a question, issuing a command, etc.). (1B) below and (18), (21), and (26) in Chapter 2 are examples of answer fragments, which are phrases uttered as answers to their preceding *wh*-questions. The examples in (2B) are clarification fragments, which are phrases uttered to clarify the preceding statement or question. The examples in (3) below and in (23) in Chapter 2 are discourse-initial fragments, for which there is no prior linguistic context in response to which the fragment is uttered.

(1) answer fragment
   A: What did Pat buy? (Culicover and Jackendoff 2005: 233)
   B: A motorcycle.

(2) clarification fragments
    A: Pat bought something.   A: Pat bought. something.   A: Did Pat buy a bicycle?
    B: A motorcycle.   B: A motorcycle?   B: No, a motorcycle.

(3) discourse-initial fragments
  a. (Abby and Ben see a man with Beth, a mutual friend of theirs. Abby turns to Ben with a puzzled look on her face. Ben says to Abby: making an assertion)
    "Some guy she met at the park."   (Merchant 2004: 661)
  b. (A wife sees her husband coming in with a letter in his hand and says: asking a question)
    "From Colombia?"   (Stainton 2004: 268)
  c. (A mother says to her children who are watching TV late at night: giving an order)
    "To your bedroom. Right now."   (Stainton 2004: 268)
  d. (A wife gives her husband, who is often late for dinner, a familiar nasty look, as he goes out the door. He says: making a promise)
    "Seven o'clock. Without fail."   (Stainton 2004: 285 note 7)
  e. (A and B are looking at a tote board, watching the progress of shares in Acme Internet, and A says to B: making an exclamative assertion)
    "Moving pretty fast!"   (Stainton 2004: 267)

Let us first consider the simplest case: answer fragments. In (1), B is understood to have performed a speech act of assertion by uttering the NP *a motorcycle* with falling intonation. What B meant was 'Pat bought a motorcycle' and A and the other audience understood the NP as such. In semantic/pragmatic terms, A provided a propositional function $P(x)$ (= 'Pat bought x') and sought a value a that would make the proposition $P(a)$ true. B simply provided such a value a instead of providing the whole proposition $P(a)$. Answer fragments, just as full sentential answers to *wh*-questions, do not impose exhaustivity on their interpretation (i.e., providing at least one value that makes $P(x)$ true is sufficient, and providing all the values that make $P(x)$ true is not required) (Merchant 2001: 119). Note also that the existential presupposition of a *wh*-question (Levinson 1983: 184) is defeasible, and "Nothing" counts as an answer to (1A) "What did Pat buy?"

As discussed in 2.2, fragments uttered in discourse are not simply ignored by the hearer as ungrammatical or gibberish. When a fragment utterance U is directed by the speaker to the hearer, U conveys to the hearer a presumption of its own optimal relevance by the Communicative Principle of Relevance (Chapter 2 (6)), because U is uttered as part of ostensive-inferential communication, and therefore the hearer expects that U is relevant enough to be worth processing by the Presumption of optimal relevance (Chapter 2 (7)). This triggers in the hearer an inferential comprehension process of constructing interpretive hypotheses about U by supplying the fragment U with missing elements and testing them in order of accessibility by the Relevance-guided comprehension heuristic (Chapter 2 (8)).

3.2 Explaining Fragment Interpretation

As an example of the inferential interpretation process of an answer fragment, let us revisit the following exchange discussed in 2.2.

(4) (Context: The following exchange takes place in a cafeteria, where Mary has almost finished eating breakfast when John comes in and talks to her.) (= Chapter 2 (18))
John: What did you have?
Mary [happily]: A steak.

Following the discussion in 2.1, we assume that the Language Module (LM) is one of the input systems and that it is equipped with the current version of Automodular Grammar (AMG). The LM decodes a sentential utterance U on the basis of the information of the lexical items in U, and computes the syntax, F/A, E/R, and IS of U. We call the ordered set (the syntax of U, the F/A of U, the E/R of U, the IS of U) the decoded four-tuple representations of U, the decoded four-tuple of U, for short. This decoded four-tuple of U consisting of the decoded syntax, F/A, E/R, and IS of U is in turn input to the Inferential Comprehension Module (ICM), another module where non-demonstrative inference is performed on decoded four-tuples of utterances and their interpretive hypotheses are constructed through development (e.g., disambiguation, referent assignment, and enrichment) (Chapter 2 (9)). This process is guided by the Relevance-guided comprehension heuristic (Chapter 2 (8)). The output of the ICM is the explicatures and implicatures of utterances (expressed in Mentalese). This process is shown in (5a).

In the case of a fragment utterance U, the decoded four-tuple of U is input to the ICM, just as in the case of (5a). The ICM first constructs the inferred four-tuple of U (consisting of the inferred syntax, F/A, E/R, and IS of U), based on the decoded four-tuple of U, default correspondences between the linguistic modules, and the (decoded/inferred) four-tuples of the prior discourse, and then constructs the explicatures and implicatures of U on the basis of the set of contextual assumptions through non-demonstrative inference including development of the inferred four-tuple. The final output of the ICM is, of course, the explicatures and implicatures (expressed in Mentalese) of the fragment utterance U. This process is shown in (5b).

(5) a. Utterance comprehension process in the case of sentential utterance (= Chapter 2 (3)) sentential utterance U → ⎿LM⏋ → decoded four-tuple of U → ⎿ICM⏋ → developed four-tuple of U → explicatures and implicatures of U (in Mentalese)
  b. Utterance comprehension process in the case of fragment utterance fragment utterance (U) → ⎿LM(AMG)⏋ → decoded four-tuple of U → ⎿ICM⏋ → inferred four-tuple of U → developed four-tuple of U → explicatures and implicatures of U (in Mentalese)
  c. Procedure for fragment comprehension
     The hearer follows the Relevance-guided comprehension heuristic and executes the following steps.
     (i) The LM computes the decoded four-tuple of a fragment utterance U and its skeletal four-tuple.
     (ii) By non-demonstrative inference, the ICM constructs the inferred syntactic structure of U on the basis of the skeletal syntax obtained in (i) and the contextual information.
     (iii) The ICM constructs the inferred four-tuple of U on the basis of the skeletal four-tuple obtained in (i), the inferred syntax obtained in (ii), and the contextual information.
     (iv) The ICM develops the inferred four-tuple of U obtained in (iii) on the basis of the contextual information.
     (v) The ICM constructs the explicatures and implicatures of U on the basis of the developed four-tuple obtained in (iv) and the contextual information.

When Mary hears John's *wh*-question in (4), her LM decodes it into the four-tuple of the *wh*-question. Her ICM develops the decoded four-tuple through reference assignment, disambiguation, and enrichment, as in the first part of (6), and constructs its explicatures and implicatures. When John hears Mary say happily "A steak," his LM first computes the decoded four-tuple of the fragment and his

ICM then constructs its inferred four-tuple and further constructs its explicatures and implicatures, as in the second part of (6).

(6) John: What did you have?
    Mary's interpretation process
        development of the decoded four-tuple representation of the *wh*-question
            reference assignment = *you* refers to Mary.
            disambiguation = *have* means 'eat.'
            enrichment = narrowing the past tense to 'this morning' and adding 'for breakfast'
        basic explicature: 'What did Mary eat for breakfast this morning?'
        higher-level explicatures:
            'John asks Mary what she ate for breakfast this morning.'
            'John does not know what Mary ate for breakfast this morning.'
            'John wants to know what Mary ate for breakfast this morning.'
    Mary: [happily] A steak.
    John's interpretation process
        decoded four-tuple: (8a)
        skeletal four-tuple: (8b)
        inferred four-tuple: (8c)
        development of the inferred four-tuple of "A steak"
            basic explicature: 'Mary ate a steak for breakfast this morning.'
            higher-level explicature: 'Mary is happy that she ate a steak for breakfast this morning.'
            implicatures: 'Mary is full.,' 'Mary was so hungry as to be able to eat a steak for breakfast.' etc.

(7) interpretive process of Mary's NP fragment "A steak" in (6)
    STEP 1: The LM computes the decoded four-tuple of the fragment utterance "A steak" from the lexical entries of *a* and *steak*, from the default correspondences between syntax, F/A, and E/R (NP ↔ ARG ↔ ROLE), and from the fact that the NP fragment is intended as an answer to a *wh*-question (i.e., FOC in IS): ([$_{\text{NP[DET]}}$ [$_{\text{DET}}$ a] [$_{\text{NP}}$ steak]], [$_{\text{ARG}}$ STEAK], ROLE, [$_{\text{U}}$ [$_{\text{FOC}}$ "a steak"]]).
    STEP 2: Because of the default correspondences (S ↔ PROP ↔ EV ↔ [$_{\text{U}}$ FOC, BI]) and the facts that the NP must be an NP of some S, that the ARG must be an argument of some proposition (PROP) and that

the ROLE must be a role of some event (EV), the ICM computes the skeletal four-tuple (8b).

STEP 3: The LM sends this skeletal four-tuple to the ICM. The ICM, following the Relevance-guided comprehension heuristic, accesses the most accessible information, namely, the four-tuple of the preceding *wh*-question and its explicatures and implicatures.

STEP 4: The ICM first constructs the inferred four-tuple of the NP fragment, namely, the four-tuple of *I had a steak*, develops it, and then constructs its explicatures (e.g., 'Mary is happy that she ate a steak for breakfast this morning.') and implicatures (e.g., 'Mary is full.') by referring to the contextual information and the explicatures and implicatures of the *wh*-question.

As discussed in Chapter 2, a skeletal four-tuple is computed automatically from every NP fragment, as follows. When the fragment in question is an NP, its decoded four-tuple is computed automatically by the default categorial correspondences (NP ↔ ARG ↔ ROLE ↔ FOC), which require that the NP correspond to an ARG in F/A, to a ROLE in E/R, and to a focus (FOC) in IS. On the one hand, this ARG must be an argument of some proposition (PROP) and this ROLE must be a participant role of some event (EV). On the other, this FOC must be new information against the phonologically unrealized old information (i.e., background information (BI)), as in [$_U$ FOC BI]. This much information in turn induces the intermodular default correspondences S ↔ PROP ↔ EV ↔ [$_U$ FOC BI]. Therefore, every time an NP fragment is uttered, a skeletal four-tuple ([$_S$ ... NP ...], [$_{PROP}$ ... ARG ...], [$_{EV}$ ... ROLE ...], [$_U$ ... FOC ...]) is computed automatically. This triggers an inferential comprehension process that leads to identifying the S, PROP, and EV in which the NP, ARG, and ROLE are properly situated, respectively. The skeletal four-tuple in question is shown in (8b).

(8) a. decoded four-tuple of "A steak"

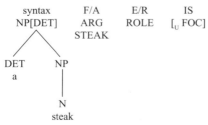

b. skeletal four-tuple of "A steak"

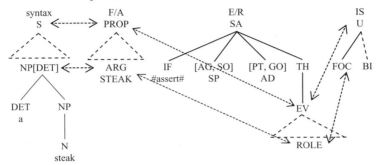

c. inferred four-tuple of "A steak"
the syntax, F/A, E/R, and IS of *I had a steak*

In (4), the speaker (SP) Mary happily uttered the NP fragment *a steak* with falling intonation, which indicates that it was a speech act (SA) of assertion with its illocutionary force (IF) #assert#, as in (8b) (Chapter 2 (36a)). If, on the other hand, SP had uttered the fragment with rising intonation ("A steak?"), SP would have performed to the addressee (AD) John a speech act of asking a question, whose IF in E/R is #inquire# (Chapter 2 (36b)). In that case, SP's intended meaning must have been either 'Did I eat a steak for breakfast this morning?' or, more contextually appropriate, 'Was it a steak?' where the pronoun *it* refers to *something* in the existential presupposition of John's *wh*-question 'You ate something.'

What AD and the other audience members need to do to properly interpret a fragment such as the NP fragment in (4) is to situate the "orphan" NP fragment in a contextually appropriate sentence in syntax (the S in the inferred syntax of (8c)), in its corresponding proposition in F/A (the PROP in the inferred F/A of (8c)), and in its corresponding speech act (the SA in the inferred E/R of (8c)), based on the prior and present linguistic and non-linguistic contextual information.

As shown in (8b, c), a fragment is inferentially interpreted as an S in syntax, a PROP in F/A, and an SA in E/R. This is supported by the following phenomena. First, a fragment can be used as the complement of the matrix verb that takes a clausal complement. This observation was originally due to Jerry Morgan (1973). In (9B), the verb *imagine* appears to take an AP *poached* as its complement, which clearly violates its subcategorization requirement in (10). However, (9B) is not excluded as ungrammatical or gibberish, because it is uttered as part of ostensive-inferential communication and the Communicative Principle of Relevance guarantees that it is worth processing. This triggers non-demonstrative inference.

100   3 AN AUTOMODULAR VIEW OF FRAGMENTS

(9) (McCawley 1998: 4)
A: Does anyone know how Reagan likes his eggs?
B: Bush imagines poached.
    basic explicature: 'Bush imagines Reagan likes his eggs poached.'
    higher-level explicature: 'B believes that Bush imagines Reagan likes his eggs poached.'

(10) lexical entries for *imagine*
syntax: V in [__, {CP[*that*]] | S[FIN]}]   syntax: V in [__, NP]
F/A: Fpa   F/A: Faa
E/R: [$_{TYPE}$ "imagine"] in   E/R: [$_{TYPE}$ "imagine"] in
   [__ [AG, LO] [$_{[PT, TH]}$ EV]]   [__ [AG, LO] [PT, TH]]

Because the AP *poached* corresponds to an Fa in F/A by default, the decoded four-tuple of (9B) leads to the following skeletal four-tuple.

(11) skeletal four-tuple of "Bush imagines poached"

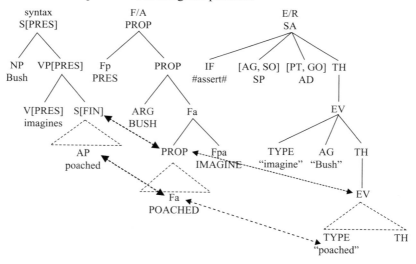

As a result of non-demonstrative inference, a contextually appropriate embedded S *Reagan likes his eggs poached* and its corresponding PROP and EV are inferred. This inferred embedded S satisfies the lexical entry for *imagine*.

Second, a fragment can co-occur with a sentence-modifying PP or a sentential adverb as in (12B) and (13aB).

(12) (McCawley 1998: 4)
    A: Would you like that with ice?
        reference assignment: *that* refers to coffee.
    B: Without, if you don't mind.
        inferred four-tuple of *I would like it without ice, if you don't mind*
        basic explicature: 'B would like coffee without ice.'
        higher-level explicature: 'B politely requests that she would like coffee without ice.'

In (12B), the conditional *if you don't mind* does not directly modify the PP[*without*] whose complement is elided. It is an illocutionary adverbial (Ueno 2014: 370) and modifies the SA superstructure [$_{SA}$ [$_{IF}$ #request#] SP AD EV] and indicates that a request is being made politely. This triggers non-demonstrative inference, which leads to identifying what request is being made politely. In (13aB), the illocutionary adverb *confidentially* cannot modify a fragment NP directly. This triggers non-demonstrative inference and as a result, it is taken as modifying the SA superstructure [$_{SA}$ [$_{IF}$ #assert#] SP AD EV].

(13) a. A: What did John buy?
       B: Confidentially, a bicycle.
          basic explicature: 'John bought a bicycle.'
          higher-level explicature: 'B tells A confidentially that John bought a bicycle.'
   b. A: Was the server polite about it?
      B: Very. He apologized for interrupting us.
   c. A: Did anyone forget themselves and reflexively reach for their cellphones?
      B: Almost. I could see a couple of my pals start to fidget and eye their phones nervously.

Furthermore, an adverb itself appears as a fragment. Since adverbs must modify VP, AP, or S, such an adverb fragment must modify one of these constituents in its inferred syntactic structure. This is shown in (13b, c).

    Third, an NP fragment can co-occur with the focus particle *only* as in (14B). Again, *only* cannot modify a fragment NP directly, because it needs a proposition to have scope over (McCawley 1993a: 193–194, 1998: 641–642). This triggers non-demonstrative inference.

(14) A: What did John buy?
B: Only a bicycle.
basic explicature: 'John bought only a bicycle.' = 'John bought a bicycle and he did not buy anything else.'

Fourth, a fragment can co-occur with such expressions as parenthetical *I think* and *I suppose* as in (15B). This shows yet again that there must be a proposition that can serve semantically as the complement of these expressions.

(15) A: What did John buy?
B: A bicycle, I suppose.
basic explicature: 'John bought a bicycle.'
higher-level explicature: 'I suppose it is a bicycle that John bought.'

Fifth, the adverb *respectively* can appear with a coordinate fragment as in (16B), which forces between the two NP-coordinate structures the pairing of *John* and *Susan* on the one hand and *Bill* and *Helen* on the other.

(16) (McCawley 1998: 296; quoted from Stockwell et al. 1973: 399)
A: Who married [Susan and Helen]?
B: [John and Bill], respectively.
basic explicature: 'John and Bill married Susan and Helen, respectively.'

In other words, (16B) is interpreted as the proposition 'John and Bill married Susan and Helen, respectively.' On a similar note, the following dialogue is semantically odd, because it is impossible to pair *Susan* with someone and *Helen* with someone else in the inferred message.

(17) (Jerry Sadock (p.c.))
A: Who did John marry?
B: #[Susan and Helen], respectively.
basic explicature: #'John married Susan and Helen, respectively.'

Note that the semantic anomaly observed in (17B) is the same as that observed in its basic explicature. This again shows that the fragment (17B) is interpreted as a proposition.

Sixth, a reduced form of an idiom chunk can appear as an NP fragment as in (18B) and (19B). For example, to properly interpret the fragment *Mary's* in (18B) as part of the idiom *pull X's leg*, we need to infer that *Mary's* represents *Mary's leg* and that this is intended as the syntactic structure of *John pulled Mary's leg*. Without this inferred syntactic structure, we would not be able to recover the idiom interpretation of the fragment. The lexical entry for this idiom is repeated in (20).

(18) A: Whose leg did John pull at the party?
B: Mary's.
inferred syntax of the fragment:
[$_{S[PAST]}$ John pulled Mary's leg at the party.]
basic explicature: 'John teased Mary at the party.'

(19) A: Whose goose did John cook?
B: Mary's.
inferred syntax of the fragment:
[$_{S[PAST]}$ John cooked Mary's goose.]
basic explicature: 'John spoiled Mary's plans.'

For this type of idiom, bi-partite lexical entries were proposed in Ueno (2014), following Sadock (2012: 59–60).

(20) bi-partite lexical entry for *pull X's leg* (Chapter 2 (29))
syntax: [$_{VP}$ [$_V$ pull] [$_{NP[DET, 3SG]}$ NP[POS], [$_{NP[3SG]}$ leg]]]
F/A: [$_{Fa}$ [$_{Faa}$ TEASE], ARG]
E/R: [$_{EV}$ [$_{TYPE}$ "tease"] AG PT]

syntax: V in [__, NP[DET, 3SG]]
F/A: Faa
E/R: TYPE in [$_{EV}$ __ AG PT]
morph: V[0]

Seventh, a fragment utterance can consist of two phrases, NP and PP. In such a case, Culicover and Jackendoff (2005) observed that the order of the two phrases (NP < PP) reflects the default order NP < PP in syntax (Sadock 2012: 115, Ueno 2014: 39, Chapter 1 (59b)).

(21) (Culicover and Jackendoff 2005: 246)
A: Harriet's been drinking again.
B: Yeah, {scotch on the weekend | *on the weekend scotch}.

inferred syntax: Harriet has been drinking [NP scotch] [PP on the weekend]
basic explicature: 'Harriet has been drinking scotch on the weekend.'

The acceptability of *scotch on the weekend* and the unacceptability of *on the weekend scotch* in (21B) reflect the default linear order NP < PP in VP. However, if we bring in contrastive pairs of day and beverage, the PP < NP order becomes acceptable, as in *Yeah, on the weekend scotch but on weekdays wine*, whose intended meaning is 'Yeah, on the weekend he's been drinking scotch but on weekdays he's been drinking wine.' (Note how similar this is to the gapping construction such as *On the weekend he's been drinking scotch but on weekdays wine*.) Furthermore, a list of two-phrase fragments is possible. In (22), what A said provides the propositional function $P(x, y) =$ 'x brought y to the potluck' and B gives a list of answers in the form of coordinated two-tuples (x_1, y_1), (x_2, y_2), and (x_3, y_3).

(22) A: Everybody brought their favorite food to the potluck.
 B: I know. John sandwiches, Tom sushi, and Mary an apple pie.
  cf. *Sandwiches John, sushi Tom, and an apple pie Mary.
   inferred syntax: John brought sandwiches to the potluck, Tom brought sushi to the potluck, and Mary brought an apple pie to the potluck.
   basic explicature: 'John brought sandwiches to the potluck, Tom brought sushi to the potluck, and Mary brought an apple pie to the potluck.'

Recall that the order of constituents is only relevant to syntax and information structure (IS) and that F/A and E/R structures are order-free. The unacceptable examples in (21B) and (22B) show that not only semantic structures (F/A and E/R) but also (inferred) syntactic structures (and IS) are relevant in interpreting fragments.

So far, we have presented seven pieces of evidence that fragments are interpreted as contextually appropriate S in syntax, PROP in F/A, and SA in E/R. This interpretation is arrived at by non-demonstrative inference (2.1) guided by the Relevance-guided comprehension heuristic (Chapter 2 (8)), which produces the contextually appropriate, most accessible inferred four-tuple of a fragment U and its explicatures and implicatures. Some of these pieces of evidence, especially the fifth, sixth, and seventh, clearly show that fragment interpretations and their acceptability are not only a matter of semantics (F/A and E/R in AMG), but are also crucially relevant to inferred syntactic structures.

(23) and (24) below are dialogues, in which a series of fragments occur sequentially.

(23) (context: Participants A, B, and C share the knowledge that John used to have a drinking problem.)
    A: Have you heard about your friend?
    B: About John?   [fragment]
    A: Yes. He's started again.
    B: Whiskey?   [fragment]
    A: No, beer.   [fragment]
    B: Every morning?   [fragment]
    A: Yes.
    C: {I didn't know that | That's true | That's false}.

The demonstrative *that* in (23C) refers to 'John has started drinking beer every morning.' The information needed to determine what *that* refers to is spread all over the prior discourse including the participants' shared knowledge and hence it is impossible to construct what *that* refers to only from the immediately preceding utterance. Furthermore, the verb *drink* contained in the referent of *that* does not occur anywhere in the discourse. However, there are two factors in the discourse that make *drink* salient: (i) the participants share the knowledge that John used to have a drinking problem, that is, he used to drink too much alcohol, and (ii) the words *whiskey* and *beer* mean at least 'something to drink.' Under normal circumstances, (ii) is sufficient to trigger the interpretation 'start drinking beer/whiskey' just by hearing "start." For example, Mary and John are talking in a restaurant with a glass of beer in their hand, and Mary says "We've just started" to Tom, who has just shown up. What Mary meant and Tom understood was 'We've just started drinking beer.' Example (23) is in marked contrast with the answer fragment example (1), in which all the information needed to interpret what B meant by the NP "A motorcycle" was given in the immediately preceding utterance by A. (24) is another example in which the information needed to recover what C's demonstrative *that* refers to is again spread all over the discourse.

(24) A: I hear there have been some serious binges going on around here.
      B: Not my favorite bottle of scotch, I hope.   [fragment]
      A: No, Tom's, I suppose.   [fragment]

B: Every night? [fragment]
A: Yes, from seven to twelve. [fragment]
C: {I didn't know that | That's true | That's false}.

The demonstrative *that* in (24C) refers to 'People have been drinking (too much of) Tom's favorite bottle of scotch every night from seven to twelve.' Again, there is no mention of the verb *drink* in the discourse, although it is understood in the referent of *that*. This verb is made salient by the knowledge that scotch is 'something to drink' and that binge is 'a period of time in which people drink too much.' Multiple fragments occur in a dialogue, as in (23) and (24), which shows that fragment interpretation must apply successively, cumulatively, and incrementally.

To illustrate how this successive, cumulative, and incremental fragment interpretation is carried out, let us examine the interpretation process of (23).

(25) (= (23)) (context: Participants A, B, and C share the knowledge that John used to have a drinking problem.)
  A: Have you heard about your friend?
  B: About John? [fragment]
   inferred syntax: Is it about John?
   explicature: 'Is it about John?' (where *it* refer to what A has in mind)
  A: Yes. He's started again.
   explicatures: 'A asserts that it is about John.'
       'A asserts that John has started drinking again.' (enrichment)
  B: Whiskey? [fragment]
   inferred syntax: Has John started drinking whiskey?
   explicature: B asks A if John has started drinking whiskey.
  A: No, beer. [fragment]
   inferred syntax: No, John has started drinking beer.
   explicatures: 'A asserts that John has not started drinking whiskey.'
       'A asserts that John has started drinking beer.'
  B: Every morning? [fragment]
   inferred syntax: Has he started drinking beer every morning?
   explicature: 'B asks A if John has started drinking beer every morning.'
  A: Yes.
   basic explicature: 'John has started drinking beer every morning.'

higher-level explicature: 'A asserts that John has started drinking beer every morning.'
C: {I didn't know that | That's true | That's false}.

C's *that* refers to the immediately preceding basic explicature. A series of fragments are interpreted online successively, cumulatively, and incrementally through non-demonstrative inference. For example, to interpret the fragment "Yes" uttered by A, we need to interpret the previous fragment "Every morning?" by B. But to interpret B's fragment, we need to interpret the previous fragment "No, beer" by A. But to interpret A's fragment, we need to interpret the previous fragment "Whiskey?" by B. But to interpret B's fragment, we need to interpret the previous utterance "Yes. He has started again" by A. But to interpret B's utterance, we need to interpret the previous fragment "About John?" by B. But to interpret B's fragment, we need the interpretation of the previous utterance "Have you heard about your friend?" by A.

Every time a fragment U is uttered, the hearer's Language Module (LM) first decodes U into its four-tuple representations (decoded four-tuple) and computes its skeletal four-tuple. The LM then sends it to the Inferential Comprehension Module (ICM), which in turn constructs the inferred four-tuple of U through non-demonstrative inference performed on the contextual information and also constructs the explicatures and implicatures of U by non-demonstrative inference on the basis of the contextual information and the explicatures and implicatures of the prior discourse. During this process, the decoded four-tuple of U is turned into the inferred four-tuple of U. This inferred four-tuple is indispensable for, among other things, the interpretation of idiom chunk fragments, as illustrated in (18) and (19) and in Chapter 2 (26), repeated here as (26). The explicature of the idiom chunk fragment *Bill's* in (26) below can be constructed through its inferred four-tuple, especially through its inferred syntax constructed form the passive lexical entry for *pull X's leg* (Chapter 2 (28)).

(26) (= Chapter 2 (26))
    John: Whose leg was pulled at the party?
    Mary [happily]: Bill's.
        John's interpretation
            inferred syntax: Bill's leg was pulled at the party.
            basic explicature: 'Bill was teased at the party.'

higher-level explicatures: 'Mary asserts that Bill was teased at the party.'
'Mary is happy that Bill was teased at the party.'

Here is an example in which both context and real world knowledge are essential to inferring what B meant.

(27) (context: Without saying anything, a regular customer holds out his empty glass to the bartender (B), who is very busy at the moment and says to the customer:)
B: In a minute, OK?
   inferred syntax: I will fix you a drink in a minute. Would that be OK with you?
   explicatures: 'B promises that he will fix the customer a drink as soon as possible.'
   'B asks the customer if that would be OK with him.'
   implicatures: 'B asks the customer to be patient.'
   'B claims that he is very busy at the moment.' etc.

The explicatures and implicatures of a fragment could not be inferred appropriately, if it were not for information about the context (in which a regular customer finishes his drink and holds out his empty glass to the bartender) or the relevant real world knowledge (such as that if a customer puts his empty glass in front of the bartender, the customer is asking for another drink). The same is true of the discourse-initial fragments in (3).

Here are some French and German examples of PP fragments. To properly interpret the PP[*parce*] in (28a) and the PP[*wenn*] in (28b), we need non-demonstrative inference based on our real world knowledge.

(28) a. A: En général, où est-ce que tu vas le week-end?
        B: Je vais au cinéma ou au café, près de chez moi.
        A: Parce que la serveuse est jolie?
        B: Non, non! Parce que c'est calme!
           (*Everyday French*, by NHK, December 2011, p. 38)
    b. Gen: Frau Ohm ... mir ist schlecht.
       Frau Ohm: Gen! Immer ruhig! Wir sind doch zweit.
       Gen: Und was machen wir, wenn sie bewaffnet ist?
       Frau Ohm: Keine Angst! Ich habe ja meinen Regenschirm.

Gen: Aber wenn sie uns einsperren will?
(Tatsuya Ota and Marco Raindl. 2009. *Das Geheimnis der Geige*, NHK, p.154)

In (28a), although B's first reply contains the disjunction *au cinéma ou au café*, the second half of the dialogue only concerns *Je vais au café* and the second B *c'est calme* concerns *le café* and not *le cinéma* in the first B. In the second half of the dialogue, A's intended meaning is 'Tu vas au café parce que la serveuse est jolie?' and B's intended meaning is 'Je vais au café parce que c'est calme!' The matrix clause to which the PP[*parce*] is interpreted as being adjoined, namely, *Je vais au café* or *Tu vas au café*, is not found verbatim in the preceding context. In (27b), Gen's "Aber wenn sie uns einsperren will?" must be interpreted as an adjunct to Gen's prior "Was machen wir?"

The notion of "script" (Schank and Abelson 1977) plays an important role not only in interpreting a fragment sequence but also in determining the case and discourse referent of an NP contained in it (McCawley 1993a: 366, Merchant 2004: 730). In the following dialogue, the fragments are underlined.

(29) (context: at a hotel reception desk, where A is a receptionist and B is a guest)
A: Moment ... Nur noch ein Doppelzimmer.
B: Äh ... na gut. Dann ein Doppelzimmer, bitte.
A: Mit oder ohne Frühstück?
B: Mit Frühstück, bitte. Für eine Nacht.
(Ota and Raindl. 2009. *Das Geheimnis der Geige*, NHK, p.68)

Without any knowledge of where this dialogue is taking place and its related script, (29) would be incomprehensible.

3.3 Properties of Fragments

In this section, we will examine interesting properties of fragments and consider how they can be understood from the AMG perspective.

3.3.1 Fragments with parentheticals
As shown in (12), (13), and (15), a fragment can consist of a fragment proper and one or more parentheticals. Here is another example.

(30) a. A: I hear John's been drinking again.
B: Frankly, not beer, I hope.
inferred syntax: Frankly, it is not beer, I hope.
basic explicature: 'It is not beer.' where *it* refers to some alcohol in A's explicature
'A hears that John has been drinking some alcohol again.'
higher-level explicatures: 'B hopes that the alcohol John has been drinking is not beer.'
'B tells A as a frank comment that the alcohol John has been drinking is not beer.'

b. A: Now that we've interviewed the shortlisted candidates, I'd like to hear your take on them.
B: In my opinion, quite an eclectic bunch, don't you think?
inferred syntax: In my opinion, they are quite an eclectic bunch, don't you think?
basic explicature: 'They are quite an eclectic bunch,' where *they* refers to the shortlisted candidates.
higher-level explicature: 'B thinks that they are quite an eclectic bunch.'
'B asks A if A does not think that they are quite an eclectic bunch.'
implicature: B wants A to agree with his opinion that they are quite an eclectic bunch.

c. E/R of (30aB)

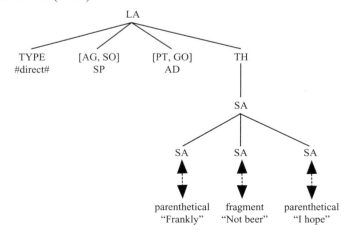

We claim that parentheticals such as *frankly* and *I hope* in (30aB) and *in my opinion* and *don't you think* in (30bB) constitute a separate speech act (SA) in E/R, just like style disjuncts (McCawley 1985, Ueno 2014: 371) and that the whole utterance by B in (30a) and in (30b) is a single locutionary act (LA) consisting of three speech acts, as in (30c) (cf. Ueno 2014: 359 (8c)). What B meant in (30a) is best paraphrased as 'I tell you this as a frank comment. It is not beer that John has been drinking. I hope so.' Note that the focus of negation is on *beer*. As for the interpretation of (30bB), the first part *in my opinion* contributes 'I think' to the higher-level explicatures, the second part, the NP fragment, conveys the basic explicature 'the shortlisted candidates we've interviewed are quite an eclectic bunch,' and the third part *don't you think* conveys the speaker's asking for agreement with what she just asserted.

3.3.2 Ban on complementizer deletion

Merchant (2004) observed that "complementizer deletion" is not allowed when the answer fragment is clausal.

(31) (Merchant 2004: 690)
    A: What does no one believe?
    B: {That I'm taller than I really am | #I'm taller than I really am}.
        (i) inferred syntax: No one believes (that) I'm taller than I really am.
            basic explicature: 'No one believes (that) I'm taller than I really am.'
        (ii) inferred syntax: It is *(that) I'm taller than I really am, where *it* refers to *something* in the existential presupposition 'No one believes something' of A's *wh*-question.
            basic explicature: 'What no one believes is that B is taller than B really is.'

There are two possibilities (i) and (ii) about the inferred syntax of B's clausal fragment. As for (ii), note that a pronoun can refer to the existential quantifier in the presupposition of the preceding *wh*-question, as in "What did they do and why did they do it?" (Ueno 2014: 291).

First, consider (i). There are three reasons why the deletion of *that* in (31B) is not felicitous when the clausal fragment is uttered as an answer to A's *wh*-question. The first reason is that a stand-alone declarative S[FIN] in syntax corresponds by default to a speech act of assertion as in (32), which is contrary to speaker B's intention.

112   3 AN AUTOMODULAR VIEW OF FRAGMENTS

(32) default correspondences between declarative S[FIN] in syntax and the other modules (= Chapter 2 (36a))

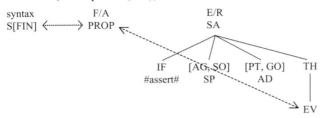

phonology: falling intonation

In relevance-theoretic terms, uttering an S[FIN] instead of a CP[*that*] as an answer to the *wh*-question (31A) increases the processing effort because of the availability of the irrelevant assertion interpretation, and hence decreases the relevance of the S[FIN] utterance. The second reason why *that* deletion is not allowed in (31B) is that the speaker B needs to make her intention clear by uttering a CP[*that*] that the clausal fragment is intended as the complement of the preceding verb *believe*. By doing so, she can forestall the irrelevant interpretation from the default correspondences (32) at the same time. The third reason is that in order for an S[FIN] to be interpreted as the complement of a verb, it must be adjacent to the verb, as shown in (33). Therefore, uttering a fragment S[FIN] in (31B) violates this lexical requirement.

(33) partial lexical entry for *believe*
     syntax: V in [__, CP[*that*]], [__ ⩽ S[FIN]], where A ⩽ B means A immediately precedes B.
     F/A: Fpa

Now consider (ii) in (31). The first reason above also holds in this case. Furthermore, *that*-deletion is impossible in the inferred syntax of (ii). Therefore, in either (i) or (ii), *that*-deletion is not felicitous in (31B). (34) is a similar example and is explained in the same way.

(34) (Merchant 2004: 690)
     A: What are you ashamed of?
     B: {That I ignored you | #I ignored you}.
         cf. I'm ashamed (*of) that I ignored you.
         cf. *(That) I ignored you, I'm ashamed of.

3.3.3 Apparent c-selection

Merchant (2004) claimed that he observed c-selectional effects in fragments. In (35a, b), it looks as if the VFORM value is maintained between the antecedent VP in A and the VP fragment in B.

(35) (Merchant 2004: 696 (121))
    a. A: What is John doing?
       B: Washing his car.
    b. A: John is doing something.
       B: Yes. Washing his car.

However, a VP[PRP], a VP headed by a verb in the present participle form (V[PRP]), occurs discourse-initially as in (3e), or when Mary sees John doing something and asks him: "Washing your car?" These are examples of discourse-initial VP[PRP] and there is no prior linguistic context from where the present participle requirement comes. Rather, a VP[PRP] headed by a non-stative verb expresses the progressive aspect in its own right, just as in "Going, going, going, gone!" at a baseball game or at an auction site. (36) is a similar example.

(36) A: What happened to John?
     B: Hit by a car.

In (36), B utters a VP[PAS], a passive VP, to mean 'John was hit by a car.' The VP[PAS] expresses the passive meaning in its own right, and there is nothing in the prior linguistic context that triggers the c-selection of a VP[PAS].

3.3.4 Fragments as focus

In the Information Structure module (IS) of (8), a fragment represents focus (FOC), a type of foreground information (FI). This is supported by Merchant's (2004) observation that when a pronoun is used as a fragment, it must be a strong form (an accusative pronoun in the case of English). In French, *moi* is a strong form of the first person singular whereas *me* is a weak form.

(37) a. (Merchant 2004: 701–2 (143) (147))
       A: Il voulait qui?
       B: {Moi | *Me}.   cf. Il {*moi | me} voulait.

b. {Moi | *Me}, il me voulait. (Merchant 2004: 702 (151))
   c. C'est {moi | *me} qui ai proposé ce film.

The strong form also appears as the left dislocation topic as in (37b) and as the focus of a cleft sentence as in (37c). In English, too, the strong form *me* must be used as a fragment, left dislocation topic, and the focus of cleft sentence, as in (38).

(38) a. (Merchant 2004: 703 (154))
         A: Who watered the plants?
         B: {Me | *I}.   cf. {*Me | I} watered the plants.
      b. {Me | *I}, I watered the plants. (Merchant 2004: 703 (156))
      c. It's {me | *I} who watered the plants. (colloquial)

The pronouns in (37aB) and (38aB) are used as fragments and they must be strong pronouns. This shows that they correspond to FI, and FOC in particular, in IS and carry stress in phonology.

3.3.5 Controlled VPs as fragments

Merchant (2004) also observed a difference between raising and control verbs when their VP complements are used as fragments. As shown in (39a, b), a VP[*to*] fragment is acceptable if it is intended as the complement of a control verb but unacceptable if it is intended as the complement of a raising verb. Of course, an NP fragment is acceptable if it is intended as the object NP of a transitive verb, as in (39c).

(39) (cf. Merchant 2004: 698 (134) and (135))
      a. A: How does Mary tend to behave? (*tend* raising verb)
         B: *To go slow.
      b. A: How does Mary want to behave? (*want* control verb)
         B: To go slow.
      c. A: What does Mary want? (*want* transitive verb)
         B: A car.

In (39c), when B hears A say "What does Mary want?," B accesses the lexical entry for *want* (40c) and utters the NP fragment "A car" intending it to be the

3.3 PROPERTIES OF FRAGMENTS

object of the transitive verb *want*. In this case, the NP fragment corresponds to the object NP in the inferred syntax, to the lower ARG in the inferred F/A, and to the TH role in the inferred E/R. (Access to lexical entries in fragment interpretation will be discussed in 3.4.)

The case of control verb (39b) is quite similar to the transitive verb case (39c). The VP[*to*] fragment in (39b), which is intended to be the complement of *want*, corresponds to the VP[*to*] complement in the inferred syntax, to the complement PROP in the inferred F/A, and to the [TH EV] role in the inferred E/R. In a sense, in (39b, c), the fragments' relationships with the verb are maintained between their inferred syntax, F/A, and E/R. This is shown in (42a, b). See 1.7 for a brief discussion on control verbs.

(40) lexical entries for *tend* and *want*

    a. *tend* (raising verb)
       syntax: V in [__, VP[*to*]]
       F/A: Fp
       E/R: [$_{TYPE}$ "tend"] in
         [$_{EV}$ __ [$_{TH}$ EV]]

    b. *want* (control verb)
       syntax: V in [__, VP[*to*]]
       F/A: Fpa
       E/R: [$_{TYPE}$ "want"] in
         [$_{STATE}$ __ PT [$_{TH}$ [$_{SITU}$ HAR]]]

       (coreference requirement)

    c. *want* (transitive verb)
       syntax: V in [__, NP]
       F/A: Faa
       E/R: [$_{TYPE}$ "want"] in [$_{STATE}$ __ PT TH]

(41) the inferred syntax, F/A, and E/R of "To go slow" in (39a)

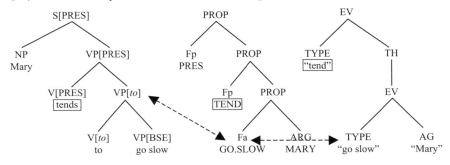

116   3 AN AUTOMODULAR VIEW OF FRAGMENTS

(42) a. the inferred syntax, F/A, and E/R of "To go slow" in (39b)

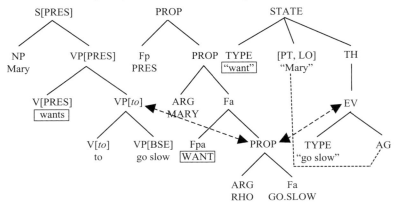

b. the inferred syntax, F/A, and E/R of "A car" in (39c)

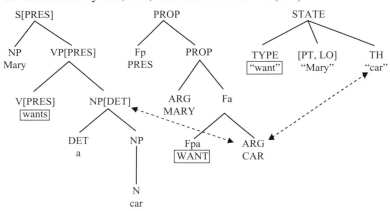

By contrast, in the case of the raising verb *tend* in (39a), the VP[*to*] fragment is intended as its complement. This VP[*to*] in the inferred syntax does not correspond to the complement PROP in the inferred F/A nor to the [_TH_ EV] role in the inferred E/R. This is shown in (41). In other words, although the VP[*to*] *to go slow* is a complement of the raising verb *tend* in the inferred syntax, this head-complement relationship does not isomorphically translate into the equivalent functor-argument or type-role relationships in the inferred F/A and E/R. This is the source of the ungrammaticality of B's utterance in (39a). See 1.6.1 for a brief discussion on subject raising verbs.

3.3.6 Three types of inferred syntax

There are three types of inferred syntax constructed from a fragment. In (43), B's NP fragment "Japanese" is understood in three ways depending on what inferred syntax is constructed from the NP fragment. Its inferred syntax can be constructed from the global domain (44a), from the local domain (44b), or by directly referring to the antecedent NP, as in (44c).

(43) (context: A and B share the knowledge that Japanese is a foreign language.)
A: Mary said John is learning a foreign language.
B: Yes. Japanese.

(44) a. inferred syntax from global domain: Mary said John is learning Japanese.
a'. B: Yes. Japanese. That's what I hear Mary said.
b. inferred syntax from local domain: John is learning Japanese.
b'. B: Yes. Japanese. That's what I know.
c. inferred syntax by direct reference: It is Japanese.
where *it* refers to a foreign language in (43A).

The difference between (44a) and (44b) is that (44a) can be followed by "That's what I hear Mary said" as in (44a'), whereas (44b) can be followed by "That's what I know" as in (44b'). The interpretation (44c) is only available in the case of matching fragments, in which a fragment has an antecedent or a related NP in the preceding discourse.

The inferred syntax of a fragment constructed from the global domain (44a) is a method of interpreting it by replacing the corresponding NP in the preceding utterance (*a foreign language*) with the NP fragment (*Japanese*). On the other hand, the inferred syntax of a fragment constructed from the local domain (44b) is a method of interpreting it relative to the local domain (i.e., the smallest clause in the prior discourse that contains the phrase corresponding to the fragment in question). In (44b'), the NP fragment is interpreted relative to the embedded clause. In (44a), B asserts what A said and adds more relevant information that A may not know. This is shown in (44a'). In (44b), by contrast, B asserts what he knows. This is shown in (44b'). The inferred syntax of a fragment constructed by direct reference (44c) is a method of interpreting it as if it consisted of pronoun + *be* +

fragment, in which the pronoun refers to the most salient NP in the immediately preceding utterance (*a foreign language*). In (44c), the pronoun *it* refers to *a foreign language* in what A said.

There are two cases of fragment use in which its inferred syntax is only constructed by direct reference. The first case is when an NP fragment with rising intonation is uttered (as a question) in response to a statement (45) or a *wh*-question (46). The symbol # indicates semantic/pragmatic anomaly.

(45) A: Mary said John bought something.
  B: A car?
    by direct reference: Is it a car?
      (*it* refers to *something* in the antecedent.)
    from global domain: #Did Mary say John bought a car?
    from local domain: #Did John buy a car?

(46) A: What did Mary say John bought?
  B_1: A car?
    by direct reference: Is it a car?
      (*it* refers to *something* in the existential presupposition 'Mary said John bought something' of the antecedent *wh*-question.)
    from global domain: #Did Mary say John bought a car?
    local domain: #Did John buy a car?
  B_2: Not a car, I'm sure.
    by direct reference: It is not a car, I'm sure.
    from global domain: #Mary didn't say John bought a car, I'm sure.
    from local domain: #John didn't buy a car, I'm sure.

In (45) and (46), neither the inferred syntax from the global domain nor the one from the local domain is felicitous.

Second, the inferred syntax of a fragment by direct reference (pronoun + *be* + fragment) is required when the antecedent NP of the fragment is modified by an adjective and the fragment has the form of *how* + adjective.

(47) A: I saw a drunken man.
  B: How {drunk | *drunken}?

by direct reference: 'How drunk was he?' (where *he* refers to *a drunken man* in what A said)
cf. How {drunken | *drunk} a man did you see?

Only the inferred syntax constructed by direct reference (pronoun subject + *be* + AP headed by a predicative adjective) can explain the acceptability of *How drunk?* and the unacceptability of *How drunken?* This is further supported by the data below, in which the meaning of the adjective in the antecedent NP differs between attributive use and predicative use. For example, *He is a tall man* and *The man is tall* are both fine but while *He is a big fan of Madonna* is fine, *The fan of Madonna is big* is not. This contrast between *big* and *tall* is seen in (48) and (49). (50) is the same type of example as (48).

(48) A: I met a big fan of Madonna.
B: #How big?
inferred syntax by direct reference: #How big was he?
(*he* refers to *a big fan of Madonna* in what A said.)
cf. How big a fan?

(49) A: I met a tall man.
B: How tall?
inferred syntax by direct reference: How tall was he?'
(*he* refers to *a tall man* in what A said.)

(50) A: He gave me a tall order.
B: #How tall?
inferred syntax by direct reference: #How tall was it?
(*it* refers to *a tall order* in what A said.)
cf. How tall an order?

Only the inferred syntax constructed by direct reference can explain the infelicity of *How big?* in (48) and *How tall?* in (50). These pieces of evidence show that the construction of inferred syntax by direct reference is independently required.

3.3.7 Quantifier fragments

Merchant (2004) observed that a quantifier answer fragment, a quantified NP (QNP) used as an answer fragment, such as a in (51B), exhibits the same ambiguity as a full sentential answer, such as b in (51B).

(51) (Merchant 2004: 681 (65))
    A: How many diplomats did every translator greet? (ambiguous)
    B: a. Three. (ambiguous)
        b. inferred syntax: Every translator greeted three (diplomats). (ambiguous)

However, question (51A) itself is ambiguous between a reading of *how many* > *every* and that with *every* > *how many*, where A > B indicates that B is within the scope of A. Furthermore, the ambiguity of question (51A) and that of answer fragment (51Ba) are closely related. If B interprets A's question as *how many* > *every* (52a), then B utters "three" intending it to mean *three* > *every* (53a). On the other hand, if B interprets A's question as *every* > *how many* (52b), then B utters "three" intending it to mean *every* > *three* (53b).

(52) F/A structures of *How many diplomats did every translator greet?*
    a. [$_{QPy}$ how many diplomats] [$_{QPx}$ every translator] [PAST(x GREET y)]
    b. [$_{QPx}$ every translator] [$_{QPy}$ how many diplomats] [PAST(x GREET y)]

(53) inferred F/A structures of answer fragment *Three*
    a. [$_{QPy}$ ∃ three (diplomats)] [$_{QPx}$ every translator] [PAST(x GREET y)]
    b. [$_{QPx}$ every translator] [$_{QPy}$ ∃ three (diplomats)] [PAST(x GREET y)]

More specifically, when B hears A's question, interprets it as (52a), and answers "Three," what B intends to convey is the F/A structure (53a), in which [$_{QPy}$ how many diplomats] is replaced by the existential QP [$_{QPy}$ ∃ three]. (Note that the noun *diplomats* is omitted in (51Ba), because it is part of old information and that this will be recovered by development when the explicature of the answer fragment is constructed.) However, when B hears A's question and interprets it as (52b), B's answer "Three" is intended to convey the F/A structure (53b), in which [$_{QPy}$ how many diplomats] is replaced by the existential QP [$_{QPy}$ ∃ three].

3.3.8 Bound variables in fragments

Merchant (2004) observed that the bound variable interpretation of a pronoun is possible in fragment answers as in (54B), just as pronouns can be interpreted as bound variables in full sentences with QNP subjects, as in (55).

(54) (Merchant 2004: 681 (66))
    A: Who does every Englishman$_x$ admire?
    B: His$_x$ mother.

(55) inferred syntax of (54B): Every Englishman$_x$ admires his$_x$ mother.

When B hears A's question in (54), interprets it as the F/A structure (56a) with its E/R (56b), and answers *His mother*, B's intention is to convey the F/A structure (57a) with its E/R (57b) by replacing *who* in the E/R (56b) with *his mother*.

(56) F/A and E/R of A's question *Who does every Englishman admire?* with *every > who*
    a. [$_{QPx}$ every Englishman] [$_{QPy}$ who] [PRES(x ADMIRE y)]
    b. [$_{EV}$ [$_{TYPE}$ "admire"] [$_{AG}$ "every Englishman"] [$_{PT}$ "who"]]

(57) inferred F/A and E/R of B's answer fragment *His mother*
    a. [$_{QPx}$ every Englishman] [PRES(x ADMIRE x's MOTHER)]
    b. [$_{EV}$ [$_{TYPE}$ "admire"] [$_{AG}$ "every Englishman"] [$_{PT}$ "his mother"]]

It has been claimed since Reinhart (1983: 122) that bound variable pronouns must be c-commanded by their binder QNPs in syntax (Ueno 2014: 291). To the extent that this condition is syntactic, the fragment answer in (54B) provides evidence for the psychological reality of the inferred syntactic structure (55), where Reinhart's syntactic condition is met.

In fact, A's question in (54) is ambiguous. When B interprets it as (58a), B can answer "The Queen" by replacing "who" in (58a, b) by "the Queen," as in (59a, b). In addition, B's reply in (54) can also be ambiguous. The bound variable interpretation of *his* in (54B) is prevented if it refers to a previously established discourse topic, as in (59c).

(58) a. [$_{QPy}$ who] [$_{QPx}$ every Englishman] [PRES(x ADMIRE y)]
    b. [$_{EV}$ [$_{TYPE}$ "admire"] [$_{AG}$ "every Englishman"] [$_{PT}$ "who"]]

(59) a. [$_{QPy}$ the Queen] [$_{QPx}$ every Englishman] [PRES(x ADMIRE y)]
    b. [$_{EV}$ [$_{TYPE}$ "admire"] [$_{AG}$ "every Englishman"] [$_{PT}$ "the Queen"]]
    c. B: Prof. Jones is very famous because his wife is stunningly beautiful.
       A: Who does every student$_x$ admire?
       B: His wife, of course.

3.3.9 Fragments and pronouns

Merchant (2004) observed that fragments exhibit the same distributional restrictions of NPs and pronouns as regulated by Binding Theory, if Binding Theory is applied to the inferred syntax of the fragment in question. The unacceptable PP fragment in (a) of (60B) is an example of "Principle C effect."

(60) (Merchant 2004: 679 (57))
    A: Where is he$_2$ staying?
    B: a. *In John$_2$'s apartment.
       b. inferred syntax: *He$_2$ is staying in John$_2$'s apartment. ("Principle C effect")

There are three reasons why the PP fragment in (60Ba) is unacceptable. First, when the audience interprets this fragment, their Language Module (LM) decodes it and computes the decoded four-tuple of the fragment. The Inferential Comprehension Module (ICM) applies non-demonstrative inference to the fragment and constructs its inferred four-tuple, whose syntax is (60Bb), which violates the syntactic condition (what McCawley (1998: 359 (30)) called "Conditions on surface structure"), which says in part that an anaphoric device (AD) may not precede and c-command its antecedent.

Second, when B hears A say "Where is he staying?" B accesses the lexical entry for *stay* and computes the E/R (61a) of question (60A). B utters the PP fragment, intending to give the value of "where" as "in John's apartment" with the E/R (61b) in mind, in which "where" is replaced by "in John's apartment." Alternatively, by uttering the PP fragment, B can compute the E/R (61b) through the default correspondences between E/R and the inferred syntax (60Bb). Either way, the resultant E/R (61b) violates the condition that if X and

Y are coreferential and X outranks Y, then Y must be a pronoun (McCawley 1998: 362, Sag et al. 2003: 522, Bresnan 1995: 247). (The exact formulation of this condition does not concern us here.) See Chapter 1 (56) for the definition of outrank.

(61) a. [$_{EV}$ [$_{TYPE}$ "stay"] [$_{[AG, TH]}$ "he$_2$"] [$_{LO}$ "where"]]
 b. *[$_{EV}$ [$_{TYPE}$ "stay"] [$_{[AG, TH]}$ "he$_2$"] [$_{LO}$ "in John$_2$'s apartment"]]

Third, when A asks question (60A), A uses the pronoun *he* to refer to *John*, which shows that *John* must already have been introduced into the discourse between A and B and they both treat *John* as old information. However, when B answers A's question in (60), B utters "In John's apartment" (instead of "In his apartment"), as if *John* is new information. This unmotivated inconsistency is another source of the unacceptability of (60Ba). When there is some pragmatic/discourse motivation, as in (62B), for using *John* instead of *he*, the use of *John* is allowed.

(62) (context: A and B have been talking about John.)
 A: Where is he$_2$ staying now?
 B: Not in Bill's apartment and not in Tom's apartment, either.
 Probably, in John$_2$'s own apartment.
 cf. *Probably, he$_2$ is staying in John$_2$'s own apartment.

The pronoun fragment *Him* in (63Ba) below is said to involve a "Principle B" violation.

(63) (Merchant 2004: 680 (59))
 A: Who did John$_1$ try to shave?
 B: a. *Him$_1$.
 b. inferred syntax: *John$_1$ tried to shave him$_1$. ("Principle B effect")

When the audience hears the pronoun fragment in (63Ba), they construct the inferred syntax in (63Bb). They compute its corresponding E/R (65b) by accessing the lexical entry for the subject-control verb *try* (64). In the E/R field of (64), a coreference requirement is stated between the AG of *try* (the controller) and the highest associable role (HAR) of the subordinate event (EV) (Sadock 2012: 89, Ueno 2014: 187).

124   3   AN AUTOMODULAR VIEW OF FRAGMENTS

(64) lexical entry for *try* (cf. Ueno 2014: 204)
    syntax: V in [__, VP[*to*]]
    F/A: Fpa
    E/R: [$_{VA}$ [$_{TYPE}$"try"] [AG, SO] [$_{PT, GO}$ [$_{EV}$ TYPE HAR…]]]

When B hears A say "Who did John$_1$ try to shave?," B intends to give the value of "who" as "John$_1$," as in (65b).

(65) a. the E/R of the question in (63)
    [$_{VA}$ [$_{TYPE}$"try"] [$_{[AG, SO]}$"John$_1$"] [$_{PT, GO}$ [$_{VA}$ [$_{TYPE}$"shave"] AG$_1$ [$_{PT}$"who"]]]]
    b. the inferred E/R of the answer fragment in (63)
    [$_{VA}$ ["try"] ["John$_1$"] [$_{PT, GO}$ [$_{VA}$ ["shave"] AG$_1$ [$_{PT}$ {"*John$_1$" | "*him$_1$" | "himself$_1$"}]]]]

However, B cannot simply say "John" because "John" was already mentioned in A's question in (63), and hence is discourse-old. Furthermore, because the matrix subject "John" outranks the embedded object "John" in (65b), B needs to use a pronoun, *him* or *himself*, due to the above outrank condition. Let us assume that all the anaphoric devices (ADs) including non-reflexive and reflexive pronouns are subject to a common condition along the lines of McCawley's "Conditions on surface structure" (cited above). But reflexive pronouns are more special than non-reflexive pronouns in that they require a local antecedent, namely, in E/R terms, that a reflexive must have its outranking antecedent within the same event (EV). Because of this more specific requirement on reflexives, non-reflexive pronouns cannot occur where reflexives can, due to the Elsewhere Principle (McCawley 1998: 163, Ueno 2014: 11). Based on the E/R (65a), B intends to express the E/R (65b), in which only *himself* is grammatical.

Merchant (2004) also observed a set of "apparent non-connectivity effects" between answer fragments such as B's answer fragments in (66) and their inferred syntactic structures in (66). Although the answer fragments (66Ba) sound perfect, their inferred syntactic structures (66Bb) are pretty bad.

(66) (Merchant 2004: 682–683 (67) and (68))
    A: Who did you tell about Bill$_2$'s raise?

B: a. {Him$_2$ | Bill$_2$}.
   b. inferred syntax: {*I told him$_2$ about Bill$_2$'s raise | ??I told Bill$_2$ about Bill$_2$'s raise}.

After B has heard A's *wh*-question, B holds the presupposition '(A thinks that) I told someone about his$_2$ raise' and identified the 'someone' as *him$_2$* or *Bill$_2$*. Note that *Bill's* in question (66A) is turned into the pro-form *his* in B's presupposition, because it is old information for B after B has heard A's question.

(67) a. E/R of A's question
      [$_{EV}$ [$_{TYPE}$ "tell"] [$_{[AG, SO]}$ "you"] [$_{[PT, GO]}$ "who"] [$_{TH}$ "about Bill$_2$'s raise"]]
   b. E/R of B's presupposition
      [$_{EV}$ [$_{TYPE}$ "tell"] [$_{[AG, SO]}$ "I"] [$_{[PT, GO]}$ "someone"] [$_{TH}$ "about his$_2$ raise"]]
   c. inferred E/R of B's answer "{him | Bill}"
      [$_{EV}$ [$_{TYPE}$ "tell"] [$_{[AG, SO]}$ "I"] [$_{[PT, GO]}$ "{him$_2$ | Bill$_2$}"] [$_{TH}$ "about his$_2$ raise"]]

On the one hand, by replacing "someone" in (67b) with "him" and answering "him," B directly refers to "Bill" in A's question in (66). On the other hand, by replacing "someone" in (67b) with "Bill" and answering "Bill," B treats "Bill" as addressee-new because it was the focus of A's *wh*-question.

3.3.10 Island insensitivity of fragments

Culicover and Jackendoff (2005) showed that fragments are insensitive to islands by giving fragment examples that would involve island violations if they were analyzed purely syntactically in terms of A'-movement and deletion. (For a full discussion on various types of island, see 6.1.3 and 6.1.4 in Ueno (2014). For a brief discussion on the CNPC, see Chapter 1 (102).)

(68) Complex NP Constraint (CNPC) (cf. Culicover and Jackendoff 2005: 245) (context: A and B share the knowledge that Albanian is a very unusual language.)
   A: Mary said John met a guy who speaks a very unusual language.
   B$_1$: Which language?
      [cf. *Which language did Mary say John met a guy who speaks?]
   B$_2$: Yes, Albanian.
      [cf. *Albanian, Mary said John met a guy who speaks ___.]

B_3: Albanian?
[cf. *Is it Albanian that Mary said John met a guy who speaks __?]

(69) Coordinate Structure Constraint (CSC) (cf. Culicover and Jackendoff 2005: 245)
(context: A and B share the knowledge that Kennedy and Hatch are senators.)
A: Mary said they persuaded Kennedy and some other senator to jointly sponsor the legislation.
B_1: Which senator?
[cf. *Which senator did Mary say they persuaded Kennedy and __ to jointly sponsor the legislation.]
B_2: Yeah, Hatch.
[cf. *Hatch, Mary said they persuaded Kennedy and __ to jointly sponsor the legislation.]
B_3: Hatch?
[cf. *Is it Hatch that Mary said they persuaded Kennedy and __ to jointly sponsor the legislation?]

(70) Sentential Subject Constraint (Culicover and Jackendoff 2005: 245)
A: For John to flirt at the party would be scandalous.
B: Even with his wife?
[cf. *Is it even with his wife that for John to flirt __ at the party would be scandalous?]

These examples show that a purely syntactic approach based on A'-movement such as topicalization or *wh*-movement followed by deletion cannot adequately account for these fragments.

As discussed in relation to (43) and (44), there are three ways of constructing the inferred syntax of ($68B_2$), which are given in (71).

(71) inferred syntactic structures of ($68B_2$)
   a. 'Yes, Mary said John met a guy who speaks Albanian' (from global domain).
   b. 'Yes, he speaks Albanian' (from local domain; the pronoun *he* refers to 'a guy who speaks an unusual language' in the antecedent).

c. 'Yes, it was Albanian' (by direct reference; the pronoun *it* refers to *an unusual language* in the antecedent).

In (68B$_2$) with the inferred syntax (71a), the fragment *Albanian* replaces the NP *a very unusual language* in the antecedent (68A). In this exchange, B asserts what A said and adds more relevant information that A may not know. In the inferred syntax (71b), the fragment is interpreted within the relative clause. The three types of inferred syntax give essentially the same information, namely that the very unusual language in question is Albanian. Similarly, (69B$_2$) can be interpreted in three ways.

(72) inferred syntactic structures of (69B$_2$)
  a. 'Yeah, Mary said they persuaded Kennedy and Hatch to jointly sponsor the legislation.' (from global domain)
  b. 'Yeah, they persuaded Kennedy and Hatch to jointly sponsor the legislation.' (from local domain)
  c. 'Yeah, he is/was Hatch.' (by direct reference; *he* refers to *some other senator* in the antecedent)

We claim based on (71) and (72) that the island insensitivity of fragments is due to the fact that there is no "A'-movement" (or in more general terms, unbounded dependencies) involved in fragment interpretation.

Merchant (2004: 689) claimed contrary to Culicover and Jackendoff (2005) that answer fragments are sensitive to islands. If his conclusion were correct, it would erroneously predict that quiz questions in which a *wh*-phrase is within an island could not be answered with fragments, which is blatantly false. This is illustrated in (73).

(73) (Ueno 2014: 297)
  a. A: For $100,000, Andy Griffith starred in CBS's *Andy Griffith Show* and played what role? (CSC)
     B: Sheriff Andy Taylor.
  b. A: For $100,000, Andy Griffith played the role of a prominent defense attorney in Atlanta whose favorite food was what? (CNPC)
     B: Hotdogs.
  c. A: For $100,000, the report that Andy Griffith passed away at what age shocked the entire nation last week? (Subject Condition)
     B: 86.

3.4 Access to Lexical Entries

In this section, we will show that accessing appropriate lexical entries is essential to interpreting fragments. In (74), which Culicover and Jackendoff (2005: 257) called sprouting (the term originally due to Chung et al. 1995), they pointed out (p. 260) that when we hear the intransitive *drink* in (74aA) and (74bA), it activates not only the lexical entries for intransitive *drink* (75a) and (75b) but also the lexical entry for the transitive *drink* (75c), so that the hearer can easily access the transitive lexical entry. In general, access to a lexical entry activates the lexical entries for the semantically related lexical items. This phenomenon is known as spreading activation (Anderson 2010: 159, Eysenck and Keane 2010: 266, Hakoda et al. 2010: 196, Michimata et al. 2011: 212). Without accessing the transitive lexical entry (75c), it is impossible to incorporate B's NP fragment into B's intended meaning, which is 'Mary has been drinking scotch' in (74a) and 'Mary has been drinking espresso' in (74b).

(74) (cf. Culicover and Jackendoff 2005: 6, 239, 257)
    a. (context: A and B share the knowledge that Mary used to have a drinking problem.)
        A: I hear Mary's been drinking again.
        B: Yeah, {scotch | #espresso}.   [sprouting fragment]
           inferred syntax: Mary has been drinking {scotch | #espresso} again.
           (from local domain)
    b. (context: A and B share the knowledge that Mary used to be addicted to caffeine.)
        A: I hear Mary's been drinking again.
        B: Yeah, {espresso | #scotch}.   [sprouting fragment]
           inferred syntax: Mary has been drinking {espresso | #scotch} again.
           (from local domain)

The verb *drink* has two intransitive uses (Jerry Sadock (p.c.), Huddleston and Pullum 2002: 304). In (75a, b), the angle brackets indicate an unassociable role, a role in E/R that does not correspond to anything in syntax or in F/A (Sadock 2012: 82, Ueno 2014: 98, 102). (75a) is the lexical entry for intransitive *drink* whose unassociable role is indefinite and represents ALCOHOL, a "specific category" of SOMETHING TO DRINK. (75b) is the other intransitive lexical entry whose unassociable role is indefinite and represents a "normal" category of SOMETHING TO DRINK. In this latter use of intransitive *drink*, the meaning

SOMETHING TO DRINK of the unassociable role serves as selectional restriction in the corresponding transitive verb (75c). In fact, there is a productive lexical process (Huddleston and Pullum 2002: 304) that turns a transitive verb into an intransitive verb by making the outranked role(s) unassociable and keeping the semantic information intact. This productive lexical process is captured by the lexical rule (76).

(75) a. partial lexical entry for intransitive *drink*
   syntax: V in [__]
   F/A: Fa
   E/R: [$_{TYPE}$ "drink"] in [__ [AG, GO] <[PT, TH; ALCOHOL]>]
   b. partial lexical entry for intransitive *drink*
   syntax: V in [__]
   F/A: Fa
   E/R: [$_{TYPE}$ "drink"] in [__ [AG, GO] <[PT, TH; SOMETHING TO DRINK]>]
   c. partial lexical entry for transitive *drink*
   syntax: V in [__, NP]
   F/A: Faa
   E/R: [$_{TYPE}$ "drink"] in [__ [AG, GO] [PT, TH; SOMETHING TO DRINK]]

(76) Intransitivization Lexical Rule
   syntax: V in [__, NP]   →   V in [__]
   F/A: Faa   →   Fa
   E/R: TYPE in [__ AG PT]   →   TYPE in [__ AG <PT>]

The [PT, TH] role is specified as ALCOHOL in (75a) and as SOMETHING TO DRINK in (75b), but it is an unassociable role, as indicated by the angle brackets. In the transitive (75c), the [PT, TH] role is specified as SOMETHING TO DRINK, which serves as selectional restriction. In (74a), B confirms the truth of what A heard by saying "yeah" and adds more relevant information that A may not have. B's intended meaning in (74a) is 'Mary has been drinking scotch (again)' and not 'A hears Mary has been drinking scotch (again).' B's intended meaning cannot be constructed without inference, which takes discourse and pragmatic factors (including participants' discourse roles and shared knowledge) into account. Furthermore, if B replied "espresso" in (74a), it would not be felicitous in view of the shared knowledge at hand. Although "espresso" meets the selectional restriction of the transitive *drink*, SOMETHING TO DRINK, it does not qualify as ALCOHOL, which is required by the intransitive *drink* (75a) and the shared knowledge.

The following set of examples can be explained in the same way, that is, by accessing the lexical entry for the verb in each exchange.

(77) a. (Culicover and Jackendoff 2005: 249)
   A: I hear Harriet has been flirting again.
   B: Yeah, {with Ozzie | *Ozzie}. [sprouting fragment]
      inferred syntax: Harriet has been flirting with Ozzie (again).
 b. (Culicover and Jackendoff 2005: 248, quoted from Hankamer 1979: 394)
   A: Wem folgt Hans?
   B: {*Der | Dem |*Den} Lehrer. [matching fragment]
      inferred syntax: Hans folgt dem Lehrer.
 c. (Culicover and Jackendoff 2005: 248, quoted from Hankamer 1979: 394)
   A: Wen sucht Hans?
   B: {*Der | *Dem | Den} Lehrer. [matching fragment]
      inferred syntax: Hans sucht den Lehrer.

In (77a), when B hears A say "… flirting…," B accesses the lexical entry for this verb, which contains V in [__, (PP[*with*])] in its syntactic field. By uttering a PP[*with*] fragment, B makes clear his intention that he is giving information about the optional complement PP[*with*] of the verb *flirt*. What is remarkable about this case is that even in English, which is a preposition-stranding language, the preposition is required in this sprouting case. If B simply replied "Ozzie," it would be interpreted as 'Ozzie has been flirting again,' a correction of what A said, as in "Nope, Ozzie." In (77b), when B hears what A says, B accesses the lexical entry for *folgen*, whose syntactic field contains V in [__, NP[DAT]]. By uttering an NP fragment in the dative (NP[DAT]), B makes clear his intention that he is giving information about the complement of the verb *folgen*. In (77c), B accesses the lexical entry for *suchen*, whose syntactic field is V in [__, NP[ACC]]. By uttering an NP fragment in the accusative (NP[ACC]), B makes clear his intention that he is giving information about the complement of the verb *suchen*. Therefore, syntactic and morphosyntactic connectivities between antecedents and fragments can be explained by assuming that hearers/interpreters access the lexical entry for the relevant lexical item.

Here is another piece of evidence that shows the same point. The morphological case ending of *jemand* (accusative *jemand(en)* and dative *jemand(em)*) is often dropped, particularly when the indefinite pronoun is followed by *anders*. In (78a, b), *jemand anders* ('someone else') lacks its overt case ending but the distinction between accusative and dative is maintained in the subsequent part of the discourse.

(78) a. A: Hans folgt jemand anders.
       B: {Wem | *Wen}?   [sluicing]
       A: {Dem Lehrer | *Den Lehrer}.   [fragment]
   b. A: Hans sucht jemand anders.
       B: {*Wem | Wen}?   [sluicing]
       A: {*Dem Lehrer | Den Lehrer}.   [fragment]

This pair of examples shows that the case distinction between dative and accusative is maintained not by copying the case feature on the antecedent NP onto the fragment NP but by accessing the lexical entries for *folgen* and *suchen*.

The process of access to and retrieval of the relevant lexical entry is also required to account for the following examples.

(79) (Culicover and Jackendoff 2005: 261)
   a. Would you hand me <u>those</u>, please?   [gesturing toward scissors]
   b. <u>Those</u> look great on you.   [gesturing toward pants]

The referent of *those* (*scissors* in (79a) and *pants* in (79b)) is a noun that is syntactically plural in its lexical entry. This plurality, the value PL of the number (NUM) feature on *those*, is only available through access to the lexical entry for the respective noun. Not only the value of the NUM feature but also that of the gender (GEN) feature are determined by accessing the lexical entry in question. For example, in (80), the demonstrative pronoun *den* (singular masculine accusative) in (80A) refers to *Rock* 'skirt' (singular masculine), and it is therefore third person singular masculine in the accusative. The demonstrative *der* (third person singular masculine nominative) in (80B) also refers to the skirt. Note that it is possible to use *der* and *den* just by pointing to a skirt. The choice of these forms would be impossible without access to the lexical entry for *Rock*.

(80) (context: A and B are at a shopping mall. A points to a skirt and says:)
      A: Schau mal. Wie findest du den?
      B: Der ist hübsch! Was kostet der denn?

The VFORM value on VP fragments is explained in the same way by accessing the lexical entry of the verb in the prior discourse that takes a VP complement.

(81) (Merchant 2004: 696)
   A: What did you make Bob do?
   B: (*To) leave the house.
      inferred syntax: I made him (*to) leave the house.

(82) (Merchant 2004: 696)
   A: What did you force Bob to do?
   B: *(To) leave the house.
      inferred syntax: I forced him *(to) leave the house.

This pair of examples is accounted for by B's access to the lexical entries for *make* and *force*. The former contains V in [__, NP, VP[BSE]] and the latter V in [__, NP, VP[*to*]]. So, for example, by choosing a VP[BSE] and saying "Leave the house," B in (81) is making clear his intention that he is adding information about the VP[BSE] complement of the verb *make*. On the other hand, by choosing a VP[*to*] and saying "To leave the house," B in (82) is making clear his intention that he is adding information about the VP[*to*] complement of the verb *force*.

The following data about predicate answers are also explained in the same way.

(83) a. (Merchant 2004: 698)
       A: What did he do to the car?
       B: Totaled *(it).   [VP[PAST] in syntax]
         cf. A: What happened to the car?
              B: Totaled (*it).   [VP[PAS] in syntax]
    b. (Merchant 2004: 698)
       A: What did she do with the spinach?
       B: Washed *(it).   [VP[PAST] in syntax]
    c. A: What happened to the spinach?
       B: Washed (*it).   [VP[PAS] in syntax]

In (83a), when B accesses the lexical entry for the verb *total*, he finds the lexical requirement V in [__, NP]. Therefore, if B said "Totaled," he would violate this subcategorization requirement in syntax. In addition, note that *do what* is an interrogative action VP (an interrogative form to ask about an action VP), just like *do it* and *do so* are pro-forms for action VPs. Therefore, an answer to a *do what* question must be a VP (in this case, VP[PAST]) and cannot be a head verb alone. (83b) is explained in the same way. In (83c), *washed* is a passive participle, whose lexical entry is V[PAS] in [__]. Recall that each passive participle (V[PAS]) has its own lexical entry in the lexicon and is related to the lexical entry for its corresponding transitive verb by the Passive Lexical Rule (Sadock 2012: 83, Ueno 2014: 98, Chapter 1 (88)). B's utterance in (84a) is the same kind of example. Therefore, the speaker and the hearer can directly access passive verb lexical entries, and under appropriate conditions, an active entry can activate its corresponding passive entry and vice versa.

(84) a. (Merchant 2004: 699 note 11)
    A: Was hat er für seine Schwester getan?
    B: i. Finanziell unterstützt hat er sie.
       ii. *Finanziell unterstützt.
  b. A: Ich kenne sie nur dem Namen nach. Sie ist Solo-Geigerin, oder?
     B: Ja. Die Arme, jemand soll ihre Geige gestohlen haben.
     A: Was? Gestohlen?
     (Ota, Tatsuya, and Marco Raindl. 2009. *Das Geheimnis der Geige*. NHK. p. 98)

B's utterance (ii) in (84aB) is ungrammatical, because it violates the lexical requirement for the transitive *unterstützen*, namely, V in [__, NP[ACC]], which B must have accessed. In (84b), the past participle *gestohlen* is interpreted as passive (*Wurde ihre Geige gestohlen?*), and therefore it satisfies its subcategorization, namely, V[PAS] in [__].

3.5 Language Acquisition and Preposition (Non)Stranding

So far, we have shown (i) that we need to assume the Inferential Comprehension Module (ICM) in addition to the Language Module (LM) to account for the speaker's intended meaning of a fragment utterance U, (ii) that the ICM collects relevant information from the discourse context in which U occurs and processes it online successively, cumulatively, and incrementally, (iii) that the ICM makes non-demonstrative inference, (iv) that the ICM constructs the inferred four-tuple of U, (v) that the ICM constructs the explicatures and implicatures of U. From this emerges a concept of the language faculty that although the LM is purely representational without derivation such as movement and deletion, the ICM is fully derivational and dynamic with many processes and steps involved.

3.5.1 Fragments and acquisition of syntax

Culicover and Jackendoff (2005) claimed that children at the one-word stage are in effect using fragments, in that their single-word utterances are intended to be interpreted richly, with the context filling in the details (p. 255). They also claimed that every language uses fragments (p. 255, attributed to Jason Merchant). Based on these points, they concluded that the use of subsentential fragments is "most robustly supported by UG and pragmatics" (p. 255). To the extent that their conclusion is correct, the ability to produce and interpret fragments is acquired before the acquisition of clausal syntax. Furthermore, as discussed in 2.1, the ability to infer the communicator's intention is acquired before the one-word stage of language acquisition. Therefore, the process of language acquisition should look as follows.

(85) | ability to infer intentions and meanings (non-demonstrative inference) | →
| ability to produce and interpret fragments | → | acquisition of clausal syntax |

The ability to infer intended meanings of fragments from linguistic and nonlinguistic context (i.e., to determine the explicatures and implicatures of fragments) is indispensable for producing and interpreting fragments. This ability of non-demonstrative inference is acquired very early in childhood, because it is needed to produce and interpret one-word utterances at the initial stage of language acquisition.

By contrast, Merchant (2004: 662) pursued a purely syntactic account of fragments, what he called the ellipsis approach, according to which fragments are accounted for by means of applying A'-movement to an XP in an underlying sentential structure, moving it to a clause-peripheral position, and deleting the rest of the sentence. The ellipsis approach would predict just the opposite of (85), namely, that the use of fragments starts only after the acquisition of A'-movement such as *wh*-movement and topicalization. However, this prediction is incompatible with the one-word stage of language acquisition.

3.5.2 Acquisition of preposition stranding

Preposition languages, those languages that employ prepositions and not postpositions, are divided into two subgroups: preposition stranding languages, such as English and Swedish, and preposition pied-piping languages, such as German and French. In the former subgroup, preposition stranding is allowed. This is shown in (86b). In a "*wh*-movement" metaphor, when a preposition takes a *wh*-NP as its

3.5 LANGUAGE ACQUISITION AND PREPOSITION (NON)STRANDING

complement, "*wh*-movement" can move only the *wh*-NP and strand the preposition at its original place. By contrast, in the latter subgroup, preposition stranding is prohibited and preposition pied-piping is required. This is shown in (87b). Again, in a "*wh*-movement" metaphor, when a preposition takes a *wh*-NP as its complement, "*wh*-movement" cannot move the *wh*-NP alone and must accompany the preposition to the clause-initial position.

(86) preposition stranding in English
 a. Mary was talking to someone.
 b. Who was Mary talking to?
 c. [$_{PP[to, WH[Q]]}$ P[*to*] NP[WH[Q]]]

(87) preposition pied-piping in German
 a. Maria hat mit jemandem gesprochen.
 b. Mit wem hat Maria gesprochen?
  cf. *Wem hat Maria mit gesprochen?
 c. [$_{PP[mit, WH[Q]]}$ P[*mit*] NP[DAT, WH[Q]]]

According to Merchant (2001: 92), only a very small number of preposition languages allow preposition stranding, whereas the majority of them are preposition pied-piping languages.

Merchant (2004: 685–6) observed that in preposition stranding languages, an answer fragment to a *wh*-question with a PP *wh*-phrase (PP[WH[Q]]) can be a bare NP, whereas in preposition pied-piping languages, an answer fragment cannot be a bare NP but must be a PP headed by the same preposition that heads the preceding PP *wh*-phrase. That is, the same preposition must be repeated in answer fragments. This is shown in (88B).

(88) (Merchant 2004: 686)
 A: Mit wem hat Anna gesprochen?
 B: {Mit dem Hans | *Dem Hans}.

Fragments in preposition pied-piping languages, such as German and French, exhibit a property of what I will call P-repeating, which requires the repetition of the same preposition when the fragment in question expresses information about a PP in the prior discourse. This is further illustrated in (89) and (90), in which the prepositions required by the P-repeating property are underlined.

(89) a. A: Weißt du, Anna hat mit jemandem gesprochen?
    B: Genau. {<u>Mit</u> ihrem Bruder | *Ihrem Bruder}. [matching fragment]
  a'. A: Weißt du, Anna hat gesprochen?
    B: Genau. {Mit ihrem Bruder | *Ihrem Bruder}. [sprouting fragment]
  b. A: Sind Sie mit der Bahn gefahren?
    B: Nein, <u>mit</u> dem Auto.
  c. Empfangschef: Ach, Moment. Sie sind Herr Aoki? Hier wurde etwas für Sie abgegeben.
    Aoki: <u>Für</u> mich? Von wem?
    Empfangschef: <u>Von</u> Frau Professor Schütz. Eine Geige, glaube ich.
  d. A: Kommen Sie aus China?
    B: <u>Aus</u> China? Nein, <u>aus</u> Japan.

(90) a. A: Anne a parlé avec quelqu'un.
    B: {<u>Avec</u> son frère | *Son frère}. [matching fragment]
  a'. A: Anne a parlé.
    B: {Avec son frère | *Son frère}. [sprouting fragment]
  b. A: Ah, vous êtes Japonaise. Et vous êtes de quelle ville?
    B: <u>De</u> Tokyo.
  c. A: Vous allez comment à Nice? En voiture?
    B: Non, <u>en</u> train ou <u>en</u> avion.
  d. A: Qu'est-ce que vous faites? Vous êtes étudiante?
    B: Non, je travaille dans une pharmacie.
    A: <u>Dans</u> une pharmacie? C'est bien, ça.
  e. A: Où est-ce que tu habites à Tokyo?
    B: J'habite à Shibuya avec ...
    A: <u>Avec</u> ta petite copine ?!
    B: Non, <u>avec</u> mon chat.

Note that this P-repeating property manifests itself in a matching PP fragment, in which an antecedent PP is available in the prior discourse.

The P-repeating property of a PP fragment presumably derives both (i) from the speaker's need to meet the subcategorization requirement of a verb if the PP fragment in question is intended as a complement of the verb, and (ii) from the speaker's intention to make clear which argument or adjunct of the verb she is expressing information about. For example, in (89a), a case of matching fragment, when B hears A say "mit jemandem gesprochen," B accesses the lexical entry for *sprechen*, which specifies that the verb takes a PP[*mit*] complement, which A has just respected. B adds information more specific than *jemand(em)* by uttering the NP *ihr(em) Bruder*, but she needs to repeat the preposition *mit*, on the one hand, to meet the lexical requirement of the verb *sprechen* and, on the other, to make clear her intention that she is adding information about the argument expressed by a PP[*mit*]. Factor (i) is also observed in cases of sprouting PP fragments: (89a'), (90a'), and (77a). Note that even preposition stranding languages such as English exhibit the P-repeating property optionally.

(91) A: Mary was talking about someone.
    B: {About whom | Who}?

On the other hand, fragments in preposition stranding languages exhibit what I will call the P-dropping property (in addition to the P-repeating property), namely, when there is an antecedent PP in the prior discourse (in the case of matching PP fragments), the preposition need not be repeated and can thus be dropped as in (91B) and (92a). However, when there is no antecedent PP in the prior discourse (in the case of sprouting PP fragments), the preposition cannot be dropped, as shown in (92c). Note that in German and French, the preposition cannot be dropped, regardless of whether there is an antecedent PP in the prior discourse or not.

(92) a. A: I hear John has been flirting <u>with someone</u>.
        B: Yes. <u>Mary</u>. [matching fragment] (by the P-dropping property)
    b. A: I hear John has been flirting <u>with someone</u>.
        B: Really? <u>Who</u>? [matching fragment] (by the P-dropping property)
    c. A: I hear John has been flirting.
        B$_1$: Yes. {With Mary | *Mary}. [sprouting fragment]
        B$_2$: Really? {With who(m)? | *Who(m)}. [sprouting fragment]

The P-dropping property might look as if it is a preposition "deletion" rule on the basis of the identity between the preposition of a PP fragment and the preposition of the antecedent PP in the prior discourse. Therefore, this property only appears in cases of matching PP fragments. We formulate this property not as a "deletion" rule but as a rule that licenses an NP fragment under certain conditions. That is, in preposition stranding languages, the speaker can choose an NP fragment if she intends it as the complement of the same preposition as that of the antecedent PP in the prior discourse.

138   3 AN AUTOMODULAR VIEW OF FRAGMENTS

Based on these sets of data, we hypothesize that at an early stage of acquisition of preposition languages, when children learn to use fragments, they first learn the P-repeating property, whether the language in question is preposition pied-piping or preposition stranding, based on positive evidence such as (89), (90), and (91) and also based on the two factors (i) and (ii). Children then learn the P-dropping property based on positive evidence such as (92a, b).

If children learn the P-repeating property but not the P-dropping property, their language will develop into a preposition pied-piping language. For example, after children have learned the P-repeating property and a basic clause structure but before they learn "*wh*-movement," or in AMG terms, the clause structure [$_{CP[WH[Q]]}$ XP[WH[Q]] S] with a clause-initial *wh*-phrase (Chapter 1 (100)), their inferred syntax of a *wh*-PP fragment is (93a). After they learn "*wh*-movement" or the clause structure [$_{CP[WH[Q]]}$ XP[WH[Q]] S], the inferred syntax of a *wh*-PP fragment is (93b), a clause structure with preposition pied-piping. The comparison between the two inferred syntactic structures in (93a, b) shows that this language is a preposition pied-piping language.

(93) A: Maria hat <u>mit jemandem</u> gesprochen.
 B: Mit wem ? (by the P-repeating property)
  a. inferred syntax of „Mit wem?" before learning [$_{CP[WH[Q]]}$ XP[WH[Q]] S]: Maria hat mit wem gesprochen?
  b. inferred syntax of „Mit wem?" after learning [$_{CP[WH[Q]]}$ XP[WH[Q]] S]: Mit wem hat Maria PP[*mit*, G] gesprochen?

On the other hand, if children learn the P-dropping property in addition to the P-repeating property, their language will develop into a preposition stranding language. For example, after children have learned the P-dropping property and a basic clause structure but before they learn "*wh*-movement," their inferred syntax of a *wh*-NP fragment is (94a). After they learn "*wh*-movement," the inferred syntax of a *wh*-NP fragment is (94b), a clause structure with preposition stranding. (94a, b) shows that this language is a preposition stranding language.

(94) A: Mary was talking <u>to someone</u>.
 B: Who ? (by the P-dropping property)
  a. inferred syntax of "who?" before learning [$_{CP[WH[Q]]}$ XP[WH[Q]] S]: Mary was talking to who ?
  b. inferred syntax of "who?" after learning [$_{CP[WH[Q]]}$ XP[WH[Q]] S]: Who was Mary talking to NP[G]?

Therefore, in preposition pied-piping languages, children are able to learn the preposition pied-piping property manifested in *wh*-questions through the acquisition of the P-repeating property of PP fragments even before they learn "*wh*-movement" itself. By contrast, in preposition stranding languages, children are able to learn the preposition stranding property manifested in *wh*-questions through the acquisition of the P-repeating and P-dropping properties of PP fragments even before they learn "*wh*-movement" itself.

Based on the discussion so far, we claim that what separates preposition stranding languages from preposition pied-piping languages is the P-dropping property that appears in matching PP fragments. In the pied-piping language group, only the P-repeating property must be learned. In the preposition stranding language group, not only the P-repeating property but also the P-dropping property must be learned. In this respect, preposition stranding languages are more complex than preposition pied-piping languages. Furthermore, in terms of the dominance path conditions for *wh*-questions (Chapter 1 (100)), the dominance path conditions for preposition pied-piping languages are simpler than those for preposition stranding languages. For example, if we compare the two types of languages with respect to the PP complement of a verb, preposition pied-piping languages allow their dominance paths to end in VP PP[G] whereas preposition stranding languages allow them to end in VP PP[G] and VP PP NP[G]. Preposition stranding languages are more complex than preposition pied-piping languages in this respect, too. These two factors explain why preposition stranding languages are so limited in the world's preposition languages.

Chapter 4

An Automodular View of Sluicing

> In this chapter, we will examine various properties of sluicing, including its island insensitivity, and explain these properties from our AMG and Relevance Theoretic perspectives. We claim that sluicing is merely the embedded fragment of a *wh*-phrase and thus term it *wh*-fragment. Therefore, we will treat sluicing exactly the same way as fragments, which were discussed in Chapter 3.

4.1 Preliminary Description of Sluicing

(1a, b) below are examples of sluicing, which was first discussed in Ross (1969). In these examples, a *wh*-phrase (XP[WH[Q]]) is interpreted as a full *wh*-question (CP[WH[Q]]). (See 1.9 for a summary of AMG analyses of *wh*-questions and Ueno (2014: 253ff.) for details.) I will henceforth call sluiced *wh*-phrases such as those in (1a, b) *wh*-fragments in view of the striking similarities between sluiced *wh*-phrases and fragments such as (1c, d). Fragments were discussed in Chapter 3. Regarding the three types of inferred syntax (from the global domain, the local domain, and by direct reference), see 3.3.6.

(1) a. Mary said John was drinking something, but I don't know [what].
 (embedded *wh*-fragment)
   (i) syntax inferred from global domain
    but I don't know [what Mary said John was drinking].
   (ii) syntax inferred from local domain
    but I don't know [what John was drinking].

(iii) syntax inferred by direct reference
but I don't know [what it was]. (*it* refers to *something*.)
b. A: Mary said John was drinking something.
B: [What], I wonder. (*wh*-fragment)
(i) syntax inferred from global domain
[What did Mary say John was drinking], I wonder.
(ii) syntax inferred from local domain
[What was John drinking], I wonder.
(iii) syntax inferred by direct reference
[What was it], I wonder. (*it* refers to *something*.)
c. A: Mary said John was drinking something.
B: [Beer], I guess. (clarification fragment)
(i) syntax inferred from global domain
[Mary said John was drinking beer], I guess.
(ii) syntax inferred from local domain
[John was drinking beer], I guess.
(iii) syntax inferred by direct reference
[It was beer], I guess. (*it* refers to *something*.)
d. A: What is John drinking?
B: [Beer], I guess. (answer fragment)

The *wh*-fragment *what* in (1a, b) can be interpreted in three ways depending on what inferred syntax the hearer/interpreter constructs from the *wh*-fragment, just as the NP fragment in (1c). Recall that an NP fragment allows three types of inferred syntax (cf. 3.3.6). The syntax inferred from the global domain in (1a) is the syntactic structure obtained by non-demonstrative inference from the decoded syntax of the *wh*-fragment in (1a) and the context. This inferred syntactic structure is constructed from the preceding utterance ("Mary said John was drinking something."), which I will call the antecedent of the *wh*-fragment, by replacing the relevant phrase in it ("something") with the *wh*-fragment in question ("what"). The second inferred syntax in (1a), what I will call the syntax inferred from the local domain, is obtained by replacing the relevant phrase ("something") with the *wh*-fragment ("what") within the local domain of its antecedent (i.e., within the innermost clause of the antecedent). The third inferred syntax in (1a), what I will call the syntax inferred by direct reference, is of the form *wh*-phrase + *be* verb + pronoun, in which the pronoun refers to the most salient NP, the focus (FOC) in Information Structure (IS), in the prior discourse ("something").

4.1 PRELIMINARY DESCRIPTION OF SLUICING

In the following discussion, we assume the same general picture of fragment interpretation as we presented in Chapter 3 (5b, c), repeated here as (2).

(2) a. fragment utterance U → LM → decoded four-tuple of U → ICM → inferred four-tuple of U → development of inferred four-tuple → explicatures and implicatures of U (in Mentalese)
  b. Procedure for fragment comprehension
    The hearer follows the Relevance-guided comprehension heuristic and executes the following steps.
    (i) The LM computes the decoded four-tuple of a fragment utterance U.
    (ii) By non-demonstrative inference, the ICM constructs the inferred syntactic structure of U on the basis of the decoded syntax obtained in (i) and the contextual information.
    (iii) The ICM constructs the inferred four-tuple of U on the basis of the inferred syntax obtained in (ii) and the contextual information.
    (iv) The ICM develops the inferred four-tuple of U obtained in (iii) on the basis of the contextual information.
    (v) The ICM constructs the explicatures and implicatures of U on the basis of the developed four-tuple obtained in (iv) and the contextual information.

In (2), LM is the Language Module, which we have been assuming is equipped with the current version of AMG, and ICM is the Inferential Comprehension Module, in which non-demonstrative inference is performed on the decoded four-tuple (syntax, F/A, E/R, IS) of the *wh*-fragment in question.

It is not true that the three types of inferred syntax (and their corresponding explicatures) are always available for every instance of a *wh*-fragment. In (3), the syntax inferred from the global domain is impossible, while in (4), it is semantically odd.

(3) Bill wondered how many papers Sandy had read, but he didn't care [which ones]. (Chung et al. 1995: 257)
  syntax inferred from global domain:
    *but he didn't care [which ones he wondered how many papers Sandy had read]
    *but he didn't care [which ones he wondered Sandy had read]

syntax inferred from local domain:
  but he didn't care [which ones Sandy had read]
syntax inferred by direct reference:
  but he didn't care [which ones they were]
  (*they* refers to 'a certain number of papers Sandy had read' in the existential presupposition of *how many papers Sandy had read*)

(4) He announced he would marry the woman he loved most. None of his relatives could figure out [who]. (ibid.)
syntax inferred from global domain:
  #None of his relatives could figure out [who he announced he would marry].
syntax inferred from local domain:
  None of his relatives could figure out [who he would marry].
syntax inferred by direct reference:
  None of his relatives could figure out [who she was].
  (*she* refers to *the woman he loved most* in the preceding utterance.)

Interpreting *wh*-fragments is very similar to interpreting fragments, which we discussed in Chapter 3. To interpret an answer fragment such as (1dB), we need to find a propositional function $P(x)$ such that the answer fragment a is combined in such a way that $P(a)$. The propositional function $P(x)$ is provided by the immediately preceding *wh*-question. In the same way, in order to interpret a *wh*-fragment, we need to find a propositional function $P(x)$ with which the *wh*-fragment is interpreted as $[[_{QP_x} [_Q \text{WH}] \ x = \ldots] [_{PROP} P(x)]]$ in F/A. For example, the *wh*-fragment in (1a, b) is interpreted as 'For which thing x, $[_{P(x)}$ Mary said John was drinking $x]$' (based on the syntax inferred from the global domain) or 'For which thing x, $[_{P(x)}$ it was $x]$' (based on the syntax inferred by direct reference), and the propositional function of the former is provided by the prior utterance "Mary said John was drinking something." Because of the similarities between fragments and *wh*-fragments, we will explore an explanation of sluicing by treating *wh*-fragments essentially as ordinary fragments and relying as much as possible on what is needed to interpret fragments.

In addition to interrogative *wh*-fragments, exclamative *wh*-fragments are also observed. They are interpreted with the understood null subject/topic and *be* (i.e., interpreted through their syntax inferred by direct reference).

(5) (Huddleston and Pullum 2002: 921)
    a. What nonsense!   b. What a strange thing for him to say!
    c. How fantastic!   d. How incredibly unlikely!

4.2 Syntax of *Wh*-Fragments

The internal syntax of *wh*-fragments is the same as that of interrogative *wh*-phrases XP[WH[Q]] (Ueno 2014: 281). As for its external syntax, Ross (1969), Merchant (2001: 40ff.), and Culicover and Jackendoff (2005: 268–269) showed that a *wh*-fragment behaves syntactically as a *wh*-interrogative clause (CP[WH[Q]]). The first piece of evidence concerns subject-verb agreement. Although the subject *wh*-phrase in (6a) is in the plural, the agreeing verb is in the singular, just like a subject *wh*-clause. The second piece of evidence concerns the possibility of the extraposition of a *wh*-fragment. The *wh*-phrase in (6b) is extraposed, again just like a subject *wh*-clause.

(6) (Culicover and Jackendoff 2005: 268 (52))
    We were supposed to do some problems for tomorrow,
    a. but [which problems] {isn't | *aren't} clear.   (subject-verb agreement)
       cf. but [which problems we were supposed to do for tomorrow] {isn't | *aren't} clear.
         (syntax inferred from global/local domain)
       cf. but [which problems they were] {isn't | *aren't} clear.
         (syntax inferred by direct reference; *they* refers to *some problems*.)
    b. but it isn't clear [which problems].   (extraposition)
       cf. but it isn't clear [which problems we were supposed to do for tomorrow].
         (syntax inferred from global/local domain)
       cf. but it isn't clear [which problems they were].
         (syntax inferred by direct reference; *they* refers to *some problems*.)

The third piece of evidence concerns the distribution of *wh*-fragments with respect to a verb-particle construction. In (7a) below, the *wh*-phrase *what*, which is apparently an NP, cannot occur between the verb and the particle, as is expected of NPs.

(7) a. He was doing something illegal, but I never {found out [what] | *found [what] out}. (Culicover and Jackendoff 2005: 269 (54a))
   cf. inferred syntax: I never {found out [what he was doing] | *found [what he was doing] out}
   cf. inferred syntax: I never {found out [what it was] | *found [what it was] out}
      (*it* refers to *something*.)
   b. He was doing something illegal, and I discovered immediately what.
   cf. He was doing something illegal, and I discovered immediately {*the thing | *it}.

The fourth piece of evidence is based on the distribution of NPs in English: that a light NP object must immediately follow a transitive verb, and that an adverb cannot intervene between a transitive verb and its light NP object. In (7b), although the light NP object *the thing* cannot occur after *immediately*, the interrogative *what* can, just like a *wh*-clause. This shows again that the *wh*-fragment *what* serves not as an NP but as a clause. The fifth way to show that a *wh*-fragment behaves syntactically as a CP[WH[Q]] is to use a verb that can take a CP[WH[Q]] complement but cannot take an NP object. The best example of such a verb is *wonder* (Ueno 2014: 122).

(8) He was doing something illegal, but I wonder [what].
   cf. inferred syntax: but I wonder [{what he was doing | what it was}].

The sixth way is coordination. A *wh*-fragment can be coordinated with a full *wh*-question.

(9) a. There are guidelines in the company dress code for [$_{\text{CP[WH[Q]]}}$ when women can use perfume] and [$_{\text{NP[WH[Q]]}}$ how much].
   b. Languages differ widely on [$_{\text{CP[WH[Q]]}}$ what sort of material can appear in the COMP field] and [$_{\text{PP[WH[Q]]}}$ under what circumstances]. (Merchant 2001: 61)
   c. Mary invited someone, but I don't know [$_{\text{NP[WH[Q]]}}$ who] or [$_{\text{CP[WH[Q]]}}$ when she invited them].

The seventh piece of evidence is case-marking (Ross 1969, Merchant 2001: 42). In (10), the German verb *schmeicheln* ('flatter') takes a dative NP and *wissen* ('know') either an accusative NP or a clause.

(10)   Er will jemandem schmeicheln, aber sie wissen nicht, {wem | *wen}.

In (10), the dative *wem* is grammatical but the accusative *wen* is not, which shows that the *wh*-fragment is interpreted as the dative object of *schmeicheln*, as in *Sie wissen nicht, wem er schmeicheln will*. Because of these pieces of evidence, we follow Ross (1969) and others and conclude that a *wh*-fragment (syntactically XP[WH[Q]]) is perceived by the hearer/interpreter to be dominated by a CP[WH[Q]] node in syntax.

From our perspective, this conclusion demonstrates how psychologically real the inferred syntax of a *wh*-fragment is. When the hearer/interpreter hears a *wh*-fragment (XP[WH[Q]] in syntax), the hearer's LM decodes it into the four-tuple (XP[WH[Q]], QP, ROLE, $[_U$ FOC]), according to the fragment comprehension process in (2). Because the hearer/interpreter knows the syntactic rule $[_{CP[WH[Q]]}$ XP[WH[Q]] S] (Chapter 1 (100)), the F/A rule $[_{PROP}$ QP PROP], the E/R rule $[_{EV}$ TYPE ROLE], and the IS rule $[_U$ FOC < BI] (i.e., the focus (FOC) precedes the background information (BI) in an utterance (U)), this much knowledge leads to the skeletal four-tuple of a *wh*-fragment (11) and triggers non-demonstrative inference in the hearer/interpreter's ICM, resulting in a suitable S in syntax, a suitable PROP in F/A, a suitable EV in E/R, and a suitable BI in IS that properly situate the *wh*-fragment in question. This process will be elaborated in the next section.

4.3 Interpreting *Wh*-Fragments

The skeletal four-tuple of a *wh*-fragment is given in (11) below. As was shown at the end of the previous section, the intermodular correspondences are established based on the decoded four-tuple (XP[WH[Q]], QP, ROLE, $[_U$ FOC]) and the knowledge of $[_{CP[WH[Q]]}$ XP[WH[Q]], S] in syntax, $[_{PROP}$ QP, PROP] in F/A, $[_{EV}$ TYPE ROLE] in E/R, and $[_U$ FOC < BI] in IS. As a result, the *wh*-fragment XP[WH[Q]] is perceived to be dominated by a CP[WH[Q]] in syntax, corresponds to a QP_x headed by the quantifier $[_Q$ WH] in F/A (Ueno 2014: 256, 290), and serves a certain ROLE in E/R if the *wh*-fragment is interpreted as an argument. Note that the speech act (SA) superstructure with the illocutionary force (IF) #inquire# (Chapter 1 (99), Ueno 2014: 257, 357) is only present when the *wh*-fragment is not embedded.

(11) skeletal four-tuple of *wh*-fragment (cf. Chapter 3 (8b))

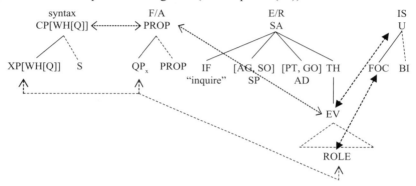

As discussed at the end of 4.2, in order to properly interpret a *wh*-fragment, the hearer/interpreter needs to determine a propositional function *P(x)* with which the *wh*-fragment is combined, namely, the S in (11) that goes with the *wh*-fragment, the PROP that goes with the QP_x, and the EV in which the *wh*-fragment carries a ROLE. Based on the relevant discussion on fragments in Chapter 3, we claim that this is achieved by non-demonstrative inference in the ICM, exactly in the same way as fragments are inferentially interpreted. The whole process of fragment interpretation was shown in (2). Let us look at the interpretation process of (1b) more closely.

(12) (= (1b)) (context: A and B are police officers and discussing what happened at the party two hours ago, when John suddenly died with a glass in his hand.)
    A: Mary said John was drinking something.
    B: [What], I wonder. (*wh*-fragment)
        inferred syntax:
            from global domain: #What did Mary say John was drinking?
            from local domain: What was John drinking?
            by direct reference: What was it? (*it* refers to *something*.)
        explicature: B wonders what John was drinking at the party two hours ago when he died. (after enrichment)

implicatures: B wants to know what John was drinking at the party when he died.

B thinks John was drinking something poisonous at the party. etc.

In the process of *wh*-fragment interpretation in (2), there are cases in which inferring the contextually appropriate S in syntax (the inferred syntax) that goes with the *wh*-fragment in question must precede the construction of the corresponding F/A and E/R. For example, to properly interpret B's *wh*-fragment *whose* in (13) below, B's inferred S must be determined first before the corresponding F/A and E/R are constructed. Without this inferred S, the idiom interpretation (in F/A and E/R) of the *wh*-fragment cannot be recovered.

(13) (cf. Chapter 3 (18), (20))
      A: Mary pulled someone's leg.
      B: Tell me [whose].
      inferred syntax: Tell me [whose leg Mary pulled].
      explicature: 'B tells A to tell him who Mary teased.'

4.4 *Wh*-Fragments and Inference

Just as is the case with fragments (e.g., Chapter 3 (23) and (24)), the propositional function that combines with a *wh*-fragment is not always available from the immediately preceding utterance, but rather it must be inferred from pieces of information spread across the prior discourse. B's *wh*-fragments in (14), especially the last one, are such examples.

(14) (context: The participants A and B share the knowledge that John used to have a drinking problem.)
      (cf. Chapter 3 (23))
      A: Have you heard about your friend?
      B: Which friend?
          inferred syntax: Which friend are you asking me about?
      A: John.
          inferred syntax: I'm asking you about John.
      He has started again.
          inferred syntax: He has started drinking again.

explicature (after reference assignment and enrichment): 'John has started drinking too much alcohol again.'
B: Which alcohol this time?
inferred syntax: Which alcohol has he started drinking this time?
Whisky?
inferred syntax: Has he started drinking whisky this time?
explicature: 'B asks A if John has started drinking too much whisky this time.'
A: No, beer.
inferred syntax: No, he has started drinking beer this time.
explicatures: 'A asserts that John has not started drinking too much whisky this time.'
'A asserts that John has started drinking too much beer this time.'
B: When?
inferred syntax: When did he start drinking beer?
A: Two weeks ago.
inferred syntax: He started drinking beer two weeks ago.
explicature: 'A asserts that John started drinking too much beer two weeks ago'

To determine the propositional function (John started drinking beer at x) that combines with B's "when," A and the other audience need to understand the prior discourse. Note that the verb *drink* in the inferred syntax of B's "Which alcohol this time?" does not appear overtly anywhere in the discourse and only exists in the shared knowledge that John used to drink too much. See the discussion on this point in Chapter 3 (23). (15) is another example in which the interpretation of a *wh*-fragment cannot be recovered from the immediately preceding utterance. The intended interpretation of "Guess who" at the end is 'Guess who did not read the textbook and finish the assignment.' (The other possibility is that "Guess who" is interpreted as 'Guess who he is' (syntax inferred by direct reference), in which *he* refers to *someone who didn't*.)

(15) A: Did you read the textbook?
B: Yes, I did. [VP ellipsis]
inferred syntax: Yes, I read the textbook.
And I finished the assignment too.
Did you? [VP ellipsis]
inferred syntax: Did you read the textbook and finish the assignment?'

C: Of course, I did. [VP ellipsis]
    inferred syntax: Of course, I read the textbook and finished the assignment.
    I'm sure everyone did. [VP ellipsis]
    inferred syntax: I'm sure everyone read the textbook and finished the assignment.
D: That's not true.
    I know someone who didn't. [VP ellipsis]
    inferred syntax: I know someone who didn't read the textbook and finish the assignment.
    Guess who. [*wh*-fragment]
    inferred syntax: Guess who didn't read the textbook and finish the assignment.

(16) is still another example.

(16) A: I'm sure John isn't seeing a girl.
    B: But I hear Tom is. [VP ellipsis]
    inferred syntax: But I hear Tom is seeing a girl.
    A: Yeah.
    B: But do you know where? [*wh*-fragment]
    inferred syntax: But do you know where Tom is seeing a girl?
    A: In his apartment, I guess. [answer fragment]
    inferred syntax: Tom is seeing a girl in his apartment, I guess.
    C: Tell me which girl. [*wh*-fragment]
    inferred syntax: Tell me which girl Tom is seeing in his apartment.

The intended interpretation of (16C) is 'Tell me which girl Tom is seeing in his apartment.' Note that *which girl* in C asks about *a girl* in the antecedent of the VP ellipsis in B's *Tom is*, namely, *Tom is seeing a girl* (cf. missing antecedent phenomenon (5.5)). (17) is an example similar to (16).

(17) A: John isn't seeing a girl but Tom is. [VP ellipsis]
    inferred syntax: but Tom is seeing a girl.
    B: Do you know how often? [embedded *wh*-fragment]
    inferred syntax: Do you know how often Tom is seeing the girl?
    A: I suppose twice a day. [embedded answer fragment]
    inferred syntax: I suppose Tom is seeing the girl twice a day.

C: Do you know where? [embedded *wh*-fragment]
  inferred syntax: Do you know where Tom is seeing the girl twice a day?

Examples (14)–(17) also show that the on-line inferential discourse comprehension process proceeds successively, cumulatively, and incrementally, which was illustrated in 3.2 and summarized in 3.5.

In (18) below, just like Chapter 3 (27), real world knowledge is needed to infer what the bartender meant, which is 'Which beer would you like this time?' or something like it. The discourse-initial, non-embedded *wh*-fragment in (18) receives its interpretation directly from the nonlinguistic context, just like the examples in (19).

(18) (context: The regular customer A enjoys various kinds of beer at the bar every night. A holds out an empty glass to the bartender B without saying anything. B says to A.)
  B (with an embarrassed smile): Which one this time?
    explicature: 'B asks A which beer A would like to drink this time.'
    implicature: 'A has already drunk all kinds of beer tonight.' or 'B wants A to stop drinking and go home.'

(19) (Chung et al. 1995: 264; cited from Ginzburg 1992)
  a. [said by a taxi driver] "Where to, lady?"
  b. [said by a distraught homeowner staring at the ashes of his house] "Why?"

In examples (18) and (19), there is no prior utterance in the discourse that provides the information needed to infer the intended meaning. The relevant information comes only from the nonlinguistic context including scripts stored in the memory. (See the discussion on (16a) in Chapter 2.) Therefore, this demonstrates once more that we need to assume the ICM, which is at work in constructing the utterance's inferred four-tuple, including its inferred syntax, and its explicatures and implicatures. What the non-demonstrative inference in the ICM needs to do is to arrive at a propositional function that combines with the *wh*-fragment, namely, to construct the S, PROP, and EV in (11) from the relevant linguistic and nonlinguistic context.

Recall the discussion in Chapter 2 (3) that the ICM integrates information coming from various input systems, including the LM, vision, smell, and memory, and performs non-demonstrative inference. For example, the audience who heard

4.5 Need for Syntactic Structures Inferred by Direct Reference

"Why?" in (19b) can correctly interpret it because, although they do not have any linguistic context that comes into their ICM, the sight of the distraught man standing in front of his burnt down house and the smell of burning are sufficient input to their ICM to trigger correct non-demonstrative inference.

4.5 Need for Syntactic Structures Inferred by Direct Reference

We illustrated the three types of inferred syntax of a fragment in 3.3.6: inferred from the global domain, inferred from the local domain, and inferred by direct reference. It was shown in (3) and (4) that these three types of inferred syntax are also available to *wh*-fragments. We showed in 3.3.6, particularly in Chapter 3 (45) and (46), that the syntax inferred by direct reference is independently motivated for fragments. In this section, we will present various pieces of evidence that we also need to posit this type of inferred syntax for *wh*-fragments. First, there are cases of *wh*-fragments whose interpretation requires a syntactic structure inferred by direct reference.

(20) A: John bought a book written by a famous scientist.
　　 B: By whom?
　　　　syntax inferred from global/local domain: *By whom did John buy a book written?
　　　　syntax inferred by direct reference: By whom was it written?
　　　　(*it* refers to *a book written by a famous scientist.*)

(20) shows the need to posit a syntactic structure inferred by direct reference for *wh*-fragments. Here, the syntax inferred from the global/local domain is impossible, because it violates the CNPC. Here is a German example.

(21) (= Chapter 3 (89c))
　　 receptionist: Ach, Moment. Sie sind Herr Aoki? Hier wurde etwas für Sie abgegeben.
　　 Aoki: Für mich? [fragment]
　　　　　 Von wem? [*wh*-fragment]
　　 receptionist: Von Frau Professor Schütz. [fragment]
　　　　　 Eine Geige, glaube ich. [fragment]
　　 (from Ota, Tatsuya, and Marco Raindl. 2009. *Das Geheimnis der Geige*. NHK. p.154)

The first two fragments *Für mich?* and *Von wem?* are interpreted not as 'Wurde etwas hier für mich abgegeben?' or 'Von wem wurde etwas hier für mich abgegeben?' (explicatures derived from the syntax inferred from the global/local domain) but simply as 'Ist das für mich?' and 'Von wem ist das?' (explicatures derived from the syntax inferred by direct reference). The last two fragments in (21) *Von Frau Professor Schütz* and *Eine Geige, glaube ich* are interpreted in the same way: not as 'Hier wurde etwas für Sie von Frau Professor Schütz abgegeben' or 'Hier wurde für Sie eine Geige abgegeben, glaube ich' (explicatures derived from the syntax inferred from the global/local domain) but simply as 'Das ist von Frau Professor Schütz' and 'Das ist eine Geige, glaube ich' (explicatures derived from the syntax inferred by direct reference). These fragments are of the most frequent type, in which a fragment carries foreground information (FI), or more specifically, focus (FOC), about an understood topic that is phonologically null. In (21), the understood topic is *etwas* ('something that was handed in for Aoki').

Second, Chung et al. (1995: 273) pointed out that some PPs that do not allow preposition stranding in *wh*-questions (e.g., (22a, b)) allow it in sluicing as in (22c, d). This was first observed by Rosen (1976).

(22) (Chung et al. 1995: 273)
    a. *What circumstances will we use force under?
       cf. Under what circumstances will we use force?
    b. *What sense is this theory right in?
       cf. In what sense is this theory right?
    c. We are willing to use force under certain circumstances, but we will not say in advance [which ones].
       inferred syntax by direct reference: but we will not say in advance [which ones they are].
         (*they* refers to *certain circumstances*)
    d. This theory is surely right in some sense; it's just not clear [which exactly].
       inferred syntax by direct reference: it's just not clear [which exactly it is].
         (*it* refers to *some sense*)

The syntax of (22c, d) inferred from the global/local domain would involve ungrammatical preposition stranding. By contrast, the syntax inferred by direct reference does not depend on ungrammatical preposition stranding.

4.5 NEED FOR SYNTACTIC STRUCTURES INFERRED BY DIRECT REFERENCE

Third, in regular *wh*-questions such as (23a), the variable associated with the QP *who*, whose F/A is $[_{QP_x} [_Q \text{WH}] [_{PROP} x = \text{PERSON}]]$ (Ueno 2014: 290), ranges over its own domain, namely, $[_{PROP} x = \text{PERSON}]$.

(23) "inheritance of content" (Chung et al. 1995: 260–261)
    a. Joan said she talked to some students, but I don't know who she talked to.
    b. Joan said she talked to <u>some students</u>, but I don't know [who].
        syntax inferred from local domain: but I don't know [who she talked to].
        syntax inferred by direct reference: but I don't know [who they were].
        (*they* refers to *some students*.)
    c. A: Joan said she talked to <u>some students</u>.
        B: Do you know [who]?
        syntax inferred by direct reference: Do you know [who they were]?
        (*they* refers to *some students*)

Chung et al. (1995: 260–261) observed that in *wh*-fragments such as (23b, c), the variable ranges over (i.e., the answer space of the variable is) the intersection of its own domain and the domain defined by the expression in the antecedent that corresponds to the *wh*-fragment in (23b, c) (their "inner antecedent" (p. 241)), *some students*. They claimed (p. 260) that restrictions on the range of the variable are determined jointly by the content of the inner antecedent (*some students* in (23b, c)) and that of the *wh*-fragment (*who* in (23b, c)). In fact, this is simply because *wh*-fragments such as (23b, c), as opposed to full *wh*-questions such as (23a), are dependent on the preceding context for their interpretation. Therefore, the answer space for the *wh*-fragment in question is jointly determined by both the *wh*-fragment and the inner antecedent. This "inheritance of content" is accounted for in a natural way in our approach by positing the syntax inferred by direct reference, because the variable introduced by *who* in (23b, c) ranges over the set of students referred to by the pronoun *they*. For example, in (24a, b), the answer space for the *wh*-fragment is the set of male guests at the party.

(24) a. A: Mary talked to <u>some men</u> at the party.
        B: [Which guests]?
        syntax inferred by direct reference: [Which guests were they]?
        (*they* refers to *some men* in A.)

b. Mary talked to <u>some men</u> at the party, but I don't know [which guests].
c. Mary talked to <u>some men</u> at the party, but I don't know which guests she talked to.

Chung et al. (1995: 261) observed that this "inheritance of content" is particular to sluicing, and full *wh*-questions do not show similar effects. In (24c), the *wh*-phrase *which guests* is not necessarily intended to ask about the preceding NP *some men*. On the other hand, this intention is clear with the *wh*-fragment in (24a, b).

Fourth, we need syntactic structures inferred by direct reference when the adjective in the *wh*-fragment of the form *how* + adjective is only used predicatively, such as *drunk*, as opposed to the corresponding attributive adjective *drunken*. This is the same argument we used in Chapter 3 (47) to show the need for inferred syntax by direct reference in the case of fragments.

(25) I saw a drunken man in the park, but I don't remember [how {*drunken | drunk}].
   a. syntax inferred by direct reference: but I don't remember [how {*drunken | drunk} he was].
      (*he* refers to *a drunken man* in the antecedent.)
   b. inferred syntax from global/local domain: *but I don't remember [how drunken I saw a __ man in the park].
      dominance path of *how drunken*: CP[WH[Q]] S[PAST] VP[PAST] NP A[G]

The grammaticality of *drunk* and the ungrammaticality of *drunken* in (25) are accounted for by the syntax inferred by direct reference, as in (25a). Note that the syntax inferred from the global/local domain in (25b) is ungrammatical, because the dominance path of *how drunken* violates the dominance path conditions, in which no adjective gap (A[G]) is allowed (cf. Chapter 1 (1c)). This is an instance of LBC violation. (As for the LBC, see Ueno (2014: 268).)

Fifth, we need syntactic structures inferred by direct reference when the adjective in the *wh*-fragment of the form *how* + adjective has different meanings depending on if it is used predicatively or attributively. This is the same argument we used in Chapter 3 (48) and (50).

(26) #I saw a hard worker in the room, but I don't remember [how hard].
　　cf. I saw a hard worker in the room, but I don't remember [how hard-working].
　　a. syntax inferred by direct reference: #but I don't remember [how hard he was].
　　　　(*he* refers to *a hard worker* in the antecedent.)
　　b. syntax inferred from global/local domain: *but I don't remember [how hard I saw a __ worker in the room]

The semantic oddity of *how hard* in (26) is accounted for by the syntax inferred by direct reference, as in (26a). Note again that the syntax inferred from the global/local domain in (26b) is ungrammatical, because the dominance path of *how hard* violates the dominance path conditions.

Sixth, when the adjective in the *wh*-fragment of the form *how* + adjective takes its own PP complement, we need to posit syntactic structures inferred by direct reference.

(27) a. I saw many proud parents in the graduation ceremony, but I don't know [how proud of their children].
　　　　syntax inferred by direct reference: but I don't know [how proud of their children they were].
　　　　(*they* refers to *many proud parents* in the antecedent.)
　　b. You see a proud winner of the award sitting in the front row. Guess [how proud of herself].
　　　　syntax inferred by direct reference: Guess [how proud of herself she is].

We conclude that these pieces of evidence show that syntactic structures inferred by direct reference are independently motivated to account for the acceptability and unacceptability of *wh*-fragments.

4.6 Multiple *Wh*-Fragments

Although English is not a multiple *wh*-fronting language (Ueno 2014: 284), Merchant (2001: 112) observed that it allows multiple *wh*-fragments when their antecedents have an appropriate pair-list reading. Just as in the case of multiple *wh*-questions with a pair-list reading (Ueno 2014: 285), the first *wh*-fragment has scope over the second *wh*-fragment and serves as the generator of pair-list reading, as in (28a, b). As shown in (28d), multiple fragments of pairs are also possible.

(28) a. Everyone brought something different to the potluck, but I couldn't tell you [{(?)who what | *what who}]. (Merchant 2001: 112, 113)
    inferred syntax: but I couldn't tell you [who brought what to the potluck].
 b. Everybody said he'd bring something different to the potluck. But I can't remember [who what]. (Merchant 2001: 113)
    inferred syntax from global domain: But I can't remember [who said he'd bring what to the potluck].
    inferred syntax from local domain: But I can't remember [who would bring what to the potluck].
 c.
 d. (= Chapter 3 (22))
    A: Everyone brought their favorite food to the potluck, didn't they?
    B: Yes. John sandwiches, Tom sushi, and Mary an apple pie.
 e. #Everyone came to the party, but I couldn't tell you who.
 f. A: Everyone came to the party.
    B: #Do you remember who?
 g. A: Who came to the party?
    (presupposition: 'Someone came to the party.')
    B: {Everyone | #Someone}.
 h. A: Everyone brought {something | their favorite food} to the potluck.
    B: Do you remember [who what]?

We claim that the syntactic structure of these multiple *wh*-fragments in (28a, b) is (28c), in which a single CP[WH[Q]] node directly dominates the left *wh*-phrase and an S node, the latter in turn directly dominating the right *wh*-phrase. This structure is due to the syntactic rule [$_{\text{CP[WH[Q]]}}$ XP[WH[Q]] S] (Chapter 1 (100)).

Note that because the left *wh*-phrase asymmetrically c-commands the right *wh*-phrase in (28c), the latter is in the scope of the former, which correctly captures the pair-list reading of multiple *wh*-questions, as discussed in Ueno (2014: 285).

In (28e, f), the *wh*-phrase *who* has the existential presupposition 'someone' and this conflicts with the universal quantifier in *everyone*, resulting in a semantic anomaly. However, when a pair-list reading is available, as in (28a, b, h), this anomaly vanishes. In a sense, this oddity is overridden by the pair-list reading.

Note that a *wh*-question with *who* can be answered with *everyone*, as long as the speaker and hearer understand what set of people *everyone* ranges over, i.e., the set of people referred to by *them* in *every one of them*. This is shown in (28g).

4.7 The Hell

Merchant (2001: 121) observed that an aggressively non-D-linked *wh*-phrase (e.g., *who the hell*) generally cannot occur in sluicing, as shown in (29a, b, c).

(29) a. Someone dented my car last night. I wish I knew who (*the hell)! (Merchant 2001: 122)
    b. A: <u>Someone</u> bought a car yesterday.
       B: Who (*the hell)?   cf. Who the hell bought it?
    c. Mary bought <u>something</u> yesterday, but I don't know [what (*the hell)].
       inferred syntax: but I don't know [what she bought yesterday].
       syntax inferred by direct reference: but I don't know [what it was].
         (*it* refers to *something*)

There seem to be two reasons why the aggressively non-D linked *wh*-phrases *who/what the hell* are unacceptable in (29). First, the interpretation of *wh*-fragments is entirely dependent on their antecedent, and in this respect, *wh*-fragments are "D-linked" and it is not appropriate for the aggressively non-D-linked *the hell* to appear with them. This is similar to the fact that *the hell* is not appropriate with the inherently D-linked *which*.

(30) (Pesetsky 1987; cited in Lasnik and Saito 1992: 173)
    a. [$_{NP[WH[Q]]}$ What the hell book] did you read that in?
    b. *[$_{NP[WH[Q]]}$ Which the hell book] did you read that in?

Second, an aggressively non-D-linked *wh*-phrase must c-command a gap (XP[G]) (i.e., its extraction site) in the decoded syntax of a CP[WH[Q]] in which it occurs: [_CP[WH[Q]]_ XP[WH[Q]] [_S_ ... XP[G] ...]]. This is shown in (31b, c), in which an *in-situ wh*-phrase cannot occur with the aggressively non-D-linked *the hell* (Ueno 2014: 260).

(31) a. Who read what?
           decoded syntax: [_CP[WH[Q]]_ [_NP[WH[Q]]_ who] [_S[PAST]_ NP[G] [_VP[PAST]_ read who]]]
      b. *Who read what the hell? (Lasnik and Saito 1992: 173)
      c. Who the hell read what?
      d. decoded syntax of the *wh*-fragments *who* in (29a, b) and *what* in (29c)
           [_CP[WH[Q]]_ [_NP[WH[Q]]_ {who | what}] S]

In the decoded syntax (a part of the output of the LM) of the *wh*-fragment (31d), the S node does not dominate anything. Its content will be filled later by the ICM. Therefore, a *wh*-fragment does not c-command any gap in its decoded syntax. This explains why the aggressively D-linked *the hell* is not allowed to occur with a *wh*-fragment.

Merchant (2001) observed that *the hell* is acceptable if it is adjoined to a *wh*-phrase that undergoes sluiced *wh*-phrase inversion with a preposition ("swiping").

(32) a. He was talking, but God knows who the hell to. (Merchant 2001: 65 note 14)
      b. A: I'm getting married.
           B: Who the hell to?
           A: Who do you think? Rita. (from the web)
      c. Am I meant to surrender? If so, who the hell to? (from the web)
      d.
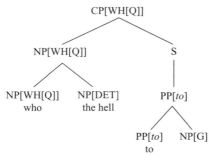

We claim that the decoded syntax of the *wh*-fragment in (32a, b, c) is (32d), in which the *wh*-phrase *who the hell* c-commands the corresponding NP gap (NP[G]). This explains their acceptability. This second reason shows that the decoded syntax and inferred syntax of a *wh*-fragment must be clearly distinguished, because *who the hell* and *what the hell* in (29a, b) c-command the corresponding NP[G] in their INFERRED syntax, but not in their DECODED syntax.

4.8 Access to Lexical Entries

As discussed in 3.4, non-demonstrative inference for utterance comprehension involves accessing the lexical entries for the words uttered and at the same time accessing the lexical entries for the closely related words (spreading activation). The following example, just like the similar example of a fragment in Chapter 3 (74), illustrates that when the lexical entry for the intransitive verb *drink* is accessed, the lexical entry for transitive *drink* is also activated and becomes available to the ICM.

(33) (Culicover and Jackendoff 2005: 266 (48b))
Harriet is drinking again, but I don't know [what]. [sprouting *wh*-fragment]
inferred syntax: but I don't know [what Harriet is drinking again]

Here is another example. When the lexical entry for intransitive *flirt* in (34A) is accessed (syntax: V in [__]), the related entry with a PP[*with*] complement is also activated (syntax: V in [__, PP[*with*]]). Therefore, in (34B), the presence of the preposition *with* is obligatory and no other preposition is possible. (See the discussion concerning Chapter 3 (77a).)

(34) (Culicover and Jackendoff 2005: 271 (58b)) (cf. Chapter 3 (77a))
    A: Harriet's been flirting again.
    B: Who *(with)?
       inferred syntax: Who has Harriet been flirting with?

Note that if B had simply said *Who?* without *with*, it would have been interpreted as 'Who is Harriet?,' which was not B's intention.

However, there seems to be a restriction, among different lexical entries for the same verb, on which lexical entry can activate which meaning. (35a, b) are examples of "matching" sluicing, the type of sluicing in which the *wh*-fragment can be matched with an overt phrase in the antecedent (Culicover and Jackendoff 2005: 257). This type of sluicing presents no problem, partly because there is an antecedent in the preceding context that the *wh*-fragment asks about and partly because the same lexical entry for the same verb ([V, NP, NP] in (35a) and [V, NP, PP[*to*]] in (35b)) is used both in the clause that contains the antecedent of the *wh*-fragment and in the inferred syntax of the *wh*-fragment.

By contrast, (35c, d) are examples of "sprouting" sluicing, the type of sluicing in which the *wh*-fragment has no matching constituent in the antecedent but only serves a suppressed/unassociable role (i.e., an implicit argument) or an adjunct in the antecedent (Culicover and Jackendoff 2005: 257). This type of sluicing is restricted, as shown in (35e).

(35) (Chung at al. 1995: 248, Merchant 2001: 33–4, and Culicover and Jackendoff 2005: 258, note 17)
    a. They served someone fish, but I don't know [who].   [matching]
       syntax inferred from global/local domain: ??but I don't know [who they served fish].
       syntax inferred by direct reference: but I don't know [who he was].
    b. They served something to the students, but I don't know   [matching] [what].
    c. She served the soup, but I don't know [to whom].   [sprouting]
    d. She served the students, but I don't know [what].   [sprouting]
    e. *She served the soup, but I don't know [who].   [sprouting]
       syntax inferred by direct reference: *but I don't know [who he was].
       (no possible antecedent for *he* available)

Note in passing that there is a restriction on the extraction of the first object NP from the ditransitive construction (Huddleston and Pullum 2002: 248–249, 2005: 72): it is difficult, if not impossible, to extract the first object NP (e.g., ??*Who did she serve __ the meal*? (Merchant 2001: 34 note 16)). The acceptability of (35a) shows that this restriction is absent in sluicing. In our approach, this is because the interpretation of the *wh*-fragment in (35a) is constructed from its syntax inferred by direct reference, which does not involve the "*wh*-movement" of the first object of the ditransitive verb. This is supported by the fact that no syntax inferred by direct reference is possible for the *wh*-fragment in (35e).

Here are four lexical entries for the verb *serve* in (35).

(36) four partial lexical entries for *serve*
   a. syntax: V in [__, NP]
      E/R: [$_{TYPE}$ "serve"] in [__ [AG, SO; SERVER] [PT, GO; DINER] <[TH; FOOD]>]
   b. syntax: V in [__, NP, NP]
      E/R: [$_{TYPE}$ "serve"] in [__ [AG, SO; SERVER] [PT, GO; DINER] [TH; FOOD]]
   c. syntax: V in [__, NP]
      E/R: [$_{TYPE}$ "serve"] in [__ [AG, SO; SEVER] [PT, TH; FOOD] <[GO; DINER]>]
   d. syntax: V in [__, NP, PP[*to*]]
      E/R: [$_{TYPE}$ "serve"] in [__ [AG, SO; SERVER] [PT, TH; FOOD] [GO; DINER]]
   e. definition of *natural extension*
      Of two lexical entries L_1 and L_2, L_2 is a natural extension of L_1 if and only if (i) the E/R of L_1 and that of L_2 have the same set of roles (and, therefore, the same outrank relations), and (ii) the role lowest in outranking is suppressed/unassociable in the E/R of L_1 but overt/associable in the E/R of L_2.

When the hearer/interpreter hears the first conjunct of (35c), he accesses the lexical entry (36c), which in turn activates (36d), which is used to infer the intended meaning of the second conjunct ('but I don't know to whom she served the soup'). I will call lexical entry (36d) a natural extension of (36c) in the sense that the suppressed/unassociable role in (36c), namely, <[GO; DINER]>, becomes overt/associable in (36d) and the outrank relations of the roles ([AG, SO] > [PT, TH] > GO) are kept intact between the two lexical entries (cf. Chung et al. 1995: 248, 262). The situation in (35d) is quite similar. When the hearer/interpreter hears the first conjunct of (35d), he accesses the lexical entry (36a), which in turn activates (36b), which is used to infer the intended meaning of the second conjunct ('but I don't know what she served the students'). Again, lexical entry (36b) is a natural extension of (36a) in exactly the same sense.

Generally, when a verb has two lexical entries L_1 and L_2, we define the binary relation of L_2 being a natural extension of L_1 as (36e). For example, if a verb has two lexical entries L_1 and L_2 with three roles R_1, R_2, and R_3 and with the outranking relations $R_1 > R_2 > R_3$ between them, and their E/Rs are [$_{EV}$ TYPE R_1 R_2 <R_3>]

for L_1 and $[_{EV}$ TYPE R_1 R_2 R_3] for L_2, then lexical entry L_2 is a natural extension of lexical entry L_1. Of the four lexical entries of the verb *serve* in (36a-d), (36b) and (36d) are natural extensions of (36a) and (36c), respectively. If a verb has two lexical entries L_1 and L_2, and L_2 is a natural extension of L_1, then the discussion so far has shown that access to L_1 can activate L_2. For example, access to (36a) and (36c) can activate (36b) and (36d), respectively.

The inferred syntax of the second conjunct of (35e) is '??but I don't know who she served the soup,' which requires lexical entry (36b). However, in the first conjunct of (35e), lexical entry (36c) is accessed, but access to (36c) in the first conjunct of (35e) cannot activate (36b) for the second conjunct, because (36b) is not a natural extension of (36c). This explains the ungrammaticality of (35e).

The verb *read* offers another example of the natural extension of a lexical entry and how it is activated. This verb has at least two lexical entries: intransitive (37a) and transitive (37b). (37b) is a natural extension of (37a). Therefore, access to (37a) in the first conjunct of (38) activates (37b) for the second conjunct, which makes the sprouting sluicing in (38) possible.

(37) a. lexical entry for intransitive *read*
 syntax: V in [__]
 E/R: [$_{TYPE}$ "read"] in [__ [AG; PERSON] <[PT, TH; INFORMATION]>]
 b. lexical entry for transitive *read*
 syntax: V in [__, NP]
 E/R: [$_{TYPE}$ "read"] in [__ [AG; PERSON] [PT, TH; INFORMATION]]

(38) She was reading, but I couldn't make out what. [sprouting] (Chung et al. 1995: 249)

On the other hand, sprouting sluicing is impossible with the verbs *bathe* and *march*, which is shown in (39).

(39) a. *She was bathing, but I couldn't make out who. [sprouting] (Chung et al. 1995: 249)
 inferred syntax: but I couldn't make out who she was bathing
 b. *They were marching, but I couldn't make out who. [sprouting]
 inferred syntax: but I couldn't make out who they were marching

c. Someone was bathing, but I couldn't make out who. [matching]
inferred syntax: but I couldn't make out who was bathing
d. Some prisoners were marching, but I couldn't [matching]
make out who.
inferred syntax: but I couldn't make out who were marching
e. She was bathing someone, but I couldn't [matching]
make out who.
inferred syntax: but I couldn't make out who she was bathing
f. The guard was marching some prisoners, but [matching]
I couldn't make out who.
inferred syntax: but I couldn't make out who the guard was marching

Although *bathe* and *march* have both intransitive and transitive uses, the transitive *bathe* and *march* are not natural extensions of the intransitive *bathe* and *march*. The transitive verbs (40b) and (41b) are causativizations of the corresponding intransitive verbs (40a) and (41a).

(40) a. partial lexical entry for intransitive *bathe*, as in *The child bathed*
syntax: V in [__]
E/R: [$_{TYPE}$ "bathe"] in [__ [AG, TH]]
b. partial lexical entry for transitive *bathe*, as in *The mother bathed the child*
syntax: V in [__, NP]
E/R: [$_{TYPE}$ "cause$_2$"]$_①$, [$_{TYPE}$ "bathe"]$_②$ in [$_{VA}$ __$_①$ AG [$_{PT}$ [$_{SITU}$ __$_②$ [AG, TH]]]]

(41) a. partial lexical entries for intransitive *march*, as in *The prisoners marched*
syntax: V in [__]
E/R: [$_{TYPE}$ "march"] in [__ [AG, TH]]
b. partial lexical entries for transitive *march*, as in *The guard marched the prisoners*
syntax: V in [__, NP]
E/R: [$_{TYPE}$ "cause$_2$"]$_①$, [$_{TYPE}$ "march"]$_②$ in [$_{VA}$ __$_①$ AG [$_{PT}$ [$_{SITU}$ __$_②$ [AG, TH]]]]

In (40b) and (41b), "cause$_2$" is a two-place predicate that takes two roles, an agent (as causer) and a caused situation, and denotes a volitional action (VA)

(McCawley 1973: 103, 157, Ueno 2014: 202). In (39a), the intended meaning of the second conjunct is 'I couldn't make out who she was bathing' with the transitive *bathe*. When the hearer/interpreter hears the first conjunct of (39a), he accesses the lexical entry for the intransitive *bathe* (40a), which does not activate the transitive *bathe* (40b), because the latter is not a natural extension of the former. Note that there is no unassociable role (i.e., implicit argument) in (40a), which becomes associable in the corresponding transitive (40b) and which successful sprouting depends on.

The same restriction on activation of lexical entries (i.e., that access to a lexical entry only activates the lexical entry for the same verb that is a natural extension of the former) also applies to fragments. This shows again a strong similarity between sluicing and fragments.

(42) restriction on lexical entry activation in fragments
    a. A: They served John fish.
        B: No, Mary.   [matching; cf. (35a)]
    b. A: They served fish to the students.
        B: No, chicken.   [matching; cf. (35b)]
    c. A: She served the soup.
        B: Yes, to John.   [sprouting; cf. (35c)]
    d. A: She served the students.
        B: Yes, fish.   [sprouting; cf. (35d)]
    e. A: She served the soup.
        B: *Yes, John.   [sprouting; cf. (35e)]
    f. A: She was bathing.
        B: *Yes, her baby. [sprouting; cf. (39a)]

4.9 Island Insensitivity

Chung et al. (1995: 273), Merchant (2001: 87), and Culicover and Jackendoff (2005: 258, note 17 and 266–267) showed that *wh*-fragments are not sensitive to islands by giving acceptable examples that would violate island constraints if a purely syntactic account, such as "*wh*-movement" followed by "deletion," were provided. Ross had already observed the weakening of island violation effects in sluicing in his seminal paper (1969: (71)–(73)). (See 3.3.10 on the island insensitivity of fragments.) These examples show that purely syntactic accounts do not fare well in accounting for the island insensitivity of sluicing.

(43) a. Bob found a plumber who fixed the sink, but I'm not sure with what.
[CNPC; sprouting] (Culicover and Jackendoff 2005: 258)
syntax inferred from global domain: *but I'm not sure with what [Bob found a plumber who fixed the sink]
syntax inferred from local domain: but I'm not sure with what [he fixed the sink]
he refers to *a plumber who fixed the sink.*
b. That Tony is eating right now is conceivable, but I'm having a hard time imagining what.
[Sentential Subject Constraint; sprouting] (Culicover and Jackendoff 2005: 258)
syntax inferred from global domain: *but I'm having a hard time imagining what [that Tony is eating right now is conceivable]
syntax inferred from local domain: but I'm having a hard time imagining what [Tony is eating right now]
c. A: Harriet drinks scotch that comes from a very special part of Scotland.
B: Where? [CNPC; matching] (Culicover and Jackendoff 2005: 267)
syntax inferred from global domain: *Where [does Harriet drink scotch that comes from]?
syntax inferred from local domain: Where [does it come from]?
it refers to *scotch that comes from a very special part of Scotland*
d. A: John met a guy who speaks a very unusual language.
B: Which language? [CNPC; matching] (Culicover and Jackendoff 2005: 267)
syntax inferred from global domain: *Which language did [John meet a guy who speaks]?
syntax inferred from local domain: Which language does he speak?
he refers to *a guy who speaks a very unusual language.*
syntax inferred by direct reference: Which language is it?
it refers to *a very unusual language.*

Although the syntax inferred from the global domain of each *wh*-fragment in (43) is not available due to an island violation, the syntactic structures inferred from the local domain or inferred by direct reference do not involve any island violation. This explains the island insensitivity of *wh*-fragments.

Although *wh*-fragments are island insensitive, VP ellipsis is island sensitive (Chung et al. 1995: 275, Merchant 2001: 4–5, 114, Merchant 2004: 705). This is because the inferred syntax of a VP ellipsis always violates the dominance path conditions, if the antecedent of the VP ellipsis contains an island. (44a) is an example of CNPC violation. (44b) is a VP ellipsis example of CNPC violation. (44c) is a *wh*-fragment example of CNPC violation.

(44) a. *They want to hire someone who speaks a Balkan language, but I don't remember which they want to hire someone who speaks. (Merchant 2001: 5)
   b. *They want to hire someone who speaks a Balkan language, but I don't remember which they do. (Merchant 2001: 5)
   antecedent of *do*: *want to hire someone who speaks a Balkan language*
   inferred syntax of *which they do*: *which they want to hire someone who speaks NP[G]
   c. They want to hire someone who speaks a Balkan language, but I don't remember which. (Merchant 2001: 4)
   syntax of *which* inferred from global domain: *which they want to hire someone who speaks NP[G]
   syntax of *which* inferred from local domain: which she speaks NP[G]
   (*she* refers to *someone who speaks a Balkan language*.)
   syntax of *which* inferred by direct reference: which it is NP[G]
   (*it* refers to *a Balkan language*.)

In our AMG approach to unbounded dependencies, island facts are captured by the dominance path conditions (Chapter 1 (100)), which formulate licit "*wh*-movement paths" by means of dominance relations, in which the top of the dominance path is CP[WH[Q]] (i.e., an interrogative *wh*-CP) and the bottom of the path is XP[G] (i.e., a gap with the syntactic category XP). Recall that the dominance path conditions (Chapter 1 (100)) are encoded as part of the lexical entry for a clause-initial ("moved") *wh*-phrase.

As discussed in 4.2, a *wh*-fragment (XP[WH[Q]]) behaves syntactically as [$_{CP[WH[Q]]}$ XP[WH[Q]] S], in which the *wh*-fragment is directly dominated by a CP[WH[Q]] node. In the decoded syntax (a part of the output of the LM) of a *wh*-fragment, this S node does not dominate anything (i.e., lacks content). However, the utterance of a *wh*-fragment is not treated as ungrammatical or gibberish, because this is part of ostensive-inferential communication and is guaranteed to be worth processing by the Communicative Principle of Relevance (Chapter 2 (6)). This triggers non-demonstrative inference in the ICM, leading to an inferred syntax that meets the dominance path conditions.

In Chapter 5, we will claim that the auxiliary verb left behind by "VP ellipsis" is a pro-VP form, and as such the ICM needs to find a suitable antecedent from the prior context and determines its reference. The ICM constructs an inferred syntax in which a pro-VP form is replaced by a full VP that is taken from its antecedent and contains a gap XP[G] if the pro-VP form is dominated by a CP[WH[Q]]. If so, this inferred syntax must meet the dominance path conditions. In either case (i.e., *wh*-fragment case (44c) or VP ellipsis case (44b)), once an inferred syntax is constructed, this syntactic structure is subject to the dominance path conditions. In other words, only the interpretations (inferred syntactic structures) of *wh*-fragments and VP ellipses that meet the dominance path conditions are available to the hearer/interpreter.

4.10 Close Examination of *Wh*-Fragment Island Insensitivity

Merchant (2001) closely examined island insensitivity in sluicing. We would like to go over the data he presented and examine from our own perspective whether syntactic structures inferred from the local domain and/or those inferred by direct reference play any role in the island insensitivity of *wh*-fragments.

4.10.1 Relative clause island

The standard cases of the Complex NP Constraint (CNPC) were discussed in Ueno (2014: 264) and accounted for in terms of the dominance path conditions. Furthermore, the cases of innocuous violation of the CNPC in light verb construction were discussed in Ueno (2014: 278) and accounted for by "role sharing" and the resultant mono-clausalization in E/R.

Merchant (2001) claimed that the effects of the relative clause island (a subcase of the CNPC) are not observed in sluicing. This is simply because, from an AMG perspective, *wh*-fragments can be interpreted through syntactic structures inferred from the local domain and/or by direct reference.

(45) indicative relative clauses (Merchant 2001: 209)
    a. They hired someone who speaks a Balkan language—guess [which]!
        syntax inferred from local domain: guess [which (Balkan language) she speaks __]
            (*she* refers to *someone who speaks a Balkan language.*)
        syntax inferred by direct reference: guess [which (Balkan language) it is __]
            (*it* refers to *a Balkan language*, based on its wide scope interpretation of *a Balkan language.*)
        syntax inferred from global domain: *guess [which (Balkan language) they hired someone who speaks __] (violation of the CNPC)
    b. They hired someone who speaks a lot of Balkan languages—guess [how many]!
        syntax inferred from local domain: guess [how many (Balkan languages) she speaks __]
            (*she* refers to *someone who speaks a lot of Balkan languages.*)
        syntax inferred by direct reference: #guess [how many (Balkan languages) they are __]
            (*they* refers to *a lot of Balkan languages*)
        syntax inferred from global domain: *guess [how many (Balkan languages) they hired someone who speaks __] (violation of the CNPC)

Merchant judged (46) ungrammatical. However, under the assumption that *a Balkan language* has wide scope over the negation, (46) seems to allow the interpretation that of all Balkan languages, they hired no Greek speaker but they hired some speakers of all the other Balkan languages, and I forgot that it was Greek that they didn't hire any speaker of. This is particularly true when the indefinite article is *a certain*, as in (47) (cf. Hornstein 1984: 21).

(46) (Merchant 2001: 211)
    They didn't hire anyone who speaks a Balkan language, but I don't remember [which].
        cf. They didn't hire any speaker of a Balkan language, but I don't remember [which].
        inferred from local domain: #but I don't remember [which (Balkan language) she speaks __]

inferred by direct reference: but I don't remember [which (Balkan language) it was __]
(*it* = *a Balkan language*, based on its wide scope interpretation)
inferred from global domain: *but I don't remember [which (Balkan language) they didn't hire anyone who speaks __] (violation of the CNPC)

(47) A: They didn't hire anyone who speaks a certain Balkan language.
B$_1$: [Which Balkan language]?
inferred by direct reference: [Which Balkan language is it __]?
(*it* = *a certain Balkan language*, based on its wide scope interpretation)
B$_2$: Greek.
inferred by direct reference: [It is Greek].
(*it* = *a certain Balkan language*, based on its wide scope interpretation)

(48) is interpreted in such a way that *someone* is *de dicto* and the quantifier phrase *a Balkan language* has wide scope over the PROP headed by WANT (Merchant 2001: 217 (167b)).

(48) subjunctive relatives and modal subordination (Merchant 2001: 217, 219)
They want to hire someone who speaks a Balkan language, but I don't know [which].
inferred from local domain: but I don't know [which (Balkan language) she should speak __]
(*she* refers to *someone who speaks a Balkan language*)
(with modal subordination)
inferred by direct reference: but I don't know [which (Balkan language) it is]
(*it* refers to *a Balkan language*, based on its wide scope interpretation)
inferred from global domain: *but I don't know [which (Balkan language) they want to hire someone who speaks __] (violation of the CNPC)

4.10.2 Conjunct Constraint

The Coordinate Structure Constraint (CSC) was discussed in Ueno (2014: 269, 303) and its standard cases and counter examples were accounted for by the dominance path conditions together with the Coordinate Structure Convention

(Ueno 2014: 305 (2), 310 (11)). The CSC is divided into two subcases (Pollard and Sag 1994: 201): (i) the Conjunct Constraint (Ueno 2014: 305) and (ii) the Element Constraint. Merchant (2001) claimed that the effects of the Conjunct Constraint are not observed in sluicing. From our perspective, this is simply because these *wh*-fragments can be interpreted through their syntactic structures inferred by direct reference.

(49) (Merchant 2001: 194)
    a. Janet and one of the boys were holding hands, but I don't remember [which one]. (Levin 1982)
        syntax inferred by direct reference: but I don't remember [which one he was]
            (*he* refers to *one of the boys*.)
        syntax inferred from global/local domain: *but I don't remember [which one Janet and __ were holding hands] (violation of the Conjunct Constraint)
    b. Ben baked the cake and something else, but I don't know [what].
        syntax inferred by direct reference: but I don't know [what it was]
            (*it* refers to *something else*.)
        syntax inferred from global/local domain: *but I don't know [what Ben baked the cake and __]
            (violation of the Conjunct Constraint)

(50) a. A: Janet and one of the boys were holding hands.
        B_1: Which one?
            syntax inferred by direct reference: Which one was he?
                (*he* refers to *one of the boys*.)
            syntax inferred from global/local domain: *Which one were Janet and __ holding hands?
                (violation of the Conjunct Constraint)
        B_2: Yeah, John.
            syntax inferred by direct reference: Yeah, he was John.
                (*he* refers to *one of the boys*.)
            syntax inferred from global/local domain: Janet and John holding were hands.
    b. A: Ben baked the cake and something else.
        B_1: What?

4.10 CLOSE EXAMINATION OF *WH*-FRAGMENT ISLAND INSENSITIVITY   173

      syntax inferred by direct reference: What was it?
        (*it* refers to *something else.*)
      syntax inferred from global/local domain: *What did Ben bake the cake and __?
        (violation of the Conjunct Constraint)
    B_2: Yeah, these bagels.
      syntax inferred by direct reference: It was these bagels.
        (*It* refers to *something else.*)
      syntax inferred from global/local domain: Ben baked the cake and these bagels.

4.10.3 Element Constraint

Merchant (2001) claimed that the effects of the Element Constraint are not observed in sluicing, either. This is again simply because *wh*-fragments can be interpreted through their syntactic structures inferred either from the local domain or by direct reference.

(51) a. Bob ate dinner and saw a movie that night, but he didn't say [which]. (Merchant 2001: 223)
      syntax inferred from local domain: but he didn't say [which (movie) he saw]
        (based on ∧-exploitation inference rule (McCawley 1993a: 65): from *Bob ate dinner and saw a movie that night*, *Bob saw a movie* is inferred)
      syntax inferred by direct reference: but he didn't say [which (movie) it was]
      syntax inferred from global domain: *but he didn't say [which (movie) he ate dinner and saw __ that night] (violation of the Element Constraint)
   b. Ben was sitting in the back and playing the trumpet, but I couldn't tell [how loudly]. (Merchant 2001: 225)
      syntax inferred from local domain: but I couldn't tell [how loudly he was playing it]
        (based on ∧-exploitation inference rule: from *Ben was sitting in the back and playing the trumpet*, *Ben was playing the trumpet* is inferred)
      syntax inferred by direct reference: *but I couldn't tell [how loudly it was]
        (*it* refers to *the trumpet.*)

syntax inferred from global domain: *but I couldn't tell [how loudly he was sitting in the back and playing it __] (violation of the Element Constraint)

(52) a. A: Bob ate dinner and saw a movie that night.
B_1: Which (movie)?
syntax inferred from local domain: Which (movie) did Bob see __ that night?
(based on ∧-exploitation inference rule: from *Bob ate dinner and saw a movie that night*, *Bob saw a movie that night* is inferred)
syntax inferred by direct reference: Which (movie) was it?
(*it* refers to *a movie*)
B_2: Yeah, *The Last Samurai*.
syntax inferred from local domain: Yeah, Bob saw *The Last Samurai* that night.
syntax inferred by direct reference: Yeah, it was *The Last Samurai*.
(*it* refers to *a movie*.)
b. A: Ben was sitting in the back and playing the trumpet.
B_1: How loudly?
syntax inferred from local domain: How loudly was Ben playing the trumpet __?
syntax inferred by direct reference: *How loudly was it? (*it* refers to *the trumpet*.)
B_2: Yeah, very loudly.
syntax inferred from local domain: Yeah, Ben was playing the trumpet very loudly.
syntax inferred by direct reference: *Yeah, it was very loudly.
(*it* refers to *the trumpet*.)

Note that in (51b) and (52b), the syntactic structures inferred by direct reference do not work, because the *wh*-fragments are an ADVP, which cannot be a complement of the *be* verb in the inferred syntax. Note furthermore that if *how loudly* in (51b) and (52b) is changed to *how loud*, the syntax inferred by the direct reference inferred becomes available, as in *How loud was it?*

Merchant (2001) judged (53) ungrammatical. However, (53) seems to allow an interpretation that describes the following situation: As for Town A, one farmer sold his farm and moved there; as for Town B, two farmers sold their farms and moved there; as for Town C, five farmers sold their farms and moved there; however, as for Town D, there was no farmer who sold his farm and moved there. This interpretation is accounted for through the syntax inferred by direct reference.

(53) No farmer sold his farm and moved to a certain town—I don't remember [which]. (Merchant 2001: 224)
    syntax inferred from local domain: *I don't remember [which (town) he moved to]
        (*he* is a bound variable, but it is not c-commanded by its quantifier *no farmer* in syntax (Ueno 2014: 291).)
    syntax inferred by direct reference: I don't remember [which (town) it was]
        (based on the fact that *a certain town* has wide scope)
    syntax inferred from global domain: *I don't remember [which (town) no farmer sold his farm and moved to __] (violation of the Element Constraint)

4.10.4 Derived position islands

The Subject Condition (SC; *aka.* the Subject Island) was discussed in Ueno (2014: 265) and was accounted for in terms of the dominance path conditions. The Topic Island can be explained in the same way, if we assume that the topic phrase is adjoined to the matrix clause.

Merchant (2001) pointed out that the effects of the topic and subject islands are not observed in sluicing, which is shown in (54). This is because, in our AMG approach, a *wh*-fragment can be interpreted through its syntax inferred by direct reference.

(54) (Merchant 2001: 185–186)
    a. A: A biography of one of the Marx brothers, she refused to read.
        B: Which one?
        syntax inferred from global domain: *Which Marx brother did a biography of __, she refuse to read?
            (violation of the topic island)
        syntax inferred by direct reference: Which Marx brother was he?
            (*he* refers to *one of the Marx brothers*, based on its wide scope reading; cf. inverse linking in Ueno 2014: 227–9 and May 1985: 68)

b. A biography of one of the Marx brothers {is going to be published | will appear} this year—guess which! (*published* passive; *appear* unaccusative)

    syntax inferred from global/local domain: *guess [[_{NP[DET]} a biography of [_{NP[WH[Q]]} which Marx brother]] {is going to be published | will appear} this year] (failure of WH[Q] percolation)

    inferred syntax from global/local domain: *guess which Marx brother [[_{NP[DET]} a biography of __] {is going to be published | will appear} this year] (violation of the SC)

    inferred syntax by direct reference: guess [[which Marx brother] he is] (*he* refers to *one of the Marx brothers*, based on its wide scope reading.)

c. A biographer of one of the Marx brothers {interviewed her | worked for her}, but I don't remember which. (*interviewed* transitive; *worked* unergative)

    inferred syntax from global/local domain: *but I don't remember [[_{NP[DET]} a biographer of [_{NP[WH[Q]]} which Marx brother]]{interviewed her | worked for her}] (failure of WH[Q] percolation)

    inferred syntax from global/local domain: *but I don't remember [which Marx brother [a biographer of __]{interviewed her | worked for her}] (violation of the SC)

    inferred syntax by direct reference: but I don't remember [which Marx brother he was]

        (*he* refers to *one of the Marx brothers*, based on its wide scope reading.)

In (54b, c), the first inferred syntax is ungrammatical, because the subject NP is not a *wh*-phrase in that the WH[Q] feature, as opposed to the WH[R] feature (Ueno 2014: 312), cannot go up from a complement or adjunct PP node to its mother NP node (Ueno 2014: 280–281, 311–312).

(55) and (56) are two more sets of examples that show that sluicing does not exhibit the effects of the topic/subject islands.

(55) (Merchant 2001: 189)
    a. Five pictures of one of the victims might be distributed to the press, but I can't remember which one.

        scope relations in F/A: [_{QP} *one of the victims*] > [_{QP} *five pictures*] > [_{Fp} *might*]

4.10 CLOSE EXAMINATION OF *WH*-FRAGMENT ISLAND INSENSITIVITY 177

syntax inferred from global/local domain: *but I can't remember [[_{NP} five pictures of [_{NP[WH[Q]]} which one]] might be distributed to the press] (failure of WH[Q] percolation)

syntax inferred from global/local domain: *but I can't remember [which one [five pictures of __] might be distributed to the press] (violation of the SC)

syntax inferred by direct reference: but I can't remember [which one he was __]

(*he* refers to *one of the victims*.)

b. Five pictures of one of the victims weren't distributed to the press, but I can't remember which one.

scope relations in F/A: [_{QP} *one of the victims*] > [_{QP} *five pictures*] > [_{Fp} *not*]

syntax inferred from global/local domain: *but I can't remember [[_{NP} five pictures of [_{NP[WH[Q]]} which one]] weren't distributed to the press] (failure of WH[Q] percolation)

syntax inferred from global/local domain: *but I can't remember [which one [five pictures of __] weren't distributed to the press] (violation of the SC)

syntax inferred by direct reference: but I can't remember [which one he was __]

(*he* refers to *one of the victims*.)

(56) (Merchant 2001: 189)

Every biography of one of the Marx brothers seemed to its author to be definitive, but I don't remember (of) which (Marx brother).

scope relations in F/A: [_{QP} *one of the Marx brothers*] > [_{QP} *every biography*] > [_{Fp} PAST]°[_{Fp} SEEM]

syntax inferred from global domain: *but I don't remember [[_{NP[DET]} every biography of [_{NP[WH[Q]]} which Marx brother]] seemed to its author to be definitive] (failure of WH[Q] percolation)

syntax inferred from global domain: *but I don't remember [which Marx brother [every biography of __] seemed to its author to be definitive] (violation of the SC)

syntax inferred by direct reference: but I don't remember [which Marx brother he was __]

(*he* refers to *one of the Marx brothers*.)

4.10.5 Adjunct Island and Sentential Subject Constraint

In Ueno (2014: 275 (1), 287 (1)), the dominance path conditions were formulated not only in syntactic terms but also in F/A terms. The Adjunct Island cases are excluded as a violation of the F/A dominance path condition. On the other hand, the Sentential Subject Constraint (SSC) is accounted for as a violation of the syntactic dominance path conditions (Ueno 2014: 265).

Merchant (2001) observed that the effects of the Adjunct Island and the SSC are not observed in sluicing. This is because, from our AMG perspective, two types of inferred syntactic structure are available to *wh*-fragments in such islands: syntax inferred by direct reference and syntax inferred from the local domain.

(57) a. If Ben talks to someone, Abby will be mad, but I don't remember [who]. (Merchant 2001: 221)
    syntax inferred from local domain: but I don't remember [who he should talk to] (with modal subordination)
    syntax inferred by direct reference: but I don't remember [who she is] based on the interpretation that *someone* has wide scope over *if* (Merchant 2001: 221 (179))
    syntax inferred from global domain: *but I don't remember [who if Ben talks to __ , Abby will be mad] (violation of the Adjunct Island)
 b. A: If Ben talks to someone, Abby will be mad.
    B_1: Who?
    B_2: Yeah, Mary.

In (58a), the first conjunct *That Maxwell killed the judge was proven* entails *Maxwell killed the judges*, due to the factivity of the sentential subject (Sadock 2012: 37, Ueno 2014: 148).

(58) a. That Maxwell killed the judge was proven, but it's still not clear [with what]. (Merchant 2001: 222)
    syntax inferred from local domain: but it's still not clear [with what Maxwell killed the judge]
    syntax inferred from global domain: *but it's still not clear [with what that Maxwell killed the judge __ was proven] (violation of the SSC)

b. A: That Maxwell killed the judge was proven.
   B₁: Really? With what?
   B₂: Yeah, I know. With a knife.

4.10.6 COMP-trace effects

The COMP-trace effects were discussed in Ueno (2014: 266) and they and their suspension/amelioration were accounted for in terms of the dominance path conditions and the lexical entry for *that*-relative clause with a subject gap (Ueno 2014: 268 (11)).

Merchant (2001) observed that the COMP-trace effects are not observed in sluicing. This is because, in AMG terms, *wh*-fragments are interpreted through their syntactic structures inferred either from the local domain or by direct reference. Recall that a syntactic structure inferred from the local domain is constructed through inference in which a *wh*-fragment is resolved locally, namely, by interpreting it relative to the innermost clause (i.e., Merchant's (2001: 208) treatment of propositional islands).

(59) (Merchant 2001: 185)
   a. It's probable that a certain senator will resign, but [which] is still a secret.
      syntax inferred from global domain: *but [which senator it is probable that __ will resign] is still a secret (COMP-trace effects)
      syntax inferred from local domain: but [which senator will resign] is still a secret
      syntax inferred by direct reference: but [which senator he will be] is still a secret
      (*he* refers to *a certain senator.*)
   b. Sally asked if somebody was going to fail Syntax One, but I can't remember [who].
      syntax inferred from global domain: *but I can't remember [who Sally asked if __ was going to fail Syntax One] (COMP-trace effects)
      syntax inferred from local domain: #but I can't remember [who was going to fail Syntax One]
      syntax inferred by direct reference: but I can't remember [who he was]
      (*he* refers to *somebody* in the antecedent, based on its wide scope reading.)

4.10.7 Weak islands

Merchant (2001: 226) pointed out that weak (selective) islands are semantic or pragmatic phenomena.

(60) implicit argument
   #Nigel never hunts, but I don't remember [what]. (Merchant 2001: 226 (196a), cited from Albert 1993)
       intended inferred syntax: #but I don't remember [what Nigel never hunts]

As discussed in 4.8, when the hearer/interpreter hears the intransitive "hunts" in the first conjunct in (60), he accesses the lexical entry for intransitive *hunt*, which in turn activates its natural extension, the lexical entry for transitive *hunt*, which is used in constructing the inferred syntax of the *wh*-fragment *what* in the second conjunct.

The first conjunct of (60) entails 'Nigel never hunts anything' (NOT > ∃), whereas *what* in the second conjunct presupposes 'Nigel never hunts something'(∃ > NOT). The conflict between these two scope relations produces the semantic anomaly in (60), exactly as in (61a).

By contrast, a quantified NP with *a certain*, for example, *a certain animal* in (61b), takes wide scope (Hornstein 1984: 21) and does not produce semantic anomaly.

(61) a. #Nigel never hunts anything, but I don't remember what he never hunts.
   b. Nigel never hunts a certain animal, but I don't remember what.
      scope relations in F/A: [$_{QP}$ *a certain animal*] > [$_{Fp}$ NOT] > [$_{QP}$ ∃ x = TIME]
      syntax inferred from global/local domain: but I don't remember what he never hunts
      syntax inferred by direct reference: but I don't remember what it is
         (*it* refers to *a certain animal*, based on its wide scope interpretation.)

Note that the negative adverb (ADV[NG]) *never* in (61b) is treated semantically as 'not at any time' (Ueno 2014: 73).

The semantic anomaly of (62), in which the *wh*-fragment is a complement PP, can be explained in the same way.

(62) #No one talked, but it's not clear [to whom]. (Merchant 2001: 226 (196d), cited from Albert 1993)

4.10 CLOSE EXAMINATION OF WH-FRAGMENT ISLAND INSENSITIVITY

The first conjunct entails 'No one talked to anyone' (NOT > ∃), whereas *to whom* in the second conjunct presupposes 'No one talked to someone' (∃ > NOT). The conflict between these two scope relations produces semantic anomaly, exactly as in (63a).

(63) a. #No one talked to anyone, but it's not clear to whom.
     b. No one talked to someone, but it's not clear to whom.

By contrast, the semantic anomaly vanishes in (63b) because the interpretation of the first conjunct and the presupposition of the second conjunct match in terms of the scope relations: ∃ > NOT.

In (64), the *wh*-fragment is an adjunct to the noun *novels* in the first conjunct.

(64) adjunct to noun
     #Reggie avoids reading novels, but I don't know what about.
         (Merchant 2001: 226 (196f), cited from Albert 1993)

The first conjunct *Reggie avoids reading novels* entails 'Reggie does not read novels,' whereas *what about* in the second conjunct presupposes 'Reggie avoids reading novels about something,' which in turn entails 'Reggie reads novels.' The two entailments are in direct conflict, resulting in the semantic anomaly of (64). The same semantic anomaly is observed in (65a). On the other hand, no semantic anomaly is observed in (65b).

(65) a. #Reggie does not read novels, but I don't know about what.
     b. Reggie avoids reading certain novels, but I don't know [about what].
        syntax inferred from global domain: but I don't know [about what
          Reggie avoids reading novels __]
        syntax inferred by direct reference: but I don't know [about what they
          are __]
        (*they* refers to *certain novels*, based on its wide scope interpretation.)

The first conjunct of (66a) is usually interpreted in such a way that the existentially quantified NP *a car* is within the negative scope of *rarely* (*rarely* > *a car*). However, the existential presupposition of *whose* in the second conjunct requires that the scope relations in the first conjunct be opposite, namely, *a car* > *rarely*. This conflict results in the semantic anomaly observed in (66a). The same semantic anomaly is also observed in (66b). Furthermore, if we change the indefinite article into *a certain*, then the semantic anomaly vanishes, as in (66c), because *a certain car* has wide scope over *rarely*, and agrees in scope relation with the existential presupposition of *whose*.

(66) possessive *wh*-fragment
    a. #Judy rarely borrows a car, but I can't recall [whose].
          (Merchant 2001: 226 (196i), cited from Albert 1993)
    b. #Judy rarely borrows any car, but I can't recall [whose].
    c. Judy rarely borrows a certain car, but I can't recall [whose].
    d. (context: John likes to borrow and drive his friends' cars.)
        John never borrows a car and I know [whose].

(66d) is acceptable in the context specified, because this context allows the scope relation *a car* > *never*, which agrees with the existential presupposition of *whose*.

Without any prior context, the first conjunct of (67a) is interpreted with the scope relations in which $\exists_{nurse}$ and implicit $\exists_{time}$ are in the scope of NOT. However, *when* in the second conjunct presupposes 'No nurse was on duty at a certain time' with the scope relations $\exists_{time}$ > NOT > $\exists_{nurse}$ (Merchant 2001: 228 (203)). This conflict produces semantic anomaly in (67a), just as in (67b).

(67) implicit time adjunct
    a. #No nurse was on duty, but we don't know when. (Merchant 2001: 227 (197a))
    b. #No nurse was on duty at any time, but we don't know when.
        scope relations: NOT > $\exists_{nurse}$, $\exists_{time}$
    c. (context: A and B know the hospital regulation that at least two nurses are on duty all the time.)
        A: There was a regulation violation yesterday. No nurse was on duty!
        B: Really? When?

If we provide a context that induces the interpretation that $\exists_{time}$ > NOT > $\exists_{nurse}$, as in (67c), the semantic anomaly disappears.

(68a) is usually interpreted as NOT > $\exists$, and semantic anomaly results, just as in (68b), because *how old* in the second conjunct presupposes the existence of *an old boat*. However, if we induce the interpretation of the first conjunct that ∃ > NOT, the semantic anomaly disappears. This is shown in (68c–e).

(68) a. #No one bought an old boat, but I don't know [how old]. (Merchant 2001: 227 (201b))
      scope relations: NOT > *an old boat*
      syntax inferred from global/local domain: *but I don't know [how old no one bought an __ boat] (violation of the LBC)
      syntax inferred by direct reference: #but I don't know [how old it was]
        (*it* cannot refer to *an old boat*, because the latter is in negative scope.)
   b. #No one bought any old boat, but I don't know [how old].
   c. No one bought a certain old boat, but I don't know [how old].
      scope relations: *a certain old boat* > NOT
      syntax inferred by direct reference: but I don't know [how old it was]
        (*it* refers to *a certain old boat*.)
   d. A: Boats were on sale last week and all the boats sold very quickly.
      B: That's not true. No one bought an old boat, but I don't know [how old].
      scope relations: *an old boat* > NOT
      syntax inferred by direct reference: but I don't know [how old it was]
        (*it* refers to *an old boat*.)
   e. (context: People who visit this car dealer are looking for expensive cars.)
      dealer: No customer of ours can buy an expensive car. Guess [how expensive].
      scope relations: *an expensive car* > NOT
      syntax inferred by direct reference: Guess [how expensive it is]
        (*it* refers to *an expensive car*.)

In (68c), the indefinite article is changed into *a certain*, which allows wide scope interpretation over NOT.

4.10.8 Left Branch Constraint

The ungrammatical examples in (69) violate the Left Branch Constraint (LBC) (Ueno 2014: 268) in their inferred syntax. In our AMG terms, they violate the dominance path conditions (Chapter 1 (100)). We claim that the ungrammaticality is also due to the fact that a stand-alone *how* cannot be an interrogative for degree or extent. See the relevant lexical entry for *how* in (71).

(69) extraction of *how* from attributive adjective within NP (Merchant 2001: 165)
    a. *He wants a detailed list, but I don't know [how].
        inferred syntax: *but I don't know [how he wants [$_{\text{NP[DAT]}}$ a [$_{\text{NP}}$ [$_A$ __ detailed] list]]]
        dominance path: *CP[WH[Q]] S[PRES] VP[PRES] NP[DET] NP A ADV[G]
        cf. but I don't know how detailed a list (he wants __)
    b. *She bought an expensive car, but I don't know how.
        inferred syntax: *but I don't know [how she bought [$_{\text{NP[DET]}}$ an [$_{\text{NP}}$ [$_A$ __ expensive] car]]]
        dominance path: *CP[WH[Q]] S[PAST] VP[PAST] NP[DET] NP A ADV[G]
        cf. but I don't know how expensive a car (she bought __)

Interrogative *how* has a wide range of uses. When used as an interrogative of degree or extent, it must be followed by an AP or ADVP ((71a), Merchant 2001: 166), as shown in (70a, b, c, d). Exceptions comprise only a few verbs such as *like*, *enjoy*, or *please*, which allow *how* instead of *how much* (70e) (Huddleston and Pullum 2002: 908).

(70) a. A: John was young.
        B: *How? (intended as a degree interrogative; cf. How young?)
           inferred syntax: *How was John [$_{\text{AP}}$ __ young]? (violation of the syntactic field of (71a))
    b. A: John was a young teacher.
        B: *How? (intended as a degree interrogative)
           inferred syntax: *How was John [$_{\text{NP[DET]}}$ a [$_A$ __ young] teacher]?
        cf. B: How young?
           syntax inferred by direct reference: How young was he [$_{\text{AP}}$ __]?
           (*he* refers to *John*.)
    c. A: John met a young teacher.
        B: *How? (intended as a degree interrogative)

4.10 CLOSE EXAMINATION OF *WH*-FRAGMENT ISLAND INSENSITIVITY

       inferred syntax: *How did John meet [$_{NP[DET]}$ a [$_A$ ___ young] teacher]?
       cf. B: How young?
          syntax inferred by direct reference: How young was he [$_{AP}$ ___]?
          (*he* refers to *a young teacher*.)
  d. A: John took it seriously.
      B: *How? (intended as a degree interrogative)
       inferred syntax: *How did John take it [$_{ADVP}$ ___ seriously]?
       (violation of the syntactic field of (71a))
       cf. How seriously?
          inferred syntax: How seriously did John take it [$_{ADVP}$ ___]?
  e. A: John likes it.
      B: How?

For the sake of concrete discussion, we propose the lexical entry for this use of *how* (71a). (71b, c) are the lexical entries for *how* used as the interrogatives of manner and means, respectively.

(71) a. partial lexical entry for degree/extent interrogative *how*
       syntax: ADV[WH[Q]] in [$_{XP[WH[Q]]}$ ___, XP], where X∈ {A, ADV}
       F/A: [$_{QPx}$ [$_Q$ WH] x = DEGREE], [$_{M\alpha}$ x], where α is a gradable F/A category.
    b. partial lexical entry for manner interrogative *how*
       syntax: ADVP[WH[Q]]
       F/A: [$_{QPx}$ [$_Q$ WH] x = MANNER], [$_{MFa}$ x]
    c. partial lexical entry for means interrogative *how*
       syntax: ADVP[WH[Q]]
       F/A: [$_{QPx}$ [$_Q$ WH] x = MEANS], [$_{MFa}$ x]

In (71a), the syntax of this use of *how* is an interrogative adverb (ADV[WH[Q]]), which is an adjunct of a gradable AP or ADVP, as in [$_{AP[WH[Q]]}$ [$_{ADV[WH[Q]]}$ *how*] [$_{AP}$ *young*]] and [$_{ADVP[WH[Q]]}$ [$_{ADV[WH[Q]]}$ how] [$_{ADVP}$ *quickly*]]. The F/A field of the entry specifies that it is a quantifier QP and its variable ranges over some degree and its corresponding variable is of the F/A category Mα, a modifier of an F/A category α. For example, the syntax and F/A of *How tall is John?* are given in (72) below.

(72) syntax and F/A of *How tall is John?*

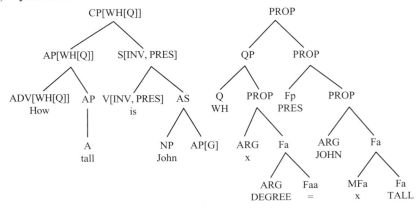

(69a, b) are ungrammatical partly because the intended inferred syntax violates the LBC (i.e., the dominance path conditions) and partly because the interrogative *how* violates its syntactic field requirement in (71a) that it be an adjunct of an AP or ADVP.

In fact, when *how* is used alone clause-initially, it serves as an interrogative of manner adjunct (*in what manner*), means adjunct (*by what means*), or predicative complement (Huddleston and Pullum 2002: 907–908) but never serves as an interrogative of degree/extent.

(73) a. A: How did John speak? (manner adjunct)
B: With a strong French accent.
b. A: How can I remove it? (means adjunct)
B: With a razor-blade.
c. A: How are you feeling? (predicative complement)
B: Fine.
d. A: How do you like your coffee? (predicative complement)
B: With cream and sugar.

Therefore, (69a, b) are acceptable either in manner interpretation or in means interpretation, which is shown below.

(74) a. He wants a detailed list, but I don't know [how]. (= (69a))
inferred syntax: but I don't know [how he [[wants a detailed list] ADVP[G]]]

4.10 CLOSE EXAMINATION OF *WH*-FRAGMENT ISLAND INSENSITIVITY

(VP-adjunct of means)
dominance path: CP[WH[Q]] S[PRES] VP[PRES] ADVP[G]
cf. He wants a detailed list <u>by applying for it</u>. (VP-adjunct of means)
b. He wants a detailed list, but I don't know [how]. (= (69a))
inferred syntax: but I don't know [how he [wants a detailed list AP[G]]]
(predicative complement)
dominance path: CP[WH[Q]] S[PRES] VP[PRES] AP[G]
cf. He wants it <u>printed on paper</u>. (predicative complement)
c. She bought an expensive car, but I don't know [how]. (= (69b))
inferred syntax: but I don't know [how she [[bought an expensive car] ADVP[G]]]
(VP-adjunct of means or manner)
dominance path: CP[WH[Q]] S[PAST] VP[PAST] ADV[G]
cf. She bought an expensive car <u>in cash</u>. (VP-adjunct of means or manner)

Recall that the interpretive hypotheses of an utterance are constructed in order of accessibility, according to the Relevance-guided comprehension heuristic (Chapter 2 (8)). If you compare the inferred syntax of the degree *how* in (69) and that of the manner/means *how* in (74), the ad-VP interpretations in (74) are more accessible than the degree interpretations in (69), because of the structural proximity between *how* and the target gap position in the inferred syntax (the gap adjoined to the matrix VP as opposed to the gap within the object NP in (69)).

The interrogative *how* in (75) is intended as an interrogative of degree. The *wh*-fragments are interpreted through their syntax inferred by direct reference.

(75) (Merchant 2001: 167)
a. He wants a detailed list, but I don't know [how detailed].
syntax inferred by direct reference: but I don't know [how detailed it should be]
(*it* refers to *a detailed list* in the antecedent; modal subordination.)
b. She bought an expensive car, but I don't know [how expensive].
syntax inferred by direct reference: but I don't know [how expensive it was]
(*it* refers to *an expensive car* in the antecedent.)

In (75a, b), an existentially quantified NP (*a detailed list* and *an expensive car*), whose F/A is roughly [$_{\text{QPx}}$ [$_\text{Q}$ ∃] PROP] (Ueno 2014: 32), is referred to by the definite pronoun *it*. See McCawley 1993a: 355–358 on how this is achieved. Recall that a syntactic structure inferred by direct reference is of the form *wh*-phrase + pronoun + *be*, in which the pronoun refers to the most salient entity (topic or focus) in the antecedent.

Merchant (2001) observed the following contrast.

(76) a. *He wants a list, but I don't know [how detailed]. (Merchant 2001: 174)
 inferred syntax: but I don't know [how detailed it should be]
 (*it* refers to *a list*; with modal subordination.)
 b. He wants a detailed list, but I don't know [how detailed]. (Merchant 2001: 167)
 inferred syntax: but I don't know [how detailed it should be]
 (*it* refers to *a detailed list*; with modal subordination.)

(77) a. *She bought a car, but I don't know [how {expensive | fast}]. (Merchant 2001: 174)
 inferred syntax: but I don't know [how {expensive | fast} it was]
 (*it* refers to *a car*.)
 b. She bought a(n) {expensive | fast} car, but I don't know [how {expensive | fast}]. (Merchant 2001: 167)
 inferred syntax: but I don't know [how {expensive | fast}) it was]
 (*it* refers to *a(n) {expensive | fast} car*.)

What seems to be at issue here is the degree to which the adjective (*detailed* in (76a) and *{expensive | fast}* in (77a)) is accessible to the hearer/interpreter (i.e., in Merchant's "given"). (76a) and (77a) improve in acceptability if we provide a context in which the adjectives in question are sufficiently primed.

(78) a. I know he needs all the information about the applicants. He says he wants a list, but I don't know [how detailed].
 syntax inferred by direct reference: but I don't know [how detailed it should be]
 (*it* refers to *a list* in the antecedent; with modal subordination.)
 (based on the knowledge that he needs all the information)

b. She bought a racing car, but I don't know [how fast].
   syntax inferred by direct reference: but I don't know [how fast it was]
   (*it* refers to *a racing car* in the antecedent.)
   (based on the knowledge that a racing car runs fast)
c. Speaking of big-ticket items, she bought a car, but I don't know [how expensive].
   syntax inferred by direct reference: but I don't know [how expensive it was]
   (*it* refers to *a car* in the antecedent.)
   (based on the knowledge that a car is a big-ticket item)

Therefore, we claim that the nature of the unacceptability of (76a) and (77a) is not grammatical but pragmatic. Compare less acceptable (79a) without priming and more acceptable (79b, c, d) with priming.

(79) a. A: Mary bought a car.
        B: {??How expensive? | ??Yeah, very expensive.}
     b. A: Mary bought an expensive car.
        B: {How expensive? | Yeah, very expensive.}
     c. A: Mary bought a Rolls-Royce.
        B: {How expensive? | Yeah, very expensive.}
     d. A: Because Mary wanted to {buy a big-ticket item | spend money lavishly}, she bought a car.
        B: {How expensive? | Yeah, very expensive.}

Merchant (2001) observed that the following *wh*-fragments are unacceptable. In each example, the inferred syntax from the global and local domains is ungrammatical, because of its LBC violation (or in AMG terms, because of its violation of the dominance path conditions).

(80) (Merchant 2001: 175)
     a. *She'll be angry if he buys <u>an expensive car</u>, but I don't know [how expensive].
        syntax inferred from global domain: *but I don't know [how expensive she'll be angry if he buys a ___ car]

syntax inferred from local domain: *but I don't know [how expensive he buys a __ car]

syntax inferred by direct reference: but I don't know [how expensive it should be __]

(*it* refers to *an expensive car*.)

b. *He got stressed because his boss wants <u>a detailed list</u>, but I don't know [how detailed].

syntax inferred from global domain: *but I don't know [how detailed he got stressed because his boss wants a __ list]

syntax inferred from local domain: *but I don't know how detailed [his boss wants a __ list]

syntax inferred by direct reference: but I don't know how detailed [it should be __]

(*it* refers to *a detailed list*.)

c. *She met a guy who bought <u>a big car</u>, but I don't know [how big].

syntax inferred from global domain: *but I don't know [how big she met a guy who bought a __ car]

syntax inferred from local domain: *but I don't know [how big he bought a __ car]

(*he* refers to *a guy who bought a big car*.)

syntax inferred by direct reference: but I don't know [how big it was __]

(*it* refers to *a big car*.)

Although the syntax of each example that is inferred by direct reference is grammatical, each example remains unacceptable. This is due to the requirement that *it* or *they* inferred by direct reference refer to the most salient NP in the prior discourse, in other words, that *wh*-fragments be about the most salient entity in the preceding context. There are two reasons for the low saliency of the antecedent NPs (underlined) in the above examples. First, an NP in the matrix clause is likely to be perceived as more salient than an NP in the subordinate clause. This point is illustrated in (81).

(81) a. Mary will be angry if John is careless, but I don't know [how {angry | #careless}].

inferred syntax: but I don't know how angry she will be

#but I don't know how careless he will be

4.10 CLOSE EXAMINATION OF *WH*-FRAGMENT ISLAND INSENSITIVITY 191

b. Mary was stressed because John was careless, but I don't know [how {stressed | #careless}].
  inferred syntax: but I don't know how stressed she was
      #but I don't know how careless he was
c. I met an old man who knew a young girl, but I don't know [how {old | #young}].
  inferred syntax: but I don't know how old he was
      #but I don't know how young she was

Second, the low saliency of the underlined NPs in (80) is also because the wide scope interpretation of these NPs is hard to come by. If we add *certain* to the underlined NPs and make them capable of wide scope interpretation (Hornstein 1984: 21, 27, Chung et al. 1995: 276), their saliency increases and the sentences improve in acceptability. This is shown in (82).

(82) a. ?She'll be angry if he buys a certain expensive car, and I don't know [how expensive].
  b. ?He got stressed because his boss wants a certain detailed list, but I don't know [how detailed].
  c. ?She met a guy who bought a certain big car, and I don't know [how big].

The following are examples in which syntactic structures inferred by direct reference do not work. Therefore, their interpretation is constructed from their syntax inferred from the global or local domain.

(83) (Merchant 2001: 181)
  a. He was short of funds, but I didn't know [how badly].
    syntax inferred by direct reference: *but I don't know [$_{\text{ADVP[WH[Q]]}}$ how badly] he was ADVP[G]]
    syntax inferred from global/local domain: but I don't know [how badly he was [$_{\text{AP}}$ ADVP[G] short of funds]
      cf. How badly was he ___ short of funds?
  b. These drugs are obtainable, but I don't want you to hear [how easily].
    syntax inferred by direct reference: *but I don't want you to hear [how easily they are ___]

192   4 AN AUTOMODULAR VIEW OF SLUICING

syntax inferred from global/local domain: but I don't want you to hear [how easily these drugs are __ obtainable]
cf. How easily are these drugs __ obtainable?
c. She was prepared—guess [how well]!
syntax inferred by direct reference: *guess [how well she was __]
syntax inferred from global/local domain: guess [how well she was __ prepared]
cf. How well was she __ prepared?

Here are the syntax and F/A of *how badly he was short of funds* in the inferred syntax of (83a). The lexical entry for the degree interrogative *how* (71a) is satisfied in (84).

(84) syntax and F/A of *how badly he was short of funds* in the inferred syntax of (83a)

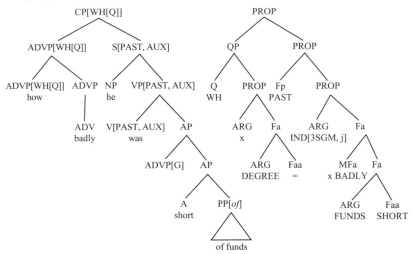

The following are examples in which all the inferred syntactic structures fail, resulting in ungrammaticality.

(85) (Merchant 2001: 181)
a. *She met a guy badly short of funds, but I didn't know [how badly].
syntax inferred by direct reference: *but I didn't know [how badly he was __]

(*he* refers to *a guy badly short of funds*.)
syntax inferred from global/local domain: *but I don't know [how badly she met a guy __ short of funds] (violation of the dominance path conditions)
cf. *How badly did she meet a guy __ short of funds?

b. *He takes easily obtainable drugs, but I don't want you to hear [how easily].
syntax inferred by direct reference: *but I don't want you to hear [how easily they are]
(*they* refers to *easily obtainable drugs*.)
syntax inferred from global/local domain: *but I don't want you to hear [how easily he takes __ obtainable drugs] (violation of the dominance path conditions)
cf. *How easily does he take __ obtainable drugs?

c. *They examined a well-prepared student—guess [how well]!
syntax inferred by direct reference: *guess [how well she was __]
(*she* refers to *a well-prepared student*.)
syntax inferred from global/local domain: *guess [how well they examined a __ prepared student] (violation of the dominance path conditions)
cf. *How well did they examine a __ prepared student?

In each of the examples in (85), the syntax inferred by direct reference is ungrammatical, because the category of the *wh*-phrase is ADVP[WH[Q]], the dominance path conditions force a gap of the category ADVP[G] as the bottom part of the dominance path, and this category cannot be a complement of the *be* verb. On the other hand, the syntax inferred from the global/local domain is ungrammatical because of its violation of the LBC, namely, violation of the dominance path conditions.

Our conclusion about the LBC is that when there are no effects of LBC violation in the interpretation of *wh*-fragments, (75) and (78) for example, this is due to the existence of syntactic structures inferred by direct reference.

4.11 A'-traces Under Sluicing

Every *wh*-question has an existential presupposition in which its *wh*-phrase corresponds to an existentially quantified NP. This existentially quantified NP can be later referred to by a definite pronoun, as in *What* did they do and why did they *do it?*, where *it* refers to *something* in the existential presupposition 'They did something' of the *wh*-question "What did they do?" (Ueno 2014: 291). In the following examples, the interpretation of a *wh*-fragment is recovered through the existential presupposition of the preceding *wh*-question.

(86) (Merchant 2001: 201–202)
    a.   The report details what IBM did and [why].
          syntax inferred from local domain: and [why IBM did it]
              (*it* refers to *something* in the presupposition 'IBM did something' of the first conjunct.)
    b.   Who did the suspect call and [when]?
          syntax inferred from local domain: and [when did the suspect call him]
              (*him* refers to *someone* in the presupposition 'The suspect called someone' of the first conjunct.)
    c.   We need to know who saw what, and [when].
          syntax inferred from local domain: and [when he saw it]
              (*he* and *it* refer respectively to *someone* and *something* in the presupposition 'Someone saw something' of the first conjunct.)

(87) (Merchant 2001: 202)
    a.   The suspect phoned everyone on this list, but we don't know [when].
          syntax inferred from local domain: but we don't know [when the suspect phoned them]
              (*them* (E-type pronoun (Evans 1980: 339)) refers to the set of people on this list.)
    b.   Every boy scout helped, though most didn't know [why]. (ambiguous)
          syntax inferred from local domain: though most boy scouts didn't know [why they helped]
              (*they* refers to the set of boy scouts who helped or to the set of people referred to by *most* ("rebinding" in Merchant 2001: 214), a subset of the above set.)

Chapter 5
An Automodular View of VP Ellipsis

> In this chapter, we will discuss various phenomena related to what has been called "VP ellipsis" and claim that they are best explained by categorizing VP ellipsis as auxiliary verbs that are used as pro-VP forms, as in (13). That is, each auxiliary verb "left behind after VP deletion" will be treated as an anaphoric device (AD).

5.1 VP Gap Analysis of VP Ellipsis

VP ellipsis, which is illustrated in (1a, b), has been treated in at least three ways: (i) as being derived by deletion transformation, (ii) as being a phonologically null VP gap (i.e., VP[G]) in syntax, or (iii) as being a pro-VP form that refers to its antecedent VP. In this chapter, we will explore option (iii).

(1) a. If Tom owns a Mercedes, Susan does too. (McCawley 1998: 30)
    b. John can't speak Japanese but Mary can.

According to option (i), the VP deletion transformation is applied to *John can't speak Japanese but Mary can speak Japanese*, deletes the non-finite VP *speak Japanese* of the finite VP of the second conjunct, and reduces the whole finite VP to the auxiliary verb *can* alone, as in (1b). As discussed in Chapter 1, the syntax module of AMG is a nonderivational mono-stratal syntax, and as such it has no transformation (movement or deletion or insertion). Hence, we cannot select option (i).

According to option (ii), the syntactic structure of *can* in (1b) is [$_\text{VP[PRES, AUX]}$ can [$_\text{VP[G]}$ ø]] and the VP gap ø is interpreted appropriately. If we take option (ii) and treat a VP ellipsis site as a phonologically null VP gap ([$_\text{VP[G]}$ ø]) in syntax, its lexical entry will have no value for the morphophonological field, but it must be given a distinct role to play in syntax, since otherwise the subcategorization requirement of the remaining auxiliary verb (*does* in (1a) and *can* in (1b)) will not be satisfied. The syntax of a VP gap, then, is a VP[G] that bears the nonfinite VFORM value that is required by the preceding/head auxiliary verb. For example, the syntactic category of the VP gap in (1a) is VP[BSE, G] because the finite auxiliary *does* takes a VP[BSE] complement (Ueno 2014: 51). However, the difficulties with this VP gap analysis are (I) that the syntactic category of the relevant gap is not always VP (McCawley 1993a: 581 note 2, McCawley 1998: 208, 214 note 27, Sadock 2012: 187, Akmajian and Wasow 1975, Baltin 1995), as illustrated in (2) and (3a), and furthermore (II) that what is supposed to be a VP gap is not always a syntactic constituent, as illustrated in (3b) and (4).

(2) *be* verb
   a. Mary will be a genius and John will be [$_\text{NP[G]}$ ø] too.
   b. Mary will be tall and John will be [$_\text{AP[G]}$ ø] too.
   c. Mary has been to Tokyo and John has been [$_\text{PP[G]}$ ø] too.

In (3b), *have* takes two complements, just like *keep* and *store*: an NP object that denotes a thing with theme role and a locative PP complement that denotes the location of the theme NP. The syntactic field of the lexical entry for this use of *have* is V[AUX] in [__, NP, PP].

(3) possessive *have* (as auxiliary verb)
   a. I haven't a clue and my wife hasn't [$_\text{NP[G]}$ ø] either. (Sadock 2012: 188)
   b. Have you a car here? If you haven't [$_\text{NP[G]}$ ø] [$_\text{PP[G]}$ ø], I have [$_\text{NP[G]}$ ø] [$_\text{PP[G]}$ ø]. (ibid.)

In the *there* construction such as (4), the VP headed by the *be* verb has a ternary branching VP structure with two complements: a theme NP and a locative PP (Ueno 2014: 75–6, McCawley 1998: 95, 635, Sadock 2012: 65, Pollard and Sag 1994: 147, Sag et al. 2003: 336, and Huddleston and Pullum 2002: 1393–5).

(4) existential *there*
They said that there [were [$_{NP}$ no errors] [$_{PP}$ in the proof]] but it turned out that there were [$_{NP[G]}$ ∅] [$_{PP[G]}$ ∅].

In these cases, (i.e., the possessive *have* and the *there* construction), the VP ellipsis site consists of two gaps, NP[G] and PP[G], that do not form a syntactic constituent. This means that we would need to add a special requirement that only under these circumstances do the two gaps occur together side by side, and that by doing so, we need to prevent an NP[G] alone or a PP[G] alone from occurring. To make matters even worse, (III) we need to explain why phonologically null VPs cannot be coordinated with overt VPs. This is illustrated in (5a).

(5) a. *John can't speak Japanese, but Mary can and read it too.
   intended VP structure: [$_{VP[AUX, PRES]}$ can [[$_{VP[G, BSE]}$ ∅] and [$_{VP[BSE]}$ read it too]]]
   ([$_{VP[G, BSE]}$ ∅] is interpreted as *speak Japanese*)
a'. John can't speak Japanese, but Mary can and reads it too.
   [$_{VP[AUX, PRES]}$ can [$_{VP[G, BSE]}$ ∅]] and [$_{VP[PRES]}$ reads it too]]
b. John can't speak Japanese, but Mary can [$_{VP[BSE]}$ speak it] and [$_{VP[BSE]}$ read it too].

To avoid problems (I), (II), and (III), we take option (iii) and treat the auxiliary verb left behind by VP ellipsis (for example, *does* in (1a) and *can* in (1b)) as a pro-VP form. (See Schachter 1978 and Napoli 1985 for similar treatments of VP ellipsis as pro-VP forms.) This option is further supported by the striking similarities between pro-VP forms and pronouns (i.e., pro-NP forms), which will be taken up in 5.3.

5.2 Pro-VP Form Analysis of VP Ellipsis

In (1a, b), *does* and *can* are pro-VP forms that are interpreted as 'owns a Mercedes' and 'can speak Japanese,' respectively. The syntax and F/A of *Susan does* in (1a) and *Mary can* in (1b) are given below in (6) and (7).

(6) syntax and F/A of *Susan does* in (1a)

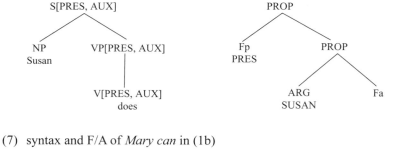

(7) syntax and F/A of *Mary can* in (1b)

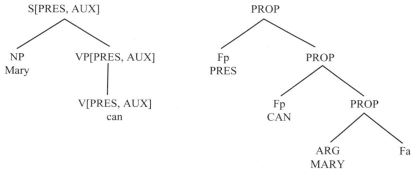

In (6), although the syntax of *Susan does* is complete, its F/A is incomplete because the Fa is not filled. However, this utterance is not treated as ungrammatical or gibberish, because it is part of ostensive-inferential communication and is guaranteed to be worth processing by the Communicative Principle of Relevance (Chapter 2 (6)). Therefore, non-demonstrative inference is triggered by this principle, on the one hand, and by the unfilled Fa, on the other. The hearer/interpreter seeks the most accessible VP that is contextually appropriate, serves as the antecedent of the pro-VP form *does*, and provides a value for the unfilled Fa. As a result, the inferred syntax of *does* turns out to be [$_{VP[PRES]}$ *owns a Mercedes*].

The same is true of (7). Although the syntax of *Mary can* is complete, its F/A is incomplete because the Fa is not filled. However, this utterance is not treated as ungrammatical or gibberish, because this is part of ostensive-inferential communication and is guaranteed to be worth processing by the Communicative Principle of Relevance. Therefore, non-demonstrative inference is triggered by this principle, on the one hand, and by the unfilled Fa, on the other. The hearer/

interpreter seeks the most accessible VP that is contextually appropriate, serves as the antecedent of the pro-VP form *can*, and provides a value for the unfilled Fa. As a result, the inferred syntax of *can* turns out to be [$_{\text{VP[PRES]}}$ *can speak Japanese*].

A pro-VP form is always interpreted as a VP that is headed by the same auxiliary verb as the pro-VP form itself together with its complement, which is inferred from the linguistic and nonlinguistic context. For example, the pro-VP form *can* in (1b) is interpreted as 'can speak Japanese,' a VP headed by the same auxiliary verb. As for the dummy *do*, *does*, and *did*, following Ueno (2014: 61, 69), we take [$_{\text{VP[PRES, AGR[3SG]]}}$ *speaks Japanese*] and [$_{\text{VP[PRES, AUX, AGR[3SG]]}}$ *does* [$_{\text{VP[BSE]}}$ *speak Japanese*]] as equivalent, because they share the same F/A and E/R. The latter is pressed into service only when the presence of an auxiliary verb is required, for example, for negation (*not [*speaks Japanese*] vs. *does* [*not* [*speak Japanese*]]) or for positive polarity emphasis (*Mary* [**DOES** [*speak Japanese*]]). Otherwise, the phonologically shorter, syntactically simpler form *speaks Japanese* is chosen over the phonologically longer, syntactically more complex form *does speak Japanese*, due to the economy of language use (Ueno 2014: 61), which says that when two expressions express the same information and compete for the same syntactic environment, the simpler expression must be chosen unless there is a special reason for choosing the more complex one.

We define the antecedent of a pro-VP form as the smallest VP that is used to determine the interpretation of the pro-VP form in question. In (1a), the VP *owns a Mercedes* is the antecedent of the pro-VP form *does*. In (1b), the VP *speak Japanese* is the antecedent of the pro-VP form *can*. Two more examples of pro-VP forms are given in (8) following.

(8) A: Which is better qualified as manager of our Tokyo office, Mary or John?
   B: Mary speaks Japanese but John <u>can't</u>.
   inferred VP: *can't speak Japanese*
   explicature: 'B asserts that Mary speaks Japanese but John can't speak Japanese.'
   implicatures: 'B thinks that John is not qualified as manager of their Tokyo office.'
   'B thinks that Mary is better qualified than John for the job.'

(9) A: Everyone must wipe their mouth with a napkin after meals.
   B: Bill has [$_{\text{NP}}$ food] [$_{\text{PP}}$ on his face] and John <u>has</u> too.
   inferred VP: *has food on his face* (sloppy identity reading of *his*)

explicature: 'B asserts that Bill has food on his face and John has food on his face too.'
implicature: 'B thinks that both Bill and John did not wipe their mouth after the meal they had just now.'
'B thinks that both Bill and John must wipe their mouth now.'

(10) syntax and F/A of *John has* in (9)

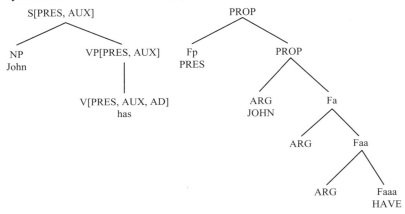

In (9), the sloppy identity reading of *his* is chosen over the strict identity reading 'John has food on Bill's face.' This is primarily because the first conjunct is interpreted as the propositional function *P(Bill)*, where $P(x) = x$ *has food on x's face*. This choice is made pragmatically, because the strict identity interpretation is odd. Note that although the syntax of (10) is complete, the corresponding F/A is not, because there are two unfilled ARGs in the F/A of (10), whose values must be determined by inference. Note that the feature AD (anaphoric device) is added to the syntactic category of the pro-VP form *has*.

It was concluded in Sadock (2012: 177–178) and Ueno (2014: 64) that all auxiliary verbs (V[AUX]), including contracted forms such as *hasn't* and *won't*, are registered in the lexicon. They can also be used as pro-VP forms. Later, we will capture the relationships between the lexical entry for an auxiliary verb (V[AUX]) and that for its corresponding pro-VP form by means of the Pro-VP Form Lexical Rule in (43). According to Merchant (2001: 3), the majority of the world's languages lack VP ellipsis. From our perspective, this means that the majority of the world's languages lack pro-VP forms in their lexicon. This is primarily due to the lack of the AUX feature in their verb feature system (Ueno 2014: 49).

What the hearer/interpreter needs to do to interpret a pro-VP form is to follow something similar to the comprehension procedure for fragments, as discussed in Chapters 2, 3, and 4, and inferentially construct the intended interpretation of the pro-VP form. Following the previous chapters, we assume that the Language Module (LM) is one of the input systems and that it is equipped with the current version of Automodular Grammar (AMG). The LM decodes an utterance U on the basis of the information of the lexical items in U, and computes the decoded syntax, F/A, E/R, and IS of U. We called the ordered set (decoded syntax, decoded F/A, decoded E/R, decoded IS) of U the decoded four-tuple of U. This decoded four-tuple of U is in turn input to the Inferential Comprehension Module (ICM), another module in which non-demonstrative inference is performed on the decoded four-tuple of U, the inferred four-tuple of U is constructed if the decoded four-tuple has missing parts, and its interpretive hypotheses are inferentially constructed through development (e.g., disambiguation, referent assignment, and enrichment) (Chapter 2 (9)). This process is guided by the Relevance-guided comprehension heuristic (Chapter 2 (8)). The final output of the ICM is the explicatures and implicatures of utterances (expressed in Mentalese). This whole process was shown in Chapter 3 (5b, c), repeated here as (11).

(11) a. Utterance comprehension process in the case of fragment utterance
fragment utterance U → ⎡LM⎤ → decoded four-tuple of U → ⎡ICM⎤ → inferred four-tuple of U → explicatures and implicatures of U (in Mentalese)
b. Procedure for fragment comprehension
The hearer follows the Relevance-guided comprehension heuristic and executes the following steps.
(i) The LM computes the decoded four-tuple of a fragment utterance U.
(ii) By non-demonstrative inference, the ICM constructs the inferred syntactic structure of U on the basis of the decoded syntax obtained in (i) and the contextual information.
(iii) The ICM constructs the inferred four-tuple of U on the basis of the inferred syntax obtained in (ii) and the contextual information.
(iv) The ICM develops the inferred four-tuple of U obtained in (iii) on the basis of the contextual information.
(v) The ICM constructs the explicatures and implicatures of U on the basis of the developed four-tuple obtained in (iv) and the contextual information.

In the case of an utterance U that contains a pro-VP form, the LM first computes the decoded four-tuple of U, whose F/A contains an unfilled Fa, as in (6) and (7) or unfilled ARGs, as in (10). The decoded four-tuple of U is, then, input to the ICM, as shown in (11a). The ICM first constructs the inferred four-tuple of U (consisting of the inferred syntax, F/A, E/R, and IS of U). In the inferred syntax of U, a full VP appears in place of the pro-VP form in U, and at the same time, the unfilled Fa and ARGs in the decoded F/A are now filled by those in the inferred VP. The inferred four-tuple of U is constructed based on the decoded four-tuple of U, default correspondences between the linguistic modules, and the contextual information. The ICM then constructs the explicatures and implicatures of U on the basis of the set of contextual assumptions through non-demonstrative inference including development of the inferred four-tuple of U. The final output of the ICM is, of course, the explicatures and implicatures (expressed in Mentalese) of the utterance U. This process is the same as that of fragment interpretation in (11a).

(12) utterance U that contains pro-VP forms → $\boxed{\text{LM}}$ → decoded four-tuple of U → $\boxed{\text{ICM}}$ → inferred four-tuple of U → explicatures and implicatures of U (in Mentalese)

More specifically, we assume the following comprehension procedure for pro-VP forms.

(13) Procedure for pro-VP form comprehension
The hearer follows the Relevance-guided comprehension heuristic and executes the following steps.
   (i) The LM computes the decoded four-tuple of an utterance U that contains pro-VP forms.
   (ii) By non-demonstrative inference, the ICM (iia) finds potential antecedents of the pro-VP forms in the linguistic and/or non-linguistic context and (iib) constructs the inferred syntactic structure of U that includes inferred VPs on the basis of the decoded syntax obtained in (i) and the contextual information.
   (iii) The ICM constructs the inferred four-tuple of U on the basis of the decoded four-tuple obtained in (i), the inferred syntax obtained in (ii), and the contextual information.
   (iv) The ICM develops the inferred four-tuple of U obtained in (iii) on the basis of the contextual information.

(v) The ICM constructs the explicatures and implicatures of U on the basis of the developed four-tuple obtained in (iv) and the contextual information.

The steps in (13) are illustrated in (14) and (15).

(14) a. *Susan* [$_{\text{VP[PRES, AUX]}}$ *does*] in (1a) →
    (i) decoded four-tuple of *Susan does*
    (iia) antecedent: *owns a Mercedes*
    (iib) inferred VP: [$_{\text{VP[PRES, AUX]}}$ *owns a Mercedes*]
    (iii) inferred four-tuple of *Susan does*: *Susan owns a Mercedes*
    (iv) development: enrichment (*now*) and assumption schema embedding (*I believe*)
    (v) explicature: 'This speaker believes that if Tom owns a Mercedes now, Susan owns a Mercedes now too.'
       implicature: 'This speaker believes that Susan is at least as rich as Tom.'

b. *Mary* [$_{\text{VP[PRES, AUX]}}$ *can*] in (1b) →
    (i) decoded four-tuple of *Mary can*
    (iia) antecedent: *speak Japanese*
    (iib) inferred VP: [$_{\text{VP[PRES, AUX]}}$ *can speak Japanese*]
    (iii) inferred four-tuple of *Mary can*: *Mary can speak Japanese*
    (iv) development: enrichment (*fluently*) and assumption schema embedding (*This speaker knows*)
    (v) explicature: 'This speaker knows that John cannot speak Japanese but Mary can speak Japanese fluently.'
       implicature: 'This speaker thinks that Mary knows a lot more about Japan than John does.'

In (15) below, the two pro-VP forms (*hasn't* and *will*) have the same VP as their antecedent (*protects our families*) and each is interpreted as the VP that is headed by the respective auxiliary verb with its complement, which is inferred from the antecedent *protects our families*.

(15) a. We need a president who protects our families. This president hasn't, but I will.
    (by Mitt Romney during his 2012 presidential campaign supporting the NRA)

b. *This president* [$_{\text{VP[PRES, AUX]}}$ *hasn't*] →
    decoded four-tuple of *This president hasn't*

antecedent: *protects our families*
inferred VP: [$_{\text{VP[PRES, AUX]}}$ *hasn't protected our families*]
inferred four-tuple of *This president hasn't protected our families*
explicature: 'Romney claims that Obama hasn't protected our families.'
implicature: 'Romney claims that Obama should not be reelected.'

c. *I* [$_{\text{VP[PRES, AUX]}}$ *will*] →
decoded four-tuple of *I will*
antecedent: *protects our families*
inferred VP: [$_{\text{VP[PRES, AUX]}}$ *will protect our families*]
inferred four-tuple of *I will protect our families*
explicature: 'Romney promises to protect our families.'
implicature: 'Romney claims that he should be elected.'

Note that in the step of constructing an inferred VP, we need to add minor changes to the antecedent VP (*protects our families*) including the form (VFORM value) of the verb and the vehicle changes (Fiengo and May 1994) of nominal expressions to obtain a contextually appropriate inferred VP. Simply copying the antecedent VP is not sufficient.

The reason why the step of constructing an inferred VP must precede the step of constructing an inferred four-tuple in (13), that is, why the syntactic structure of an inferred VP must be determined before its corresponding semantic structures in F/A and E/R are determined, is that some VP idioms, what Nunberg et al. (1994: 496) called idiomatically combining expressions (ICE), allow VP ellipsis in the active and passive. (See Ueno 2014: 126ff. for ICE idioms and their passives.)

(16) a. My goose is cooked, but yours isn't. (Nunberg et al. 1994: 501)
b. They claim that the beans were spilled by accident, and they really were.

To interpret the second conjunct *yours isn't* of (16a) as an idiom, we first need to determine syntactically that *yours* represents *your goose* and the pro-VP form *isn't* represents *isn't cooked*, and therefore the inferred syntax of the second conjunct is *your goose isn't cooked*, namely, the passive form of the VP idiom *cook NP's goose*. Without inferring this syntactic structure first, the intended idiomatic interpretation is irrecoverable, because [$_{\text{NP}}$ *your goose*] and [$_{\text{VP}}$ *isn't cooked*] are both needed for it to qualify as the passive form of the VP idiom in question. The situation is the same in (16b). To interpret its second conjunct *they really were* as an idiom, we need to determine syntactically that the pronoun *they* represents *the beans* and the pro-VP form *were* represents *were spilled by accident*, and therefore the inferred syntax of the second conjunct is *the beans really were spilled by accident*, namely, the passive form of the VP idiom *spill the beans*. See the lexical entry for this idiom in Ueno (2014: 128).

The second reason for determining the inferred VP in syntax before determining the corresponding parts in F/A and E/R is that although the VP inferred from a pro-VP form is always a syntactic constituent, namely, VP[AUX], its correspondent in F/A is not an F/A constituent. For example, in (1b), the VP inferred from the pro-VP form *can* is *can speak Japanese*, but this VP[AUX] does not correspond to a constituent in F/A. The F/A structure of the second conjunct *Mary can* of (1b) is shown below, in which the pro-VP form *can* corresponds to [$_{PROP}$ [$_{Fp}$ PRES] [[$_{Fp}$ CAN] [$_{PROP}$ [$_{ARG}$] Fa]]] excluding the subject ARG. Both a pro-VP form and its inferred VP are always constituents in syntax but never so in F/A.

(17) syntax and F/A of *Mary can* in (1b)

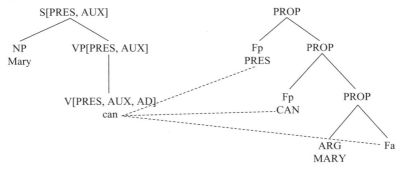

The dummy *do* (Ueno 2014: 51) is also used as a pro-VP form, as illustrated previously in (1a).

(18) a. John plays the piano and Mary <u>does</u> too.
   Mary does →
   decoded four-tuple of *Mary does*
   antecedent: *plays the piano*
   inferred VP: [$_{VP[PRES]}$ *plays the piano*]
   inferred four-tuple of *Mary plays the piano*
   explicature: 'This speaker asserts that Mary plays the piano.'

b. John DOESN'T play the piano but Mary DOES.
Mary DOES →
decoded four-tuple of *Mary does*
antecedent: *play the piano*
inferred VP: [$_{\text{VP[PRES, AUX]}}$ *does play the piano*]
inferred four-tuple of *Mary does play the piano*
explicature: 'This speaker asserts emphatically that Mary plays the piano.'

In (18a), the inferred VP can be either *plays the piano*, as shown above, or *does play the piano*. Although the latter is a regular inferred VP in that it is headed by the same auxiliary verb as the pro-VP form *does*, the former is chosen as the inferred VP, due to the economy of language use. In (18b), by contrast, the more complex *does play the piano* is chosen as the inferred VP, because *does* carries stress and therefore emphasizes the positive polarity of the second conjunct.

McCawley (1998: 217) pointed out that VP ellipsis cannot "delete" a VP with a tense. This is illustrated in (19b) and is explained by the simple fact that there is no pro-VP form left if the whole finite VP is "deleted."

(19) a. If Tom owns a Mercedes, Susan does too. (= (1a))
     b. *If Tom owns a Mercedes, Susan too. (McCawley 1998: 30)
     c. Tom owns a Mercedes, and Susan too.

Note that (19c) is not an instance of VP ellipsis but an instance of stripping (to be discussed in 6.8), whose occurrence is restricted to two-term coordinate structures (McCawley 1998: 31).

As for step (iib) in (13) of inferring a VP that is appropriate for the pro-VP form in question, there are cases of split antecedents in which no single VP in the preceding linguistic context is sufficient for determining the inferred VP of a pro-VP form and the relevant information is spread across the prior discourse. In such cases, the hearer/interpreter needs to collect the relevant pieces of information and integrate them into a single coherent inferred VP. (20) provides such examples.

(20) (context: students A, B, and C are talking to student D. They are all taking the same class.)
     A: Have you read the article for today's class?
        D's set of potential antecedents = {..., *read the article*}

B: And have you finished the assignment too?
   D's set of potential antecedents = {..., *read the article, finish the assignment*}
C: Have you brought the textbook?
   D's set of potential antecedents = {..., *read the article, finish the assignment, bring the textbook*}
D: Of course, I have. Is there anything else I have to do for today's class?
   I have →
   decoded four-tuple of *I have*
   antecedents: *read the article, finish the assignment, bring the textbook*
   inferred VP: [$_{\text{VP[PRES, AUX]}}$ *have read the article, finished the assignment, and brought the textbook*]
   inferred four-tuple of *I have read the article, finished the assignment, and brought the textbook*
   explicature: 'D asserts that he has read the article, finished the assignment, and brought the textbook for today's class.'
   implicature: 'D believes that he has done everything for today's class.'

In (20), the inferred VP for the pro-VP form *have* in D contains a coordination of three VPs. However, there is no single sentence or sentence fragment in the preceding discourse that contains all the information regarding what the pro-VP form purports to refer to. Each of the preceding VPs contributes relevant information to the pro-VP form. (21a) is a similar example.

(21) a. (context: Students A and B are talking about the reading assignment for Jim's *Syntax 1* class right before it starts.)
   A: Have you read Chapter 2?
   B: Did I have to?   [VP ellipsis]
   A: You should have finished the homework, too. It's due today.
   B: Really!?
   A: Jim told us yesterday.   [null complement anaphora]
      Don't you remember?   [null complement anaphora]
   B: No. I completely forgot I had to. [VP ellipsis]
   b. successive and cumulative online inference processes
      A: Have you read Chapter 2?
         B's set of potential antecedents = {..., *read Chapter 2*}

B: Did I have to?   [VP ellipsis]
     have to →
         decoded four-tuple of *Did I have to?*
         antecedent: *read Chapter 2*
         inferred VP: *have to read Chapter 2*
         inferred four-tuple of *Did I have to read Chapter 2?*
         explicature: 'B asks A whether B had to read Chapter 2 of the textbook for today's Jim's Syntax 1 class.' (after enrichment)
         implicature: 'B forgot to read Chapter 2 of the textbook for today's class.'
A: You should have finished the homework, too. It's due today.
     B's set of potential antecedents = {..., *read Chapter 2, finish the homework*}
B: Really!? [fragment]
A: Jim told us yesterday.   [null complement anaphora]
     told us →
         inferred syntax: *told us to read Chapter 2 and finish the homework*
    Don't you remember?   [null complement anaphora]
     remember →
         inferred syntax: *remember what Jim told us yesterday*
B: No. I completely forgot I had to.
     had to →
         decoded four-tuple of *I completely forgot I had to*
         antecedents: {*read Chapter 2, finish the homework*}
         inferred VP: *had to read Chapter 2 and finish the homework*
         four-tuple of *I completely forgot I had to read Chapter 2 and finish the homework*
         explicature: 'B asserts that he completely forgot B had to read Chapter 2 of Jim's Syntax 1 textbook and finish Jim's Syntax 1 homework.'
         implicature: 'B suggests that he was too busy doing something else.'

In (21a), B's *I completely forgot I had to* is interpreted as 'I completely forgot I had to read Chapter 2 and finish the homework.' (22) is another example.

(22) a. (context: Students A and B share the knowledge that their assignment for today's class is to read an article. A is waving the article at B and says:)
A: Unfortunately, I was too busy last night.
B: That's too bad. The article was very easy. It took me half an hour.
A: Only half an hour!? Then, maybe I could <u>have</u> if I had gotten up a little earlier this morning.

b. successive and cumulative online inference processes
A: Unfortunately, I was too busy last night.
explicature: 'Unfortunately, I was too busy last night to read this article.'
B: That's too bad. The article was very easy.
It took me half an hour.
explicature: 'It took B half an hour to read the article last night'
A: Only half an hour!?
Then, maybe I could <u>have</u> if I had gotten up a little earlier this morning.
have →
decoded four-tuple of *I could have*
antecedent: *read the article*
(from the shared knowledge, from A's and B's previous explicatures, and from the word *article*, which at least means 'something to read')
inferred VP: *could have read the article*
four-tuple of *I could have read the article if I had gotten up a little earlier this morning*
explicature: 'A thinks that A could have read the article if A had gotten up a little earlier than usual this morning.'
implicature: 'A regrets that A didn't get up a little earlier than usual and read the article.'

The pro-VP form *have* in the second A in (22a) is interpreted as 'have read the article' or 'have done the reading assignment.' Note that there is no mention in the prior discourse in (22a) of the verb *read*, which only exists in the students' shared knowledge about their assignment and in the meaning of the noun *article*. Inference is essential to deal with these cases. Non-demonstrative inference processes information online successively, cumulatively, and incrementally, as already pointed out regarding the inferential process of fragment interpretation in Chapter 3 (23), (24), and (25).

(23) provides examples of VP ellipsis whose antecedent contains a gap.

(23) (Johnson 2001: 465–466; a from Webber 1978, b and c from Hardt 1993: 15–16)
 a. China is a country that Joe wants to visit, and he <u>will</u> too if he gets enough money.
 will →
   decoded four-tuple of *he will*
   antecedent: *visit* NP[G]
   inferred VP: *will visit China*
   inferred four-tuple of *he will visit China*
 b. This is just the kind of thing that Harris could have suggested. And in fact, he <u>did</u>.
 did →
   decoded four-tuple of *he did*
   antecedent: [$_{VP[PSP]}$ *suggested* NP[G]]
   inferred VP: [$_{VP[PAST]}$ *suggested this*]
   inferred four-tuple of *he suggested this*
 c. Harry is someone they would like to send to the Olympics. And they <u>will</u> too, if they can finance it.
 will →
   decoded four-tuple of *they will*
   antecedent: *send* NP[G] *to the Olympics*
   inferred VP: *will send Harry to the Olympics*
   inferred four-tuple of *they will send Harry to the Olympics*
 d. (entailment from the first conjunct of (23a)) 'Joe wants to <u>visit China</u>.'
 e. (entailment from the first sentence of (23b)) 'Harris could have <u>suggested this</u>.'
 f. (entailment from the first sentence of (23c)) 'They would like to <u>send Harry to the Olympics</u>.'

The first conjunct or sentence of each example of (23a, b, c) entails (23d, e, f), respectively. It is very likely that when the hearer/interpreter constructs the inferred VP, he uses this entailment, which contains the inferred VP. This is further illustrated in (24).

(24) a. China is not a country that Joe wants to visit, but he <u>will</u> if his boss tells him to.
      entailment of the first conjunct: 'Joe does not want to visit China.'
      inferred VP: *will visit China*
   b. This is not the kind of thing that Harris could have suggested. But in fact, he <u>did</u>.
      entailment of the first sentence: 'Harris could not have suggested this.'
      inferred VP: *suggested this*
   c. Harry is not someone they would like to send to the Olympics. But they <u>will</u>, if they are ordered to by the committee.
      entailment of the first sentence: 'They would not like to send Harry to the Olympics.'
      inferred VP: *will send Harry to the Olympics*

To construct a contextually appropriate inferred VP, we need vehicle change and similar adjustments.

(25) a. Rusty$_1$ talked about himself$_1$ only after Holly$_2$ <u>did</u>. (ambiguous) (Johnson 2001: 468)
      did →
         antecedent: *talked about himself*
         inferred VP: *talked about him$_1$* (strict identity) or *talked about himself$_2$* (sloppy identity)
   b. We haven't decided to blackmail any firms. But there's a chance we <u>might</u>. (ambiguous) (Johnson 2001: 468, Hardt 1993: 22)
      might →
         antecedents: {*decided to blackmail any firms, blackmail any firms*}
         inferred VP: *might decide to blackmail some firms* or *might blackmail some firms*
   c. The doctor didn't do anything but the nurse <u>did</u>. (Postal 1998: 102)
      did →
         antecedent: *do anything*
         inferred VP: *did something*
   d. I could find no solution, but Holly <u>might</u>. (Johnson 2001: 468)
      might →
         antecedent: *find no solution*
         inferred VP: *might find a solution*

e. Gordon may have discovered no counterexamples but Elisa <u>did</u>.
   did →
   antecedent: *discovered no counterexamples*
   inferred VP: *discovered some counterexamples*
f. In the narrow syntactic sense, English has no interrogative or exclamative mood; in the semantic sense, at least if the mood-based semantic programme is to go through, it <u>must</u>. (Wilson and Sperber 2012: 211)
   must →
   antecedent: *has no interrogative or exclamative mood*
   inferred VP: *must have interrogative and exclamative moods*
g. They$_1$ arrested Alex$_2$, though he$_2$ thought they$_1$ <u>wouldn't</u>. (Merchant 2001: 24)
   wouldn't →
   antecedent: *arrested Alex$_2$*
   inferred VP: *wouldn't arrest him$_2$*

In (25b, c), the *some-any* alternation (cf. McCawley 1998: 581) is automatic in the sense that *some* and *any* are two alternating forms of a single lexeme, the former appearing in positive syntactic environments and the latter in negative/interrogative syntactic environments.

In (25c, d, e, f), the pro-VP forms without the negative clitic *n't* must be interpreted in such a way that they take an affirmative VP as their sister complement in the inferred VP. In other words, these pro-VP forms must be interpreted as representing an affirmative VP. For example, although the antecedent VP of (25d, e, f) contains the negative determiner *no*, each pro-VP form (*might, did, must*) is interpreted affirmatively. We can account for this effect in F/A terms. This effect is due to the F/A structures of, for example, the two pro-VP forms *did* and *didn't*, which are shown in (26).

(26)

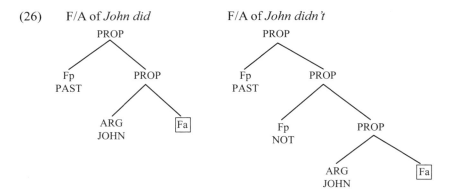

The Fa enclosed by a square in (26) is the one that is to be constructed by inference. The other part of the F/A structure is already fixed. Therefore, the pro-VP form *did* cannot be interpreted as a negative VP. If *did* was interpreted as such, there would be no room for the negative operator [$_{Fp}$ NOT] that is contained in a negative VP to be represented in the F/A structure of *John did*.

In (25f), the antecedent *has no interrogative or exclamative mood* in the negative is altered to *have interrogative and exclamative moods* in the affirmative inferred VP. This shows again the inferential nature of VP ellipsis comprehension.

In the inferred VP in (25 g), *Alex* is turned into *him*. *Alex* is first introduced in the matrix clause as discourse-new, and in the following PP[*though*], it is changed to *he* and is treated as discourse-old. Therefore, in the inferred VP, *him* must be used to refer to the same *Alex*, because it has already been established as discourse-old. On the other hand, if *Alex* was retained in the inferred VP as in *wouldn't arrest Alex*, this *Alex* would represent discourse-new information, namely, a different *Alex*. Note that a pro-VP form is a pro-form and as such carries discourse-old information by default, just as a pro-NP form (i.e., a pronoun) carries discourse-old information by default.

There are cases of VP ellipsis reported in which the antecedent of a pro-VP form contains a noun that corresponds to the head verb of the inferred VP. Note that the nouns *laugher* in (27a) and *harassment* in (27b) are morphologically transparent in that they clearly show their base verbs, *laugh* in (27a) and *harass* in (27b), from which each VP is inferred.

(27) (Johnson 2001: 470, cited from Hardt 1993: 34)
   a. David Begelman is a great laugher, and when he does, his eyes crinkle at you the way Lady Brett's did in
      The Sun Also Rises.
      does →
         decoded four-tuple of *he does*
         antecedent: *is a great laugher*
         inferred VP: *laughs (a lot)*
         inferred four-tuple of *he laughs (a lot)*
   b. Today there is little or no OFFICIAL harassment of lesbians and gays by the national government, although autonomous governments might.
      might →
         decoded four-tuple of *autonomous governments might*
         antecedent: *is little or no OFFICIAL harassment of lesbians and gays by the national government*

inferred VP: *might (officially) harass lesbians and gays*
inferred four-tuple of *autonomous governments might (officially) harass lesbians and gays*

When the hearer/interpreter of (27a, b) accesses the lexical entries for *laugher* and *harassment*, the lexical entries for their morphologically transparent base verbs *laugh* and *harass* are also activated and become accessible. In general, access to the lexical entry for a de-verbal noun activates the lexical entry for its base verb (due to spreading activation (3.4)), if the relationship between the two is morphologically transparent.

A passive VP can be the antecedent of an active VP ellipsis, as illustrated in (28). When the hearer accesses the passive verbs *released* in (28a) and *presented* in (28b), their corresponding active verbs are activated and become accessible to the hearer (spreading activation). The inference involved here depends on the synonymity between the passive in the first conjunct and its active counterpart (*Gorbachev could have*) *released this information* and (*can*) *present a lot of this material in a fairly informal and accessible fashion*.

(28) (Johnson 2001: 471, cited from Hardt 1993: 37)
    a. This information could have been released by Gorbachev, but he chose not <u>to</u>.
        to →
            decoded four-tuple of *he chose not to*
            antecedent: [$_{\text{VS[AUX, PAST]}}$ *This information could have been released by Gorbachev*]
            inferred VP: *to* [$_{\text{VP[BSE]}}$ *release this information*]
            inferred four-tuple of *he chose not to release this information*
    b. A lot of this material can be presented in a fairly informal and accessible fashion, and often I <u>do</u>.
        do →
            decoded four-tuple of *I do*
            antecedent: [$_{\text{VS[AUX, PRES]}}$ *A lot of this material can be presented in a fairly informal and accessible fashion*]
            inferred VP: [$_{\text{VP[BSE]}}$ *present a lot of this material in a fairly informal and accessible fashion*]
            inferred four-tuple of *I present a lot of this material in a fairly informal and accessible fashion*

Note that the relevant antecedents are not VPs but VSs (= Ss) in these examples. Conversely, an active VP can be the antecedent of a passive VP ellipsis.

(29) (Johnson 2001: 471, cited from Fiengo and May 1994: 203 note 10)
?John fired Max, although it was Bill who should have been.
been →
decoded four-tuple of *who should have been*
antecedent: [$_{VP[PAST]}$ *fired Max*]
inferred VP: *been* [$_{VP[PAS]}$ *fired*]
inferred four-tuple of *who should have been fired*

(28) and (29) are similar to (27) in that access to the lexical entry for a word activates the lexical entry for a related word: in (28), access to the lexical entry for a passive verb (V[PAS]) activates the lexical entry for its corresponding active verb, whereas in (29), access to the lexical entry for an active verb activates the lexical entry for its corresponding passive verb. We are claiming regarding (27)–(29) that access to a lexical entry activates other closely related lexical entries, which is known as the spreading activation model, first proposed by Collins and Loftus (1975) and discussed in Michimata et al. 2011: 212, Hakoda et al. 2010: 196, Anderson 2010: 159, Eysenck and Keane 2010: 428. See related discussion in 3.4 and 4.8.

As discussed in relation to (5), the pro-VP form analysis of VP ellipsis can explain why a "null VP" cannot be coordinated with an overt VP (Grosu 1981: 53, Merchant 2001: 195). This is because, according to the pro-VP form analysis, there is no VP gap in pro-VP forms. The second *can* in (30a, b) constitutes a VP of the category [$_{VP[AUX, PRES]}$ *can*] and *could* in (30d) [$_{VP[AUX, PAST]}$ *could*].

(30) a. *Bob can juggle, and Abby both can and sing, too. (Merchant 2001: 195)
pro-VP analysis: *[$_{VP[AUX, PRES]}$ *can*] and [$_{VP[BSE]}$ *sing*]
(ill-formed coordinate structure)
VP gap analysis: can [[$_{VP[BSE, G]}$ ø] and [$_{VP[BSE]}$ *sing*]]
(well-formed coordinate structure)
b. *Bob can juggle, and Abby can sing and, too. (ibid.)
pro-VP analysis: *[$_{VP[AUX, PRES]}$ can sing] and [ø]
(no pro-VP form)
gap VP analysis: can [[$_{VP[BSE]}$ sing] and [$_{VP[BSE, G]}$ ø]]
(well-formed coordinate structure)

c. Bob can juggle, and Abby [$_{\text{VP[AUX, PRES]}}$ can] and {can sing | sings}, too.
d. *I couldn't lift this weight, but I know a boy who could and lift a crowbar, too. (Grosu 1981: 53)
   pro-VP analysis: *[$_{\text{VP[AUX, PAST]}}$ could] and [$_{\text{VP[BSE]}}$ lift a crowbar]
   (ill-formed coordinate structure)
   VP gap analysis: could [[$_{\text{VP[BSE, G]}}$ ø] and [$_{\text{VP[BSE]}}$ lift a crowbar]]
   (well-formed coordinate structure)
e. I couldn't lift this weight, but I know a boy who [$_{\text{VP[AUX, PAST]}}$ could] and could lift a crowbar, too.

Johnson (2001) pointed out the contrast (31a, b) (attributed to Christopher Kennedy). Note that the same inference that is applied to the acceptable (31a) is also available to the unacceptable (31b). In fact, (31b) improves in acceptability when *did* is stressed and *himself too* is added to the pro-VP form as in (31c).

(31) a. Every man who said he would buy some salmon <u>did</u>. (Johnson 2001: 449)
    did →
        antecedents: {*buy some salmon, said he would buy some salmon*}
        inferred VP: *bought some salmon*
    b. *Every man who said George would buy some salmon <u>did</u>. (Johnson 2001: 449)
    c. Every man who said George would buy some salmon **DID** himself too.
    d. Every man who said George wouldn't buy any salmon **DIDN'T** himself either.

The unacceptability of (31b) seems to show that the intended interpretation of *did* is difficult to obtain simply because the subject of *would buy some salmon* and that of *did* are different.

5.3 Similarities and Differences Between Pro-VP Forms and Pronouns

There are many similarities between personal pronouns (i.e., pro-NP forms) and what we have been calling pro-VP forms, which supports our analysis of VP ellipsis as pro-VP forms. First, both personal pronouns and pro-VP forms allow inferred interpretations, those that are not found verbatim in the preceding context but are constructed by inference. For pro-VP forms, this was illustrated in

5.3 SIMILARITIES AND DIFFERENCES BETWEEN PRO-VP FORMS AND PRONOUNS   217

(22), (24), (25), (27), (28), and (29). The examples of personal pronouns in (32) illustrate the same point.

(32) inferred interpretations of personal pronouns
   a. Fry the onions in the butter till they're tender. Add the carrots, parsley, salt, and pepper, and put it all into a buttered casserole dish. Pour the cream on top, cover [$_{NP}$ ∅$_1$], and bake [$_{NP}$ ∅$_2$] at 350 for forty-five minutes. (Yamanashi 1992: 57)
   it = 'the mixture of the onions fried in the butter, the carrots, parsley, salt, and pepper'
   ∅$_1$ = 'the mixture in the buttered casserole dish of the onions fried in the butter, the carrots, parsley, salt, and pepper with cream poured on top'
   ∅$_2$ = 'the mixture in the covered buttered casserole dish of the onions fried in the butter, the carrots, parsley, salt, and pepper with cream poured on top'
   b. Which atoms make up living organisms? Where are they$_1$ found in the environment? How do they$_2$ become part of living organisms? We answer these questions next. (from a college textbook)
   they$_1$ = 'the atoms that make up living organisms'
   they$_2$ = 'the atoms that make up living organisms that are found somewhere in the environment'
   c. Mary took her nieces to Design Research, where she bought each of the girls a T-shirt. They thanked her for them. (Imanishi and Asano 1990: 60)
   them = 'the set of the T-shirts Mary bought for her nieces'
   d. A: Want to hear my scheme?
   B: Tell me, if you like it. (Yamanashi 1992: 29)
   it = 'A tells B about A's scheme' in 'I will tell you about my scheme if you want to hear my scheme' pragmatically entailed by "Want to hear my scheme?"

Second, just like personal pronouns (33a), split antecedents are possible with pro-VP forms. This was illustrated in (20) and (21). The examples in (33) are similar examples. (33b, c) are from Napoli (1985: 289, attributed to Jerry Morgan).

(33) a. John$_i$ told Sue$_j$ that they$_{\{i,j\}}$ would get married in the fall.
   b. John was going to write a letter and Sue was going to send flowers, but one of them didn't.

c. John was going to <u>write a letter</u> and Sue was going to <u>send flowers</u>, but both of them forgot <u>to</u>.
   d. Wendy is eager to <u>sail around the world</u> and Bruce is eager to <u>climb Kilimanjaro</u>, but neither of them <u>can</u> because money is too tight. (Johnson 2001: 473, cited from Webber 1978)

The explicature of the last conjunct of (33b) *one of them didn't* is 'either John or Sue didn't do what he or she was going to do' or, equivalently, 'either John didn't write a letter or Sue didn't send flowers.' Similarly, the explicature of the last conjunct of (33c) *both of them forgot to* 'both John and Sue forgot to do what they were going to do' or, equivalently, 'John forgot to write a letter and Sue forgot to send flowers.'

Third, both pronouns and pro-VP forms allow non-constituent antecedents. This was illustrated by the examples of split antecedents above and is also illustrated by (34).

(34) a. (?)**Robin** <u>slept</u> for **twelve** hours <u>in the bunkbed</u>, and **Leslie** <u>did</u> for **eight** hours. (Culicover and Jackendoff 2005: 286)
   b. <u>I</u> may <u>be wrong</u>, but I doubt <u>it</u>. (McCawley 1998: 57)

In (34a), *did* is interpreted as 'slept in the bunkbed,' which does not form a syntactic constituent. In (34b), *it* refers to 'I am wrong,' which does not form a constituent in the first conjunct, either.

Fourth, just like the personal pronoun in (35c), when there are multiple potential antecedents, ambiguity arises in the interpretation of a pro-VP form. This is shown in (35a, b).

(35) a. Although Mary could <u>have</u>, John decided to open the door. (Napoli 1985: 289)
      have → inferred VP: *have decided to open the door* or *have opened the door*
   b. John left before Mary did, and Tom <u>did</u> too.
      did → inferred VP: *left* or *left before Mary left*
   c. Although Mary hates <u>it</u>, she bought the picture of Chicago.
      it → *buying the picture of Chicago* or *the picture of Chicago* or *Chicago*

5.3 SIMILARITIES AND DIFFERENCES BETWEEN PRO-VP FORMS AND PRONOUNS

Fifth, just like personal pronouns, the syntactic relationships between pro-VP forms and their antecedents are insensitive to island constraints (Napoli 1985: 289; McCawley 1998: 521), because they are both anaphoric devices and therefore have nothing to do with unbounded dependencies, which are formulated as part of the lexical entry for the clause-initial *wh*-phrase (Chapter 1 (100)).

Sixth, ADs cannot precede and c-command their antecedent NPs (McCawley 1998: 359). This is true not only of personal pronouns but also of pro-VP forms. They cannot precede and c-command their antecedent VPs.

(36) a. *John [can if he must <u>pass the test</u>] and [is willing to prove it]. (VP-adjunct PP[*if*])
   a' John [will be able <u>to</u> if he must <u>pass the test</u>] and [is willing to prove it].
   b. John <u>can</u>, {of course | I bet}, if he must <u>pass the test</u> and he is willing to prove it. (S-adjunct PP[*if*])
   c. [If he must <u>pass the test</u>, John <u>can</u>] and he is willing to prove it.

In (36a), the second VP conjunct *is willing to prove it* is added to ensure that the PP[*if*] is not an S-adjunct but a VP-adjunct, so that the syntactic structure of the VP of the first conjunct is forced to be [$_{VP[PRES, AUX,]}$ [$_{VP[PRES, AUX]}$ can] PP[*if*]], in which the pro-VP form *can* precedes and c-commands the underlined antecedent VP. On the other hand, in (36b), because S-coordination is involved, the PP[*if*] can be interpreted as being adjoined to the first S [$_{S[PRES, AUX]}$ John can]. Therefore, *can* does not c-command the antecedent VP *pass the test*. In (36a'), the pro-VP form *to* does not c-command the underlined antecedent VP, because the PP[*if*] is adjoined to the VP *will be able to*.

(37) (Ross 1967 (5.173), 1986: 221)
   a. I'll <u>work on it</u> if I <u>can</u>.
   b. *I <u>will</u> if I can <u>work on it</u>.   cf. I <u>will</u>, {of course | absolutely}, if I can <u>work on it</u>.
   c. If I can <u>work on it</u>, I <u>will</u>.
   d. If I <u>can</u>, I will <u>work on it</u>.

In (37b), we take the PP[*if*] as being adjoined to the matrix VP *will*, which therefore c-commands the underlined antecedent VP. If we insert between *will* and *if* an ad-S adverbial such as *of course* or *absolutely*, which is adjoined to the S

I will, (37b) improves in acceptability, because *will* no longer c-commands the antecedent VP *work on it*. Another argument on the same point is given in (38).

(38) a. [NP Anyone who wants to leave] can. (Napoli 1985: 290)
b. *Can [NP anyone who wants to leave]? (ibid.)
c. A: Those of you who are going to stay tonight can pay the fee by noon.
B: Can [NP anyone who wants to leave], too?
d. Can [NP anyone who wants to] leave?

In (38a), *can* is the pro-VP form that is interpreted as 'can leave.' In the corresponding inverted clause (38b), because *can* precedes and c-commands *leave*, the pro-VP form *can* no longer takes *leave* as its antecedent and needs to find its antecedent from outside. This is shown in (38c). Of course, if we understand (38b) as (38d), in which *to* is a pro-VP form, then its antecedent can be found within the sentence, namely, *leave*. Note that *to* in (38d) does not c-command *leave*.

Seventh, just like personal pronouns, deictic use of VP ellipsis (i.e., pro-VP forms taking situational/pragmatic antecedents) is possible (pace Hankamer and Sag 1976 and McCawley 1998: 346). The following examples (39a-c) are taken from Schachter (1977: 763). More examples are found in Merchant (2004: 718–720).

(39) a. (context: John tries to kiss Mary. She says:) "John, you mustn't."
b. (context: John hands Mary the expensive present he has bought for her. She says:) "Oh, John, you shouldn't have."
c. (context: TV ad for a hair color) "Does she or doesn't she? Only her hairdresser knows for sure."
d. "Will she or won't she? Clinton sidesteps the 2016 question." (MSNBC *Morning Joe*, January 28, 2013)

In (39d), the topic is the 2016 presidential election and *she* refers to Hilary Clinton and *the 2016 question* refers to whether she will run for president or not.

Finally, both personal pronouns and pro-VP forms allow Bach-Peters sentences, in which two anaphoric devices are each contained in the other's antecedent. That is, in (40a), the two personal pronouns *it* and *he* are each contained in the other's antecedent, whereas in (40b), the two pro-VP forms *to* and *hadn't* are each contained in the other's antecedent.

5.3 SIMILARITIES AND DIFFERENCES BETWEEN PRO-VP FORMS AND PRONOUNS

(40) a. [The boy who wanted it] got [the prize that he deserved]. (McCawley 1998: 342)
antecedent of *it*: *the prize that he deserved*
antecedent of *he*: *the boy who wanted it*
b. The boy who had [wanted to] finally [got the prize that his parents mistakenly thought he hadn't]. (McCawley 1998: 376, Ueno 1997: 101)
antecedent of *to*: *got the prize that his parents mistakenly thought he hadn't*
antecedent of *hadn't*: *wanted to*
c. interpretation process of (40b)
to →
  (i) decoded four-tuple of *who had wanted to*
  (iia) antecedent of *to*: *got* [$_{NPi}$ *the prize that his parents mistakenly thought he hadn't*]
  (iib) inferred VP: *to get* [$_{NPi}$ *the prize*] (by the entailment from the antecedent)
  (iii) inferred four-tuple of *who had wanted to get the prize*
hadn't →
  (i) decoded four-tuple of *his parents mistakenly thought he hadn't*
  (iia) antecedent of *hadn't*: *wanted to get the prize* (from the inferred VP for *to*)
  (iib) inferred VP: *hadn't wanted to get the prize*
  (iii) inferred four-tuple of *his parents mistakenly thought he hadn't wanted to get* NP[G]
  inferred syntax of the whole sentence: *The boy who had wanted to get the prize finally got the prize that his parents mistakenly thought he hadn't wanted to get* NP[G].

The interpretation process of (40b) follows the same procedure for pro-VP form comprehension (13) and is given in (40c), where Step (iib) of constructing the inferred VP for the pro-VP form *to* is justified by the fact that the antecedent *got* [$_{NPi}$ *the prize that his parents mistakenly thought he hadn't*] entails *got* [$_{NPi}$ *the prize*] with the same referential index *i* on both NPs. Furthermore, when the inference of the pro-VP form *hadn't* occurs, the inference of the antecedent of *to* has already been completed and its inferred VP is available. This justifies Step (iia) of finding a potential antecedent of *hadn't*.

In the classical approach to Generative Grammar in the 1960s, pronouns were treated as being derived by the "pronominalization transformation" from copies of their antecedents (McCawley 1998: 336). This approach was abandoned partly because of the discovery of Bach-Peters sentences such as (40a), which would cause infinite regress in establishing a well-formed deep structure, which was called the "Bach-Peters paradox" (Kajita 1974: 598, McCawley 1998: 342–343, Imanishi and Asano 1990: 122). In the case of VP ellipsis, the "pronominalization transformation" corresponds to the deletion approach to VP ellipsis, in which a copy of the antecedent VP is deleted by the "VP deletion transformation." If so, the deletion approach has the same problem of infinite regress in dealing with Bach-Peters sentences with VP ellipsis such as (40b).

Note in passing that this does not apply to McCawley's approach to VP deletion, because he had his "external Q' analysis" (McCawley 1998: 630) of quantified NPs and "Q'-lowering transformation," which enabled him to account for (40b) and simultaneously maintain his "V'-deletion transformation" (personal communication from Jim McCawley on December 26, 1996). On the other hand, a reconstruction approach such as the one adopted in MGG cannot account for (40b) (Ueno 1997: 101).

Regarding the differences between pronouns and pro-VP forms, Sag (1976) pointed out the following.

(41) a. *He <u>did</u> when they asked him to <u>leave</u>. (VP-adjunct PP[*when*]; Sag 1976: 266, Johnson 2001: 448)
 b. A: Did Harry <u>leave</u>? (Sag 1976: 267)
  B: He <u>did</u> when they asked him to <u>leave</u>. (VP-adjunct PP[*when*])
  did → antecedent: *leave* in the preceding A
   inferred VP: *left*
 b'. (inferred syntax of (41bB)) He left when they asked him to leave.
 c. *<u>He</u> thinks <u>John</u> is unpopular. (Sag 1976: 266)
 d. <u>John</u> has problems. *<u>He</u> thinks <u>John</u> is unpopular. (Sag 1976: 266)
 e. <u>Mag</u> is a workaholic. *<u>She</u> will work, if <u>Mag</u> can work. (Johnson 2001: 448)

The backward anaphora relation, such as in (41a), between a pro-VP form and its following antecedent VP can be rescued by providing a preceding antecedent, as in (41b). This effect does not hold in the case of the backward anaphora relation

5.3 SIMILARITIES AND DIFFERENCES BETWEEN PRO-VP FORMS AND PRONOUNS

with a pronoun, as shown in (41d, e), where the ungrammaticality of the sentence persists even when an antecedent of the pronoun is provided in the prior discourse. We interpret this as showing that while an "r-expression" (i.e., an element that refers but is not referentially dependent (Chomsky 1995: 41)), such as *John* in (41d) and *Mag* in (41e), exhibits "the Condition C effect" ("An r-expression must be free" (Chomsky 1995: 96; that is, an r-expression cannot be c-commanded by a coreferential element)), no VP does not exhibit the similar property, as shown in (41b) and (42). In these examples, the second VP is c-commanded by the first VP, which is identical to the second except for its tense.

(42) a. John left when I told him to leave and never came back. (VP-adjunct PP[*when*])
    cf. *John left when I told John to go.
  b. Mary sang because she was told to sing and never stopped. (VP-adjunct PP[*because*])
    cf. *Mary sang because Mary was told to do something.

In (42a), *leave* is c-commanded by *left*, and in (42b), *sing* is c-commanded by *sang*. The sentences are acceptable, although they may sound redundant. This difference in the Condition C effect between pronouns and pro-VP forms is due to the difference in the nature of dependency between referential dependency (in the case of pronouns and their antecedents) and semantic dependency (in the case of pro-VP forms and their antecedent VPs). In other words, the reason why (41bB) is acceptable is that once the antecedent of the pro-VP form *did* is provided from the prior discourse, its inferred syntax (41b') is constructed and no longer violates the restriction that a pro-VP form cannot precede and c-command its antecedent VP. Furthermore, recall the outrank condition on NPs (McCawley 1998: 362, Ueno 2014: 295), which says that of two NPs X and Y, if X and Y are coreferential and X outranks Y, then Y must be a pronoun. The unacceptability of *John left when I told John to go in (42a) is also due to the violation of this condition, because the first *John* outranks the second *John*. See the definition of *outrank* in Chapter 1 (56). However, the outrank relation cannot be defined between VPs and therefore, there is no corresponding outrank condition on VPs, which explains the acceptability of *John left when I told him to leave* in (42a). More importantly, the outrank condition concerns referential dependency between two NPs but the relation between two VPs is not referential but semantic.

5.4 Lexical Entries for Pro-VP Forms

The lexical entry for each pro-VP form and the lexical entry for its corresponding auxiliary verb are related by the following lexical rule. Recall that a lexical rule is a statement that captures regular relationships between two sets of lexical entries in the lexicon. More specifically, a lexical rule says that if there is a lexical entry in the lexicon that meets its input conditions, there is another lexical entry in the lexicon that meets its output conditions.

(43) Pro-VP Form Lexical Rule
     input   output
     lexical entry for auxiliary verb   lexical entry for corresponding
                                                            pro-VP form
     syntax: V[AUX, Ψ] in [__ , XP]   →   syntax: V[AUX, AD, Ψ] in [__]
     morph: Word   →   morph: Word

In the output syntax of the lexical rule, its syntactic complement is lost and the V[AUX, AD, Ψ] constitutes its own phrase VP[AUX, Ψ]. Note that the output syntax is marked as AD (anaphoric device). The F/A and E/R fields are not specified in the lexical rule, meaning that their input information is retained intact with no change in their output. The input of this lexical rule is restricted to a full word (<BAR, 1> in morphology), meaning that a clitic auxiliary, such as *'s* in *he's*, cannot be used as a pro-VP form, as shown in (47).

This lexical rule, for example, relates the dummy *does* and the pro-VP *does* in the following way.

(44)   lexical entry for dummy *does*   lexical entry for pro-VP
       (Ueno 2014: 51)   form *does*
       (input to the lexical rule)   (output of the lexical rule)
       syntax: V[AUX, PRES, 3SG]   syntax: V[AUX, PRES, 3SG, AD]
         in [__ , VP[BSE]]   in [__]
       F/A: [$_{Fp}$ PRES]   F/A: [$_{Fp}$ PRES]
       E/R: nil   E/R: nil
       morph: V[1, PRES, 3SG]   morph: V[1, PRES, 3SG]
       mphon: [$_{V[1, PRES, 3SG]}$ /dʌz/]   mphon: [$_{V[1, PRES, 3SG]}$ /dʌz/]

In the syntactic field of the output of (43), a pro-VP form is the same syntactic category as the input auxiliary verb (V[AUX]) but lacks its original complement

5.4 LEXICAL ENTRIES FOR PRO-VP FORMS 225

XP, constituting a VP[AUX] node by itself. This captures the fact that although VP-adjuncts can be retained along with VP ellipsis, as in (45b), complements cannot, as in (45c) (Culicover and Jackendoff 2005: 286).

(45) a. John [VP[PRES] [VP[PRES] plays poker] on Fridays], and Nancy <u>does</u> too. (McCawley 1998: 55)
   b. John [VP[PRES] [VP[PRES] plays poker] on Fridays], and Nancy <u>does</u> [PP[on] on Saturdays]. (ibid.)

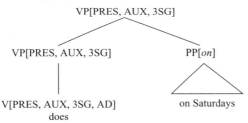

   c. *Robin [VP[PAST] put a book on the couch], while Leslie [VP[AUX, PAST] <u>did</u>] on the table. (Culicover and Jackendoff 2005: 286)

The pro-VP form *does* in (45b) constitutes its own VP[AUX], to which the temporal modifier PP[*on*] is adjoined.

Furthermore, the syntactic field of the output in (43) also captures a certain word order restriction that pertains to some VP-adverbs, including floated quantifiers (Ueno 2014: 244), whereby they must precede the pro-VP form that they modify (46a, c). The asterisked versions (46b', d') are unacceptable because the adverbs are placed after the VP. Note that if an adverb can be placed either before or after a VP, it can also be placed either before or after a pro-VP form, as shown in (46e–f').

(46) a. Mary goes to Chicago but John <u>never</u> [goes there].
   a'. *Mary goes to Chicago but John [goes there] <u>never</u>.
   b. Mary goes to Chicago but John <u>never</u> [VP[PRES, AUX] does].
   b'. *Mary goes to Chicago but John [does] <u>never</u>.
   c. The boys will not go to Chicago but the girls <u>all</u> [will go there].
   c'. *The boys will not go to Chicago but the girls [will go there] <u>all</u>.
   d. The boys will not go to Chicago but the girls <u>all</u> [VP[PRES, AUX] will].
   d'. *The boys will not go to Chicago but the girls [will] <u>all</u>.

e. Some people still think WWII is being fought. And in a way, it <u>still</u> [is being fought].
e'. Some people still think WWII is being fought. And in a way, it [is being fought], <u>still</u>.
f. Some people still think WWII is being fought. And in a way, it <u>still</u> [$_{\text{VP[PRES, AUX]}}$ is].
f'. Some people still think WWII is being fought. And in a way, it [is], <u>still</u>.

The VP gap analysis of VP ellipsis cannot account for this fact so easily. For example, the syntactic structure of the starred (46d') would be [$_{\text{VP}}$ *will* [$_{\text{VP}}$ *all* [$_{\text{VP[BSE]}}$ ø]]] (cf. *The girls* [*will* [*all* [*go there*]]]) and we would have to explain why null VPs do not allow adjunction of adverbs and floated quantifiers. The deletion approach has the same problem.

The lexical rule (43) says in its morphological field that its morphological input and output are a full-fledged word (a morphological entity with <BAR, 1> (Ueno 2014: 3)), which excludes from pro-VP forms the auxiliary verbs that lack word status such as cliticized forms like *'s, 'll, 've, 'd, 'm, 're*, which are all simple clitics in morphology (Sadock 1991: 66; cf. Huddleston and Pullum 2002: 1614, Sadock 2012: 158). In fact, they cannot be used as pro-VP forms, as shown in (47).

(47) a. *John's leaving and Mary<u>'s</u> too.   cf. John's leaving and Mary <u>is</u> too.
    b. *They've left and we<u>'ve</u> too.   cf. They've left and we <u>have</u> too.
    c. *He'll leave and she<u>'ll</u> too.   cf. He'll leave and she <u>will</u> too.

According to (13), the inferred F/A and E/R of a pro-VP form will be constructed after its inferred VP is determined in syntax. They are constructed from the syntactic structure of the inferred VP and from the lexical entries for the words in the inferred VP. The process of constructing an inferred VP is shown in (48).

(48) (McCawley 1998: 217)
    a. Fred must have been singing songs, and Nancy <u>must</u> too.
       must →
           decoded four-tuple of *Nancy must*
           antecedent: *have been singing songs*
           inferred VP: *must have been singing songs*
           inferred four-tuple of *Nancy must have been singing songs*

a'. lexical entry for *must*   lexical entry for pro-VP form *must*
    syntax: V[PRES, AUX] in   syntax: V[PRES, AUX, AD]
      [__, VP[BSE]]   in [__]
    F/A: [$_{Fp}$ PRES]∘[$_{Fp}$ MUST]   F/A: [$_{Fp}$ PRES]∘[$_{Fp}$ MUST]
    E/R: nil   E/R: nil
    morph: Word   morph: Word

b. Fred must have been singing songs, and Nancy must <u>have</u> too.
    have →
        decoded four-tuple of *Nancy must have*
        antecedent: *been singing songs*
        inferred VP: *have been singing songs*
        inferred four-tuple of *Nancy must have been singing songs*

b'. lexical entry for *have*   lexical entry for pro-VP form *have*
    syntax: V[AUX] in [__, VP[PSP]]   syntax: V[AUX, AD] in [__]
    F/A: [$_{Fp}$ PAST]   F/A: [$_{Fp}$ PAST]
    E/R: nil   E/R: nil
    morph: Word   morph: Word

c. Fred must have been singing songs, and Nancy must have <u>been</u> too.
    been →
        decoded four-tuple of *Nancy must have been*
        antecedent: *singing songs*
        inferred VP: *been singing songs*
        inferred four-tuple of *Nancy must have been singing songs*

c'. lexical entry for *be(en)*   lexical entry for pro-VP form *be(en)*
    syntax: V[PSP, AUX] in   syntax: V[PSP, AUX, AD]
      [__, VP[PRP]]   in [__]
    F/A: nil   F/A: nil
    E/R: nil   E/R: nil
    morph: Word   morph: Word

What is called "progressive *be*" in (48c, c') is in fact the empty *be* (Sadock 2012: 29, Ueno 2014: 54). See the brief discussion in relation to Chapter 1 (33c, d).

Not only finite auxiliary verbs but also nonfinite auxiliary verbs serve as pro-VP forms, as in (48b, c). This is covered by the lexical rule in (43), where the syntactic field of the input is not V[AUX, FIN] but V[AUX]. Furthermore, because pro-VP forms are syntactically VP, namely, VP[AUX], and cannot take any complement, they can only appear at the end of a string of auxiliary verbs.

To determine the inferred VP for a pro-VP form, not only the lexical entry for the pro-VP form but also the lexical entry for the corresponding auxiliary verb is used. For example, when the lexical entry for the pro-VP form *must* is accessed in (48a), the lexical entry for the corresponding auxiliary verb *must* is also activated and becomes available, due to spreading activation (3.4). The latter entry gives the information that *must* takes a VP[BSE] complement, which helps the inferential process and leads to an inferred VP in the form of VP[BSE].

The VP[*to*] allows the same possibilities of VP ellipsis as a VP (VP[AUX, FIN]) headed by a modal auxiliary verb. Compare (48) and (49). This is primarily because *to* and modal auxiliaries both take a VP[BSE] complement and, in addition, modal auxiliaries cannot occur as the complement of *to*, since they lack their base form (V[BSE]).

(49) a. Fred seems to have been singing songs, but Mary doesn't seem <u>to</u>.
    a'. lexical entry for *to*   lexical entry for pro-VP *to*
        (Chapter 1 (12c))
        syntax: V[*to*, AUX] in   syntax: V[*to*, AUX, AD]
        [__, VP[BSE]]   in [__]
        F/A: nil   F/A: nil
        E/R: nil   E/R: nil
        morph: Word   morph: Word
    b. Fred seems to have been singing songs, but Mary doesn't seem to <u>have</u>.
    c. Fred seems to have been singing songs, but Mary doesn't seem to have <u>been</u>.

Note again that the inferred VP for each pro-VP form is always a syntactic constituent (VP[AUX]), but this does not correspond to a constituent in F/A. Therefore, as claimed in (13), determining the inferred VP of a pro-VP form is primarily (but not exclusively) based on the syntactic structure of an utterance that contains a potential antecedent if relevant linguistic context is available.

The distribution of the pro-VP form *to* is very peculiar.

(50) distribution of pro-VP form *to*
     a. I wanted to take the train, but they didn't want <u>to</u>.
        to → inferred VP: *to take the train*
     b. *Mag Wildwood came to read Fred's story, and I also came <u>to</u>. (adjunct *to*, Johnson 2001: 440)

5.4 LEXICAL ENTRIES FOR PRO-VP FORMS 229

cf. Mag Wildwood came to introduce the barkeep but I came (precisely) not <u>to</u>. (Johnson 2001: 447)
  c. *You shouldn't play with rifles because <u>to</u> is dangerous. (subject *to*, Johnson 2001: 442, originally from Zwicky 1981)
      cf. You shouldn't play with rifles because it's dangerous <u>to</u>.
      (extraposed *to*, Johnson 2001: 442, originally from Zwicky 1981)
      cf. You should unload rifles because not <u>to</u> is dangerous. (Johnson 2001: 447)
      cf. For Mary to leave wouldn't bother me, but for Sally <u>to</u> would. (Johnson 2001: 474 note 7)
  d. Don't start the motor unless you're sure you know how <u>to</u>. (Johnson 2001: 474 note 5)
  e. Sally explained why we were going to arrest Holly only after the decision <u>to</u> had already been made. (Johnson 2001: 475 note 12, attributed to Chris Kennedy)

It seems that the pro-VP form *to* must be some kind of complement of a lexical head, the exact formulation of which does not concern our present purposes.

Examples of the pro-VP form *not* and its lexical entry are given in (51a, b) and (51a'), respectively. Recall that the clitic auxiliary *'s* in the second conjunct of (51a) does not serve as a pro-VP form, as shown in (47a). Note that the lexical entry for *not* and that for the corresponding pro-VP form *not* are not related by the lexical rule (43), because the syntactic category of *not* is not V[AUX]. This shows that the lexical entry for a pro-VP form is independently needed regardless of whether or not it is related to its corresponding auxiliary.

(51) *not* as pro-VP form (Johnson 2001: 440)
  a. John is leaving, but Mary's <u>not</u>.
      not →
          decoded four-tuple of *Mary's not*
          antecedent: *leaving*
          inferred VP: *not leaving*
          inferred four-tuple of *Mary's not leaving*
  a'. lexical entry for *not*   lexical entry for pro-XP form
       (Ueno 2014: 60)   *not*
       syntax: Word in [$_{XP}$ __, XP],   syntax: Word[AD] in [$_{XP}$ __],
       where XP≠VP[FIN]   where XP≠VP[FIN]

F/A: [_{Fp} NOT]   F/A: [_{Fp} NOT]
E/R: nil   E/R: nil
morph: Word   morph: Word
  b. I consider Bill intelligent and I consider Sally <u>not</u>.
not →
decoded four-tuple of *I consider Sally not*
antecedent: [_{AP} *intelligent*]
inferred AP: [_{AP} *not intelligent*]
inferred four-tuple of *I consider Sally not intelligent*

In (51b), the syntactic category of the pro-XP form *not* is AP, because, on the one hand, the subcategorization frame of *consider* requires it and, on the other, the antecedent AP *intelligent* requires it. This means that the syntax of *not* in (51b) is [_{AP} [_{Word[AD]} not]]. This syntactic structure does not violate the Head Feature Convention (HFC) (Chapter 1 (3)) for two reasons. First, this structure is not a headed local tree and hence is outside the purview of the HFC. Secondly, [_{XP} [_{Word[AD]} not]], including [_{AP} [_{Word[AD]} not]], is part of the lexical information in (51a'), and hence the HFC is not violated, thanks to its proviso "unless specified otherwise."

The examples in (52) show that the contracted forms such as *hasn't*, *isn't*, and *didn't* serve as pro-VP forms. As discussed in Sadock (2012: 177–178) and Ueno (2014: 64), all the contracted forms of finite auxiliary and *not* are registered in the lexicon. They also undergo the lexical rule in (43).

(52)   contracted forms of finite auxiliary and *not* as pro-VP forms
    a. John's eaten lunch but Mary <u>hasn't</u>.
      hasn't →
      decoded four-tuple of *Mary hasn't*
      antecedent: *eaten lunch*
      inferred VP: *hasn't eaten lunch*
      inferred four-tuple of *Mary hasn't eaten lunch*
    a'. lexical entry for *hasn't*   lexical entry for pro-VP form *hasn't*
      syntax: V[PRES, AUX, 3SG]   syntax: V[PRES, AUX, 3SG, AD]
      in [__, VP[PSP]]   in [__]
      F/A: [_{Fp} PRES]∘[_{Fp} PAST]∘   F/A: [_{Fp} PRES]∘[_{Fp} PAST]∘
      [_{Fp} NOT]   [_{Fp} NOT]
      E/R: nil   E/R: nil
      morph: Word   morph: Word

5.4 LEXICAL ENTRIES FOR PRO-VP FORMS   231

b. John's eating lunch but Mary <u>isn't</u>.
   isn't →
      decoded four-tuple of *Mary isn't*
      antecedent: *eating lunch*
      inferred VP: *isn't eating lunch*
      inferred four-tuple of *Mary isn't eating lunch*

b'. lexical entry for *isn't*   lexical entry for pro-VP form *isn't*
    syntax: V[PRES, AUX, 3SG]   syntax: V[PRES, AUX, 3SG, AD]
    in [__, VP[PRP]]   in [__]
    F/A: $[_{Fp}$ PRES$]\circ[_{Fp}$ NOT$]$ F/A: $[_{Fp}$ PRES$]\circ[_{Fp}$ NOT$]$
    E/R: nil   E/R: nil
    morph: Word   morph: Word

c. John ate lunch but Mary didn't.
   didn't →
      decoded four-tuple of *Mary didn't*
      antecedent: *ate lunch*
      inferred VP: *didn't eat lunch*
      inferred four-tuple: *Mary didn't eat lunch*

c'. lexical entry for *didn't*   lexical entry for pro-VP form *didn't*
    syntax: V[PAST, AUX]   syntax: V[PAST, AUX, AD]
    in [__, VP[BSE]]   in [__]
    F/A: $[_{Fp}$ PAST$]\circ[_{Fp}$ NOT$]$ F/A: $[_{Fp}$ PAST$]\circ[_{Fp}$ NOT$]$
    E/R: nil   E/R: nil
    morph: Word   morph: Word

As already pointed out in (34a) (repeated here as (53)), the antecedent of a VP ellipsis does not have to be a syntactic constituent.

(53) (?)**Robin** slept for **twelve** hours in the bunkbed, and **Leslie** $[_{VP[AUX, PAST]}$ did] for **eight** hours.

The pro-VP form *did* in (53) is interpreted as 'slept in the bunkbed,' which does not form a syntactic constituent in the first conjunct, whose syntactic structure is $[_{VP} [_{VP} [_{VP}$ slept] PP[*for*]] PP[*in*]]. However, the subjects in both conjuncts are contrastively stressed and so are the two *for*-phrases. The pro-VP form is taken to mean 'slept in the bunkbed,' which is the whole VP of the first conjunct except for the contrastively stressed phrase *for twelve hours*. Contrastive stress on the *for*-phrases signals difference in the two VPs, whereas the lack of contrastive stress on the verb and the PP[*in*] in the first conjunct signals that they are taken to be the same in both VPs. This example shows that the interpretation of a pro-VP form retains the interpretation of its antecedent VP as much as possible except for contrastively stressed constituents. This is shown in (54).

(54) syntax and IS of the second conjunct: ***Leslie*** *did for **eight** hours*

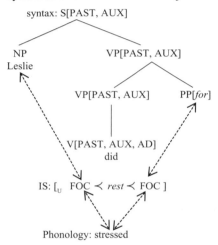

Finite auxiliary pro-VP forms also occur as inverted auxiliaries. See also (38cB) and (39c, d). In (55e, f), the two-word interrogative sentence of inverted auxiliary and subject pronoun is followed by a sluiced *wh*-phrase (*wh*-fragment), as discussed in Chapter 4.

(55) a. I can speak Japanese. <u>Can</u> you?
       can →
           decoded four-tuple of *Can you?*
           antecedent: *speak Japanese*
           inferred VP: *speak Japanese*
           inferred four-tuple of *Can you speak Japanese?*
           explicature: 'The speaker asks the addressee whether he can speak Japanese.'

5.4 LEXICAL ENTRIES FOR PRO-VP FORMS 233

implicature: 'The speaker doesn't think the addressee can speak Japanese.'
b. I've never been to Chicago. <u>Have</u> you?
c. "The most basic question of all is, do you want a referendum? I do. <u>Does</u> he?"
   (British Prime Minister David Cameron, on January 23, 2013, reported by BBC Radio 4)
d. Natalie Morales: I'm glad you lived up to your reputation.
   Savannah Guthrie: <u>Did</u> I ever?   (NBC *Today Show*, August 9, 2013)
e. I've done several triathlons but have never warmed up before a race. <u>Should</u> I, and if so, how and why? (from the web)
f. I'm thinking about doing a sport next year. <u>Should</u> I and which sport? (from the web)

The interpretations of (55e, f) clearly show that online ellipsis comprehension works successively and cumulatively. For example, the interpretation of the *wh*-fragment *which sport?* in (55f) depends on the interpretation of the pro-VP form *should*, because the former is interpreted as 'Which sport should I do next year?' and not as #'Which sport am I thinking about doing next year?' These processes are shown in (56) below.

(56) interpretation processes of <u>Should I and which sport?</u> in (55f)
      should →
         decoded four-tuple of *Should I?*
         antecedent: *doing a sport next year*
         inferred VP: *do a sport next year*
         inferred four-tuple of *Should I do a sport next year?*
      which sport? →
         decoded four-tuple of *which sport?*
         antecedent: *Should I do a sport next year?* (from the inferred syntax of the preceding pro-VP form)
         inferred syntax: *Which sport should I do next year?*
         inferred four-tuple of *Which sport should I do next year?*

We take these pro-VP forms in inversion (inverted pro-VP forms) in (55) as output of the Inversion Lexical Rule (Ueno 2014: 48). The contrast between b and c in (38) clearly shows that inverted auxiliaries function as pro-VP forms in syntax.

(57) Inversion Lexical Rule applied to pro-VP forms

input	output
lexical entry for pro-VP form *can*	corresponding inverted pro-VP form *can*
syntax: V[PRES, AUX, AD] in [__]	→ syntax: V[PRES, INV, AD] in [$_{S[INV]}$ __, NP[NOM]]
F/A: [$_{Fp}$ PRES]∘[$_{Fp}$ CAN]	→ F/A: [$_{Fp}$ PRES]∘[$_{Fp}$ CAN]
E/R: nil	→ E/R: nil
morph: Word	→ morph: Word

(58) syntax of *Can you?* in (55a)

Note that in (57) and (58), the sister of V[INV] is not an S but an NP[NOM]. There is no syntactic or semantic evidence that an inverted pro-VP form takes an S complement. If it did, S coordination (59aB1) and VP coordination (59bB) would be possible. In addition, an ad-VP (59aB2) would be possible after the subject NP.

(59) a. A: I confess. I took the money.
    B1: *Did [$_{S[BSE]}$ you [$_{VP[BSE]}$ ø] and [$_{S[BSE]}$ your wife spend it all]]? (S-coordination)
    B2: *Did you [$_{VP[BSE]}$ intentionally [$_{VP[BSE]}$ ø]]?
  b. A: You should read more Minimalist books.
    B: *Should [$_{S[BSE]}$ I [$_{VP[BSE]}$ ø] and [$_{VP[BSE]}$ waste my precious time]]? (VP-coordination)

5.5 Missing Antecedent Phenomenon

We proposed (13) to determine the intended interpretation of a pro-VP form. We called the VP inferentially constructed by (13) the inferred VP. The Missing Antecedent Phenomenon, which was first discussed by Grinder and Postal (1971) and is illustrated in (60a, b), is a phenomenon in which "the copy of the antecedent that one might regard as implied by the AD contains a constituent that serves as antecedent for another AD" (McCawley 1998: 344). For example, in (60a), the pronoun *he* finds its antecedent *an astronaut* in the inferred VP *interviewed an astronaut*.

(60) a. Barbara Walters has never interviewed an astronaut, but if she ever <u>did</u>, <u>he</u>'d probably tell her lots of interesting stories. (McCawley 1998: 344)
  (the first conjunct interpreted under the scope relation *never > an astronaut*)
  did →
   decoded four-tuple of *if she ever did, he'd probably tell her lots of interesting stories*
   antecedent of *did*: [$_{VP[PSP]}$ *interviewed an astronaut*]
   inferred VP: [$_{VP[PAST]}$ *interviewed an astronaut*]
   inferred four-tuple of *if she ever interviewed an astronaut, he'd probably tell her lots of interesting stories*
 b. Fred doesn't pick up girls, but Mark <u>does</u>, and <u>they</u>'re generally stunningly beautiful. (McCawley 1998: 344)
  (the first conjunct interpreted under the scope relation *not > girls*)
  does →
   decoded four-tuple of *Mark does*
   antecedent of *does*: [$_{VP[BSE]}$ *pick up girls*]
   inferred VP: [$_{VP[PRES, 3SG]}$ *picks up girls*]
   inferred four-tuple of *Mark picks up girls*
 c. Fred doesn't pick up girls who wear a pink skirt, but Mark <u>does</u>, and he always asks <u>them</u> where <u>they</u> bought <u>it</u>.
  does →
   decoded four-tuple of *Mark does*
   antecedent of *does*: [$_{VP[BSE]}$ *pick up girls who wear a pink skirt*]
   inferred VP: [$_{VP[PRES, 3SG]}$ *picks up girls who wear a pink skirt*]
   inferred four-tuple of *Mark picks up girls who wear a pink skirt*
 d. Harry sank <u>a destroyer</u> as soon as Bill <u>did</u>. <u>They</u> both went down with all hands.
  (based on Grinder and Postal 1971: 279 (19b))
  did →

decoded four-tuple of *Bill did*
antecedent of *did*: [$_{VP[PAST]}$ *sank a destroyer*]
inferred VP: [$_{VP[PAST]}$ *sank a destroyer*]
inferred four-tuple of *Bill sank a destroyer*

The pronoun *he* in (60a) refers to *an astronaut* in the inferred VP [$_{VP[PAST]}$ *interviewed an astronaut*]. It cannot refer to *an astronaut* in the first conjunct, because under the scope relation *never* > *an astronaut*, **Barbara Walters has never interviewed an astronaut, but he'd probably tell her lots of interesting stories*. In (60b), *they* refers to *girls* in the inferred VP *pick up girls*. In (60c), which is a generalized version of (60b), *them* and *they* refer to *girls who wear a pink skirt* and *it* refers to *a pink skirt*. The two antecedents are both in the inferred VP *picks up girls who wear a pink skirt*. In (60d), *they* has split antecedents, the destroyer sunk by Harry and the destroyer sunk by Bill, the latter being in the inferred VP *sank a destroyer*. As with other cases of VP ellipsis comprehension, inference plays an essential role in the interpretation of the Missing Antecedent Phenomenon. An example such as (60b) can be generalized to an example with a series of pro-VP forms, which is similar to (20) and (21).

(61) a. A: I have never picked up girls.
 Have you? [VP ellipsis]
 B: Yes, I have. [VP ellipsis]
 Do you know if Fred and Mark have? [VP ellipsis]
 A: I don't know about Fred but Mark has. [VP ellipsis]
 Mark once told me they were stunningly beautiful.
 b. A: Fred doesn't pick up girls but Mark does. [VP ellipsis]
 B: No, just the opposite. [fragment]
 Fred does but Mark doesn't. [VP ellipsis]
 A: No, no. You're wrong! Fred doesn't but Mark does. [VP ellipsis]
 Because Mark once told me they were stunningly beautiful.

In (61a), *they* refers to *girls* in the inferred VP (*has picked up girls* or *picks up girls*) of the immediately preceding pro-VP form (underlined).

It has been observed that the Missing Antecedent Phenomenon is impossible with *do it*, whereas it is possible with the pro-VP form *do so*.

(62) absence of Missing Antecedent Phenomenon with *do it*
   a. *My uncle didn't buy anything for Christmas, but my aunt did it for him, and it was bright red. (Bresnan 1971: 591, also cited in Johnson 2001: 456)
   a'. My uncle didn't buy anything for Christmas, but my aunt did for him, and it was bright red. (Bresnan 1971: 591)
   b. Barbara Walters has never interviewed an astronaut, but I've done it (??and he didn't have much to say). (McCawley 1998: 345)
   c. Fred doesn't pick up girls, but Mark does it (??and they're generally stunningly beautiful). (McCawley 1998: 345)

(63) Missing Antecedent Phenomenon with *do so*
   Jerry wouldn't read a book by Babel, but Meryl has done so and it was pretty good. (Johnson 2001: 466)

(64) Missing Antecedent Phenomenon with *so* + auxiliary verb + subject
   a. Harry sank a destroyer and so did Bill and they both went down with all hands. (Grinder and Postal 1971: 279)
   b. John has finished a term paper and so has Mary, and she is going to submit it today.

A pro-VP form ($[_{VP[AUX]}$ V[AUX, AD]] in syntax) undergoes the Procedure for pro-VP form comprehension (13), which constructs its inferred syntactic VP structure. By contrast, the action-denoting VP *do it* is an ordinary VP consisting of the agentive transitive *do* and the pronoun *it*. The pronoun has in its F/A, and, due to Feature Osmosis (Sadock 2012: 154, Ueno 2014: 25), in its syntax as well, the INDEX feature with referential index (i) and agreement feature value (3SGN), namely, IND[i, 3SGN]. For example, the pronoun *it* in *did it* of (62a) refers to 'the act of buying something for Christmas' not by syntactically representing a VP structure (as inferred VP) but through its referential index. In short, the transitive VP *do it* does not trigger the syntactic construction of an inferred VP.

The other action-denoting VP *do so* is different from *do it* in this respect when used as a pro-VP form, as shown in (63). (65) is the lexical entry for the agentive pro-VP form *do so*. Because of its E/R, *do so* does not directly refer to its antecedent through its referential index but rather represents the same TYPE of action as its antecedent.

(65) lexical entry for action type denoting pro-VP form *do so*
syntax: [$_{VP}$ do [$_{ADV[AD]}$ so]]
F/A: Fa
E/R: [$_{VA}$ [$_{TYPE}$ "do"] AG [$_{MANNER}$ "so"]]

5.6 Syntactic Status of Inferred VP

There are several pieces of evidence that show that inferred VPs not only exist in semantics (F/A and E/R in our AMG approach), but also exist in SYNTAX as real SYNTACTIC entities. First, recall the argument based on VP idioms and their passives in (16), which showed the SYNTACTIC existence of inferred VP, without which no idiomatic interpretation is recoverable.

Second, the contrast between the grammatical (60a) and the ungrammatical (66a) below shows that in the ordered syntactic structure of (66a) with the inferred VP *interviewed an astronaut* in place of the pro-VP form *did*, the pronoun precedes and c-commands its antecedent *an astronaut* in the inferred VP, thus violating the SYNTACTIC condition that "An AD must not precede and c-command its antecedent" (McCawley 1998: 359), which is illustrated in (66b), the inferred syntax of the second conjunct of (66a). Note that precedence (i.e., linear order) is defined on syntactic structures, but not on F/A and E/R structures, which are order-free.

(66) a. *Barbara Walters has never interviewed an astronaut, but <u>he</u>'d probably tell her lots of interesting stories, if she ever <u>did</u>.
b. *<u>He</u>'d probably tell her lots of interesting stories, if she ever interviewed <u>an astronaut</u>.
c. Barbara Walters didn't interview an astronaut yesterday. But tomorrow, because <u>he</u> is American, she definitely <u>will</u>.
will →
   decoded four-tuple of *she definitely will*
   antecedent: *interview an astronaut*
   inferred VP: *will interview an astronaut*
   inferred four-tuple: *she will definitely interview an astronaut*

Considering that (60a) and (66a) share the same F/A and E/R structures, the step in (13) of constructing an inferred VP structure in SYNTAX is justified. In (66c), *he* does not c-command *an astronaut* in the inferred VP; hence, there is no violation of the above condition. This supports our analysis of the contrast between (60a) and (66a).

Third, the same point can be shown by a quantified NP (QNP) and its bound variable pronouns, about which the SYNTACTIC condition (originally due to Reinhart (1983: 122)) has been known that a pronoun can be interpreted as a bound variable if it is c-commanded by a QNP (Ueno 2014: 291). The contrast between (67a, b) shows that in (67a), *everyone* does not c-command *he* whereas in (67b), the c-command relation holds when the PP[*because*] is adjoined to the VP.

(67) a. *Mary insulted everyone$_x$ but he$_x$ didn't insult her.
 b. Mary [$_{VP}$ [$_{VP}$ insulted everyone$_x$] [because he$_x$ insulted her too]].
 c. *Mary$_i$ didn't insult everyone$_x$, but Jane$_j$ <u>did</u> and he$_y$ insulted her$_j$ too.
 (based on Grinder and Postal 1971: 290 (56a))
 did → inferred VP: *insulted everyone$_y$*
 d. (?)Mary$_i$ didn't insult everyone$_x$ but Jane$_j$ [<u>did</u> because he$_y$ insulted her$_j$ too].
 did → inferred VP: *insulted everyone$_y$*

In (67d), where the PP[*because*] is adjoined to the VP headed by the pro-VP form *did*, if *did* is replaced by its inferred VP, *he* comes to be c-commanded by *everyone* in the inferred VP, and is thus interpreted as a bound variable, which explains its acceptability. The contrast between the acceptability of (67d) and the unacceptability of (67c) shows that the SYNTACTIC condition applies to inferred VPs, another demonstration that inferred VPs do not exist in the abstract but are real SYNTACTIC entities.

The fourth piece of evidence concerns the gender of a pronoun.

(68) My uncle doesn't have a spouse but your aunt does and {he | *she | *it} is lying on the floor. (Grinder and Postal 1971: 278)
 does → inferred VP: *has a spouse*

The pronoun in (68) refers to the NP *a spouse* in the inferred VP *has a spouse*. However, this NP does not have a definite gender. It can be either masculine or feminine, depending on the gender of the person whose spouse the speaker is talking about. To choose the pronoun with the appropriate gender in (68), the speaker and addressee need to access the whole inferred S *your aunt has a spouse*, which contains the inferred VP, because this S makes clear that the pronoun purports to refer to 'your aunt's spouse,' which is masculine. Although this may look like a semantic phenomenon, because the English gender system is based on natural gender, it is in fact more syntactic than purely semantic. The same holds in languages with grammatical gender such as German. In (69), the pronoun agrees in gender with the antecedent NP in the inferred VP.

(69) (Grinder and Postal 1971: 280)
   a. Hans wollte keinen Tisch kaufen, aber ich wollte (es) und {er | *sie | *es} war teuer.
   wollte (es) → inferred VP: *wollte einen Tisch kaufen*
   b. Hans wollte keine Lampe kaufen, aber ich wollte (es) und {*er | sie | *es} war teuer.
   wollte (es) → inferred VP: *wollte eine Lampe kaufen*
   c. Hans wollte kein Auto kaufen, aber ich wollte (es) und {*er | *sie | es} war teuer.
   wollte (es) → inferred VP: *wollte ein Auto kaufen*

The fifth piece of evidence concerns Postal's (1969) anaphoric island. It is observed that when the antecedent of a pronoun is available from linguistic context, it must be syntactically expressed (or, at least must be arrived at through inference based on syntactically expressed information). For example, although the matrix clauses of (70a, b) express the same meaning, *their* in (70b) fails to refer to *sheep*, which is part of the compound noun *sheepbreeder* and as such is not syntactically expressed. In (70d), the intended antecedent of *them* is 'parents,' a semantic constituent contained in the meaning of *orphan* ('a child whose parents are dead'), which is not expressed syntactically.

(70) (a, b from Grinder and Postal 1971: 286; c, d from McCawley 1998: 537)
   a. Harry is one who breeds sheep$_i$ because he likes <u>their</u>$_i$ smell.
   b. *Harry is a sheepbreeder because he likes <u>their</u> smell.
   c. A child whose parents are dead usually misses <u>them</u>.
   d. *An orphan usually misses <u>them</u>.

The same restriction holds of the Missing Antecedent Phenomenon, which shows again that inferred VPs are syntactic entities. In (71a), *there* refers to *in prison* in the inferred VP, whereas in (71b), *there* fails to refer to 'in prison,' which is semantically contained in *imprisoned* but is not expressed syntactically.

(71) (Grinder and Postal 1971: 286)
   a. Max wasn't put in prison, but Joe was and he is still there.
      was → inferred VP: *was put in prison*
   b. *Max wasn't imprisoned, but Joe was and he is still there.
      was → inferred VP: *was imprisoned*

(72) illustrates the same point. In (72a), *she* refers to *his wife* in the inferred VP. In (72b), the intended antecedent of *she* is 'wife,' a semantic constituent contained in the meaning of *widower* ('a person who lost his wife') that is not expressed syntactically.

(72) (McCawley 1998: 345)
   a. John hasn't lost his wife, but Bill has; she died last month.
      has → inferred VP: *has lost his wife* (with sloppy identity)
      cf. Bill has lost his wife; she died last month.
   b. ??John isn't a widower, but Bill is; she died last month.
      is → inferred VP: *is a widower*
      cf. ??Bill is a widower; she died last month.

The examples in (73) are pseudo-gapping. Still, the same point holds. In (73a), the pro-VP form *wasn't* finds its antecedent in the inferred VP *found Joan guilty* constructed from *did Joan*. In (73b), the intended antecedent of the pro-VP form *wasn't* is 'guilty,' which is a semantic constituent of the verb *convict* contained in the inferred VP *convicted Joan* but which is not syntactically expressed.

(73) (Grinder and Postal 1971: 287 (42))
   a. The jury didn't find Bill guilty, but did Joan although she wasn't.
      did Joan → inferred VP: *found Joan guilty*
      wasn't → inferred VP: *wasn't guilty*
   b. *The jury didn't convict Bill, but did Joan although she wasn't.
      did Joan → inferred VP: *convicted Joan*

The sixth piece of evidence concerns implicit arguments and adjuncts. (74b) and (74d) show that implicit arguments and adjuncts in inferred VPs cannot be referred to by a pronoun, because they are not expressed syntactically.

(74) (Grinder and Postal 1971: 289)
   a. Harry didn't eat anything, but Gladys did and it gave her heartburn.
      did → inferred VP: *ate something*
   b. *Harry didn't eat, but Gladys did and it gave her heartburn.
      did → inferred VP: *ate*
      cf. John ate *(something) and it gave him heartburn.
   c. Mary wasn't attacked by anyone, but Sally was and it was only by accident that he was caught.
      was → inferred VP: *was attacked by someone*
   d. *Mary wasn't attacked, but Sally was and it was only by accident that he was caught.
      was → inferred VP: *was attacked*
      cf. Jane was attacked *(by someone), and it was only by accident that he was caught.

Note that *ate* (intransitive) and *was attacked* (passive) entail 'ate something' and 'was attacked by someone' respectively, but 'something' and 'by someone' in the respective entailment do not qualify as the antecedents of a pronoun, because they are not expressed syntactically in their inferred VPs. In other words, the distinction between overt arguments/adjuncts and implicit arguments/adjuncts is maintained in inferred syntactic structures. If inferred syntactic structures only existed in semantics, this distinction would be lost.

The seventh piece of evidence concerns the dialects that manifest the "Pronoun Identity Conditions (PROIC)" (Grinder and Postal 1971: 298). Although they gave a description of such dialects using the form of *so* + auxiliary verb + NP, the same point holds of VP ellipsis. In these dialects, the interpretation of pro-VP forms is restricted in such a way that their inferred VPs must have the same pronoun form as that in their antecedents. For example, in the PROIC dialects, (75a) is ambiguous between strict identity reading and sloppy identity reading, but (75b) is not. It does not allow sloppy identity reading.

(75) (based on Grinder and Postal 1971: 297 (45))
   a. John painted his house and Bob did too. (ambiguous between strict identity and sloppy identity readings)
      did → inferred VP: *painted his house*
   b. John painted his house and Mary did too. (strict identity reading only)
      did → inferred VP: *painted his house*

In (75b), the inferred VP is *painted his house* and therefore, the subject *Mary* and *his* in the inferred VP cannot be coreferential. For a sloppy identity reading to obtain, *his* of the inferred VP must have been *her*, which is prohibited in these dialects. In the PROIC dialects, the sloppy identity reading is missing from (76b). Again, for it to be available, *he* in the inferred VP must be *she*, which violates the PROIC.

(76) (based on Grinder and Postal 1971: 298 (90))
    a. John said he drank wine and Bob did too. (ambiguous between strict identity and sloppy identity readings)
    b. John said he drank wine and Mary did too. (strict identity reading only)
       did → inferred VP: *said he drank wine*

For the PROIC to be effective in these dialects, inferred syntactic structures with each lexical node filled by a lexical item are required. These pieces of evidence show that inferred VPs exist in SYNTAX and count as being syntactically expressed.

5.7 Antecedent Contained Deletion

Antecedent Contained Deletion (ACD) is illustrated in (77a), (78a), and (79a), and was once said to be "one of the strongest arguments for the level of LF and its distinctive properties and operations" (Hornstein 1995: 72). ACD is another phenomenon where the step in (13) of constructing an inferred VP through non-demonstrative inference plays a crucial role in determining the intended interpretation of the pro-VP form in this construction.

(77) a. Children may not even be learning what they ought to. (ambiguous)
       (Ueno 1997: 103, McCawley 1998: 376)
       to →
       decoded four-tuple of *what they ought to*
       potential antecedents: {*learning what they ought to, be learning what they ought to*}
       inferred VPs: {[$_{VP[to, AUX]}$ *to learn* NP[G]], [$_{VP[to, AUX]}$ *to be learning* NP[G]]}
       inferred four-tuples of *what they ought to learn* and *what they ought to be learning*

b. Children are said to learn what they are interested in. But these children may not even be learning what they ought to. (ambiguous)

to →

decoded four-tuple of *what they ought to*

potential antecedents: {*are interested in, learning what they ought to, be learning what they ought to*}

inferred VPs: {*to be interested in* NP[G], *to learn* NP[G], *to be learning* NP[G]}

inferred four-tuples of *what they ought to be interested in* or *what they ought to learn* or *what they ought to be learning*

The antecedent of the pro-VP form in the ACD construction can be found locally as in (77a). However, the pro-VP form does not have to take an intra-sentential antecedent, and in fact, it can take a different antecedent from the prior discourse if an appropriate context is given. For example, in (77b), which is at least three-way ambiguous, the pro-VP form *to* takes its antecedent from the preceding sentence, as shown in the first inferred VP. The same point is also shown in (82c) and (85c, d). Furthermore, the potential antecedents of the pro-VP form *to* in (77a) contain the pro-VP form *to* itself. This situation sometimes arises with pronouns, as in [*The man next to* [*his*] *dog*] *is smiling* and [*The boy with a collar that suits* [*him*]] *is a designer* (Imanishi and Asano 1990: 120).

The NP gap (NP[G]) in each inferred VP in (77) is required by two factors: (i) through access to the lexical entry of the verb in the inferred VP, namely, *learn*, which contains the syntactic requirement V in [__, NP], and, more importantly, (ii) by the dominance path conditions (Chapter 1 (100)) triggered by the free relative *what*, which require that there be a gap (XP[G]) in the inferred VP headed by *to*. Because of these factors, the inferred VP in ACD must contain an NP[G]. Our claim here is that when a pro-VP form is dominated by a node that triggers the dominance path conditions (e.g., CP[WH[Q]] for interrogative *wh*-clauses or CP[WH[R]] for *wh*-relative clauses), its inferred VP must meet the dominance path conditions. This is a natural consequence of the fact that inferred VPs are syntactic entities, as was shown in 5.6. This will correctly predict that the available interpretations of pro-VP forms in ACD are only those in which their inferred VPs satisfy the dominance path conditions. In other words, no interpretation of the ACD construction that involves island violations in its inferred VP is available. This is shown in (78).

(78) a. Mary suspects everyone [$_{\text{S[PRES]}}$ she knows John <u>does</u>].
   does →
   decoded four-tuple of *everyone she knows John does*
   antecedent: *suspects* [$_{\text{NP}}$ *everyone she knows John does*]
   inferred VP: *suspects* NP[G]
   inferred four-tuple of *everyone she knows John suspects*
 b. Mary suspects everyone she knows John suspects NP[G].
 c. *Mary suspects everyone [$_{\text{S[PRES]}}$ she knows the report that John <u>does</u>]. (Ueno 1997: 107)
   does →
   decoded four-tuple of *everyone she knows the report that John does*
   antecedent: *suspects* [$_{\text{NP}}$ *everyone that she knows the report that John does*]
   inferred VP: *suspects* NP[G]
   inferred four-tuple of **everyone she knows the report that John suspects*
 d. *Mary suspects everyone [$_{\text{S[PRES]}}$ she knows the report that John suspects NP[G]].

(78a) does not contain an island between the top node of the relative clause (S[PRES]) and the pro-VP form *does* and between the top node of the inferred VP (VP[PRES]) and the gap (NP[G]). Therefore, (78a) is acceptable and its interpretation is the same as that of (78b). On the other hand, (78c), whose intended interpretation is the same as that of (78d), violates the CNPC in its inferred syntax and is unacceptable.

When the inferred VP of (79a) is taken as *suspects* NP[G], the sentence is acceptable with (79b) as its interpretation. However, when it is taken as *believes the report that John suspects* NP[G], as in (79c), the sentence, whose interpretation is (79d), is unacceptable, because there is a CNPC violation inside the inferred VP, as shown in (79c).

(79) a. Mary believes the report that John suspects everyone [$_{\text{CP[that]}}$ that Bill does]. (cf. Ueno 1997: 108)
   does →
   antecedent: *suspects* [$_{\text{NP}}$ *everyone that Bill does*]
   inferred VP: *suspects* NP[G]

b. Mary believes the report that John suspects everyone [$_{CP[that]}$ that Bill suspects NP[G]].
c. Mary believes the report that John suspects everyone [$_{CP[that]}$ that Bill does]. (= (a))
does →
    antecedent: *believes the report that John suspects* [$_{NP}$ *everyone that Bill does*]
    inferred VP: **believes the report that John/he suspects* NP[G]
d. *Mary believes the report that John$_j$ suspects everyone [$_{CP[that]}$ that Bill believes the report that he$_j$ suspects NP[G]].

VP ellipsis sites out of which "*wh*-movement" appears to have taken place, as seen in the ACD construction, are also observed in regular VP ellipsis cases such as (80a, b, c, d). However, if we fill these ellipsis sites with *do it* or *do so* as in (80e, f), the sentences become ungrammatical.

(80) a. I know which book Max read, and which book Oscar <u>didn't</u>. (Fiengo and May 1994: 229)
didn't →
    antecedent: [$_{VP[PAST]}$ *read* NP[G]]
    inferred VP: *didn't* [$_{VP[BSE]}$ *read* NP[G]]
b. I know what I like and what I <u>don't</u>. (Merchant 2001: 58 note 8)
don't →
    antecedent: *like* NP[G]
    inferred VP: *don't like* NP[G]
c. We need to know which languages Abby speaks, and which Ben <u>does</u>. (Merchant 2001: 115 note 5)
does →
    antecedent: *speaks* NP[G]
    inferred VP: *speaks* NP[G]
d. We know that Abby DOES speak Greek, Albanian, and Serbian—we need to find out which languages she DOESN'T. (Merchant 2001: 115 note 5, cited from Hardt 1993, 1999)

5.7 ANTECEDENT CONTAINED DELETION

       doesn't →
         antecedent: *speak* [$_{NP}$ *Greek, Albanian, and Serbian*]
         inferred VP: *doesn't speak* NP[G]
  e. *I know which book Max read NP[G], and which book Oscar didn't do it.
  f. *I know which book Max read NP[G], and which book Oscar didn't do so.

In (80d), the presence of an NP[G] in the inferred VP is required by the dominance path conditions triggered by the *wh*-phrase *which languages*. On the other hand, the second conjunct in (80e, f) is a CP[WH[Q]] that violates the dominance path conditions, which are triggered by the presence of the *wh*-phrase (NP[WH[Q]]) *which book*, because there is no gap at the bottom. The ACD construction shares this property.

(81) a. Dulles suspected everyone who Angleton <u>did</u>. (May 1985: 11)
       did →
         antecedent: *suspected* [$_{NP}$ *everyone who Angleton did*]
         inferred VP: *suspected* NP[G]
    b. *Dulles suspected everyone who Angleton <u>did it</u>. (Johnson 2001: 457)
    c. *Dulles suspected everyone who Angleton <u>did so</u>. (Johnson 2001: 457)

(82a) below is another example of ACD, in which the presence of an NP[G] in the inferred VP is again required by the lexical entry for *kiss* and, more importantly, by the dominance path conditions for *that*-relative clauses (Ueno 2014: 350).

(82) a. John kissed every guest that Sally <u>did</u>. (Hornstein 1995: 72)
       did →
         antecedent: *kissed* [$_{NP}$ *every guest that Sally did*]
         inferred VP: [$_{VP[PAST]}$ *kissed* NP[G]]

248 5 AN AUTOMODULAR VIEW OF VP ELLIPSIS

b. syntax of (82a)

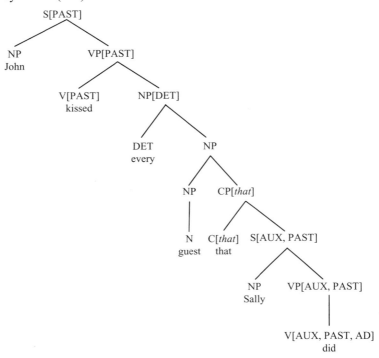

c. Because Sally told John to kiss the guests, John kissed every guest that Sally <u>did</u>. (ambiguous)

   did →

   potential antecedents: {*told John to kiss* [_{NP} *the guests*], *kissed* [_{NP} *everyone that Sally did*]}

   inferred VPs: *told him to kiss* NP[G] or *kissed* NP[G]

   inferred four-tuples of *every guest that Sally told him to kiss* or *every guest that Sally kissed*

Note that (82a) *John kissed every guest that Sally did* does not mean {guests who John kissed} = {guests who Sally kissed}, but rather {guests who John kissed} ⊇ {guests who Sally kissed}. This is shown by the fact that *John kissed every guest that Sally did but Sally didn't kiss every guest that John did* is not contradictory and simply means that {guests who Sally kissed} is a proper subset of {guests who John kissed}. (83) is the F/A structure of (82a), which captures the correct interpretation represented informally as *For every guest s.t. Sally kissed him, John kissed him.*

(83) F/A of (82a)

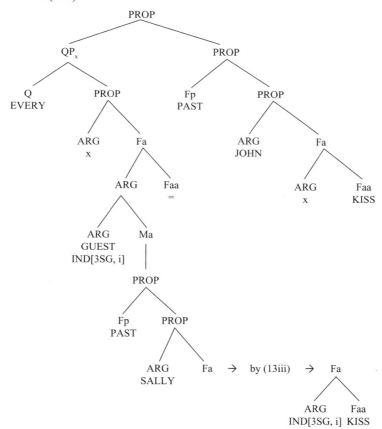

The coindexing (index sharing) in (83) between the head ARG, namely [$_{ARG}$ GUEST], and the coreferential ARG in the inferred Fa in the Ma (relative clause) is forced by the very nature of the *that*-relative clause (Ueno 2014: 331) that the head NP to which the relative clause is adjoined must corefer with an NP gap (NP[G]) that it c-commands. Note again that if we add an appropriate context to (82a), the pro-VP form *did* can take a different antecedent, as in (82c).

Here are other types of ACD.

(84) a. John persuaded everyone that you <u>did</u> to be polite. (Hornstein 1995: 74)
  did →
   antecedent: *persuaded* [$_{NP}$ *everyone that you did*] *to be polite*
   inferred VP: *persuaded* NP[G] *to be polite*
 b. John wanted to talk to everyone that Bill <u>did</u>. (Hornstein 1995: 86)
  (ambiguous)
  did →
   antecedents: *(wanted to) talk to* [$_{NP}$ *everyone that Bill did*]
   inferred VPs: *wanted to talk to* NP[G] or *talked to* NP[G]
 c. John kissed a woman who had ordered him <u>to</u>. (McCawley 1998: 638, 1993a: 205)
  to →
   antecedent: *kissed* [$_{NP}$ *a woman who had ordered him to*]
   inferred VP: *to kiss her* (Both *who* and *her* refer to the NP *woman*.)

ACD is known to occur in other environments. ACD is possible with a definite NP (85a). "Long distance" ACD is also possible ((85b), (78a)). Furthermore, it is quite possible for an ACD configuration to be only apparent in that the antecedent of its pro-VP form is found in the prior discourse, as illustrated in (77b) and (82c) and further illustrated here in (85c, d).

(85) a. Dulles suspected the spy that Angleton <u>did</u>. (Fiengo and May 1994: 242)
  did →
   inferred VP: *suspected* NP[G]
 b. John talked to everyone who Sally would have preferred that he hadn't. (Fiengo and May 1994: 250)
  hadn't →
   inferred VP: *hadn't talked to* NP[G]
 c. Blondie: Isn't that exquisite! I'd love to own it.
  Dagwood: That's the one big difference between us, honey. You always crave the things you can't have and I settle for the things I <u>can</u>.
   (Ueno 1997: 113, taken from *the International Herald Tribune* November 13, 1996)

  can →
    inferred VP: *can have* NP[G]
 d. I know which book Max read, and which book Oscar thinks that Sally
  did. (Fiengo and May 1994: 229)
  did →
    inferred VP: *read* NP[G]

As for (86b), this sentence is syntactically ambiguous between *I visited [$_{NP}$ every town in every country]* and *I [$_{VP}$ [$_{VP}$ visited every town] in every country]*, where *in every country* is part of the object NP in the former, while it is a VP adjunct in the latter. Only the latter structure allows PP-preposing, as in *In every country, I visited every town*.

(86) (Johnson 2001: 449)
 a. I visited every town I had to.
  to →
    inferred VP: *to visit* NP[G]
 b. *I visited every town in every country I had to.
  to →
    inferred VP: *to visit* NP[G]

Although Johnson claimed (86b) to be unacceptable, an interpretation of (86b) seems to be available in which the relative clause *I had to* only modifies *every country* as in (87a, b), which is not an ACD structure and means that 'In every country I had to visit, I visited every town.' For example, all the countries I had to visit were Japan, Korea, and China, and in each of these countries, I visited every town.

(87) a. ?I [[visited every town] (last year) [$_{PP}$ in every country I had to]].
  to →
    antecedent: *visited* [$_{NP}$ *every town*]
    inferred VP: *to visit* NP[G]
 b. ?In every country I had to, I visited every town.
  to →
    antecedent: *visited* [$_{NP}$ *every town*]
    inferred VP: *to visit* NP[G]

5.8 Ambiguity in Pro-VP Form Interpretations

McCawley (1993a: 261) discussed Sag's (1976) observation that (88a) is ambiguous between interpretations (88b) and (88c).

(88) a. Betsy greeted everyone when Sandy <u>did</u>. (ambiguous) (McCawley 1993a: 261, Sag 1976: 41 (1.3.12))
    b. 'Betsy greeted everyone when Sandy greeted everyone.'
        = 'Betsy said, "Hello, everyone" when Sandy said, "Hello, everyone."'
    c. 'Betsy greeted everyone$_x$ when Sandy greeted him$_x$.'
        = 'For every person, Betsy greeted him when Sandy greeted him.'

Interpretation (88b) concerns two acts of greeting everyone, one by Betsy and the other by Sandy. This interpretation is arrived at in the following way.

(89) arriving at interpretation (88b)
    did →
        decoded four-tuple of *Sandy did*
        antecedent: *greeted everyone*
        inferred VP: *greeted everyone*
        inferred four-tuple of *Sandy greeted everyone* with the corresponding inferred F/A
            $[_{QPy}$ EVERYONE] (PAST [SANDY(GREET(y))])

In general, a pro-VP form can take as its antecedent a VP that contains a quantified NP (QNP) as in (90).

(90) a. John greeted someone yesterday. Mary <u>did</u> today.
      did →
          decoded four-tuple of *Mary did today*
          antecedent: *greeted someone*
          inferred VP: *greeted someone*
          inferred four-tuple of *Mary greeted someone today*
    b. Fred talked about everything before Rusty <u>did</u>. (Johnson 2001: 469)
      did →
          decoded four-tuple of *Rusty did*
          antecedent: *talked about everything*

inferred VP: *talked about everything*
inferred four-tuple of *Rusty talked about everything*

In (90a), the person who John greeted yesterday and the person who Mary greeted today do not have to be identical. John and Mary may very well have greeted different people. This means that each sentence is interpreted with its own existential quantifier. In (88b), the first *everyone* ranges over the set of people Betsy greeted and the second *everyone* ranges over the set of people Sandy greeted, and the two sets can be distinct. Note that (90b) can also be interpreted as 'Fred talked about everything before Rusty talked about them' with the E-type pronoun *them*.

Interpretation (88c) is due to the inference process of turning a QNP into its bound variable pronoun (a kind of vehicle change) when the pro-VP form *did* is in the scope of QNP *everyone* (i.e., when the latter c-commands the former).

(91) a. arriving at interpretation (88c)
did →
decoded four-tuple of *Betsy greeted everyone when Sandy did*
(PP[*when*] as VP-adjunct)
antecedent: *greeted* [$_{NP}$ *everyone*]
inferred VP: *greeted* [$_{NP}$ *him*]
(*him* (vehicle change) as a bound variable c-commanded by *everyone*)
inferred four-tuple of *Betsy greeted everyone when Sandy greeted him*
b. F/A of *Betsy greeted everyone*

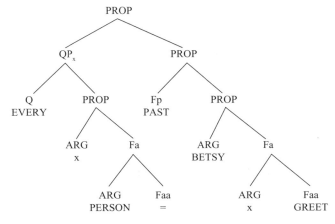

The inference process (vehicle change) of turning a QNP into a bound variable pronoun in the inferred VP, such as the inferred VP in (91a), is motivated by the fact that the pro-VP form *did* is c-commanded by the QNP *everyone* (because the PP[*when*] is a VP-adjunct), and hence within its scope. In addition, when *did* is interpreted, the matrix clause *Betsy greeted everyone* is already processed and its decoded four-tuple is available. In particular, its decoded F/A (91b) is available when *did* is interpreted. Because *did* is within the scope of *everyone*, the F/A correspondent of the PP[*when*] will modify a PROP (except for the topmost PROP) or Fa. The antecedent [$_{VP[PAST]}$ *greeted everyone*] roughly corresponds to [$_{Fa}$ [$_{ARG}$ x], [$_{Faa}$ GREET]]. This correspondence between the antecedent VP and the Fa with variable x also motivates this inference process.

This inference process is further illustrated by (92) under the assumption that the pro-VP form is in the scope of the QNP.

(92) a. Betsy greeted someone because Sandy did. (PP[*because*] as VP adjunct)
   did →
   decoded four-tuple of *Betsy greeted someone because Sandy did*
   antecedent: *greeted someone*
   inferred VP: *greeted him*
      (*him* (vehicle change) as a bound variable c-commanded by *someone*)
   inferred four-tuple of *Betsy greeted someone because Sandy greeted him*

b. We discussed everything because we wanted to. (PP[*because*] as VP adjunct)
   to →
   decoded four-tuple of *We discussed everything because we wanted to*
   antecedent: *discussed everything*
   inferred VP: *to discuss it* or *to discuss them* (E-type pronoun)
      (*it* (vehicle change) as a bound variable c-commanded by *everything*)
   inferred four-tuple of *We discussed everything because we wanted to discuss it* or
      We discussed everything because we wanted to discuss them
      (E-type pronoun)

In short, to arrive at reading (88b), the comprehension procedure (13) proceeds as usual through the syntactic structure of (88a), whereas, to arrive at reading

(88c), (13) proceeds the same way but with an additional inference (a type of vehicle change) of turning a QNP into a bound variable pronoun. For readings (88c) and (92a, b) to obtain, the PP must be adjoined to the matrix VP, because a pronoun interpreted as a bound variable must be c-commanded by its binder QNP (Ueno 2014: 291).

5.9 Strict and Sloppy Identity Interpretations

In this section, we will only consider the strict and sloppy identity interpretations of possessive determiners such as *his* or *her*. If we restrict our attention to the interpretations of (93a) in which *his* refers to *John*, then the pro-VP form *does* is interpreted in two ways: strict identity interpretation (93b), in which *his* in the inferred VP carries the same referential index as *his* in the antecedent VP, and sloppy identity interpretation (93c), in which *his* in the inferred VP carries the same referential index as its own subject *Bill*.

(93) a. John$_i$ loves his$_i$ wife and Bill <u>does</u> too. (ambiguous) (McCawley 1993a: 197)
   does →
      decoded four-tuple of *Bill does too*
      antecedent: *loves his wife*
      inferred VP: *loves his wife*
      inferred four-tuple of *Bill loves his wife too*
   b. strict identity reading: 'John$_i$ loves his$_i$ wife and Bill$_j$ loves his$_i$ wife too.'
   c. sloppy identity reading: 'John$_i$ loves his$_i$ wife and Bill$_j$ loves his$_j$ wife too.'
   d. John loves his wife and his brother <u>does</u> too. (strict identity reading > sloppy identity reading)

(93b, c) show that *his* in the inferred VP in (93a) takes as its antecedent *John* (resulting in strict identity interpretation (93b)) or *Bill* (resulting in sloppy identity interpretation (93c)).

As discussed in Ueno (2014: 25), the referential index is primarily an F/A entity and represented in F/A, but it is also represented in syntax, due to an extended interpretation of Feature Osmosis (Sadock 2012: 154, Ueno 2014: 25). We assume (I) that step (iib) in (13) of constructing an inferred VP retains by default the referential indices on the NPs in the antecedent (that is, the NPs in the inferred VP carry the same referential indices as the original NPs in the antecedent) and (II) that this retention can be overridden by other stronger semantic/pragmatic factors. For example, in sentences such as *John shook his head and Bill did too, John laughed his way out of the restaurant and Bill did too*, and *John likes his own car and Bill does too*, the retention of the same referential index on *his* in the antecedent VP and on *his* in the inferred VP is overridden by semantic/pragmatic factors. If these assumptions ((I) and (II)) are correct, strict identity interpretation holds by default.

Furthermore, strict identity interpretation is usually more accessible than sloppy identity interpretation. When the speaker utters the first conjunct of (93a), she takes John's point of view (along the lines of Kuno's (1987) empathy), because the possessive determiner *his* refers to *John*. If the speaker maintains the same point of view in the second conjunct, the strict identity interpretation (93b) obtains. By contrast, in order for the sloppy identity interpretation (93c) to obtain, the speaker has to change her point of view from John in the first conjunct to Bill in the second conjunct. Notice that the sloppy identity reading (93c) obtains under very limited circumstances such as when both John and Bill are happily married and they are equally prominent in discourse and therefore equally easy to empathize with. This line of reasoning seems to be on the right track, which is shown by (93d), where not only the first but also the second conjunct take John's point of view and as a result, a strict identity interpretation is more salient than a sloppy identity interpretation.

However, the availability of strict and sloppy identity readings is influenced by semantic/pragmatic factors. Sloppy identity interpretation is obligatory and strict identity interpretation is impossible in each example of (94). In (94a), the first conjunct makes manifest the propositional function $P(x) = x$ *loves x's wife*, and the second conjunct is simply interpreted as *P(John)*. In (94b), the inferred VP *love his own wife* forces a sloppy identity reading, because of the presence of *own*. The examples in (94) only allow a sloppy identity reading for semantic/pragmatic reasons.

(94) a. Every husband loves his wife and I'm sure John <u>does</u> too.
 b. John loves his own wife and Bill <u>does</u> too.
 c. John {raised his voice | kept his mouth shut | craned his neck} and Bill <u>did</u> too.
 d. John divorced his wife and Bill <u>did</u> too.

The availability of sloppy identity reading is pragmatically influenced. Slopping identity reading is dominant in (95a) but very weak in (95b).

(95) a. Obama loves his wife and Biden <u>does</u> too.
b. President Obama loves his wife and all the White House staffers <u>do</u> too.

Jerry Sadock (p.c.) pointed out the following example.

(96) Speaking of Fred$_k$, he$_k$ has the most beautiful wife. John$_i$ loves his$_k$ wife and Bill$_j$ <u>does</u> too. (cf. (93a))
does →
    inferred VP: *loves his$_k$ wife*
    strict identity reading: 'John$_i$ loves his$_k$ wife and Bill$_j$ loves his$_k$ wife too' (default)

In (96), the first sentence establishes *Fred* as discourse topic and the whole discourse is uttered from Fred's point of view. Therefore, *his* in the second sentence refers to Fred and this point of view is maintained throughout the second sentence including its second conjunct, namely, *Bill does too*, resulting in strict identity reading.

5.10 Restrictions on VP Ellipsis

In this section, we will consider the two types of restriction on VP ellipsis interpretation discussed in McCawley (1993a) and try to account for them from our AMG perspective.

5.10.1 VP ellipsis in *tough* construction

When a VP contains another VP, either VP can be referred to by an appropriate pro-VP form.

(97) (McCawley 1993a: 259)
    a. Sam [$_{VP[PRES]}$ wants [$_{VP[to]}$ to write a novel]], and Larry <u>does</u> also.
       does → inferred VP: *wants to write a novel*
    b. Sam [$_{VP[PRES]}$ wants [$_{VP[to]}$ to write a novel]], and Larry wants <u>to</u> also.
       to → inferred VP: *to write a novel*

This is also true of (98) but not of (99), a contrast that was originally pointed out by Sag (1976).

(98) (McCawley 1993a: 259)
  a. Peter [$_{\text{VP[PRES]}}$ is ready [$_{\text{VP[to]}}$ to give up]], and Betsy is also.
     is → inferred VP: *is ready to give up*
  b. Peter is ready to give up, and Betsy is ready to also.
     to → inferred VP: *to give up*

(99) (McCawley 1993a: 259; McCawley 1998: 738 note 9)
  a. The steak [$_{\text{VP[PRES]}}$ is ready [$_{\text{VP[to]}}$ to eat NP[G]]], and the chicken is also. (Sag 1976: 83 (2.1.51))
  b. *The steak is ready to eat, and the chicken is ready to also. (Sag 1976: 85 (2.1.61))

The difference between (97) and (98) on the one hand and (99) on the other is that in the former sentences, the smaller VPs (i.e., *to write a novel* in (97) and *to give up* in (98)) are saturated in terms of the subcategorization of the respective verbs, whereas in the latter sentences, the smaller VP (i.e., *to eat* in (99)) is not saturated in the sense that it contains an NP gap (NP[G]).

To account for the difference between (98) and (99), we need two lexical entries for the adjective *ready*. In (98), *ready* is a subject-control adjective and its lexical entry is (100a). In (99), the complement VP[*to*] of *ready* contains an NP gap (NP[G]). The lexical entry for this use of *ready* is given in (100b), which is tentative only for the present discussion. For its precise lexical entry, we would need a proper analysis of the *tough* construction and related constructions, which would take us too far afield (cf. Sadock 2012: 198).

(100) a. lexical entry for *ready* in (98) (cf. Chapter 1 (82), Chapter 3 (64))
        syntax: A in [__, VP[*to*]]
        F/A: Fpa
        E/R: [$_{\text{TYPE}}$ "ready"] in [$_{\text{STATE}}$ __ [PT, TH] [$_{\text{GO}}$ [$_{\text{EV}}$ HAR ...]]
                                                          └─────────────────────────┘

     b. lexical entry for *ready* in (99)
        syntax: A in [__, VP[*to*]]
          The VP[*to*] must dominate an NP[G].
        F/A: Fpa
        E/R: [$_{\text{TYPE}}$ "ready"] in [$_{\text{STATE}}$ __ [PT, TH] [$_{\text{GO}}$ EV]]
          [PT, TH] must corefer with the role in the EV that corresponds to the NP[G] in syntax.

5.10 RESTRICTIONS ON VP ELLIPSIS   259

The tri-modular representations of the first conjunct in (98a) are given below.

(101) tri-modular representations of first conjunct of (98a) *Peter is ready to give up*

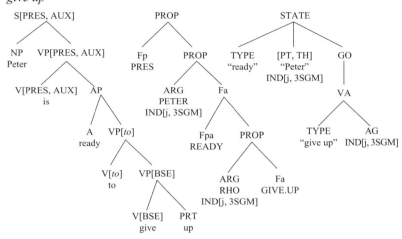

In the F/A above, PETER and RHO share the same INDEX (IND) value [j, 3SGM], which is due to the coreference requirement in the E/R field of (100a) between the [PT, TH] role of *ready* and the AG role of its VA complement. (102) is the syntax of the second conjunct of (98a) with the pro-VP form *is* and its inferential interpretation process.

(102) syntax of second conjunct of (98a) *Betsy is (also)*

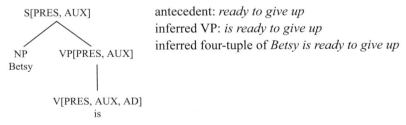

antecedent: *ready to give up*
inferred VP: *is ready to give up*
inferred four-tuple of *Betsy is ready to give up*

(103) is the syntax of the second conjunct of (98b) with the pro-VP form *to* and its inferential interpretation process.

(103) syntax of second conjunct of (98b) *Betsy is ready to (also)*

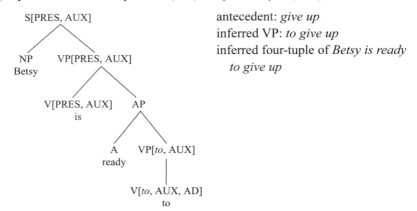

antecedent: *give up*
inferred VP: *to give up*
inferred four-tuple of *Betsy is ready to give up*

Note that the adjective *ready* in (103) takes a VP[*to*] complement and hence satisfies the syntactic field of the lexical entry for *ready* in (100a). In addition, the coreference requirement in the E/R field of the lexical entry (100a) is satisfied by the inferred syntax *Betsy is ready to give up*.

By contrast, (104) gives the tri-modular representations of the first conjunct of (99a).

(104) tri-modular representations of first conjunct of (99a) *The steak is ready to eat*

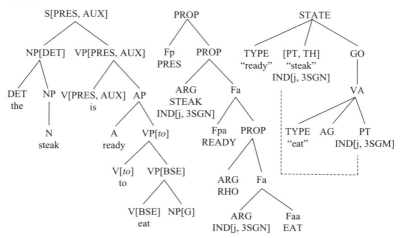

(105) is the syntax of the second conjunct of (99a) with the pro-VP form *is* and its inferential interpretation process.

(106) syntax of second conjunct of (99a) *The chicken is also*

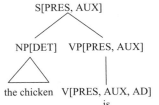

antecedent: *ready to eat NP[G]*
inferred VP: *is ready to eat NP[G]*
inferred four-tuple of *The chicken is ready to eat NP[G]*

(106) is the syntax of the second conjunct of (99b) with the pro-VP form *to* and its inferential interpretation process.

(106) syntax of second conjunct of (99b) **The steak is ready to eat NP[G] and the chicken is ready to also*

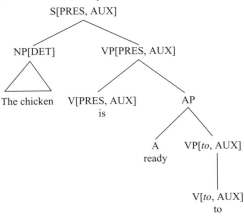

antecedent: *eat NP[G]* (from the first conjunct)
inferred VP: *to eat NP[G]*
inferred four-tuple of *The chicken is ready to eat NP[G]* (with the lexical entry (100a) *for ready*)

When the decoded syntax of the second conjunct *The chicken is ready [$_{\text{VP[to]}}$ *to*] also* of (99b) is constructed, the lexical entry for *ready* (100a) and not (100b) is chosen, because the adjective *ready* in (99b) takes a VP[*to*] complement that does not dominate an NP[G], which is shown in (106). Note that if you compare the syntactic fields of (100a) and (100b), the latter is more specific than the former. Therefore, (100b) must be chosen first before (100a) gets its chance to be chosen, according to the Elsewhere Principle. However, the condition in (100b) that the

VP[*to*] must dominate an NP[G] is not met in the second conjunct *the chicken is ready to also* of (99b). This means that (100a) is the only choice available when its decoded syntax is computed.

The construction of its inferred syntax proceeds as usual, which is indicated in (106). The end result of this is that *the chicken* is coreferential with the AG role of *eat*, due to the coreference requirement in the E/R field of (100a), there is no relation between *the chicken* and the NP[G], and hence there is no binder of the NP[G] (no role or *wh*-phrase), resulting in unacceptability. The contrast between *Peter is easy to talk to and Betsy is also* and **Peter is easy to talk to and Betsy is easy to also* (McCawley 1993a: 258–259) can also be explained in the same way.

5.10.2 Disappearance and reappearance of sloppy identity interpretation

Here is another set of examples that show a restriction on VP ellipsis. According to McCawley (1993a: 259), (107a) is three-way ambiguous with two strict identity interpretations (108a, b) and one sloppy identity interpretation (108c). But (107b), where VP ellipsis appears in the embedded clause of the second conjunct, is only two-way ambiguous: namely, while the two strict identity interpretations are retained, the sloppy identity interpretation disappears. In (107c), where VP ellipsis appears in the matrix clause of the second conjunct, the three-way ambiguity reappears.

(107)   a.   Alan said that Betsy had hit him, and Peter also said that she had hit him. (three-way ambiguous)
         b.   Alan said that Betsy had hit him, and Peter also said that she had. (two-way ambiguous)
         c.   Alan said that Betsy had hit him, and Peter did also. (three-way ambiguous)

(108)   three interpretations of (107a, c)
         a. $Alan_i$ said that Betsy had hit him_i and $Peter_j$ also said that she had hit him_i. (strict)
             direct discourse: $Alan_i$ said, "Betsy hit me_i," and $Peter_j$ also said, "She hit $\{you_i \mid him_i\}$."
         b. $Alan_i$ said that Betsy had hit him_k and $Peter_j$ also said that she had hit him_k. (strict)
             direct discourse: $Alan_i$ said, "Betsy hit him_k," and $Peter_j$ also said, "She hit him_k."

c. Alan$_i$ said that Betsy had hit him$_i$ and Peter$_j$ also said that she had hit him$_j$. (sloppy)
   direct discourse: Alan$_i$ said, "Betsy hit me$_i$," and Peter$_j$ also said, "She hit me$_j$."

The unavailability of a sloppy identity reading (108c) in the second conjunct of (107b) is due to a certain grammatical condition on the availability of sloppy identity reading in VP ellipsis. It was argued in 5.9 that strict identity reading holds by default and that sloppy identity reading is available under very limited circumstances.

(109) a. John$_i$ loves his$_i$ wife and Bill$_j$ does too. (= (93a))
      b. John$_i$ loves his$_i$ wife and Bill$_j$ loves his$_j$ wife too. (sloppy identity reading of (109a))

The sloppy identity reading of (109a) obtains if it is possible for the hearer/interpreter to take (109a) as *P(John) and P(Bill)*, where $P(x) = x$ *loves x's wife*. Let us call the value of x of the propositional function $P(x)$ (*John* in the first conjunct and *Bill* in the second) the controller of a sloppy identity reading. The condition on the sloppy identity reading of a pro-VP form is that the controller of a sloppy identity reading must be the subject of the pro-VP form in question. This must be so, because a pro-VP form signals that it and its subject must be interpreted in the same way as the antecedent VP and its subject, which in turn provide a possibility of taking them as a propositional function $P(a)$, where a is the subject NP of the antecedent VP.

If we take the first conjunct of (110a) as *P(Alan)*, where $P(x) = x$ *said that Betsy had hit x*, the controller of the sloppy identity reading is *Alan* and the second conjunct of (110a) is *P(Peter)*, where the controller *Peter* is the subject of the pro-VP form *did*, as required by the above condition. By contrast, this possibility is not available in (110b), where if we take the second conjunct as *P(Peter)*, the controller *Peter* is not the subject of a pro-VP form. Therefore, a sloppy identity reading does not obtain in (110b).

(110) a. Alan said that Betsy had hit him, and Peter did also. (= 107c))
      b. Alan said that Betsy had hit him, and Peter also said that she had. (= (107b))

Chapter 6
An Automodular View of Gapping

> In this chapter, we will examine various properties of gapping (both S-level gapping and VP-level gapping) and claim that they are best explained by formulating gapping as a construction, as in (33), that involves a coordinate structure. We will also show that non-demonstrative inference plays an important role in the interpretation of the gapping construction and propose the Procedure for gapping comprehension (24), which is common in large measure to all types of ellipsis comprehension. Finally, we will extend this approach to stripping.

6.1 Preliminary Description of Gapping

According to McCawley (1998: 287), gapping applies to a coordinate structure in which the conjuncts are identical except for two contrasting constituents, one constituent being outside the topmost VP constituent (subject NP or adverbial S-adjunct) and the other being contained in the topmost VP constituent, and deletes everything except those nonidentical constituents from all conjuncts other than the first. In the following examples, contrastively focused phrases are enclosed in square brackets. (1) is an example of gapping. The second conjunct (gapped conjunct) consists of two remnant NPs and is considered in derivational approaches to have been derived from [*Bernice*] *sent the President* [*a bomb*]. The two remnant phrases of the gapped conjunct are contrastively focused with the corresponding phrases of the first conjunct: in (1), the first remnant phrase *Bernice* is contrastively focused with *Fred* and the second remnant phrase *a bomb* with *a nasty letter*.

(1) [$_S$ [Fred] sent the President [a nasty letter]], and [$_S$ [Bernice] [a bomb]]. (McCawley 1998: 280)

We will enumerate here ten descriptive observations of gapping that have often been pointed out. First of all, the method of combining the first S, which is a full (gapless) sentence, and the second gapped S, which consists of two remnant phrases, is coordination. This is clear, for one thing, from the use of the coordinating conjunction *and* in (1). More importantly, the whole structure obeys the Coordinate Structure Constraint (CSC) (Ueno 2014: 262, 270), which is illustrated in (2). This shows that, if considered in derivational terms, a coordinate structure is required as input to the "gapping transformation" and is maintained in its output.

(2) a. [Fred] sent her [reports of this case] and [Bernice] [articles about that case].
  b. *Which case did [Fred] send her [reports of __] and [Bernice] [articles about that case]?
  b. *Which case did [Fred] send her [reports of this case] and [Bernice] [articles about __]?
  c. Which case did [Fred] send her [reports of __] and [Bernice] [articles about __]?
  d. Which case did [Fred] persuade her to read [reports of __] and [Bernice] to write [articles about __]?

In fact, (3) shows that gapping is restricted to coordinate structures.

(3) (McCawley 1998: 281)
  a. *That [Alice] ordered [turnips] makes it likely that [Fred] [artichokes].
  b. *Although [Alice] ordered [turnips], [Fred] [artichokes].

Second, the constituents of the first (gapless) conjunct that are contrastively focused with one of the remnant constituents in the gapped conjuncts must be "major constituents," which are phrases directly dominated by S, VP, or AP (Hankamer 1973: 18 note 2). In other words, the remnant constituents in the gapped conjuncts must be interpreted as major constituents. (4a) is unacceptable because *memorizing* of the first conjunct, which is intended to be contrastively focused with *reciting* of the gapped conjunct, is not a major constituent. Although it is directly dominated by a VP (i.e., [$_{VP}$ memorizing limericks]), it is not a phrase (i.e., not a VP). Compare this with (4a'), where *eating* in the first conjunct constitutes a VP. (4b, c) are unacceptable for the same reason.

6.1 PRELIMINARY DESCRIPTION OF GAPPING

(4) a. *[John] enjoys [memorizing] limericks, and [Mary] [reciting]. (McCawley 1998: 287)
(= the intended interpretation of the second conjunct: Mary enjoys reciting limericks)
a'. [John] continued [$_{VP}$ eating], and [Mary] [$_{VP}$ sleeping]. (McCawley 1998: 287)
b. *[John] [likes] Mary and [Bill] [loves]. (Hudson 1989: 70)
c. ??[George] became [ashamed] of the Washington family's past, and [Martha] [proud]. (McCawley 1998: 287)

As opposed to the unacceptable (4c), (5a) is acceptable because the AP of the first conjunct, directly dominated by a VP, is a major constituent. (5b) is also acceptable, because the PP of the first conjunct, directly dominated by an AP (i.e., [$_{AP}$ ashamed of his past]), is a major constituent.

(5) (McCawley 1998: 287)
a. [George] became [$_{AP}$ ashamed of the Washington family's past], and [Martha] [$_{AP}$ proud of it].
b. [George] became ashamed [$_{PP}$ of his past], and [Martha] [$_{PP}$ of her taste in men].

In (9d) below, the PP[*on*] of the first conjunct is a major constituent, because it is directly dominated by an AP (i.e., [$_{AP}$ keen on Mary]).

Third, gapping is applicable not only to two-term coordinate structures as in (1) and (5), but also to coordinate structures of three terms or more.

(6) a. [John] gave [$50] to the Cancer Foundation, [Mary] [$100], and [Ted] [$75]. (McCawley 1998: 62)
b. [Alice] ordered [turnips], [Ed] [artichokes], and [Bernice] [zucchini]. (McCawley 1998: 280)
c. [Paul Schachter] has informed me [that the basic order in Tagalog and related languages is VOS], [Ives Goddard] [that the unmarked order in Algonquian is OVS], and [Guy Carden] [that the basic order in Aleut is OSV]. (Ross 1970: 250)

Fourth, the phrase of the first conjunct that is contrastively focused with the second remnant phrase of the gapped conjuncts can be deeply embedded. In other words, the second remnant phrase of the gapped conjuncts can be interpreted as being deeply embedded.

(7) a. [John] managed to find time to start writing [a novel], and [Mary] [a movie script]. (McCawley 1998: 62)
   b. [I] want to try to begin to write [a novel], and [Mary] [a play]. (Ross 1970: 250)
   c. [Fred] tried to talk the dean into recommending that the linguistics department teach [semiotics], and [Wilma] [dialectology]. (McCawley 1998: 287)

However, the "deleted parts" of the gapped conjuncts (i.e., the noncontrastive parts of the first conjunct) do not have to be contiguous, let alone a single constituent. In (6a), for example, the deleted parts of each conjunct are the verb (*gave*) and the PP[*to*] (*to the Cancer Foundation*), which are not adjacent or a constituent of the first conjunct.

Fifth, the phrase of the first conjunct that is contrastively focused with the first remnant phrase of the gapped conjuncts can be an ad-S (i.e., sentence-modifying) adverb phrase (ADVP) or PP. In other words, the first remnant phrase of the gapped conjuncts can be interpreted as an ad-S adjunct. This type of gapping is covered by McCawley's description given above. In (8a), the two ad-S adverbs are contrastively focused, as are the two ad-S PPs in (8b, c).

(8) (McCawley 1998: 287)
   a. [Frequently] Max eats [herring], and [occasionally] [oysters].
   b. [On Tuesday] Max ate [herring], and [on Thursday] [oysters].
   c. [In Canada] they drive [on the right], and [in Japan] [on the left].

Sixth, the coordinated Ss can be nonfinite clauses. (2c, d) are such examples. They are instances of S[BSE]-coordination. Regarding the syntax of inverted clauses, see Chapter 1 (16).

(9) a. Will [$_{S[BSE]}$ [$_{S[BSE]}$ [John] watch [the Red Sox game]] and [$_{S[BSE]}$ [Lucy] [the quiz show]]]?
   (S[BSE]-coordination; McCawley 1998: 306)
   a'. Did [$_{S[BSE]}$ [$_{S[BSE]}$ [Bill] eat [the peaches]], or [$_{S[BSE]}$ [Harry] [the grapes]]]?
   (S[BSE]-coordination; Jackendoff 1971: 23)

6.1 PRELIMINARY DESCRIPTION OF GAPPING   269

    a". It is past time that [$_{S[BSE]}$ [$_{S[BSE]}$ [the power of presidency] be [reduced]] and [$_{S[BSE]}$ [the power of congress] [restored]]]. (S[BSE]-coordination; Imanishi and Asano 1990: 367)
    b. Painters want to see the world afresh, and to discard all the accepted prejudices about [$_{S[PRP]}$ [$_{S[PRP]}$ [flesh] being [pink]] and [$_{S[PRP]}$ [apples] [red]]]. (S[PRP]-coordination)
    b'. With [$_{S[PRP]}$ [$_{S[PRP]}$ [Pollini] playing [the Brahms Second]] and [$_{S[PRP]}$ [Arran] [the Beethoven Fourth]]], we're going to have a great week of concerts. (S[PRP]-coordination; McCawley 1983: 273)
    c. For [$_{S[to]}$ [$_{S[to]}$ [Jack] to hate [swimming]] and [$_{S[to]}$ [Fred] [fishing]]] would be a tremendous surprise. (S[*to*]-coordination; Jackendoff 1977: 45)
    c'. Mary wants [$_{S[to]}$ [$_{S[to]}$ [Tom] to cook [the egg]] and [$_{S[to]}$ [Nancy] [the eggplant]]]. (S[*to*]-coordination; Imanishi and Asano 1990: 366; Chapter 1 (6b), Ueno 2014: 181)
    d. With [$_{AS}$ [$_{AS}$ [John] keen [on Mary]] and [$_{AS}$ [Mary] [on Bill]]], the holiday that the three of them are planning looks doomed to failure. (AS-coordination; Hudson 1989: 86)

The syntactic structures of S[*to*] in (9c, c') and AS in (9d) are as follows: [$_{S[to]}$ NP [$_{VP[to]}$ V[*to*] VP[BSE]]] (cf. Chapter 1 (6b)) and [$_{AS}$ NP AP] (cf. Chapter 1 (2)).

Seventh, coordinated imperatives, which lack overt subjects, can be gapped.

(10) a. [Always] do it [with your left hand], [never] [with your right]. (Huddleston and Pullum 2002: 1338)
    b. [Always] eat [slowly], [never] [noisily], and [sometimes] [moderately]. (Hudson 1989: 86)

Eighth, McCawley's description above excludes cases of gapping in which the two remnant phrases of the gapped conjuncts are contrastively focused with two phrases of the first conjunct that are both outside the topmost VP.

(11) a. ??[On Tuesdays], [Lucy] handles customers' complaints, and [on Wednesdays] [George]. (McCawley 1998: 63)
    b. ??[At 11], [John] was summoned to the dean's office, and [at 12], [Bill]. (McCawley 1998: 288)

cf. [At 11], the dean summoned [John] to his office, and [at 12], [Bill]. (McCawley 1998: 288)
c. ??[In China], [wine] is served in small cups, and [in Turkey], [coffee]. (McCawley 1998: 288)
cf. [In China], they serve [wine] in small cups, and [in Turkey], [coffee]. (McCawley 1998: 288)
d. *[Which book] did [Mary] buy, and [which record] [Bill]? (Hudson 1982: 549)

However, some speakers accept this type of gapping, which is shown in (12) below.

(12) a. [On Sundays], [Robin] speaks French to Bill, and [on Mondays], [Leslie]. (Culicover and Jackendoff 2005: 273)
b. [Yesterday], [Tom] came to see me, and [today], [Mary]. (Kuno 1976: 301, note 4)
c. [In most households] [the adults] make these decisions, but [in ours] [the kids]. (Huddleston and Pullum 2002: 1339)

In this type of gapping, the first remnant phrase (e.g., [*on Mondays*] in (12a)) is contrastively focused with the ad-S PP or adverb before the subject of the first conjunct, and the second remnant phrase (e.g., [*Leslie*] in (12a)) is contrastively focused with the subject NP of the first conjunct, and the topmost VP is "deleted."

Ninth, gapping is island insensitive in the sense that the phrase in the first conjunct that is contrastively focused with the second remnant phrase of the gapped conjuncts can be located within an island, as Culicover and Jackendoff (2005: 274) observed. In other words, the second remnant phrase of the gapped conjuncts can be interpreted as if it is contained in an island. For example, if the second remnant phrase in (13a), *German*, were moved by "A-bar movement," it would violate the CSC. If the second remnant phrase in (13b), *Ann Tyler*, were moved by "A-bar movement," it would violate the CNPC.

(13) Culicover and Jackendoff (2005: 273 (62) and (63))
a. CSC
[Robin] wants to wake up in the morning and be able to speak [French], and [Leslie], [German].

b. CNPC
      [Robin] is reading a book written by [John Updike], and [Leslie], [Ann Tyler].
   c. Adjunct Island
      [Robin] believes that everyone pays attention to you when you speak [French], and [Leslie], [German].
   d. *Wh*-island (and the CNPC)
      [Robin] knows a lot of reasons why [dogs] are good pets, and [Leslie], [cats].
   e. *that*-trace effect
      [Robin] thinks that [Ferraris] are cool, and [Leslie], [Maseratis].

These examples show the difficulties inherent in approaches to gapping that resort to "A-bar movement" and "deletion."

Tenth, some speakers do not allow deletion of a preposition that would leave behind its object NP as a remnant phrase, as shown in (14a, b). This restriction is due to the major constituent requirement illustrated in (4). Note that although the PP in the structure [$_{VP}$ V [$_{PP}$ P NP]] is a major constituent, its NP complement is not. However, some speakers allow this type of gapping, as shown in (13b) and (14c–e).

(14) a. John studied with Mary, and Tom *(with) Jane. (Kuno 1976: 301, note 3)
     b. John went to Miami and Mary ??(to) Detroit. (McCawley 1998: 307, ex 10)
     c. John thought about Jane and Bill, Betty. (Hudson 1989: 59)
     d. Fred has been working on semantics and Bill, syntax. (Hudson 1989: 60)
     e. Fred sat on a chair, Mary a stool, and Bill a bench. (Hudson 1989: 64)

6.2 Gapping and Inference

Gapping interacts with phenomena such as VP ellipsis, discussed in Chapter 5, and sluicing (*wh*-fragments), discussed in Chapter 4, which have been shown to involve the extragrammatical/pragmatic process of non-demonstrative inference. For example, to understand what C meant in (15a), we need to understand what B meant, but to determine what B meant, we need to revert to what A said at the beginning. The inferred syntactic structure of C is *What else does Tom like?*

(15) a. A: [John] likes [steak and raw fish] ...
  B: And [Tom] [teriyaki chicken and ...] [gapping]
  C: What else? [*wh*-fragment]
 b. A: Did you know [John] visited [Tokyo] and
   [Mary] [Kyoto]? [gapping]
  B: When? [*wh*-fragment]
  C: Well, [John] did [last month] [VP ellipsis + gapping]
   and [Mary] [this month].

In (15b), to understand C's second conjunct *Mary this month*, we need to refer back to the first conjunct with the pro-VP form *did*. The inferred syntax of the second conjunct is *Mary did this month* with another pro-VP form *did*. These two pro-VP forms have different antecedents. The antecedent of *did* in *John did last month* is *visited Tokyo*, whereas the antecedent of *did* in the inferred *Mary did this month* is *visited Kyoto*. Therefore, the inferred syntax of C's second conjunct *Mary this month* is *Mary visited Kyoto this month*. (16) provides some similar examples.

(16) a. A: Speaking of sports, John likes to play
   baseball, and Mary tennis. [gapping]
  B: Really? I don't think she does. [VP ellipsis]
  A: What sport, then? [*wh*-fragment]
 b. A: John gave her a novel and Tom a music CD. [gapping]
  B: Tell me when. [*wh*-fragment]
  C: John did on Monday and Tom on Tuesday. [VP ellipsis + gapping]
  D: Tom on Tuesday? Are you sure? [null complement
   On Wednesday, I guess.   anaphora + fragment]

The inferred syntax of A's *What sport, then?* in (16a) is *What sport do you think Mary likes to play, then?* The inferred syntax of D's *On Wednesday, I guess* in (16b) is *Tom gave her a music CD on Wednesday, I guess*. Here again, the antecedent of *did* in C's first conjunct and that of the inferred *did* in the second conjunct are different. The former is *gave her a novel* and the latter is *gave her a music CD*.

Second, the Missing Antecedent Phenomenon, which was discussed in 5.5, also appears in the gapping construction. This is illustrated in (17). To understand what *they* in the second sentence in (17a) refers to, the hearer/interpreter needs to posit an inferred syntax of the second conjunct *and Mary in New York* of the first sentence, which is *and Mary interviews artists in New York*. This provides the antecedent of *they*.

(17) Missing Antecedent Phenomenon in gapping
    a. Tom$_i$ interviewed artists in Chicago and Mary$_j$ in New York. She$_j$ knows they were generally more prolific than those he$_i$ interviewed in Chicago.
    b. Tom bought a picture in Chicago and Mary in New York. They were both very beautiful.

Third, the remnant phrases of gapped conjuncts can be *wh*-fragments, which need their inferred syntax for their interpretation. (18a) is an example of gapping in which the second remnant phrase of the gapped conjunct is a *wh*-fragment. The inferred syntax of *Mary how many girls* is *Mary knows how many girls are taking the course*.

(18) a. [John] knows [how many boys] are taking the course, and [Mary] [how many girls].
    b. A: I was told we have an important meeting today, but I don't know when or where.
       B: Ask John and Mary. [John] knows [when] and   [gapping + [Mary] [where].   *wh*-fragments]

The inferred syntax of the second sentence in (18bB) is *John knows when we have it and Mary knows where we have it* (or *John knows when it is and Mary knows where it is*), in which *it* refers to *an important meeting* in what A said. The first remnant phrase of gapped conjuncts can also be a *wh*-fragment, as shown in (19). The inferred syntax of the second conjunct is [*which girl*] *is taking algebra is known to Mary*.

(19) [Which boy] is taking algebra is known [to John] and [which girl] [to Mary].

Fourth, idiom chunks appear in gapped conjuncts. The VP idiom *cook someone's goose*, which means 'to spoil someone's plans,' is passivizable (Chapter 5 (16a)).

The VP idiom *pull someone's leg*, which means 'deceive someone playfully,' is also passivizable (Ueno 2014: 129–30).

(20) a. [John's goose] was cooked [by accident] and [Mary's] [by design].
 b. [John's leg] was pulled [by his brother] and [Mary's] [by her sister].

To understand the second conjunct *Mary's by design* of (20a), the hearer/interpreter needs to determine its inferred syntax by referring to the first conjunct. The first remnant phrase *Mary's* of the gapped conjunct represents *Mary's goose* and therefore the inferred syntax of the gapped conjunct is *Mary's goose was cooked by design*. Once the hearer/interpreter has determined its inferred syntax, he can interpret the gapped conjunct as the passive of VP idiom *cook someone's goose*. Without determining its inferred syntax, the hearer/interpreter cannot recover the idiomatic interpretation of the second conjunct, because he needs both *Mary's goose* and *was cooked* (*by design*) to interpret the second conjunct as the idiom.

Finally, gapping is similar to VP ellipsis in that it creates ambiguity between strict and sloppy identity readings (5.9) and requires vehicle change (Chapter 5 (25)).

(21) sloppy identity reading in gapping
 a. [John] loved his wife [five years ago] and [Max] [ten years ago]. (ambiguous)
  strict identity reading: 'John$_i$ loved his$_i$ wife five years ago and Max$_j$ loved his$_i$ wife ten years ago.'
  sloppy identity reading: 'John$_i$ loved his$_i$ wife five years ago and Max$_j$ loved his$_j$ wife ten years ago.'
 b. [John] introduced his wife [to the President] and [Max] [to the First Lady]. (ambiguous)
  strict identity reading: 'John$_i$ introduced his$_i$ wife to the President and Max$_j$ introduced his$_i$ wife to the First Lady.'
  sloppy identity reading: 'John$_i$ introduced his$_i$ wife to the President and Max$_j$ introduced his$_j$ wife to the First Lady.'
 c. [John] talked about himself [to me] and [Max] [to you]. (ambiguous)
  strict identity reading: 'John$_i$ talked about himself$_i$ to me and Max$_j$ talked about him$_i$ to you.'
  sloppy identity reading: 'John$_i$ talked about himself$_i$ to me and Max$_j$ talked about himself$_j$ to you.'

(22) vehicle change in gapping (cf. (21c))
   a. Mary and John$_i$ have different opinions about him$_i$. [She] thinks of him [as a fool] but [he] [as a genius].
   he as a genius → inferred syntax: *he thinks of* {**John* | **him* | *himself*} *as a genius*
   b. Mary and John$_i$ were worried about his$_i$ health. [She] talked about him [to a counselor] and [he] [to a doctor].
   he to a doctor → inferred syntax: *he talked about* {**John* | **him* | *himself*} *to a doctor*

The cases of gapping we have examined so far in this section show that non-demonstrative inference is essential to interpreting gapped conjuncts. As in other ellipsis comprehension, we assume the following process.

(23) a. Utterance comprehension process (cf. Chapter 3 (5b))
      elliptic utterance U → Language Module (LM) → decoded four-tuple of U → Inferential Comprehension Module (ICM) → inferred four-tuple of U → developed four-tuple of U → explicatures and implicatures of U (in Mentalese)
   b. Procedure for inferential comprehension of ellipsis (= Chapter 3 (5c))
      The hearer follows the Relevance-guided comprehension heuristic and executes the following steps.
      (i) The LM computes the decoded four-tuple of an elliptic utterance U.
      (ii) By non-demonstrative inference, the ICM constructs the inferred syntactic structure of U on the basis of the decoded syntax obtained in (i) and the contextual information.
      (iii) The ICM constructs the inferred four-tuple of U on the basis of the inferred syntax obtained in (ii) and the contextual information.
      (iv) The ICM develops the inferred four-tuple of U obtained in (iii) on the basis of the contextual information.
      (v) The ICM constructs the explicatures and implicatures of U on the basis of the developed four-tuple obtained in (iv) and the contextual information.

More specifically, we assume the comprehension procedure that is almost identical to the Procedure for pro-VP form comprehension (Chapter 5 (13)).

(24) Procedure for gapping comprehension
The hearer follows the Relevance-guided comprehension heuristic (Chapter 2 (8)) and executes the following steps.
  (i) The LM computes the decoded four-tuple of the gapped conjunct.
  (ii) By non-demonstrative inference, the ICM constructs the inferred syntactic structure of the gapped conjunct on the basis of the decoded syntax obtained in (i), the developed four-tuple of the first conjunct, and the contextual information.
  (iii) The ICM constructs the inferred four-tuple of the gapped conjunct on the basis of its inferred syntax obtained in (ii), the developed four-tuple of the first conjunct, and the contextual information.
  (iv) The ICM develops the inferred four-tuple of the gapped conjunct obtained in (iii) on the basis of the contextual information.
  (v) The ICM constructs the explicatures and implicatures of the whole gapping construction on the basis of the developed four-tuple obtained in (iv) and the contextual information including the developed four-tuple of the first conjunct.

Step (ii) of (24) involves supplying the gapped conjunct(s) with the information in the first conjunct that is not contrastively focused. (25) is an example of inferential interpretation of a gapping construction.

(25) (at a party) (cf. Chapter 2 (30))
Hostess: Come to the table and help yourself.
Host: The food will get cold and the beer lukewarm.
  and the beer lukewarm →
  (i) decoded four-tuple of *and the beer lukewarm*:
    ([$_{S[and]}$ and [$_S$ [$_{NP[DET]}$ the beer] [$_{AP}$ lukewarm]]], [$_{PROP}$ ARG Fa], [$_{EV}$ ROLE TYPE], [$_U$ FOC FOC])
  (ii) inferred syntax: *and the beer will get lukewarm*
  (iii) inferred four-tuple of *and the beer will get lukewarm*
  (iv) development of inferred four-tuple:
    enrichment of *will*: immediate future 'will very soon'
    reference assignment: *the beer* refers to 'the beer on the table where the food is put'

(v) explicature and implicatures

explicature: 'The host believes that the food on the table will get cold very soon and the beer on the table will get lukewarm very soon.'

implicature: 'The host tells the guests to come to the table and have the food and beer before the food gets cold and the beer gets lukewarm.'

Step (ii) of (25) is schematically shown in (26).

(26) before and after step (ii) of inferring syntactic structure of gapped conjunct

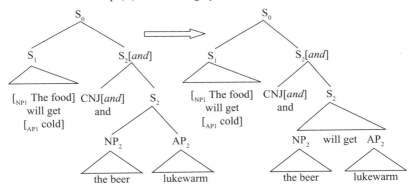

Before step (ii), NP_1 *the food* of the first conjunct and NP_2 *the beer* of the second conjunct are contrastively focused. In addition, AP_1 *cold* of the first conjunct and AP_2 *lukewarm* of the second conjunct are contrastively focused. The inferred syntactic structure of the gapped conjunct is obtained by filling it with the noncontrastive information (*will get*) of the first conjunct.

As shown in (26), when the first conjunct is not gapped, it is the antecedent of the gapped conjuncts. However, the first conjunct itself can be gapped, as illustrated in (27). In (27aB) and (27bB), a series of gapped conjuncts appear without a gapless conjunct as an answer to a multiple *wh*-question. Note that when the answer consists of only one gapped conjunct, it sounds quite awkward. This is because the speaker who chooses this way of answering usually intends to give a list of pairs. In these cases, the multiple *wh*-question serves as the antecedent of gapped conjuncts.

(27) a. A: [Who] brought [what] to the potluck?
　　　B: (i) [John] [a bottle of wine], [Mary] [a six-pack of beer], [Tom] [potato salad], ….
　　　　 (ii) [John] [a bottle of wine] and [Mary] [a six-pack of beer].
　　　　 (iii) ??[John] [a bottle of wine].
　　b. A: [What] did Fred bring [to whom]?
　　　B: (i) [A bottle of wine] [to John], [a six-pack of beer] [to Mary], [potato salad] [to Tom], ….
　　　　 (ii) [A bottle of wine] [to John] and [a six-pack of beer] [to Mary].
　　　　 (iii) ??[a bottle of wine] [to John].

In (28), B's part is uttered as an answer to A's question and is not a gapping construction. However, the explicature of B's first conjunct (*Yeah* in (28a), *Yeah, scotch* in (28b), and *no* in (28c)) provides a gapless antecedent of his second gapped conjunct.

(28) (Culicover and Jackendoff 2005: 276)
　　a. A: Are you going to invite [Robin]?
　　　B: Yeah, and [tomorrow night], [Leslie].
　　　Yeah →
　　　　　explicature: 'Yeah, tonight I am going to invite Robin.' (after enrichment with *tonight*) *and tomorrow night, Leslie* →
　　　　　decoded four-tuple of *and tomorrow night, Leslie*
　　　　　inferred syntax: *and tomorrow night, I am going to invite Leslie* (from the explicature)
　　　　　inferred four-tuple of *and tomorrow night, I am going to invite Leslie*
　　b. A: Does [Robin] drink?　　(cf. lexical entry for intransitive *drink* in Chapter 3 (75a))
　　　B: Yeah, [scotch], and [Leslie], [gin].
　　　Yeah, [scotch] →
　　　　　explicature: 'Yeah, Robin drinks scotch.'
　　　　　(The transitive *drink* is activated by the preceding intransitive *drink* and becomes accessible.)
　　　and Leslie, gin →
　　　　　decoded four-tuple of *and Leslie, gin*
　　　　　inferred syntax: *and Leslie drinks gin* (from the explicature)
　　　　　inferred four-tuple of *and Leslie drinks gin*

c. A: Does [Robin] speak [French]?
B: No, but [Leslie], [German].
No →
    explicature: *No, Robin does not speak French*
but Leslie, German →
    decoded four-tuple of *but Leslie, German*
    inferred syntax: *but Leslie speaks German*
        (from the explicature and pragmatic knowledge about *but*)
    inferred four-tuple of *but Leslie speaks German*

6.3 Gapping as Construction

In the first part of this section, we will present three pieces of evidence that show that we need to formulate gapping not as some kind of deletion rule, but as a construction, which is something to be registered in the lexicon (1.5, Ueno 2014: 43). In the second part, we will propose a lexical entry for the gapping construction and discuss various conditions imposed on it.

The first piece of evidence for treating gapping as a construction is that there are cases of gapping for which it is very difficult, if not impossible, to assume a full-fledged sentence for the gapped conjunct. In this respect, Hankamer's observation (1973: 24) that "every elliptical sentence consists of constituents which can occur as parts of some ordinary sentence" is wrong.

(29) a. [Kim] didn't [play bingo] or [Sandy] [sit at home all evening]. (Culicover and Jackendoff 2005: 279)
    b. Kim didn't play bingo or Sandy didn't sit at home all evening.
    c. [Mary] supports [John], not [John], [Mary]. (Klima 1964: 301)
    d. *Mary supports John, not John supports Mary.
    e. [Robin] speaks [French], {but | and} not [Leslie], [German]. (Culicover and Jackendoff 2005: 278, 281)
    f. *Ozzie said Harriet is beautiful {but | and} not Ricky was handsome. (Culicover and Jackendoff 2005: 281)
    g. [Sam] doesn't play [sousaphone], nor [Medusa] [sarrussophone]. (Jackendoff 1971: 22)
    h. Sam doesn't play sousaphone, nor does Medusa play sarrussophone.
    i. [Max] hadn't finished [his assignment], nor [Jill] [hers]. (Huddleston and Pullum 2002: 1339)
    j. Max hadn't finished his assignment, nor had Jill finished hers.

In (29a), *didn't* in the first conjunct is interpreted to have scope over the entire coordinate S with the second conjunct in its scope. That is, (29a) is interpreted as ¬(P∨Q), which is deductively equivalent to (¬P) ∧ (¬Q) (de Morgan law, McCawley 1993a: 78). In F/A terms, the composite functor [$_{Fp}$ PAST]∘[$_{Fp}$ NOT] that corresponds to *didn't* in the syntax of (29a) takes as its complement a coordinated PROP, namely, [$_{PROP}$ KIM(PLAY(BINGO))] OR [$_{PROP}$ SANDY(SIT. AT.HOME.ALL.EVENING)]. In this sense, *didn't* is shared between the first and second conjuncts. (See 6.7 for details on operator sharing.) Note that (29a) is semantically different from (29b) and hence cannot be assumed to have been derived from (29b).

In (29c) without a coordinating conjunction (CNJ) and in (29e) with a CNJ, the second gapped conjunct is immediately preceded by *not*, which is used as metalinguistic contrastive negation (cf. McCawley 1998: 613). Note that *not* cannot be adjoined to an S, as is shown in (29d, f). In these cases, there is no well-formed inferred syntax of gapped conjuncts, but they do have well-formed explicatures such as 'As for who supports who, a true proposition is that Mary supports John and not that John supports Mary' for (29c) and 'As for who speaks what language, a true proposition is that Robin speaks French but/and not that Leslie speaks German' for (29e).

In (29g, i), gapping occurs with the negative CNJ *nor*. However, the full sentence of the second conjunct must have negative inversion with the auxiliaries *does* and *had* as in (29h, j), whereas the auxiliaries in the first conjunct are *doesn't* and *hadn't*. If we took a deletion approach to gapping, deriving (29 g) from (29h) and (29i) from (29j) would complicate the formulation of a "gapping deletion rule."

The second piece of evidence for formulating gapping as a construction is that the case of a subject pronoun in a gapped conjunct may be either nominative or accusative, as shown in (30). Of course, the accusative subject of a finite clause is ungrammatical: **Me took the lower one* and **Them try to treat him*.

(30) a. [Kim] took [the upper route], [{I | me}] [the lower one]. (Huddleston and Pullum 2002: 1339)
b. [Fred] tries to treat [his parents] well, and [{they | them}] [him]. (Hudson 1989: 57)

The reason why an accusative pronoun is allowed to appear as a remnant of gapped conjuncts is that because remnant phrases are foci and focused pronouns are in the strong form (i.e., in the accusative case in the case of English), the accusative pronoun is allowed to appear in (30) as a strong form of the nominative pronoun. See Chapter 3 (37) and (38).

The third piece of evidence concerns *John did on Monday and Tom on Tuesday* in (16b), repeated below. Its inferred syntax is *John gave her a novel on Monday and Tom gave her a music CD on Tuesday*.

(31) A: John gave her a novel and Tom a music CD. [gapping]
    B: Tell me when. [*wh*-fragment]
    C: John did on Monday and Tom on Tuesday. [VP ellipsis + gapping]
    D: Tom on Tuesday? Are you sure?
       On Wednesday, I guess. [null complement anaphora + fragment]

Suppose we took deletion approaches to gapping and VP ellipsis, and tried to derive *John did on Monday and Tom on Tuesday* in (31C) from its full-fledged sentence *John gave her a novel on Monday and Tom gave her a music CD on Tuesday*. As for the first conjunct *John gave her a novel on Monday*, VP deletion is applicable because its antecedent *gave her a novel* is in what A said previously (*John gave her a novel and Tom a music CD*). However, VP deletion is not applicable to the second conjunct *Tom gave her a music CD*, because there is no prior VP antecedent (*gave her a music CD*). Note that the second conjunct of A is already gapped and *gave a music CD* is reduced to *a music CD*. This shows that if we took deletion approaches to gapping and VP ellipsis, there would be no way of deriving *John did on Monday and Tom on Tuesday* in (31C) from its full-fledged sentence. On the other hand, if we formulate gapping as a construction, this example will be licensed by the lexical entry for the gapping construction (to be given as (33)) and its intended interpretation will be recovered by inference.

Although gapping is said to occur in coordinate structures, the set of coordinating conjunctions that appear with gapped conjuncts is much larger than the set of such pure coordinating conjunctions as *and*, *or*, *but*, and includes such connectives as *as well as*, *not to mention*, *let alone*, the positive degree *as*, the comparative degree *than*, *instead of*, and *rather than*.

(32) a. [Robin] speaks [French], {<u>as well as</u> | <u>not to mention</u>} [Leslie], [German]. (Culicover and Jackendoff 2005: 278)
    b. [Robin] doesn't speak [French], <u>let alone</u> [Leslie], [German]. (Culicover and Jackendoff 2005: 278)

b'. They couldn't make [John] eat [the shrimp], <u>let alone</u> [Lucille] [the squid]. (Fillmore et al. 1988: 514)
c. [Robin] tried harder to learn [French] <u>than</u> [Leslie], [German]. (Culicover and Jackendoff 2005: 278)
d. [Robin] tried to learn [French] <u>as hard as</u> [Leslie], [German].
e. [She] paid [for him] <u>instead of</u> [him] [for her]. (Hudson 1989: 73)
f. [He] helped [her] <u>rather than</u> [her], [him] (Hudson 1989: 73)

These coordinating connectives (CCs) therefore must include in the syntactic field of their lexical entries the statement that their complement allows a gapped conjunct consisting of two remnant phrases.

The gapping construction is understood in the most general terms as the syntactic structure $[_S \ldots XP \ldots YP \ldots] [CC [_S XP\ YP]]^n$ (i.e., any number of $[CC [_S XP\ YP]]$), in which the first conjunct is a gapless full clause and is followed by any number of gapped conjuncts that consist of two phrases XP and YP that are contrastively focused with the corresponding XP and YP in the first conjunct. (33) is the lexical entry for the gapping construction.

(33) lexical entry for gapping (as a construction)
The gapping construction is a coordinate structure of conjuncts with the syntactic category C, where C is clausal (<BAR, 2>, cf. Chapter 1 (2)) or VP (cf. 6.4).

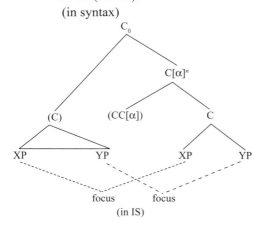

(i) Each gapped conjunct consists of two remnant phrases XP and YP.
(ii) The antecedent of the gapped conjuncts is the first conjunct if it is not gapped. Otherwise, it is in the prior discourse.
(iii) XP and YP in the antecedent must be major constituents.
(iv) The antecedent is the smallest CP[WH[Q]], S, or VP that dominates both XP and YP.
(v) XP and YP of the gapped conjuncts are contrastively focused with XP and YP in the antecedent, respectively.

The gapping construction is limited to the coordinate structure, as was discussed in (1), (2), and (3). In the syntactic structure of (33), the coordinating connective (CC) includes those in (32) that take a gapped conjunct as its complement. Technically, α is a value of the CCFORM feature. For example, CC[*and*] is a CC with the CCFORM feature whose value is *and*, namely {<POSP, CC>, <BAR, 0>, <CCFORM, *and*>}. Therefore, S[*and*] is an S with the CCFORM feature value *and*, namely {<POSP, V>, <BAR, 2>, <CCFORM, *and*>}. To guarantee such syntactic structures as [$_{S[and]}$ CC[*and*] S] and [$_{VP[but]}$ CC[*but*] VP], we would need new PS rules [$_{S[α]}$ CC[α], S] and [$_{VP[α]}$ CC[α], VP] in addition to those in Chapter 1 (1). However, we don't need to do so. These rules must be stated in the syntactic field of each coordinating connective as part of its lexical information. Note also that the linear order between CC and S (or VP) is determined by Chapter 1 (59).

The syntax of (33) covers such gapping cases as (34), in which XP is an ad-S adjunct or subject and YP is a VP that is the complement of a finite auxiliary verb (V[FIN, AUX]). Both XP and YP are major constituents, because the former is directly dominated by S and the latter by VP[FIN, AUX].

(34) a. [John] will [$_{VP[BSE]}$ sing] and [Mary] [$_{VP[BSE]}$ dance]. (Hudson 1976: 543)
 b. [Tom] will [play the guitar] and [Mary] [sing]. (Huddleston and Pullum 2002: 1542)
 c. [Today] I will [play the guitar] and [tomorrow] [sing].

Furthermore, the superior *n* to the constituent C[α] in the syntactic structure of (33) shows a possibility of three or more terms of coordination in the gapping construction, as was discussed in (6).

The syntactic structure of (33) requires of each conjunct that the linear order between XP and YP be fixed (i.e., XP must precede YP). However, this linear order requirement is relaxed when the gapping construction consists of two conjuncts and one of the remnant phrases is an ad-S adjunct.

(35) a. Max ate [herring] [on Tuesday], and [on Thursday] [oyster]. (Sobin 1981: 489)
 b. [In the morning] [John] washes up, and [Mary] [in the afternoon]. (Imanishi and Asano 1990: 331)
 c. [A policeman] walked in [at 11], and [at 12], [a fireman]. (Sag et al. 1985: 158)
 d. [A blossom] fell [from the tree] and [from the sky] [a snow flake]. (Imanishi and Asano 1990: 331)

In each example in (35), the PP of the first conjunct is an ad-S adjunct. These adjuncts can appear either at the S-initial or S-final position. Note that the PP[*from*] of the first conjunct of (35d) is taken as a complement, and the second conjunct is interpreted as an instance of locative inversion *and from the sky fell a snow flake*. In either case, we claim that the order between XP and YP in the gapped conjuncts is allowed to change as long as XP and YP in that order have a well-formed inferred syntax as a result of step (ii) of (24).

The syntactic structure in (33) correctly predicts several points. First, it excludes cases such as (36a), in which XP and YP of the gapped conjunct are embedded and something (*it seems that*) other than the two contrastively focused phrases appears. However, as shown in (36a'), a parenthetical can appear in the gapped conjunct, since it constitutes a separate speech act (cf. Ueno 2014: 324, 371). In (36b, c), the complementizers *that* and *for* cannot be remnants in gapping, because all remnants in gapped conjuncts must be phrases, as required by (33i). In (36d), the inverted auxiliary cannot be a remnant in gapping for the same reason.

(36) a. *[Alan] went [to New York] and it seems (that) [Betsy] [to Boston]. (Sag 1976)
   a'. [Alan] went [to New York] and, {probably | I suppose | if I'm not wrong}, [Betsy] [to Boston].
   b. Betsy said that [Alan] went [to the ballgame], and (*that) [Sandy] [to the movie]. (Sag 1976)
      cf. Betsy said that [$_{S[PAST]}$ [$_{S[PAST]}$ [Alan] went [to the ballgame]], and [[Sandy] [to the movie]]].
   c. For [Jack] to hate [swimming] and (*for) [Fred] [fishing] would be a tremendous surprise. (Jackendoff 1977: 45)
      cf. For [$_{S[to]}$ [$_{S[to]}$ [Jack] to hate [swimming]] and [[Fred] [fishing]]] would be a tremendous surprise.
   d. Did [Bill] eat [the pears] or (*did) [Harry] [the grapes]? (Jackendoff 1971: 23, note 2)
      cf. Did [$_{S[BSE]}$ [$_{S[BSE]}$ [Bill] eat [the pears]] or [[Harry] [the grapes]]]?

Note that (36b) without the second *that* is a coordination of the embedded S[PAST], (36c) without the second *for* is a coordination of S[*to*], and (36d) without the second *did* is a coordination of S[BSE]. Furthermore, when an ad-S adjunct precedes XP in the first conjunct, it must be interpreted as modifying not the first conjunct S but the whole coordinate structure. This is shown in (37), where the adjunct in question is underlined.

(37) a. <u>According to a recent report</u>, [$_S$ [$_{XP}$ the number of dogs] fell by 2 million and that of cats by 3 million].
b. <u>From 2010 to 2013</u>, [$_S$ [$_{XP}$ the number of dogs] fell by 2 million and that of cats by 3 million].
c. <u>In Japan</u>, [$_S$ [$_{XP}$ the number of dogs] fell by 2 million and that of cats by 3 million].

Second, as long as (33) is satisfied, there are multiple possibilities of YP of the gapped conjunct.

(38) a. (Ross 1970: 250)
[I] want to try to begin to write a novel, and [$_{XP}$ Mary] [$_{YP}$ {to try to begin to write a play | to begin to write a play | to write a play | a play}].
b. (Jackendoff 1971: 25)
[Max] seemed to be trying to begin to love Harriet, and [$_{XP}$ Fred] [$_{YP}$ {to be trying to begin to love Sue | to begin to love Sue | to love Sue | Sue}].

Third, the syntactic structure in (33) requires that gapping apply across-the-board, that is, gapped Ss must appear in all conjuncts but the first.

(39) (McCawley 1998: 289)
a. Tom ordered a daiquiri, Alice a manhattan, and Jane a screwdriver.
b. ??Tom ate a hamburger, Alice a Polish sausage, and Jane drank a beer.
c. *Tom ate a hamburger, Alice drank a martini, and Jane a beer.
d. The cost per click has been declining largely because [$_{S1}$ advertisers pay less for mobile ads], and [$_{S2}$ more people are using Google on their mobile devices] and [$_{S3}$ fewer on their desktop computers]. (*The New York Times*, January 23, 2013)

(39a–c) are instances of three-term S-coordination ([$_S$ S$_1$, S$_2$, *and* S$_3$]). In (39a), the second and third Ss are both gapped. This ATB application of gapping in a coordinate structure is guaranteed in (33), where the second and later conjuncts consist of two remnant phrases. (39d) is not a three-term S-coordination, but a two-term S-coordination, in which the second term is itself a two-term S-coordination ([$_S$ S$_1$, and [$_S$ S$_2$ and S$_3$]]), and gapping is applied to the second term [$_S$ S$_2$ and S$_3$].

Some remarks are in order about each condition in (33). Regarding condition (i), some speakers generalize gapped conjuncts to those consisting of three or four remnant phrases, as illustrated in (40) below.

(40) a. *[Alec] gave [money] [to the Alumni Fund], and [Nancy] [books] [to the library]. (McCawley 1998: 211, note 5)
   b. *[John] talked [with his father] [about politics], and [Mary] [with her mother] [about religion]. (McCawley 1998: 63)

(41) gapped conjunct = subject + object or PP-complement + adjunct
   a. [Bill] went [to Nikko] with Mary [yesterday], and [Tom] [to Kamakura] [the day before yesterday]. (Imanishi and Asano 1990: 302)
   b. [Peter] talked [to his boss] [on Tuesday], and [Betsy], [to her supervisor], [on Wednesday]. (Sag 1976: 164)
   c. [Robin] speaks [French] [on Tuesdays], and [Leslie], [German], [on Thursdays]. (Culicover and Jackendoff 2005: 273)
   d. [A businessman] will drink [a martini] [to relax], and [a health nut], [a glass of wine], [just to remain healthy]. (Sag et al. 1985: 157)
   e. [Charlie] entered [the bedroom] [at 5:30], and [Vera] [the kitchen] [at 6:00]. (Sag 1976: 211)
   f. [Ed] had given me [earrings] [for Christmas] and [Bob] [a necklace] [for my birthday]. (Huddleston and Pullum 2002: 1339)

(42) gapped conjunct = subject + object or PP-complement + PP-complement
   a. [John] talked [to his supervisor] [about his thesis], and [Erich], [to the dean], [about departmental politics]. (Sag 1976: 164)
   b. [John] gave [a Ford] [to Mary] and [Harry], [a Cadillac], [to Susan]. (Abbott 1976: 642)
   c. *?[Willy] put [the flowers] [in a vase], and [Charlie] [the book] [on the table]. (Sag 1976: 211)

(43) gapped conjunct = subject + adverb + object
   a. [Monk] [probably] enjoyed [epistrophy], and [Albert Ayler], [almost certainly], [ghosts]. (Sag 1976: 164)

b. [Max] [sometimes] beats [his wife], and [Ted] [frequently] [his dog]. (Imanishi and Asano 1990: 316)

(44) gapped conjunct = subject + object or manner-adjunct + place-adjunct + time-adjunct
   a. [Mary] played [the piano] [on the stage] [on Monday], and [Betsy] [the violin] [in the pit] [on Wednesday]. (Imanishi and Asano 1990: 373)
   b. [Betsy] dances [with a parasol] [in the living room] [on Fridays], and [Peter] [with a meat cleaver] [in the bar] [on Saturday nights]. (Sag 1976: 212)

When a gapped conjunct consists of three remnant NPs, which result from a ditransitive construction, it is unacceptable even to speakers who accept three-remnant gapped conjuncts.

(45) *[John] gave [Mary] [a Ford] and [Harry], [Susan], [a Cadillac]. (Abbott 1976: 642)

As for condition (33ii), when the first conjunct of the gapping construction is a gapless conjunct, this is the antecedent of the second and later gapped conjuncts, as was discussed in (26). However, if the first conjunct is already gapped, the antecedent of the gapped conjuncts should be found in the prior discourse, as was illustrated in (27) and (28).

Condition (33iii) was illustrated in (4) and (5) and is further illustrated in (46) and (47) below. In (46a'), the PP[*on*] in the first conjunct is a major constituent, because it is adjoined to the first conjunct S, but the NP *Winthrop Street* in (46a) is not. In (46b', c'), the subject NP in the first conjunct is a major constituent, but the bracketed PP in the first conjunct of (46b, c) is not. However, (46d) is a counterexample to (33iii).

(46) a. *On [Winthrop Street] Jim saw [the boy], and [Hooker Street] [the girl].
   a'. [On Winthrop Street] Jim saw [the boy], and [on Hooker Street] [the girl].
   b. *The vice-president [of IBM] met [John], and [of Xerox] [Betsy].
   b'. [The vice-president of IBM] met [John], and [the vice-president of Xerox] [Betsy].
   c. *A boy [with red hair] met [Peter], and [with black hair] [John].
   c'. [A boy with red hair] met [Peter], and [a boy with black hair] [John].

d. His criticisms [of Kim] were [inaccurate] and [of Pat] [irrelevant]. (Huddleston and Pullum 2002: 1339)

(47) a. *[Jim] was hassled on [Winthrop Street], and [Norma] [Hooker Street]. (Sag 1976)
  a'. [Jim] was hassled [on Winthrop Street], and [Norma] [on Hooker Street].
  b. *[John] met the vice-president [of IBM], and [Betsy] [of Xerox]. (Sag 1976)
  b'. [John] met [the vice-president of IBM], and [Betsy] [the vice-president of Xerox].
  c. *[Peter] met a boy [with red hair], and [John] [with black hair]. (Neijt 1979: 126)
  c'. [Peter] met [a boy with red hair], and [John] [a boy with black hair].

In (47a), YP is *Winthrop Street*, which is not a major constituent, and hence this example is unacceptable. However, the PP[*on*] *on Winthrop Street* is a major constituent, and (47a') is acceptable. Similarly, in (47b', c'), *the vice-president of IBM* and *a boy with red hair* are major constituents, but *of IBM* and *with red hair* in (47b, c) are not. Furthermore, this restriction takes care of (14a, b), those cases where gapping cannot delete a preposition if its object NP is left behind. This also applies to combinations of V+P or V+N+P that constitute a single semantic unit, as in (48).

(48) a. [Tom] listened [to the radio] and [Jack] [*(to) the records]. (Imanishi and Asano 1990: 385)
  b. [John] paid attention [to Tom's suggestion], and [Mary] [*(to) Bill's suggestion]. (Imanishi and Asano 1990: 385)
    cf. [$_{VP}$ [$_V$ *pay*] [$_{NP}$ *attention*] [$_{PP[to]}$ *to* NP]] in syntax
  c. [John] took advantage [of Mary], and [Mary] [*(of) John]. (Bresnan 1976: 15)
    cf. [$_{VP}$ [$_V$ *take*] [$_{NP}$ *advantage*] [$_{PP[of]}$ *of* NP]] (Ueno 2014: 131–2)

Regarding condition (33iv), the domain of the gapping construction is not only S-coordination but also CP[WH[Q]]-coordination (49) and VP-coordination (50). The former type was also illustrated in (19). We will call the latter type, which is illustrated in (64)–(70), VP-level gapping.

(49) gapping in CP[WH[Q]]-coordination
    a. [$_{CP[WH[Q]]}$ [Which students] can speak [French]], and [$_{CP[WH[Q]]}$ [which professors] [German]]? (McCawley 1998: 288)
    b. You and I will see in the years ahead [which of us] was [right] and [which] [wrong]. (Imanishi and Asano 1990: 364)

(50) gapping in VP-coordination (VP-level gapping) (McCawley 1998: 63)
    a. John [$_{VP[PAST]}$ donated [$50] [to the Anti-Vivisection Society]] and [$_{VP[PAST]}$ [$75] [to the Red Cross]].
    b. I didn't put [potatoes] [in the pantry] or [milk] [in the refrigerator].

Regarding condition (33v), which was illustrated in (1), contrastive focus is a semantic and pragmatic notion. If the XP (or YP) in the first conjunct and XP (or YP) in the second conjunct are contrastively focused, they are usually of the same syntactic category, but do not have to be, as illustrated in (57) and (58). Furthermore, this identity in syntactic category is not sufficient. Such gapping cases as (51) are unacceptable. In (51a), the YP in the first conjunct and YP in the gapped conjunct are coreferential and do not count as being contrastively focused. In (51b, c), the XP in the first conjunct and XP in the second conjunct are coreferential and do not count as being contrastively focused.

(51) a. *[Jack] likes [Sue$_j$] and [Mike] [her$_j$]. (Imanishi and Asano 1990: 301)
    b. *[Jack$_i$] likes [Sue] and [he$_i$] [Betsy]. (ibid.)
    c. *[Tom$_k$] will [play the guitar] and [he$_k$] [sing too]. (Huddleston and Pullum 2002: 1543)

However, the following examples are acceptable, because the contrastive focus requirement is satisfied between the XPs of both conjuncts and between the YPs of both conjuncts.

(52) a. Before their arguments, [John$_i$] had usually agreed [with Mary$_j$], and [she$_j$] [with him$_i$]. (Kuno 1976: 309, note 18)
    b. [Susan$_i$] loves [John$_j$], {and | but} not [he$_j$] [her$_i$]. (Culicover and Jackendoff 2005: 282)

In (53), the YP of the gapped conjunct is a pronoun and is coreferential not to the YP of the first conjunct but to a part of it. Nevertheless, the two remnant phrases count as being contrastively focused.

(53) (Sag et al. 1985: 161)
   a. [You] talked to [John's mother], and [I] [him].
   b. I gave [a book] [to John's mother] and [a magazine] [to him]. (VP-level gapping)

Furthermore, (54) and (55) show again that partial contrast is sufficient for the corresponding remnant phrases to be contrastively focused. This was also shown in (46b', c'), (47b', c').

(54) a. [I] want [to try to begin to write a novel], and [Mary] [to try to begin to write a play]. (Ross 1970: 250)
   b. [Max] seemed [to be trying to begin to love Harriet], and [Fred] [to be trying to begin to love Sue]. (Jackendoff 1971: 25)

(55) a. [The professor of physics] wants [to try to begin to write a novel], and [the professor of mathematics]
   [to try to begin to read a novel].
   b. [The boy with long hair] wants [to try to begin to write a novel], and [the boy with short hair]
   [to try to continue to write a novel].
   c. Bill expects [Harry] [to find the way to the party], and [Sue] [to find the way home].
   (VP-level gapping, Hankamer 1973: 26)

In order for two phrases to qualify as being contrastively focused, we claim that they must serve the same semantic function (i.e., must be of the same category in F/A and E/R). Therefore, the following examples in (56) are excluded.

(56) a. *[Sam] hates [reptiles], and [Sandy] [to talk to Oh]. (Sag 1976)
   b. *He blamed [his wife] [for the debts] and [the untidy state of the house] [on the boys]. (Huddleston and Pullum 2002: 1341)
   c. *[Fred] gave [Mary] a pencil and [Bill], [to Jane]. (Hudson 1989: 67)
   d. *Beth ate [yogurt], and Norma [at midnight]. (Sag 1976)
   e. *[This door] can open [at any moment], and [John] [any door]. (Grosu 1985: 234)

In (56a), the syntactic field of the lexical entry for *hate* in the first conjunct is V in [__, NP], whereas the second conjunct requires a different syntactic field: V in [__, VP[*to*]] for its inferred S. These two are distinct lexical entries for *hate*. More importantly, *reptiles* of the first conjunct is ARG in F/A but *to talk to Oh* in the second conjunct is PROP. In (56b), the syntactic field of the lexical entry for *blame* in the first conjunct is V in [__, NP, PP[*for*]], whereas the second conjunct requires a different syntactic field: V in [__, NP, PP[*on*]]. Again, these two are distinct lexical entries for *blame*. Furthermore, the PPs of the first and second conjuncts carry different roles. In (56c), the syntactic field of the lexical entry for *give* in the first conjunct is V in [__, NP, NP], whereas the second conjunct requires a different syntactic field: V in [__, NP, PP[*to*]]. Again, these two are distinct lexical entries for *give* (Chapter 1 (53), (54)). At the same time, the intended contrastive pair, *Mary* of the first conjunct and *to Jane* of the second conjunct, are of different syntactic categories and carry different roles (the former being [PT, GO] and the latter being GO). In (56d), the syntactic field of the lexical entry for *eat* of the first conjunct is V in [__, NP] (transitive), whereas the second conjunct requires a different syntactic field: V in [__] (intransitive). These two are distinct lexical entries for *eat*. In addition, the YP of the first conjunct is an object NP, but the YP of the second conjunct is an adjunct. In (56e), the syntactic field of the lexical entry for *open* of the first conjunct is V in [__] (unaccusative), whereas the second conjunct requires a different syntactic field: V in [__, NP] (transitive). These two are distinct lexical entries for *open*. Furthermore, the first contrastive pair (*This door* and *John*) is semantically different, and so is the second contrastive pair (*at any moment* and *any door*).

(57b) below is almost acceptable with two kinds of *leave* that share roughly the same meaning: V in [__, NP, NP] of the first conjunct and V in [__, NP, PP[*to*]] of the second conjunct. This high acceptability is because the NP-PP[*to*] order of the second conjunct is motivated by the fact that the antecedent of *half that amount* is the immediately preceding NP *$20,000*, namely, the NP and PP[*to*] carry old and new information, respectively. On the other hand, there is no such motivation in (57c) for using a different VP syntax for each conjunct.

(57) a. He left [$20,000] [to his daughter] and [half that amount] [to each of his grandchildren].
 b. ?He left [his daughter] [$20,000] and [half that amount] [to each of his grandchildren]. (Huddleston and Pullum 2002: 1342, note 64)
 c. *He left [$20,000] [to his daughter] and [each of his grandchildren] [half that amount]. (Huddleston and Pullum 2002: 1342, note 64)

(58a, b) look like the unacceptable (56d) in that the verb of the first conjunct is transitive and the verb in the inferred syntax of the second conjunct is intransitive.

(58) a. [John] can drink [anything] and [Mary] [with anybody]. (Grosu 1987: 451)
  b. [John] drinks [only the best wine] and [Mary] [only in the best company]. (ibid.)
  c. ??[John] can drink [anything] and Mary [only in the best company].
  d. ??[John] drinks [only the best wine] and Mary [with anybody].

However, the crucial difference between the unacceptable (56d) and the acceptable (58a, b) is that in the latter, the object NP of the first conjunct and the adjunct PP of the second conjunct qualify semantically/pragmatically as being contrastively focused with each other in the sense that they both purport to denote different ways of drinking: John's way of drinking (*drink anything* in (58a) and *drink only the best wine* in (58b)) is contrasted with Mary's way of drinking (*drink with anybody* in (58a) and *drink only in the best company* in (58b)). Note also that in (58a, b), the YPs in both conjuncts are very similar in form: *any* in (58a) and *only the best* in (58b), which helps make the contrast more manifest. Compare (58a ,b) with the less acceptable (58c, d).

In (59a), although *rather foolish* and *a complete idiot* are of different syntactic categories, they serve the same semantic function: Fa in F/A. Furthermore, they are both the complement of the same empty *be* verb (Ueno 2014: 54). (59b) is of the same type as (59a). The VP[PRP] and the predicative PP are of different syntactic categories but both serve as Fa and are the complement of the empty verb *be*. (To be precise, the VP[PRP] *surviving* in (59b) serves not only as Fa but also as [$_{Fp}$ PROG], just as an intransitive verb in the present tense serves as Fa and [$_{Fp}$ PRES]. See Chapter 1 (33c, d) and the related discussion.) In (59c), the AP and NP are in contrast. Again, they are both Fa and the complement of *become*. What is interesting about (59d) is that although *in good spirits* is a predicative PP and hence Fa in F/A, this is unacceptable because *become* takes as its complement AP and NP, but not a predicative PP (Pollard and Sag 1994: 105).

(59) a. Leslie is [$_{AP}$ rather foolish], and Lou [$_{NP[DET]}$ a complete idiot]. (Sag et al. 1985: 160)
  b. Kim seems to be [$_{VP[PRP]}$ just surviving], and Terry [$_{PP}$ in dire need of our help]. (ibid.)

c. Pat has become [_AP_ crazy], and Chris [_NP[DET]_ an incredible bore]. (ibid.)
d. *Pat has become [crazy], and Chris [in good spirits]. (ibid.)
   cf. *Chris has become in good spirits.
d'. Pat has become [_AP_ crazy], and Chris more and more [_PP_ like his father].
    cf. Chris has become more and more [like his father]. (cf. Pollard and Sag 1994: 105)

The contrast between (59d, d') shows yet again that the interpretation of gapping involves a step in which a full syntactic structure of the gapped conjunct is inferentially constructed, namely, step (ii) of (24).

To account for such unacceptable gapping cases as (56), (57c), and (59d) as well as the acceptable gapping examples we have examined thus far, we assume that the lexical entries accessed when the first conjunct is processed are retained in working memory (Michimata et al. 2011: 187, Gray 2011: 311, Anderson 2010: 152, Eysenck and Keane 2010: 211) while the second and later gapped conjuncts are being processed. This means that the lexical entries for the words in the first conjunct are available when the hearer/interpreter inferentially constructs the syntactic structures of gapped conjuncts (step (ii) of (24)).

There is a wide range of idiolectal variation in the acceptability of the gapping construction. First, some speakers accept a non-major constituent NP as XP or YP in (33), when it is the complement of a major constituent PP. This is especially true if the PP itself is a complement. This was shown in (14c-e), in which the YP is a non-major constituent NP. (60) provides such examples with VP-level gapping, as will be discussed below. In these examples, the XP is a non-major constituent NP.

(60) VP-level gapping
  a. Bill is [_VP[PRP]_ depending [_PP[on]_ on Harry] [to find the way to the party], and [_VP[PRP]_ [_NP_ Sue] [to find the way home]]. (Kuno 1976: 301)
  b. Mary [_VP[PRES]_ thinks [_PP[of]_ of Japan] [as a beautiful country]] and [_VP[PRES]_ [_NP_ Britain] [as a democratic country]].
  c. We'll [_VP[BSE]_ be [_PP[in]_ in Paris] [for a week]] and [_VP[BSE]_ [_NP_ Bonn] [for three weeks]]. (Huddleston and Pullum 2002: 1343, note 65)

Second, some speakers accept the gapping construction in which XP and YP in the first conjunct are outside the topmost VP, as was shown in (12). Third, as pointed out in Imanishi and Asano (1990: 375), some speakers accept the gapping construction in which XP is an ad-S adjunct and YP is the topmost VP, as illustrated in (61b) below.

(61) a. *[On Tuesday], Sam [must have seemed happy] and [on Wednesday] [must have seemed sad]. (Sag 1976: 202)
b. [On Tuesday] Linda [washed the car], and [on Wednesday] [cleaned the stove]. (Sobin 1981: 490)

Fourth, although the acceptability of two-remnant gapped conjuncts is quite stable and unanimous, there is considerable idiolectal variation in the acceptability of gapped conjuncts with three or more remnant phrases (McCawley 1998: 83 note 4). In fact, some speakers generalize the gapping construction to cases where there are three or more remnant phrases in gapped conjuncts, as was illustrated in (40)–(45).

In (33), we provided the lexical entry for the gapping construction, whose syntax covers not only S-coordination but also VP-coordination, as illustrated in (60). In fact, Sag et al. (1985: 158) divided gapping into two cases: S-level gapping and VP-level gapping. (62) provides more examples of VP-level gapping.

(62) VP-level gapping
a. Bill is depending on [Harry] [to find the way to the party], and [Sue] [to find the way home]. (= (60a))
cf. [$_{VP}$ depending on [Harry] [to find the way to the party]], and [$_{VP}$ [Sue] [to find the way home]]
b. Max seemed to be trying to force [Ted] [to leave the room], and [Walt] [to stay a little longer]. (Kuno 1976: 301)
cf. [$_{VP}$ force [Ted] [to leave the room]], and [$_{VP}$ [Walt] [to stay a little longer]]
c. The court declared [Edward] [insane], and [his mother] [morally bankrupt]. (Kuno 1976: 303)
cf. [$_{VP}$ declared [Edward] [insane]], and [$_{VP}$ [his mother] [morally bankrupt]]
d. Max sent Sally [the messenger] [last week], and [Susan] [yesterday]. (Kuno 1976: 304)
cf. [$_{VP}$ sent Sally [the messenger] [last week]], and [$_{VP}$ [Susan] [yesterday]]

e. Max wanted Ted to persuade [Alex] to see [Mary], and [Walt], [Ira]. (Kuno 1976: 301)

cf. [$_{VP}$ persuade [Alex] to see [Mary]], and [$_{VP}$ [Walt], [Ira]]

When the phrase (*Terry* in (63a) below) that is contrastively focused with the first remnant (*Tracy* in (63a)) of the gapped conjunct is outside the VP, S-coordination is involved. On the other hand, when the phrase (*the book* in (64a)) that is contrastively focused with the first remnant (*the records* in (64a)) of the gapped conjunct is inside the VP, VP-coordination is involved.

(63) a. [$_S$ [Terry] likes [Stacy]] [$_{S[and]}$ and [$_S$ [Tracy] [Lee]]]. (S-level gapping, Sag et al. 1985: 163)
 b. *[$_S$ John didn't see Mary] and [$_S$ Bill Sue]. (Sag et al. 1985: 158)

(64) a. Sandy [$_{VP}$ gave [the book] [to Lee]] [$_{VP[and]}$ and [$_{VP}$ [the records] [to Kim]]. (VP-level gapping, Sag et al. 1985: 163)
 b. John didn't [$_{VP}$ give the books to Mary] and [$_{VP}$ the papers to Sue]. (Sag et al. 1985: 158)

S-level gapping and VP-level gapping are distinct types of gapping. For example, Sag et al. (1985) observed that although coordinated negative sentences cannot undergo S-level gapping, which was originally observed by Ross (1970) and is illustrated in (63b), VP-level gapping is possible in coordinated negative sentences, as shown in (64b). Although Sag et al. (1985) did not give any evidence for the difference in constituent structure between (63a) and (64a), their claim can be justified by means of VP ellipsis. The pro-VP form *did* in (65a) can refer to the entire VP [$_{VP}$ *gave books to Lee*] [$_{VP}$ *and (gave) pictures to Kim*]. Furthermore, their claim is also supported by the fact that VP-level gapping still undergoes S-level gapping as in (65b, c).

(65) a. Sandy [$_{VP}$ gave books to Lee] [$_{VP}$ and pictures to Kim], and Mary did too. (VP-level gapping in the first conjunct + VP ellipsis in the second conjunct)
 b. [$_S$ Sandy gave books to Lee and pictures to Kim], and [$_S$ Mary a notebook to John and a music CD to Tom]. (S-level gapping of VP-level gapping conjuncts)

b'. decoded syntax of second conjunct of (65b)

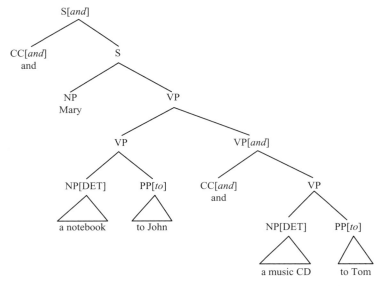

c. [$_S$ Max ate herring on Tuesday and oyster on Thursday], and [$_S$ Mary tuna on Monday and squid on Wednesday]. (S-level gapping of VP-level gapping conjuncts)

Note that in (65b'), the two instances of [$_{VP}$ NP[DET] PP[*to*]] do not violate the HFC (Chapter 1 (3)). Because there is no lexical head in this structure (i.e., this is not a "headed local tree"), the HFC does not apply. Another property of VP-level gapping is that it is possible with embedded VPs, just as S-level gapping is possible with embedded Ss. This is shown in (62b, e) and (66a). In (66b), a pro-VP form *to* appears at the end of the *but*-conjunct, and its inferred VP is *to persuade Alex to get lost, and persuade Susan to stay.*

(66) a. Max wanted to [$_{VP[BSE]}$ persuade [Alex] [to get lost]], [$_{VP[BSE, and]}$ and [$_{VP[BSE]}$ [Susan] [to stay]]. (VP-level gapping applied to the embedded VP[BSE]-coordination)
 b. Max wanted to persuade Alex to get lost, and Susan to stay, but his wife didn't want to.

Finally, VP-level gapping does not allow the option of putting *both* or *either* before the XP of the first conjunct (Postal 1974: 419, McCawley 1998: 63, Ueno 2014: 172).

(67) a. John [$_{VP[PAST]}$ donated [$50] [to the Anti-Vivisection Society]] and [$_{VP[PAST]}$ [$75] [to the Red Cross]]. (McCawley 1998: 63)
b. ??John [$_{VP[PAST]}$ donated both [$50] [to the Anti-Vivisection Society]] and [$_{VP[PAST]}$ [$75] [to the Red Cross]]. (ibid.)
c. John both [$_{VP[PAST]}$ donated [$50] [to the Anti-Vivisection Society]] and [$_{VP[PAST]}$ [$75] [to the Red Cross]].

(68) a. I didn't put [potatoes] [in the pantry] or [milk] [in the refrigerator]. (McCawley 1998: 63)
b. ??I didn't put either [potatoes] [in the pantry] or [milk] [in the refrigerator]. (McCawley 1998: 64)
c. I didn't either put [potatoes] [in the pantry] or [milk] [in the refrigerator].

The reason why (67b) and (68b) are unacceptable is that *both* and *either* in *both* A *and* B and *either* A *or* B require that A be a syntactic constituent, which is violated in (67b) and (68b). By contrast, the acceptability of (67c) and (68c) shows that *donated $50 to the Anti-Vivisection Society* in (67a) and *put potatoes in the pantry* in (68a) are constituents, namely VPs.

6.4 Speaker's Intention in Gapping

The speaker chooses the gapping construction, whose lexical entry was given in (33), when she wants to compactly express by uttering a series of two-remnant conjuncts those conjoined propositions that are identical to the proposition expressed in the first conjunct except for two contrasting phrases. It is the speaker's responsibility, therefore, to make clear which phrase in the first conjunct each of the two remnant phrases XP and YP in the gapped conjuncts [$_{C[\alpha]}$ CC[α] [$_C$ XP YP]] in (33) is contrastively focused with. For this purpose, when the XP or YP is an NP, she uses the same case marking as on the corresponding NP in the first conjunct, if the language in question has morphological case marking.

(69) (Hankamer 1973: 20)
a. [$_{NP[NOM]}$ Das Kind] folgte [$_{PN[DAT]}$ mir], und [$_{NP[NOM]}$ der Hund] [$_{NP[DAT]}$ meinem Vater].
b. [$_{NP[NOM]}$ Das Kind] hat [$_{PN[ACC]}$ mich] gebissen, und [$_{NP[NOM]}$ der Hund] [$_{NP[ACC]}$ meinen Vater].

The verb *folgen* in (69a) takes a nominative NP subject and a dative NP complement, as shown in the first conjunct in (69a). In the gapped conjunct, two NPs are expressed, the first in the nominative and the second in the dative. By using the same case marking on the remnant NPs, the speaker is making clear her intention regarding which NP in the gapped conjunct corresponds to and is contrastively focused with which NP in the first conjunct. By contrast, the verb *beißen* in (69b) takes a nominative NP subject and an accusative NP object. In the gapped conjunct, two NPs are expressed, one in the nominative and the other in the accusative.

Furthermore, when complement PPs are contrastively focused in gapping and the PP in the first conjunct requires a specific PFORM value, the same PFORM value is required of the PP in the gapped conjunct. This is shown in (70a, c).

(70) (Hankamer 1973: 21–22)
    a. [Bill] depends [$_{PP[on]}$ on Alex], and [Alex] [$_{PP[on]}$ on Bill].
    b. partial lexical entry for *depend on*
       syntax: V in [__, PP[*on*]]
       F/A: Faa
       E/R: [$_{TYPE}$ "depend-on"] in [$_{EV}$ TH LO]
    c. [Das Kind] fürchtet sich [$_{PP[vor]}$ vor dem Hund], und [die Frau] [$_{PP[vor]}$ vor der Maus].
    d. partial lexical entry for *fürchten*
       syntax: V in [__, RPN[ACC], PP[*vor*]]   (RPN = reflexive pronoun)
       F/A: Faa
       E/R: [$_{TYPE}$ "afraid"] in [$_{STATE}$ __ [PT, LO] GO]

The verb *depend* in the first conjunct of (70a) takes a PP[*on*] complement, which is shown in its lexical entry (70b). The speaker chooses the same PFORM value *on* for the PP in the gapped conjunct in (70a), because she wants to make clear by doing so that the PP of the gapped conjunct is the complement of *depend*. At the same time, the speaker respects the major constituent requirement in (33iii). The morpho-syntactic connectivity of CASE and PFORM values observed in the gapping construction is quite natural if we consider the speaker's intention. While producing the gapped conjuncts, the speaker needs to retain in her working memory the lexical entry for the verb she accessed in the production of the first conjunct. (70c) with *fürchten*, which takes a complement PP[*vor*], is the same type of example. Note also that just as in the case of fragments, the P-repeating property (Chapter 3 (88)-(90)) is at work by default, which requires that the preposition be maintained along with its NP object. From the hearer's point of view, the connectivity of CASE and PFORM values in the gapping construction (i.e., the same CASE and PFORM values in the gapped conjuncts) serves as priming (Michimata et al. 2011: 191, Anderson 2010: 204) and makes it easier for the hearer/interpreter to access the lexical entry for the verb that is retained in his working memory.

Hankamer (1973: 22) pointed out that in the gapping construction such as *#Jack admires chastity, and sincerity the bedpost*, the gapped conjunct obeys the same selectional restrictions as when the same verb *admire* is supplied to it, as in *#Sincerity admires the bedpost*. (See (75) for details.) Again, this is accounted for if we assume that the lexical entry for *admire* is accessed when the first conjunct is processed and retained in working memory while the gapped conjunct is processed. (A more complex case will be discussed at the end of this section.) On a related note, if a reference transfer coercing function such as [$_{ARG}$ PERSON CONTEXTUALLY ASSOCIATED WITH __] (Ueno 2014: 315) is applied to the first conjunct of the gapping construction, it is retained in working memory and optionally applied to the gapped conjunct, as in *The hamburger at Table One wants a beer, and {the ham sandwich at Table Two | John} a coffee.*

Since it is a type of ellipsis, gapping is a construction that maximizes both the speaker's economy of expression and the hearer's recoverability of meaning. The maximization of the speaker's economy of expression is achieved by only expressing new/contrastive information in the form of a two-remnant conjunct (i.e., by uttering the gapped conjuncts) instead of uttering full propositions that contain repeated parts. The maximization of the hearer's recoverability of meaning is achieved by the speaker's clear expression of which phrase in the first conjunct each of the two remnant phrases in the gapped conjuncts is contrastively focused with. A common way of achieving this is the speaker's use of the same case marking and the same PFORM value between the contrastively focused phrases by accessing and retaining the relevant lexical entry. The hearer can infer and recover a full-fledged S from a gapped conjunct by supplying it with the noncontrastive information in the first conjunct on the basis of the Procedure for gapping comprehension (24). In 3.4, the connectivity of CASE and PFORM values in answer fragments was explained in the same way, i.e., by accessing and retaining the lexical entry of the relevant verb.

As was discussed at the beginning of this section, the speaker chooses the gapping construction, whose lexical entry was given in (33), when she wants to concisely express by uttering a series of two-remnant conjuncts those conjoined propositions in the case of S-level gapping and those conjoined Fa predicates in the case of VP-level gapping that are identical to the proposition or predicate expressed in the first conjunct except for two contrasting phrases. This implies that the gapping construction is (part of) a single speech act. This implication is correct, which is confirmed by looking at ad-S adverbs that form a separate speech act. (See the lexical entry for *fortunately* in Ueno 2014: 374, for example.) On the face of it, (71a) looks like an instance of the gapping construction, but it is not. First, (71a) is not acceptable and it sounds much better if *too* is added at the end, as in (71b). This reminds us of stripping, which will be discussed in 6.8. Second, as (71c) shows, the second ad-S adverb can be dropped, which leaves us with an instance of stripping. Finally, a regular gapping construction appears together with an ad-S adverb in each conjunct, as shown in (71d) below.

(71) a. ??Fortunately, John found sweet cookies in the fridge and unfortunately, sour milk.
  b. Fortunately, John found sweet cookies in the fridge and unfortunately, sour milk, too.
  c. Fortunately, John found sweet cookies in the fridge and sour milk, too.
  d. Fortunately, John found sweet cookies in the fridge and unfortunately, Mary sour milk.

This set of data confirms that ad-S adverbs that constitute a separate speech act cannot be XPs or YPs of the gapping construction and only serve as parentheticals. In other words, all XPs and YPs in (33) must be part of the same speech act. See Chapter 2 (34a).

6.5 Interpreting Gapped Conjuncts

The gapped conjuncts in (33) have a constituent structure of $[_{C[\alpha]}$ CC$[\alpha]$ $[_C$ XP YP]], where the gapped conjunct of the syntactic category C$[\alpha]$ (with CCFORM value α) consists of the coordinating connective (CC) α and a nonce constituent C that directly dominates two remnant phrases XP and YP. This structure not only appears as the second and later gapped conjuncts in the standard gapping construction such as (63a) and (64a), but also as an answer to a yes/no question and multiple *wh*-question, as pointed out in (33ii) and illustrated in (27) and (28).

6.5 INTERPRETING GAPPED CONJUNCTS

These cases are allowed by the Procedure for gapping comprehension (24) and the lexical entry for the gapping construction (33).

We proposed in the Procedure for gapping comprehension (24) that inferentially constructing the syntactic structure of the gapped conjuncts (step ii) precedes constructing its corresponding F/A and E/R (step iii). As for the syntactic nature of inferentially recovered conjuncts, we presented several pieces of evidence in 6.2. Here we review a piece of evidence for step ii in (24) of constructing the inferred syntax of a gapped conjunct. This concerns the interaction between gapping and VP ellipsis in (72a) (= (16a)), and that between gapping and *wh*-fragment in (72b) (= (16b)). Inferences (i.e., the inferred syntactic structures obtained by (24) for gapping and by Chapter 5 (13) for VP ellipsis) are indicated by →.

(72) a. A: Speaking of sports, John likes to play [gapping]
baseball, and Mary tennis.
→ *and Mary likes to play tennis*
B: Really? I don't think she does. [VP ellipsis]
→ *I don't think she likes to play tennis.*
A: What sport, then? [sluicing]
→ *What sport do you think she likes to play, then?*
b. A: John gave her a novel and Tom a music CD. [gapping]
→ *and Tom gave her a music CD*
B: Tell me when. [sluicing]
→ *Tell me when John gave her a novel and Tom gave her a music CD.*
C: John did on Monday and Tom on Tuesday. [VP ellipsis + gapping]
→ *John did on Monday and Tom did on Tuesday.*
[undoing gapping]
→ *John gave her a novel on Monday and Tom gave her a music CD on Tuesday.*
[undoing VP ellipsis]
D: Tom on Tuesday? [fragment]
→ *Tom gave her a music CD on Tuesday?*
Are you sure? [null complement anaphora]
→ *Are you sure that Tom gave her a music CD on Tuesday?*
On Wednesday, I guess. [fragment]
→ *Tom gave her a music CD on Wednesday, I guess.*
c. [$_S$ [$_{NP}$ John] [[$_{VP[AUX]}$ did] [$_{PP}$ on Monday]]] [$_{S[and]}$ and [$_S$ [$_{NP}$ Tom] [$_{PP}$ on Tuesday]]].

In (72aB), to infer the syntactic structure (*likes to play tennis*) of the pro-VP form *does*, the hearer/interpreter should have inferred beforehand the syntactic structure (*and Mary likes to play tennis*) of the gapped conjunct (*and Mary tennis*) in (72aA). This shows that step (ii) of Chapter 5 (13) for VP ellipsis requires a syntactic structure to which step (ii) of (24) for gapping has already been applied. Otherwise, the proper interpretation of *does* in (72aB) cannot have been obtained. A similar argument can be constructed based on sluicing (*wh*-fragment). To infer the syntactic structure (*when John gave her a novel and (when) Tom gave her a music CD*) of the *wh*-fragment *when* in (72bB), the hearer/interpreter should have inferred beforehand the syntactic structure (*and Tom gave her a music CD*) of the gapped conjunct (*and Tom a music CD*) in (72bA). This shows that the step of inferring a syntactic structure for the *wh*-fragment requires a syntactic structure to which step (ii) of (24) for gapping has already been applied. Otherwise, the proper interpretation of *when* in (72bB) cannot have been obtained. Note in passing that in (72bC), the pro-VP form *did* undergoes gapping. The decoded syntax of (72bC) is given in (72c), in which the PP of the first conjunct is an S-adjunct or VP-adjunct. (72c) meets the lexical entry for the gapping construction (33). After step (ii) of (24), the inferred syntactic structure for the second conjunct of (72c) is *and Tom did on Tuesday* with another pro-VP form *did*. The pro-VP form *did* in the first conjunct and that in the inferred conjunct have a different VP as their antecedent. Everything conforms to the constructional view of gapping and the pro-VP form analysis of VP ellipsis.

Here we will present three pieces of evidence for step iii of (24) (i.e., constructing the inferred four-tuple (syntax, F/A, E/R, IS), especially the inferred F/A and the inferred E/R). The first evidence concerns *de re* and *de dicto* interpretations. In (73), the intentional predicate *look for* in the first conjunct allows *de re* and *de dicto* readings (cf. McCawley 1993a: 210–211) of its object NP.

(73) [Pat] is looking for [a piece of paper], and [Chris], [a pencil]. (Sag et al. 1985: 162, note 29)

Sag et al. (1985: 162) observed that it is not necessarily the case that both conjuncts in (73) are interpreted uniformly *de re* or uniformly *de dicto*. They claimed that (73) allows interpretations in which one object NP is interpreted *de re* and the other *de dicto*. If so, this shows that after the inferred gapless S-conjunct is constructed for the second conjunct (*Chris is looking for a pencil*), the F/A structures of the two conjuncts are constructed independently of each other from their respective syntactic structure.

6.5 INTERPRETING GAPPED CONJUNCTS

The second piece of evidence concerns interpretation of quantifier scope. Recall that the scope of a quantified NP is represented in the F/A module (Chapter 1 (36), (37)). (74A) is a gapping example with two quantified NPs in each conjunct. The inferred syntax for the second conjunct is *every woman likes a man*. The first conjunct and the second inferred conjunct are both ambiguous in terms of scope relations between *every* and *a* (Chapter 1 (38), (41)).

(74) A: [Every man] likes [a woman] and [every woman] [a man].
B: Really?
C: Yes. Every man likes his mother and every woman the President.

After the inferred syntactic structure of the gapped conjunct is constructed in step (ii) of (24), the F/A structures of both conjuncts must be constructed independently, because C's answer "Yes. Every man likes his mother and every woman the President" indicates that when C interpreted what A said ("Every man likes a woman and every woman a man"), she must have interpreted it to mean $[_{QP_x}$ every man] $[_{QP_y}$ a woman] [x likes y] for the first conjunct and $[_{QP_y}$ a man] $[_{QP_x}$ every woman] [x likes y] for the second conjunct.

Third, Hankamer (1973: 22–23) observed that selectional restriction is violated in the second conjunct of the gapping construction in (75a). This is the same selectional restriction violation that is observed in (75b), the inferred syntax of the second conjunct of (75a).

(75) a. [Chastity] is believed to have been admired [by the Romans], and #[the bedpost] [by sincerity]. (Hankamer 1973: 23)
b. #The bedpost is believed to have been admired by sincerity. (Hankamer 1973: 22)
c. E/R of first conjunct

$[_{EV}$ "believe" <AG> $[_{PT}$ $[_{EV}$ "cause" $[_{AG}$ "Romans"] $[_{EV}$ "admire" <AG> $[_{PT}$ "chastity"]]]]]

d. E/R of second conjunct based on its inferred syntactic structure

#$[_{EV}$ "believe" <AG> $[_{PT}$ $[_{EV}$ "cause" $[_{AG}$ "sincerity"] $[_{EV}$ "admire" <AG> $[_{PT}$ "bedpost"]]]]]

What is called "selectional restriction" is not a syntactic but a semantic notion (McCawley 1973: 134, McCawley 1998: 51 note 9) (i.e., a semantic restriction on the denotation of, say, an NP), and is closely related to the participant roles that NPs bear, which are represented in the E/R module. (In fact, we represented the selectional restriction of the transitive verb *drink* in the E/R field of its lexical entry in Chapter 3 (75c).) When the hearer/interpreter hears (75a), he first infers the gapless S for the second conjunct, namely, the inferred syntactic structure (75b), by step (ii) of (24), and then constructs by step (iii) the E/R (75c) of the first conjunct and the E/R (75d) of the inferred syntactic structure of the second conjunct. The double-headed arrow in (75c, d) indicates "role sharing," that is, that the agent of "cause" and the agent of "admire" are shared (unified) (Ueno 2014: 278–9). (75d) explains the selectional restriction violation observed in (75a, b). For one thing, the abstract noun *sincerity* is difficult to perceive as the causer of the event [$_{EV}$ "admire" <AG> [$_{PT}$ "bedpost"] and, simultaneously, as the agent of the event type "admire." For another, the noun *bedpost* is difficult to perceive as the patient of "admire." Note, however, that if (75a, b) are interpreted with respect to such a fairy-tale world as *Beauty and the Beast*, in which a spoon and a teapot act and speak, their semantic anomaly vanishes. This shows the semantic/pragmatic nature of selectional restrictions. (See Sadock (2012: 94–95) and Ueno (2014: 106) for the treatment of the passive *by*-phrase.)

We observed that gapping interacts with VP ellipsis and *wh*-fragments in (72). Gapping also interacts with Right Node Raising (RNR) and "*wh*-movement."

(76) gapping and RNR
    a. *[Fred] sent [the President] [a nasty letter], and [Bernice] [the governor] [a bomb]. (gapping with three NP remnants) (McCawley 1998: 280)
    b. [Fred] sent [the President], and [Bernice] [the Vice President], [a nasty letter about the CIA].
    c. [Harry] told [Sue], and [Tom] [Sally], [that Albania is a lovely place for a vacation]. (Jackendoff 1971: 25)
    d. decoded syntax of (76b)

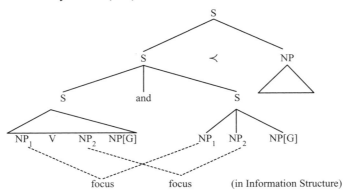

(76a) is unacceptable to those speakers who only accept two-remnant gapped conjuncts in the gapping construction. It is also unacceptable to those who accept three-remnant gapped conjuncts, because the gapped conjunct consists of three NPs, as was shown in (45). On the other hand, in (76b), the third NP (i.e., the theme NP) undergoes RNR and thereby the second conjunct consists of two remnant NPs. The NP gap (NP[G]) in the first and second conjuncts of (76d) does not count as a third remnant phrase, because it is phonologically null and therefore they cannot be contrastively focused with each other. In (76d), A < B means A precedes B. We take the RNR-ed phrase in (76b, d) as adjoined to the S node that dominates the coordinate structure. (See Chapter 7 (22).) (76c) is a similar gapping example in which a CP[*that*] is RNR-ed out of both conjuncts and two remnant NPs are retained in the gapped conjunct.

(77) provides examples that show the interaction between gapping and "*wh*-movement."

(77) gapping and "*wh*-movement"
 a. Which nasty letters did [Fred send the President NP[G]] and [Bernice the Vice President NP[G]]? (ATB "*wh*-movement")
 b. These are the nasty letters about the CIA that [Fred sent the President NP[G]] and [Bernice the Vice President NP[G]].
 c. I wonder what John [$_{VP}$ gave NP[G] to Mary on Tuesday], and [$_{VP}$ NP[G] to Sue on Friday]. (VP-level gapping, Schachter and Mordechay 1983: 263)
 d. decoded syntax of (77b)

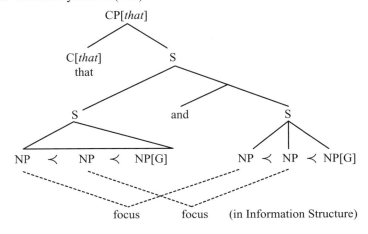

Without the "*wh*-movement" in (77a) or relativization in (77b), the gapping construction would have been unacceptable with three remnant NPs in the gapped conjunct.

Recall that the Relevance-guided comprehension heuristic (Chapter 2 (8)) says that the construction of an interpretation of an utterance proceeds along "a path of least effort." This entails that the first interpretation the hearer/interpreter constructs is the one that is most easily available to him. In the remainder of this section, we will discuss Kuno's (1976) processing strategies for gapping interpretation, which determine the most easily available interpretation, namely, the interpretation accessible with least effort.

Imanishi and Asano (1990: 375ff.) observed, citing (78) and (79), that there are cases of the gapping construction that satisfy the lexical entry for the gapping construction (33), but are judged unacceptable.

(78) a. *[Max] gave Sally [a nickel], and [Harvey] [a dime]. (Hankamer 1973: 26)
 b. *[Max] wanted to put the eggplant [on the table], and [Harvey] [in the sink]. (Hankamer 1973: 31)
 c. *[Max] seemed to want Alex [to get lost] and [Susan] [to stay]. (Hankamer 1973: 25)

(79) (Kuno 1976: 304)
 a. *[Max] wanted [Ted] to persuade Alex to see Mary, and [Walt], [Ira].
 b. *[Max] wanted Ted to persuade [Alex] to see Mary, and [Walt], [Ira].
 c. *[Max] wanted Ted to persuade Alex to see [Mary], and [Walt], [Ira].
 d. *Max wanted [Ted] to persuade [Alex] to see Mary, and [Walt], [Ira].
 e. *Max wanted [Ted] to persuade Alex to see [Mary], and [Walt], [Ira].

However, Imanishi and Asano (1990: 376) pointed out that each sentence in (78) and (79) is acceptable under the interpretation indicated in (80).

(80) a. Max gave [Sally] [a nickel], and [Harvey] [a dime]. (cf. (78a))
 b. #Max wanted to put [the eggplant] [on the table] and [Harvey] [in the sink]. (cf. (78b))
 c. Max seemed to want [Alex] [to get lost] and [Susan] [to stay]. (cf. (78c))
 d. Max wanted Ted to persuade [Alex] to see [Mary], and [Walt], [Ira]. (Kuno 1976: 304) (cf. (79))

The contrast between (78) and (79) on the one hand and (80) on the other shows that in addition to the lexical entry for the gapping construction (33), the hearer/interpreter needs an extragrammatical processing strategy for gapping interpretation that seeks the most accessible interpretation that meets the Relevance-guided comprehension heuristic (Chapter 2 (8)). Kuno (1976: 306) proposed several such processing strategies, one of which is his "Minimal Distance Principle," restated in our terms in (81) below.

(81) Minimal Distance Principle (MDP)
The most accessible association in (33) of XP and YP of the gapped conjunct with XP and YP of the first conjunct is when XP and YP of the first conjunct are its rightmost phrases.

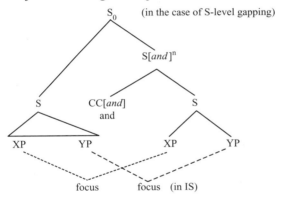

This MDP effect is explained, according to Kuno (1976), by two factors, one being about processing effort and the other about a general feature of discourse structures. The first factor concerns the amount of processing effort needed to recall XP and YP of the first conjunct when the gapped conjunct is being processed. Kuno (1976: 306) observed that the later the constituents of the first conjunct are processed, the easier it is to recall them while the gapped conjunct is being processed. In other words, the least amount of effort will be expended if the last two eligible phrases of the first conjunct are taken as being contrastively focused with the two remnant phrases XP and YP of the gapped conjunct. The other factor concerns the general feature of discourse structures that in terms of information flow in a sentence, old information tends to appear sentence-initially and new/focused information tends to appear sentence-finally (Chapter 1 (61), Kuno and Takami 2007: 163). Because of this general tendency, if there is no prior context, the hearer/interpreter of a gapping construction tends to interpret the last phrases as the locus of contrastive focus (Kuno and Takami 2007: 163). In other words, the later XP and YP appear in the first conjunct, the easier it is to interpret them as focused.

For example, in a gapping construction of the form (82a), interpretation (82b), which meets the MDP (81), is most readily available. Therefore, this is chosen over the nonMDP interpretation (82c) (i.e., a gapping interpretation that does not meet the MDP (81)), as long as the former interpretation is not anomalous semantically or pragmatically.

(82) illustrations of MDP (81)
    a. NP V NP PP and NP PP (gapping construction)
    b. MDP interpretation: NP [$_{VP}$ V [NP] [PP]] and [$_{VP}$ [NP] [PP]] (VP-level gapping)
    c. nonMDP interpretation: [$_S$ [NP] V NP [PP]] and [$_S$ [NP] [PP]] (S-level gapping)

In a gapping construction of the form (83a), interpretation (83b) is most readily available and overrides (83c) and (83d), as long as (83b) is not anomalous semantically or pragmatically.

(83) illustrations of MDP (81)
    a. NP V NP NP and NP NP (gapping construction)
    b. MDP interpretation: NP [$_{VP}$ V [NP] [NP]] and [$_{VP}$ [NP] [NP]] (VP-level gapping)
    c. nonMDP interpretation: [$_S$ [NP] V NP [NP]] and [$_S$ [NP] [NP]] (S-level gapping)
    d. nonMDP interpretation: [$_S$ [NP] V [NP] NP] and [$_S$ [NP] [NP]] (S-level gapping)

Note that the examples in (78) and (79) with the indicated interpretations violate the MDP (81). On the other hand, those in (80) satisfy the MDP and are the most readily available interpretations.

An MDP interpretation is arrived at by default. For a nonMDP interpretation to be available, the hearer/interpreter needs some positive evidence that overrides the default MDP interpretation and supports the nonMDP interpretation: (i) the

6.5 INTERPRETING GAPPED CONJUNCTS

semantic/pragmatic oddity in the MDP interpretation and the lack thereof in the nonMDP interpretation, as in (84), (ii) the similarity in form and meaning between phrases contrastively focused with each other in the nonMDP interpretation, and the lack thereof in the MDP interpretation, as in (84) and (85), (iii) the speaker's empathy agrees with the nonMDP interpretation, as in (86), and (iv) the focus and presupposition of a *wh*-question agree with those of its answer in the gapping construction, as in (87).

For example, in each of (84a, b, c), the first remnant phrase of the gapped conjunct (e.g., *Mr. Brown* in (84a)) has the same kind of form and meaning as the subject NP in the first conjunct (e.g., *Mr. Smith* in (84a)). Although contrasting these NPs violates the MDP, the resultant nonMDP interpretation is semantically and pragmatically more acceptable than the MDP interpretation shown in (84a', b', c'), which are all semantically and pragmatically odd.

(84) a. [Mr. Smith] will teach Spanish [to our class] and [Mr. Brown] [to your class]. (Imanishi and Asano 1990: 377)
   a'. #Mr. Smith will teach [Spanish] [to our class] and [Mr. Brown] [to your class]. (MDP interpretation)
   b. On my birthday, [Tom] gave me [a book] and [Nancy] [a doll]. (Imanishi and Asano 1990: 377)
   b'. #On my birthday, Tom gave [me] [a book] and [Nancy] [a doll]. (MDP interpretation)
   c. [Harry] told this story [to his mother], and [Tom] [to his father]. (Kuno 1976: 307–308)
   c'. #Harry told [this story] [to his mother], and [Tom] [to his father]. (MDP interpretation)
   d. Of the people polled, [80%] believe the president to be [guilty], and [20%] [innocent]. (Kuno 1976: 307–308)
   d'. #Of the people polled, 80% believe [the president] to be [guilty], and [20%] [innocent]. (MDP interpretation)
   e. Of the 100 people contacted, [70] promised the fund raiser to donate [$100], and [30] [$200]. (Kuno 1976: 307–308)
   e'. #Of the 100 people contacted, 70 promised [the fund raiser] to donate [$100], and [30] [$200]. (MDP interpretation)
   f. [Some Republicans] want [Ford] to run for the Presidency in 1976, and [others] [Reagan]. (Kuno 1976: 307–308)
   f'. #Some Republicans want [Ford] to run for [the Presidency] in 1976, and [others] [Reagan]. (MDP interpretation)

(84a, b, c, d, e, f) are understood unambiguously in the nonMDP interpretation, because their MDP interpretation is rejected due to its semantic or pragmatic anomaly. For example, in (84a), *Mr. Brown* of the gapped conjunct contrasts with *Mr. Smith* of the first conjunct in form and meaning. At the same time, if we try its MDP interpretation (84a'), we will end up with #*Mr. Smith will teach Mr. Brown to your class*. In (84b), *Nancy* of the gapped conjunct contrasts with *Tom* of the first conjunct, due to the similarity in form and meaning (i.e., both are one-word names). The pronoun *me* usually carries old information and does not qualify as a contrastively focused XP or YP in the gapping construction (33). Furthermore, the MDP interpretation would produce #*On my birthday, Tom gave me a book, and he gave Nancy a doll* in spite of the hearer's expectation that the sentence will concern who gave me what present on my birthday.

What is interesting about (85a) below is that it is judged ambiguous between the MDP interpretation (85b) and the nonMDP interpretation (85c).

(85) a. Bob will interview some candidates this morning and Peter this afternoon. (ambiguous) (Quirk et al. 1972: 580)
 b. Bob will interview [some candidates] [this morning] and [Peter] [this afternoon]. (MDP interpretation)
 c. [Bob] will interview some candidates [this morning] and [Peter] [this afternoon]. (nonMDP interpretation)
 d. The examiner will interview some candidates this morning and Peter this afternoon. (not ambiguous)

The MDP interpretation (85b) of (85a) is semantically and pragmatically normal and hence is not rejected. It simply entails that Peter is another candidate. On the other hand, *Peter* and *Bob* are similar in form and meaning in that both are one-word names. Therefore, the nonMDP interpretation (85c), which is also semantically and pragmatically normal, is motivated, which explains the ambiguity of (85a). Furthermore, if we change the subject of the first conjunct in (85a) from *Bob* to *the examiner*, as in (85d), the sentence loses its ambiguity and can only be understood in the MDP interpretation, because there is no similarity in form and meaning between *Peter* and *the examiner*. The nonMDP interpretation is no longer motived.

(86) provides some examples in which nonMDP interpretation is motivated by the speaker's "empathy" (Kuno 1987: 206). Kuno (1976: 307, note 12) judged (86a) ambiguous between readings (86b) and (86c) without any comment. Note that *Bill* of the gapped conjunct can equally contrast with *Mary*

(MDP interpretation, as in (86c)) or with *John* (nonMDP interpretation, as in (86b)) of the first conjunct, as far as their form and meaning are concerned. They are one-word personal names.

(86) a. John comes to see Mary every day, and Bill every other day. (ambiguous) (Kuno 1976: 307) (nonMDP interpretation > MDP interpretation)
 b. [John] comes to see Mary [every day], and [Bill] [every other day]. (nonMDP interpretation)
  cf. [John] comes to see me [every day], and [Bill] [every other day].
 c. John comes to see [Mary] [every day], and [Bill] [every other day]. (MDP interpretation)
 d. John goes to see Mary every day, and Bill every other day. (ambiguous) (nonMDP interpretation < MDP interpretation)

However, the nonMDP interpretation (86b) seems to be more prominent (i.e., more readily available) than the MDP interpretation (86c). This difference in the availability of interpretations is due to the verb *come*. Kuno (1987: 225) observed that "*X comes to Y* if the speaker is closer to Y than to X such that X moves toward the speaker (as well as toward Y)." In other words, the speaker's empathy is with Y rather than with X. That is, the speaker takes Y's point of view. In (86a), the speaker's empathy is with *Mary*. This implies that *Mary* is presupposed and the speaker's interest when uttering the first conjunct is in *Who comes to see Mary when?* rather than *Who does John come to see when?*. The nonMD interpretation (86b) maintains the speaker's empathy with *Mary* throughout the two conjuncts, thus satisfying the speaker's interest in *Who comes to see Mary when?* On the other hand, the speaker, when uttering (86a) with the MDP interpretation (86c) in mind, has to change her locus of empathy from *Mary* in the first conjunct to *Bill* in the gapped conjunct. However, under this interpretation, the sentence as a whole is understood to be about the discourse topic *John*, which usually requires the speaker's empathy. Because of this empathy conflict, (86c) is more difficult to perceive than (86b). Note furthermore that if we change the verb from *come* to *go*, as in (86d), the availability of the two interpretations reverses. This is because in *John goes to see Mary every day*, the speaker's empathy is with *John* and the speaker's interest when uttering the first conjunct is in *Who does John go to see when?*.

A nonMDP interpretation of a gapping construction can be motivated for discourse reasons. In (87aB) and (87bB), *Mary*, which is already mentioned in the preceding question (87aA) and (87bA), is part of the presupposition *Someone hit Mary with something* and *Someone persuaded someone to examine Mary*, and represents old information. As such, it cannot be stressed, let alone contrastively focused with something else.

(87) Kuno 1976: 308
  a. A: With what did John and Bill hit Mary?
     B: [Jóhn] hit Măry [with a stíck] and [Bíll] [with a bélt]. (nonMD interpretation)
  b. A: Who persuaded who to examine Mary?
     B: [Jóhn] persuaded [Dr. Thómas] to examine Măry, and [Bíll] [Dr. Jónes]. (nonMD interpretation)

The MDP interpretation *Jŏhn hit [Máry] [with a stíck] and [Bíll] [with a bélt]* of (87aB) is not available, because the old information *Mary* is contrastively focused with *Bill*, and this answers the question *With what did John hit Mary and Bill?* rather than the question (87aA). By the same token, the MDP interpretation *John persuaded [Dr. Thómas] to examine [Máry], and [Bíll] [Dr. Jónes]* of (87bB) is not available. So far, we have looked at four factors that increase the availability of the nonMDP interpretation of a gapping construction: (i) the semantic/pragmatic oddity in the MDP interpretation and the lack thereof in the nonMDP interpretation, (ii) the similarity in form and meaning between phrases contrastively focused with each other in the nonMDP interpretation, and the lack thereof in the MDP interpretation, (iii) the speaker's empathy agrees with the nonMDP interpretation, and (iv) the focus and presupposition of a *wh*-question agree with those of its answer in the gapping construction.

Kuno (1976) and Kuno and Takami (2007) proposed another processing strategy, which we will call the Semantic Relatedness Principle (SRP), to account for the contrast between (88) and (89).

(88) (Kuno and Takami 2007: 165–166)
  a. Mary persuaded John to donate $100, and Bill $200.
  b. Mary persuaded [John] to donate [$100], and [Bill] [$200]. (MDP interpretation, VP-level gapping)
       cf. Mary persuaded [John] that he donate [$100], and [Bill] [$200].
  c. *[Mary] persuaded John to donate [$100], and [Bill] [$200]. (nonMDP interpretation, S-level gapping)
       cf. *[Mary] persuaded John that he donate [$100], and [Bill] [$200].

(89) (Kuno and Takami 2007: 166)
   a. Mary promised John to donate $100, and Bill $200.
   b. *Mary promised [John] to donate [$100], and [Bill] [$200]. (MDP interpretation, VP-level gapping)
      cf. *Mary promised [John] that she would donate [$100], and [Bill] [$200].
   c. [Mary] promised John to donate [$100], and [Bill] [$200]. (nonMDP interpretation, S-level gapping)
      cf. [Mary] promised John that she would donate [$100], and [Bill] [$200].

Here is the restatement of Kuno and Takami's SRP in our terms.

(90) Semantic Relatedness Principle (SRP)
   The most accessible association in (33) of XP and YP of the gapped conjunct with XP and YP of the first conjunct is when XP of the first conjunct is s-related to its YP.

(91) definition of *semantic relatedness* (*s-relatedness*)
   Of two phrases XP and YP of a sentence, XP is s-related to YP if and only if
   (i) The F/A correspondent of XP is PROP-mates with the F/A correspondent of YP, or
   (ii) The F/A correspondent of XP is coreferential with an ARG that is PROP-mates with the F/A correspondent of YP.

(92) definition of *PROP-mates*
   a. definition of *x-command* (Chapter 1 (19), Ueno 2014: 21)
      For two nodes X and Y in a given tree, X x-commands Y if and only if (i) the first (lowest) non-adjoined node that dominates X and is a member of $\phi(x)$, the set of bounding nodes for x, also dominates Y, and (ii) X does not dominate Y.
   b. definition of *non-adjoined node* (Chapter 1 (20), Ueno 2014: 21)
      The non-adjoined node in an adjunction structure is the node that dominates all the adjoined nodes.
   c. definition of *PROP-command* (cf. definition of *S-command* in Chapter 1 (23), Ueno 2014: 22)
      For two nodes X and Y in a given F/A structure, X PROP-commands Y if and only if X x-commands Y, where $\phi(x) = \{\text{PROP}\}$.

d. definition of *PROP-mates* (cf. definition of *S-mates* in Chapter 1 (24), Ueno 2014: 22)

For two nodes X and Y in a given F/A structure, X and Y are PROP-mates if and only if X and Y PROP-command each other.

For example, when (93a) is interpreted as (93b), *Fred* and *a nasty letter* are s-related by (91i). Note that (93b) violates MDP but is still acceptable.

(93) a. Fred sent the President a nasty letter, and Bernice a bomb. (= (1))
  b. [$_S$ [Fred] sent the President [a nasty letter]], and [$_S$ [Bernice] [a bomb]]. (S-level gapping)
  b'. F/A of the first conjunct
    [$_{PROP}$ [$_{Fp}$ PAST] [$_{PROP}$ [$_{ARG}$ FRED] [$_{Fa}$ [$_{ARG}$ PRESIDENT] [$_{Faa}$ [$_{ARG}$ NASTY.LETTER] [$_{Faaa}$ SEND]]]]]
  c. On Mondays Fred eats lunch in the classroom, and on Tuesdays in the canteen.
  d. [$_S$ [On Mondays] Fred eats lunch [in the classroom]], and [$_S$ [on Tuesdays] [in the canteen]]. (S-level gapping)
  d'. F/A of the first conjunct (cf. Chapter 1 (31b))
    [$_{PROP}$ [$_{Fp}$ PAST] [[$_{Mp}$ MONDAYS] [[$_{Mp}$ IN.CLASSROOM] [[$_{ARG}$ FRED] [$_{Fa}$ [$_{ARG}$ LUNCH] [$_{Faa}$ EAT]]]]]]

(93c) is interpreted as (93d), in which the two PPs in the first conjunct are s-related by (91i).

Going back to (88a) with the object control verb *persuade* (Chapter 1 (81)), (88b), the MDP interpretation of (88a), is favored over (88c) not only by satisfying the MDP but also by satisfying the SRP, because in the first conjunct, *John* is s-related to *$100* by (91ii). Interpretation (88c) violates both the MDP and SRP. Note that in the first conjunct of (88c), *Mary* is not s-related to *$100*. On the other hand, (89a) with the subject control verb *promise* (Chapter 1 (82)) is interpreted as (89c), which violates the MDP but satisfies the SRP, because in the first conjunct, *Mary* is s-related to *$100*. Recall that the MDP is a default processing strategy and can be overridden by some other factor. In (89c), the MDP is overridden by the SRP. However, the SRP is simply another processing strategy that is useful for the hearer/interpreter to find the most readily available interpretation (i.e., the interpretation accessible with least effort), and hence it is not absolute, as shown in (7c).

Here are two more examples of the SRP (90). Hankamer (1973) took (94a) as an instance of gapping. If so, this satisfies the SRP, because *Mike* is s-related to *to wash himself* by (91i). However, recall that *want* takes an S[*to*] complement (Chapter 1 (6), Ueno 2014: 17, 181), whose constituent structure is [$_{S[to]}$ NP, VP[*to*]]. Therefore, (94a) is not a gapping construction but simply a coordination of S[*to*]. Still, the gapping construction lexical entry (33) is applied vacuously to (94a) in the sense that the bracketed phrases are contrastively focused, just as the subject NP and its predicate VP can be contrastively focused in ordinary sentences such as (94b).

(94) a. Jack wants [Mike] [to wash himself], and [Arnie] [to shave himself]. (Hankamer 1973: 25)
 b. [Mike] [washed himself] and [Arnie] [shaved himself].
 c. [John] struck Mary [as being honest], and [Bill] [as being sincere]. (S-level gapping, Kuno 1976: 312)

(94c) is a gapping example with raising verb *strike* (Ueno 2014: 157). Although it violates the MDP, it satisfies the SRP because in the first conjunct, *John* is s-related to *as being sincere* by (91i).

Kuno (1976) also pointed out the contrast between (95bB) and (95cB).

(95) (Kuno 1976: 314)
 a. A: Who persuaded who to examine Mary?
  B: [Jóhn] persuaded [Dr. Thómas] to examine Măry, and [Bíll] [Dr. Jónes].
 b. A: Who persuaded Dr. Thomas to examine who?
  B: *[Jóhn] persuaded Dr. Thŏmas to examine [Jáne], and [Bíll] [Mártha].
 c. A: Who promised Bill to examine who?
  B: [Dr. Thómas] promised Bĭll to examine [Jáne], and [Dr. Jónes] [Mártha].

In the acceptable (95aB), *John* and *Dr. Thomas* of the first conjunct satisfy the SRP, but violate the MDP. In addition, in the acceptable (95cB), *Dr. Thomas* and *Jane* satisfy the SRP. In the unacceptable (95bB), *John* and *Jane* in the first conjunct violate both the MDP and the SRP.

In (96a), *Bill* and *his father* of the first conjunct satisfy the SRP. In (96b), because *want*, *try*, and *begin* are all subject control verbs, *I* and *a novel* of the first conjunct satisfy the SRP. In (96c), *seem* is a subject raising verb and *try* and *begin* are subject control verbs, and therefore, *Max* and *Harriet* of the first conjunct satisfy the SRP by (91ii). In (96d), *John* and *Mary* of the first conjunct satisfy the SRP, because *try* is a subject control verb.

(96) a. ?[Bill] visited Boston to see [his father], and [John] [his uncle]. (Kuno 1976: 315)
   b. [I] want to try to begin to write [a novel], and [Mary] [a play]. (= (7b))
   c. [Max] seemed to be trying to begin to love [Harriet], and [Fred] [Sue]. (= (38b))
   d. [John] has tried to persuade [Mary] to accept his hand in marriage and [Bill], [Jane]. (Hudson 1989: 61)

In (97a), if we take *today* and *tomorrow* as modifiers of (the event structure of) *cook*, the intended gapping interpretation is not available. Note that *wonder* is not a unique control verb and an infinitival *wh*-question is not a unique control structure (Ueno 2014: 341–2). Therefore, *John* and *today* of the first conjunct violate the SRP. In addition, they violate the MDP. On the other hand, *John* and *what to cook today* of the first conjunct in (97b) satisfy the SRP. What is interesting about (97a) is that if we take *today* and *yesterday* as modifying (the event structure of) *wondered*, then *John* and *today* of the first conjunct satisfy the SRP, and hence (97c) is acceptable under this interpretation. For example, (97c) is intended as an answer to the multiple *wh*-question *Who wondered what to cook when?*.

(97) a. *[John] wondered what to cook [today], and [Peter] [tomorrow]. (Neijt 1979: 138)
   a'. John wondered what fish to cook today and what meat tomorrow. (VP-level gapping)
   b. [John] wondered [what to cook today], and [Peter] [what to cook tomorrow].
   c. [John] wondered what to cook [today], and [Peter] [yesterday].

6.6 Gapping and Speech Acts

In the gapping construction, the first conjunct and the second and later gapped conjuncts can be uttered by different speakers, as in (98a) below. (15a) was such an example. In these cases, the second speaker, who utters the gapped conjunct, also commits himself to the truth of the first conjunct (McCawley 1998: 743). In (99), for example, the first speaker Jorge, who utters a false proposition, and the second speaker Ivan, who utters a true proposition, are both liars, because gapping indicates that Ivan is a "coprincipal" of the first conjunct and hence responsible for the first assertion (McCawley 1998: 743). Here, the role of *speaker* is regarded, following Goffman (1981: 144ff.), McCawley (1998: 741), and McCawley (1999), as conflating the roles of *author*, the person who composes the text, *animator*, the person who utters the text, and *principal*, the person "whose beliefs have been told" and "who is committed to what the words say" (Goffman 1981: 144).

(98) a. (McCawley 1998: 742; taken from Hankamer and Sag 1976: 410)
 Jorge: Ivan is now going to peel an apple.
 Ivan: And Jorge an orange.
 b. Jorge: Ivan is now going to peel an apple.
 Ivan: And Jorge an orange?

(99) (McCawley 1998: 743)
 Jorge: Detroit is in Nebraska. (false proposition)
 Ivan: And Boston in Massachusetts. (true proposition)

With this in mind, the modular representations of (98a) are given in (100), in which the first part of (98a) is asserted by both Jorge and Ivan (i.e., it is a speech act (SA) of assertion by them both) but its locutionary act (LA) is performed by Jorge alone. (See Chapter 2 (37) for SA and LA superstructures.) Note that the E/R representation in (100) allows a possibility as in (98b) that the first conjunct is a declarative and the second gapped conjunct is an interrogative. In such a case, the illocutionary force (IF) of the second SA is #inquire# instead of #assert#.

(100) syntax (ordinary gapping syntax)

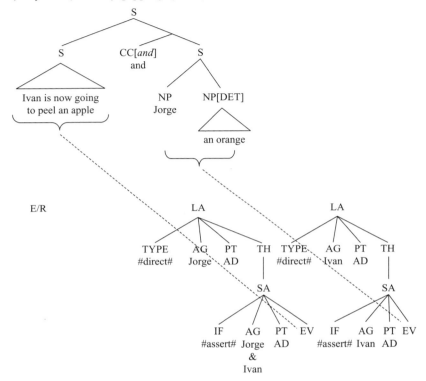

Sag et al. (1985: 160) pointed out a gapping example that exhibits the "shift in deixis" (shift between the first and second person singular).

(101) a. (Sag et al. 1985: 160)
    A_i: [I_i] shall miss [you$_j$].
    B_j: And [I_j] [you$_i$].
  b. (Huddleston and Pullum 2002: 1542)
    A_i: [I_i] will now show you how to make [clafouti].
    B_j: And [I_j] [custard].

Each instance of the same first- or second-person pronoun can be contrastively focused with each other as long as each instance refers to a different person. However, Hudson (1989: 69) observed that speakers can change freely in the middle of any utterance, provided that there is a pragmatic reason for doing so. In (102), the reflexive pronoun coreferential with speaker A is uttered by speaker B. Therefore, although the syntactic requirement to use a reflexive pronoun is met, the deixis is shifted from the first to the second person.

(102) (Hudson 1989: 69)
    a. A_i: I_i looked in the mirror and saw ...
        B_j: Yourself$_i$.
    b. A_i: I've fallen down again.
        B_j: And hurt yourself$_i$, I suppose.

Even when a gapping construction is uttered by two speakers, the nature of its construction is retained intact and must satisfy its lexical entry (33). For example, the second conjunct must be adjacent to the first conjunct and no material can intervene between the first and second conjunct, as was shown in (36).

(103) (Hudson 1989: 70)
    A_i: [I_i] shall miss [you$_j$].
    B_j: (*That's funny) and [I_j] [you$_i$].

6.7 Operator Sharing in Gapping

In this section, we will discuss what is called "operator sharing" in the gapping construction, which was first observed and investigated by McCawley (1993b). McCawley (1993b: 249) and Culicover and Jackendoff (2005: 278) pointed out that such elements as auxiliary verbs, subject raising verbs, and ad-S adverbs can have the whole coordinate structure within their scope, when used in the first conjunct of the gapping construction. Recall that auxiliary verbs and subject raising verbs are Fp in F/A (i.e., a functor category that takes PROP as its complement and returns PROP: [$_{PROP}$ Fp, PROP]), whereas ad-S adverbs are Mp in F/A (i.e., a category that modifies PROP: [$_{PROP}$ Mp, PROP]). (See Chapter 1 (27d), (28a), and (31).)

For example, in (104a), the contracted form *can't* of modal *can* and negative *not* takes scope over the entire coordinated proposition 'John eat steak and Mary eat just spam.' The intended interpretation is not 'John can't eat steak and Mary can't eat just spam' but 'for John to eat steak and Mary to eat just spam is impossible.' Note that the pronoun *it* in (104a) refers to this coordinated proposition. In (104b), the contracted form *didn't* takes scope over the entire conjoined proposition 'Kim play bingo or Sandy sit at home all evening.'

(104) a. [John] <u>can't</u> eat [steak] and [Mary], [just spam]—it's not fair. (Culicover and Jackendoff 2005: 278)
     b. [Kim] <u>didn't</u> [play bingo] or [Sandy] [sit at home all evening]. (= (29a))
     c. The Yankees <u>have often</u> finished first and the White Sox last. (McCawley 1993b: 249)
     d. John <u>happened</u> to be in the bathroom and Mary in the basement when the phone rang. (McCawley 1993b: 249)
     e. I tried it in both positions, one of which <u>must have</u> been the locked position and the other one the unlocked position, but it wouldn't work either way. (McCawley 1993b: 249)
     f. Many linguists can't read German, and many musicians can't read French. (McCawley 1993b: 248)
     g. *Many linguists can't read German, and/or many musicians French. (McCawley 1993b: 248)
     h. John didn't go to the laundromat, nor Betsy to the grocery store. (Sag 1976: 139)
     h'. I didn't eat fish, nor Bill ice cream. (Sag 1976: 143)

Recall that negative elements such as *not* cannot be "deleted" in the S-level gapping, as was shown in (65b) and is illustrated again in (104g). (However, *not* can be "deleted" in the VP-level gapping, as was illustrated in (66b).) Therefore, (104a, b) cannot be interpreted as being "derived" from coordinated negative sentences. This point was discussed in relation to (29a). In other words, gapping requires that *not* have scope over the entire coordinate structure, which does not contradict our constructional view of gapping (33).

Because the underlined parts in (104a–e) are shared semantically with the gapped conjunct of each sentence and hence there are no multiple occurrences of them semantically, these examples cannot involve the regular gapping. However, McCawley (1993b: 249) pointed out that the conditions on the gapping construction in (33) still hold in the examples in (104). For example, the two remnant phrases of the gapped conjuncts are required to contrast with the two phrases of the first conjunct, just as in the regular gapping. Note also that when the second remnant phrase of the gapped conjuncts is a VP, its VFORM value is determined by the shared auxiliary verb. For example, in (104b), the second remnant phrase of the gapped conjunct is VP[BSE]. This VFORM value BSE is imposed by the shared auxiliary *didn't*, which takes a VP[BSE] complement.

The intended interpretation of (104a, b), for instance, can be arrived at as usual by the Procedure for gapping comprehension (24). However, there are two differences in the interpretation procedure of the operator-sharing cases. The first difference is that step (ii) of constructing the inferred syntactic structure of the gapped conjunct is not complete, because there is no well-formed inferred syntactic structure for these gapped conjuncts. The second difference is the way of constructing the inferred F/A of the gapped conjunct. When the inferred F/A of the gapped conjunct of such operator-sharing gapping cases as (104a, b) is constructed (step (iii) of (24)), it is coordinated with the inner PROP of the first conjunct and this coordinated PROP is in turn embedded under the shared operators. (105) provides examples of the comprehension procedure of gapping constructions with shared operators.

(105) John can't eat steak and Mary, just spam. (= (104a))
and Mary, just spam →
  (i) decoded four-tuple of *and Mary, just spam*
  (ii) inferred syntax of gapped conjunct: *and Mary eat just spam*
       (incomplete; only supplying the main verb *eat*)
  (iii) inferred four-tuple of gapping construction
    1. computing decoded F/A of first conjunct
       $[_{Fp} \text{PRES}] \circ [_{Fp} \text{NOT}] \circ [_{Fp} \text{CAN}]([_{PROP} (\text{JOHN}(\text{EAT}(\text{STEAK})))])$
    2. computing F/A of gapped conjunct on the basis of its inferred syntax
       $[_{PROP} (\text{MARY}(\text{EAT}(\text{JUST.SPAM})))]$
    3. coordinating this F/A with inner PROP of first conjunct
       $[_{PROP} (\text{JOHN}(\text{EAT}(\text{STEAK})))]$ AND $[_{PROP} (\text{MARY}(\text{EAT}(\text{JUST.SPAM})))]$
    4. embedding coordinated PROP under shared operators
       $[_{Fp} \text{PRES}] \circ [_{Fp} \text{NOT}] \circ [_{Fp} \text{CAN}]([_{PROP} (\text{JOHN}(\text{EAT}(\text{STEAK})))]$ AND $[_{PROP} (\text{MARY}(\text{EAT}(\text{JUST.SPAM})))])$
  (iv) explicatures and implicatures:
       higher-level explicature: 'The speaker thinks that it should not be allowed for John to eat steak and Mary to eat just spam.'
       implicature: 'The speaker believes that John and Mary should eat the same food.'

(106) Kim didn't play bingo or Sandy sit at home all evening. (= (104b))
or Sandy sit at home all evening →
  (i) decoded four-tuple of *or Sandy sit at home all evening*
  (ii) inferred syntax of gapped conjunct: *or Sandy sit at home all evening* (= decoded syntax of (i))
  (iii) inferred four-tuple of gapping construction
    1. computing decoded F/A of first conjunct
       $[_{Fp} \text{PAST}] \circ [_{Fp} \text{NOT}] ([_{PROP} (\text{KIM}(\text{PLAY}(\text{BINGO})))])$
    2. computing decoded F/A of gapped conjunct
       $[_{PROP} (\text{SANDY}(\text{SIT.AT.HOME.ALL.EVENING}))]$
    3. coordinating this F/A with inner PROP of first conjunct
       $[_{PROP} (\text{KIM}(\text{PLAY}(\text{BINGO})))]$ OR
       $[_{PROP} (\text{SANDY}(\text{SIT.AT.HOME.ALL.EVENING}))]$
    4. embedding coordinated PROP under shared operators
       $[_{Fp} \text{PAST}] \circ [_{Fp} \text{NOT}] ([_{PROP} (\text{KIM}(\text{PLAY}(\text{BINGO})))]$ OR
       $[_{PROP} (\text{SANDY}(\text{SIT.AT.HOME.ALL.EVENING}))])$
  (iv) explicatures and implicatures
       higher-level explicature: 'The speaker knows that Kim didn't play bingo and Sandy didn't sit at home all evening.'
       implicature: 'The speaker wonders what Kim and Sandy did all evening.'

The comprehension steps in (105iii) and (106iii) of constructing the inferred F/A of the gapping construction demonstrate that the F/A module is autonomous in and of itself and separate from the syntax module.

To arrive at explicatures and implicatures of the gapping construction, inferring its syntactic structure, however incomplete it may be, is still essential. This is especially true of VP idioms, which were illustrated in (20). In (107), *can't have*, which corresponds to $[_{Fp} \text{PRES}] \circ [_{Fp} \text{NOT}] \circ [_{Fp} \text{CAN}] \circ [_{Fp} \text{PAST}]$ in F/A, is shared between both conjuncts.

(107) John's leg <u>can't have</u> been pulled by his brother or Mary's by her sister. (cf. (20b))

Exactly as in (20), to arrive at a proper interpretation of (107), the hearer/interpreter needs to infer that *Mary's* represents *Mary's leg* in syntax and therefore the gapped conjunct at least represents *Mary's leg pulled by her sister* in syntax, and that it is a passivization of the VP idiom *pull someone's leg*, just as the first conjunct is.

McCawley (1993b) and Culicover and Jackendoff (2005: 279) pointed out a similar phenomenon in which the quantifier, including the definite article and possessive NP of the subject NP of the first conjunct is shared by and takes scope over the gapped conjuncts. The shared operators are underlined in (108).

(108) a. [Not every girl] ate [a green banana] and [her mother] [a ripe one]. (Culicover and Jackendoff 2005: 279)
 b. [No one's duck] was [moist enough] or [his mussels] [tender enough]. (McCawley 1993b: 248)
 b'. *No one's duck was moist enough or/and his mussels were tender enough. (McCawley 1993b: 248)
 c. [NP Too many Irish setters] are named [Kelly] and [NP German shepherds] [Fritz]. (Culicover and Jackendoff 2005: 279)
 d. [Too many Irish setters] are named [Kelly], [German shepherds] [Fritz], and [huskies] [Nanook]. (McCawley 1993b: 245)
 d'. *Too many Irish setters are named Kelly, German shepherds are named Fritz, and huskies are named Nanook. (McCawley 1993b: 245)
 e. [The duck] is [dry] and [mussels] [tough], but Bocuse D'Or rehearsal goes well for chef Bumbaris. (McCawley 1993b: 245)
 f. [How many good students] did he give [Fs] to and [bad students] [As]? (McCawley 1993b: 246)
 g. [Italy's red wines] are [outstanding] and [white wine] [excellent]. (McCawley 1993b: 246)
 h. Martha Washington, [whose husband's honesty] was [legendary] and [courage] [justly famous], was herself a remarkable person. (McCawley 1993b: 246)
 i. [Not enough linguists] study [Russian], [literary scholars] [French], or/??and [engineers] [Japanese]. (McCawley 1993b: 247)
 i'. Not enough linguists study Russian, not enough literary scholars French, *or/and not enough engineers Japanese. (McCawley 1993b: 247)
 j. [Too few fathers] had been rostered [for Saturday] and [mothers] (*had been rostered) [for Sunday]. (Huddleston and Pullum 2002: 1339)

Gapping is required here, too, for operator sharing to take place, as shown in (108b, b', d, d', i, i'). In (108b), for example, gapping is required for *his* in the second conjunct to be interpreted as a variable bound by *no one* in the first conjunct. This does not contradict our constructional view of gapping but a deletion approach to gapping would encounter serious problems.

The F/A of (108a) is easy to determine, because *her* in the gapped conjunct is clearly interpreted as a variable bound by the quantified NP *every girl* in the first conjunct. The comprehension process of (108a) on the basis of Procedure for gapping comprehension (24) proceeds as follows.

(109)   Not every girl ate a green banana and her mother a ripe one. (= (108a))
        and her mother a ripe one →
   (i) decoded four-tuple of *and her mother a ripe one*
   (ii) inferred syntax of gapped conjunct: *and her mother ate a ripe banana*
   (iii) inferred four-tuple of gapping construction (cf. (105iii) and (106iii))
   1. computing decoded F/A of first conjunct:
      NOT([$_{QPx}$ EVERY x = GIRL] PAST [$_{PROP}$ [$_{ARG}$ x] EAT [$_{ARG}$ GREEN BANANA]])
   2. computing F/A of gapped conjunct on the basis of its inferred syntax:
      AND PAST [$_{PROP}$ [$_{ARG}$ HER MOTHER] EAT [$_{ARG}$ RIPE BANANA]]
   3. inferred F/A of gapped conjunct from that of first conjunct:
      AND PAST [$_{PROP}$ [$_{ARG}$ x's MOTHER] EAT [$_{ARG}$ RIPE BANANA]]
   4. coordinating inner PROP of this F/A with inner PROP of first conjunct
      [$_{PROP}$ x EAT GREEN.BANANA] AND [$_{PROP}$ x's MOTHER EAT RIPE.BANANA]
   5. embedding coordinated PROP under shared QP and Fp's
      NOT [$_{QPx}$ EVERY x = GIRL] PAST ([$_{PROP}$ x EAT GREEN.BANANA] AND [$_{PROP}$ x's MOTHER EAT RIPE.BANANA])

As for the F/A of (108c), its intended interpretation of the second conjunct is 'too many German shepherds are named Fritz.' However, the determiner *too many* is shared between the first conjunct and the gapped conjunct. That is, there is a single occurrence of *too many* in (108c) that goes over to both conjunct propositions. In other words, (108c) reports not two separate judgments of *too many* but a single judgment of *too many* in which *Irish setters* and *German shepherds* are pooled (cf. McCawley 1993b: 248). To arrive at a proper F/A of (108c), the hearer/interpreter needs two variables, one ranging over the set of Irish setters and the other ranging over the set of German shepherds.

6.7 OPERATOR SHARING IN GAPPING

Following one of McCawley's two suggestions (McCawley 1993b: 248), we adopt his "polyadic quantifier" approach, in which a single quantifier is allowed to bind multiple variables. (See McCawley (1993a: 240ff.) for details on polyadic quantifiers.)

(110) Too many Irish setters are named Kelly and German shepherds Fritz. (= (108c))
and German shepherds Fritz →
  (i) decoded four-tuple of *and German shepherds Fritz*
  (ii) inferred syntax of gapped conjunct: *and German shepherds are named Fritz* (from first conjunct)
  (iii) inferred four-tuple of gapping construction
    1. computing decoded F/A of first conjunct
       [$_{QPx}$ [$_Q$ TOO MANY] x = IRISH.SETTERS] PRES [$_{PROP}$ [$_{ARG}$ x] NAMED KELLY]
    2. computing F/A of gapped conjunct on the basis of its inferred syntax
       PRES [$_{PROP}$ [$_{ARG}$ GERMAN.SHEPHERDS] NAMED FRITZ]
    3. inferring F/A of gapped conjunct from that of first conjunct
       [$_{PROP}$ [$_{ARG}$ y] NAMED FRITZ]
    4. coordinating this F/A with inner PROP of first conjunct
       [$_{PROP}$ [$_{ARG}$ x] NAMED KELLY] AND [$_{PROP}$ [$_{ARG}$ y] NAMED FRITZ]
    5. embedding coordinated PROP under shared Fp and polyadic quantifier QP

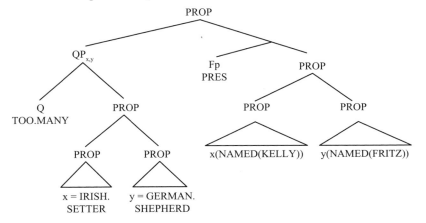

There is a general tendency in gapping interpretation that the remnant phrases XP and YP of the gapped conjunct are contrastively focused with [XP + α] and [YP + β] of the first conjunct. That is, XP and YP of the gapped conjunct are interpreted as (elliptic forms of) [XP + α] and [YP + β]. In a sense, these α and β are interpreted as being shared between the first conjunct and the gapped conjunct.

(111) a. [John] will find [a man <u>who can speak Japanese</u>], and [Bill] [a girl]. (Imanishi and Asano 1990: 386)
b. [John] tried to find [a girl <u>with blue eyes</u>], and [Mary] [a boy].
c. You and I will see in the years ahead [which <u>of us</u>] was [right], and [which] [wrong]. (= (49b))
d. [Which dress <u>to wear</u>] is a problem [for Sue] and [which tie] [for John]. (Neijt 1979: 174)
d'. [Which dress <u>to wear</u>] is a problem for Sue while [which tie] is a problem for John.
e. [Charles] may decide [which boys <u>are coming along</u>] and [Max] [which girls]. (Neijt 1979: 142)
e'. Charles may decide [which boys <u>are coming along</u>] as soon as Max decides [which girls].
f. [<u>His criticisms</u> of Kim] were [inaccurate] and [of Pat] [irrelevant]. (= (46d))

For example, in (111a), the second remnant phrase *a girl* of the gapped conjunct is contrasted with the NP *a man who can speak Japanese* of the first conjunct, and can optionally be interpreted as being modified by the same relative clause, namely, as an elliptic form of *a girl who can speak Japanese*. Note that *a girl* of the gapped conjunct of (111a) cannot be contrasted with *a man* of the first conjunct, because *a man* is not a major constituent, let alone a constituent, of the first conjunct. Recall that a restrictive relative clause (RRC) is adjoined to the head NP, as in [$_{NP[DET]}$ DET [$_{NP}$ NP RRC]] (Chapter 1 (1b, c)). By the same token, *a boy* of the gapped conjunct in (111b) can optionally be interpreted as an elliptic form of *a boy with blue eyes*. In (111c), *which* of the gapped conjunct is contrastively focused with *which of us* in the first conjunct, and hence interpreted as an elliptic form of *which of us*.

(111d, e) are examples in which one of the two remnant phrases of the gapped conjuncts is a *wh*-fragment, which is interpreted according to the Fragment comprehension procedure (Chapter 3 (5b)). The *wh*-fragment *which tie* in (111d) is contrastively focused with *which dress to wear* of the first conjunct and hence interpreted as an elliptic form of *which tie to wear*. Similarly, *which girls* in (111e) is contrastively focused with *which boys are coming along* of the first conjunct and hence interpreted as an elliptic form of *which girls are coming along*. Example (18a) was of the same type. Note (pace Imanishi and Asano 1990: 386) that the interpretations of *which tie* in (111d) as *which tie to wear* and of *which girls* in (111e) as *which girls are coming along* are independent of an occurrence of the gapping construction in (111d, e), as shown in (111d', e').

These examples in (111) show that there is a "parallelism constraint" at work in the gapping construction to the effect that phrases contrastively focused with each other tend to be interpreted in as parallel a way as possible. Going back to the cases of quantifier sharing in (108), the examples in (108c–j) can also be seen as instances of gapping in which this parallelism constraint is at work.

6.8 Stripping

Stripping is a two-term coordinate structure in which the first conjunct is a full sentence and the second conjunct (stripped conjunct) consists of a single constituent that is contrastively focused with a constituent in the first conjunct, as in (112a) (McCawley 1998: 62, 281–282). The constituents that are contrastively focused are in brackets.

(112) stripping
- a. [The audience] listened to the speaker, and [the ushers] too. (McCawley 1998: 30)
- b. [Tom] owns a Mercedes, and (*I'm pretty sure that) [Susan] too. (McCawley 1998: 30)
- b'. [Tom] owns a Mercedes, and, I'm sure, [Susan] too.
- b". [Tom] owns a Mercedes, and, as far as I know, [Susan] too.
- c. If [Tom] owns a Mercedes, [Susan] *(does) too. (McCawley 1998: 30)
- c'. *That Fred sent [a threatening letter] to the President makes it likely that [a bomb] too. (McCawley 1998: 281)
- c". *Although Fred sent [a bomb] to the President, [a nice letter] too. (ibid.)
- d. John drives [from Boston to New York] in three hours, but not [from Chicago to St. Louis]. (McCawley 1998: 56)
    cf. It is [from Boston to New York] that John drives in three hours. (cf. McCawley 1998: 66)

d'. ??John talks [to his father about politics], but not [to his mother about religion]. (ibid.)
  cf. John talks [to his father] about politics, but not [to his mother].
  John talks to his father [about politics], but not [about religion].
d". ??Smith sells [luxury cars to insurance executives], but not [pick-up trucks to farmers]. (McCawley 1998: 62)
  cf. Smith sells [luxury cars] to insurance executives, but not [pick-up trucks].
  Smith sells luxury cars [to insurance executives], but not [to farmers].
e. ??Smith sells [luxury cars] to insurance agents, [pick-up trucks] too, and [mobile homes] as well. (McCawley 1998: 62)
e'. *Smith sells [luxury cars] to insurance agents, but not [pick-up trucks], and [mobile homes] too.
e". ?Smith sells [luxury cars] to insurance agents, and [[pick-up trucks] too but not [mobile homes]].
e'". Smith sells [luxury cars] to insurance agents, but [not [pick-up trucks] and not [mobile homes] either].

(112b) shows that the second conjunct must only consist of a contrastive constituent (together with *too* or *not*), and therefore, the second conjunct cannot be embedded. The same property is shared by the gapping construction, which was illustrated in (36a). However, a parenthetical, which constitutes a separate speech act, can be inserted immediately before the second conjunct, as shown in (112b', b"). This property is also shared by the gapping construction, which was illustrated in (36a'). (112c, c', c") show that stripping is restricted to coordinate structures. (112d) shows that since the sequence PP[*from*] PP[*to*] forms a single constituent, it appears as the second conjunct in stripping. On the other hand, (112d', d") show that the sequences PP[*to*] PP[*about*] and NP PP[*to*] do not make up a single constituent and hence stripping is impossible. (112e, e') show that stripping is restricted to two-term coordinate structures. By contrast, (112e", e'") are much better than (112e, e'). This is because it is easy to interpret *pick-up trucks too, but not mobile homes* as making up a single constituent in (112e"), hence resulting in a two-term coordinate structure as a whole. The same is true of *but not pick-up trucks, and not mobile homes either* in (112e'").

The phrase in the first conjunct in the stripping construction that is contrastively focused with the second conjunct must be a major constituent (i.e., a constituent directly dominated by S, VP, or AP), as shown in (113a, b), (114a, b), and (115a, b). Note that in the b-examples, the first contrastive phrase is not a major constituent. This is again similar to the gapping construction ((4), (5), (46), (47), (48)).

(113) a. John borrows [novels by Hemingway] from the library, but not [plays by Shakespeare].
b. ??John borrows novels [by Hemingway] from the library, but not [by Faulkner].
c. John collects books [by Hemingway] but not [by Faulkner]. (McCawley 1998: 696)

In (113c), the first PP[*by*] is not a major constituent, because it is directly dominated by an NP. This is not an instance of stripping, contrary to McCawley's claim that it is (McCawley 1998: 696), but a mere instance of coordinate structure [$_{PP[by]}$ PP[*by*] *but not* PP[*by*]].

(114) a. John looked at the ship [through a telescope] yesterday, but not [through binoculars].
b. *John looked at the ship through [a telescope] yesterday, but not [binoculars].

(115) a. [The participants from China] stayed in the assembly hall, but not [those from Korea].
b. *The participants [from China] stayed in the assembly hall, but not [from Korea].

Furthermore, just like a gapped conjunct ((98), (99)), the stripped conjunct can be uttered by a different speaker in a different speech act.

(116) A_i: I_i'll have Japanese food for lunch. (assertion)
B_j: And Chinese food too? (question)
→ *And will you$_i$ have Chinese food for lunch too?*

(117) A: Detroit is in Illinois. (false proposition)
B: And Chicago too. (true proposition)
→ *And Chicago is in Illinois too*

In (117), not only A but also B is a liar, because B is also a coprincipal of the coordinated proposition (cf. (99)).

As with the gapping construction (6.7), the stripping construction allows operator sharing. (118a) is ambiguous between two readings. One is 'either one of them hadn't complied with the regulations' just like (118b), in which *or* is unstressed and the stripped conjunct *or her secretary* is outside the negative scope. The other is 'Neither of them had complied with the regulations,' in which *or* is stressed, *or her secretary* is inside the negative scope, and *hadn't* serves as a shared operator. The latter interpretation is more readily available.

(118) a. [Jill] hadn't complied with the regulations—or [her secretary]. (ambiguous) (Huddleston and Pullum 2002: 1346)
b. Jill or her secretary hadn't complied with the regulations.

To capture these similarities between stripping and gapping, we would like to formulate stripping as a construction, along the lines of gapping.

(119) lexical entry for stripping construction
(in syntax)

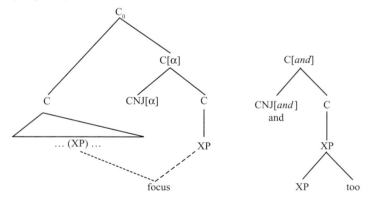

(in syntax)
(i) C_0 is a nonce coordinate structure of the syntactic category C with a coordinate conjunction (CNJ) $\alpha \in \{and, or, but\}$.
(ii) The left conjunct C is the smallest CP[WH[Q]], S, or VP that contains XP.
(iii) The right conjunct consists of a single constituent XP.

(iv) XP of the first conjunct, if present, is a major constituent.
(in Information Structure)
  (v) XP of the left conjunct and XP of the right conjunct are contrastively focused.
  (vi) XP of the right conjunct is often added as an afterthought.

Sag et al. (1985) claimed that stripping is a special case of gapping, specifically, the minimal case of gapping in the sense that the number of gapped conjuncts is limited to only one, and at the same time the number of the remnant phrases of each gapped conjunct is again limited to just one. However, because of a different type of stripping, which will be discussed later in relation to (136), we follow McCawley (1998) and Huddleston and Pullum (2002) and claim that it is a construction different from the gapping construction.

We claim that the interpretation of the stripping construction is arrived at by the same five-step procedure that is applied to fragments, sluicing, VP ellipsis, and gapping. To be more specific, what the hearer/interpreter has to do to determine the intended meaning of the stripped conjunct is to apply the five steps given in (120) and compute the explicatures and implicatures of the whole coordinate structure.

(120) Procedure for stripping comprehension (cf. (24))
The hearer follows the Relevance-guided comprehension heuristic (Chapter 2 (8)) and executes the following steps.
  (i) The LM computes the decoded four-tuple of the stripped conjunct.
  (ii) By non-demonstrative inference, the ICM constructs the inferred syntactic structure of the stripped conjunct on the basis of the decoded syntax of the stripped conjunct obtained in (i), the developed four-tuple of the first conjunct, and the contextual information.
  (iii) The ICM constructs the inferred four-tuple of the stripped conjunct on the basis of the inferred syntax obtained in (ii), the developed four-tuple of the first conjunct, and the contextual information.
  (iv) The ICM develops the inferred four-tuple of the stripped conjunct obtained in (iii) on the basis of the contextual information.
  (v) The ICM constructs the explicatures and implicatures of the whole stripping construction on the basis of the developed four-tuple obtained in (iv) and the contextual information including the developed four-tuple of the first conjunct.

Condition (v) in (119) entails that the first conjunct of the stripping construction is always the antecedent of the stripped conjunct. For example, (121b) shows the comprehension process of the stripping construction in (121a). The inferred syntax of the stripped conjunct *and Jerry too* is *and Jerry owns a Rolls-Royce too*. The object NP *a Rolls-Royce* of the inferred syntactic structure provides an antecedent of *Jerry's* in the second sentence.

(121) a. A: Are Tom and Jerry rich?
B: Tom owns a Rolls-Royce, and Jerry too. But Jerry's is much more expensive than Tom's.
b. [$_S$ [$_{NP}$ Tom] owns a Rolls-Royce], [$_{S[and]}$ and [$_S$ [$_{NP}$ Jerry] too]]]. (S-level stripping)
and Jerry too →
   (i) decoded four-tuple of *and Jerry too*
   (ii) inferred syntax: *and Jerry owns a Rolls-Royce too*
   (iii) inferred four-tuple of *and Jerry owns a Rolls-Royce too*
   (iv) explicatures and implicatures
      higher-level explicature: 'B knows Tom owns a Rolls-Royce and Jerry owns a Rolls-Royce too.'
      implicature: 'B thinks Tom and Jerry are both rich but Jerry is much richer than Tom.'

When step (ii) of (120) is applied to the stripped conjunct, lexical information accessed during the interpretation of the first conjunct is retained in working memory. For example, in the comprehension process of (122a) and (123a), the lexical entry for *perjure* with a fake reflexive and that for *count* with a PP[*on*] complement are accessed while processing the first conjunct and they are retained in working memory until the inferred four-tuple of the stripped conjunct is constructed.

(122) a. [Tom] perjured himself, and [Jerry] too. (S-level stripping)
→ *and Jerry perjured himself too*
b. lexical entry for *perjure*
syntax: V in [__, [$_{NP}$ *oneself*]]
F/A: Fa
E/R: [$_{TYPE}$ "perjure"] in [$_{EV}$ __ [AG, SO]]

(123) a. Tom [$_{VP}$ counts [$_{PP[on]}$ on your help] too often], [$_{VP[and]}$ and [$_{VP}$ [$_{PP[on]}$ on your money] too]]. (VP-level stripping)
→ *and counts on your money too often too*

b. lexical entry for *count on*
syntax: V in [__, PP[*on*]]
F/A: Faa
E/R: [$_{TYPE}$ "count-on"] in [$_{EV}$ __ [AG, TH] [PT, GO]]

Constructing the inferred syntactic structure of the stripped conjunct (step ii of (120)) is needed to deal with the following four cases, which motivated the same step in the comprehension procedure of fragments, sluicing, VP ellipsis, and gapping. The first case is idiom chunks.

(124) a. [John's leg] was pulled yesterday, and [Mary's] too. (S-level stripping)
→ *and Mary's leg was pulled yesterday too.*
b. [John's goose] was cooked yesterday, and [Mary's] too. (S-level stripping)
→ *and Mary's goose was cooked yesterday too.*

To interpret the stripped conjunct in (124a, b), the hearer/interpreter needs first to infer that *Mary's* in (124a, b) represents *Mary's leg* and *Mary's goose*, respectively, and then to infer the syntactic structure of the respective stripped conjunct. Without these inferred syntactic structures, the idiom interpretation would not be recoverable. (125b) is the passive lexical entry for the idiom *pull X's leg*, which is the output of the Passive Lexical Rule (Chapter 1 (88)) that is applied to the active lexical entry (125a).

(125) a. bipartite lexical entry for *pull X's leg* (as ICE) (Chapter 2 (28), Ueno 2014: 129)

syntax: [$_{VP}$ [$_V$ pull] [$_{NP[DET, 3SG]}$ syntax: V in [__, NP]
    [$_{NP[POS]}$ NP, CL[POS]],   F/A: Faa
    [$_{NP[3SG]}$ leg]]]   E/R: TYPE in [$_{EV}$ __ AG PT]
F/A: [$_{Fa}$ [$_{Faa}$ TEASE], ARG]
E/R: [$_{EV}$ [$_{TYPE}$ "tease"] AG PT]

b. bipartite passive lexical entry for *pull X's leg* (as ICE) (Chapter 2 (29), Ueno 2014: 129)

syntax: [$_{VP}$ [$_V$ pull] [$_{NP[DET, 3SG]}$ syntax: V[PAS] in [__]
    [$_{NP[POS]}$ NP, CL[POS]],   F/A: Fa
    [$_{NP[3SG]}$ leg]]]   E/R: TYPE in [$_{EV}$ __ <AG> PT]
F/A: [$_{Fa}$ [$_{Faa}$ TEASE], ARG]
E/R: [$_{EV}$ [$_{TYPE}$ "tease"] AG PT]

Second, the stripping construction exhibits the Missing Antecedent Phenomenon, just as VP ellipsis (5.5) and gapping (17).

(126) a.   John visited a temple [in Kyoto] last year, and [in Nara] too. (VP-level stripping)
           They are both more than 800 years old.
           → *and (he) visited a temple in Nara last year too.*
    a'.   John didn't visit a temple [in Kyoto] last year, but [in Nara] instead. (VP-level stripping)
           It is more than 800 years old.
           → *but (he) visited a temple in Nara last year instead.*
    b.   [John] visited a temple in Kyoto, and [Mary] too. (S-level stripping)
           They are both more than 800 years old.
           → *and Mary visited a temple in Kyoto too*
    b'.   [John] didn't visit a temple in Kyoto, but [Mary] instead. (S-level stripping)
           It is more than 800 years old.
           → *but Mary visited a temple in Kyoto instead*
    c.   [Tom] pulled a guest's leg at the party, and [Jerry] too. They were both from Japan.
    c'.   [Tom] didn't pull a guest's leg at the party, but [Jerry] instead. She was from Japan.

The antecedent of *They* in the second sentence in (126a, b) can be recovered only when the inferred syntactic structure of the stripped conjunct is constructed: *(John) visited a temple in Nara last year too* in (126a), and *(Mary) visited a temple in Kyoto too* in (126b). In (126a', b'), the antecedent of *it* in the second sentence is found in the inferred syntax of the stripped conjunct. Note that a missing antecedent can be an idiom chunk, as shown in (126c, c').

Third, when the stripped conjunct is in the form of *but XP instead* and the first conjunct is a negative sentence in which its focus of negation is on XP, as in (127a), the XP of the stripped conjunct must be interpreted with respect to the corresponding affirmative sentence. The polarity is reversed between the first conjunct (antecedent) and the inferred syntax of the second conjunct. Note again that XP can be an idiom chunk, as shown in (127b).

(127) a. John didn't put [garlic] in the meatloaf, but [anise] instead.
(VP-level stripping, the focus of negation is on *garlic*)
→ *but (he) put anise in the meatloaf instead*
b. Tom didn't pull [Mary's leg] at the party, but [Jane's] instead.

Finally, stripping interacts with VP ellipsis and sluicing, which require inferred syntactic structures.

(128) A: John bought a new PC, didn't he?
B: Yes, he did, and Mary too.   [VP ellipsis + stripping]
→ *and Mary did too*
→ *and Mary bought a new PC too*
A: Really? When?   [*wh*-fragment]
→ *When did Mary buy a new PC?*
B: Last month.   [fragment]
→ *Mary bought a new PC last month.*

(129) A: Did John buy a new car?
B: Yes, he did. But I don't remember   [VP ellipsis + *wh*-fragment + when and my wife either.   stripping]
he did → *he bought a new car*
I don't remember when → *I don't remember when he bought a new car*
and my wife either → *and my wife doesn't remember when he bought a new car, either*

Thus far, we have seen S-level stripping (126b, b') and VP-level stripping (126a, a'). In the comprehension process of each example, an inferred S or VP is constructed in step (ii) of (120). However, there are cases of stripping in which two XPs in (119) are interpreted as being directly coordinated as part of the first conjunct. That is, inference in step (ii) of (120) leads to a coordinate structure *XP and/or XP* in place of XP in the first (i.e., antecedent) conjunct. In derivational terms, the second conjunct XP[*and*] of a two-term coordinate structure originates in the first conjunct as in [$_S$ ... [$_{XP}$ XP [$_{XP[and]}$ and XP]] ...] and is moved out of the coordinated XP to the S-final position, as if in the case of Heavy Constituent Shift (HCS) (Ueno 2014: 76, 170). We will call this type of stripping interpretation XP-coordination reading.

336   6 AN AUTOMODULAR VIEW OF GAPPING

(130) cases where step (ii) of (120) leads to an NP-coordination reading within the first conjunct
   a. John gave either [Mary] a birthday gift, or [Lucille]. (McCawley 1998: 281)
      → *John gave either [[Mary] or [Lucille]] a birthday gift.*
      (inferred syntax of the whole coordinate structure)
   b. John sent [letters] by airmail, but not [parcels].
      → *John sent [[letters] but not [parcels]] by airmail.*
   c. John sent not only [letters] by airmail, but also [parcels].
      → *John sent [not only [letters] but also [parcels]] by airmail.*
   d. To which country does John send [letters] PP[G] by airmail, but not [parcels]? (McCawley 1998: 281)
      → [$_{PP[WH[Q]]}$ *To which country*] *does John send* [[*letters*] *but not* [*parcels*]] PP[G] *by airmail?*

In (130a), an NP-coordination reading is required because of *either* in the first conjunct, which demands the structure *either* A *or* B. In (130b, d), the negation in A *but not* B is a contrastive negation (McCawley 1998: 613) and B is its focus. Here are two more examples that require an NP-coordination reading.

(131) a. They hadn't issued [sheets] to the new recruits—or [towels]. (Huddleston and Pullum 2002: 1347)
   a'. They hadn't [$_{VP}$ [$_{VP}$ issued [$_{NP}$ sheets] to the new recruits]—[$_{NP[or]}$ or [$_{NP}$ towels]]].
      → *They hadn't issued* [[*sheets*] *or* [*towels*]] *to the new recruits.*
   b. How many had they issued [sheets] to, but not [pillow-slips]? (Huddleston and Pullum 2002: 1347)
   b'. How many had they [$_{VP}$ [$_{VP}$ issued [$_{NP}$ sheets] to NP[G]], [$_{NP[but]}$ but not [$_{NP}$ pillow-slips]]]?
      → *How many had they issued* [[*sheets*] *but not* [*pillow-slips*]] *to* NP[G]?

(131a) is interpreted as a single negative statement to the effect that 'they had issued neither sheets nor towels to the new recruits.' The second conjunct NP[*or*] is coordinated with the lowest VP that contains its correspondent NP *sheets*, as in (131a'). (131b) is a single question asking the number of people to whom only sheets had been issued. The second conjunct NP[*but*] is coordinated with the lowest VP that contains its correspondent NP *sheets*, as in (131b'). In these cases of stripping in which XP-coordination reading obtains, we will take their syntactic structure as (132).

(132) lexical entry for the stripping construction with XP-coordination reading

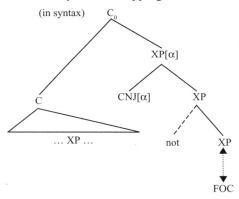

(in syntax)
(i) C_0 is a nonce coordinate structure dominating C and XP[α].
(ii) The left conjunct C is the smallest S or VP that contains XP.
(iii) The right conjunct consists of a single constituent XP.
(iv) XP of the left conjunct is a major constituent.
(in IS)
(v) XP of the right conjunct is focused à la HCS.

By contrast, in (133a, b), an NP-coordination interpretation is hard to come by.

(133) a. Jill must have told them, or else her secretary. (Huddleston and Pullum 2002: 1346)
 a'. [$_S$ [$_S$ [Jill] must have told them], [$_{NP[or]}$ or else [her secretary]]].
  → *Jill must have told them, or else her secretary must have told them.*
  ??*Jill or <u>else</u> her secretary must have told them.* (NP-coordination reading)
 b. [Jill] has been charged with perjury, and [her secretary] too. (Huddleston and Pullum 2002: 1346)

→ *Jill has been charged with perjury, and her secretary has been charged with perjury too.*
??*Jill and her secretary <u>too</u> have been charged with perjury.* (NP-coordination reading)

(133a, b) are interpreted as each S-conjunct making an affirmative assertion. (134a) is similar to (133b) in this respect. If we try putting the second conjunct in (134a) *anise too* immediately after its corresponding NP *garlic*, the resultant interpretation is not quite acceptable, unless we treat it as a parenthetical and separate it by comma intonation, as in (134b). *Do so* in (134c) refers to the act of *always putting garlic in meatloaf and putting anise in it too*. This shows that the relevant coordination is VP-coordination.

(134) a. John put garlic in the meatloaf, and anise too. (McCawley 1998: 31)
→ *John put garlic in the meatloaf, and put anise in the meatloaf too.*
??*John put garlic and anise <u>too</u> in the meatloaf.*
b. John put garlic, and anise too, in the meatloaf.
c. John always puts garlic in meatloaf, and anise too. So does Mary.
John [$_{VP}$ [$_{VP}$ puts garlic in meatloaf], [$_{VP[and]}$ and anise too]].

(135a) is ambiguous between an NP-coordination reading and S-level stripping.

(135) a. Did [Jill] tell you that, or [her secretary]? (ambiguous; Huddleston and Pullum 2002: 1346)
b. Did [$_S$ [$_S$ [$_{NP}$ Jill] tell you that], [$_{S[or]}$ or [$_S$ [$_{NP}$ her secretary]]]]? (S-level stripping reading; syntax by (119))
→ inferred syntax: *Did [Jill] tell you that, or [her secretary] tell you that?* (S[BSE]-coordination)
c. Did [$_S$ [$_S$ [$_{NP}$ Jill] tell you that], [$_{NP[or]}$ or [$_{NP}$ her secretary]]]? (syntax by (132))
→ inferred syntax: *Did [Jill] or [her secretary] tell you that?* (NP-coordination reading)

The S-level stripping reading of (135a) *Did Jill tell you that or her secretary tell you that?*, as in (135b), is in effect equivalent to an alternative question ('Which of them told you that?'). By contrast, its NP-coordination reading, as in (135c), *Did Jill or her secretary tell you that?* is in effect equivalent to a yes/no (polar) question ('Did either one of them tell you that?').

Huddleston and Pullum (2002) pointed out a third type of stripping, what they called "addition of a new element," which is illustrated below in (136a, b, c, d).

(136) a. I spoke to her, but only briefly. (Huddleston and Pullum 2002: 1346)
→ inferred syntax: *but spoke to her only briefly*
   a'. I spoke to her <u>only briefly</u>.
   b. The match was won by Kim, and very convincingly too. (Huddleston and Pullum 2002: 1347)
→ inferred syntax: *and won by Kim very convincingly too*
   b'. The match was won by Kim <u>very convincingly</u>.
   c. John is reading in his study, but nothing very serious.
→ inferred syntax: *but reading nothing very serious in his study*
   c'. John is reading <u>nothing very serious</u> in his study.
   d. I'll drive you there, but only if you pay for the petrol. (ibid.)
→ inferred syntax: *but I'll drive you there only if you pay for the petrol*
   d'. I'll drive you there, <u>only if you pay for the petrol</u>.

Huddleston and Pullum (2002: 1346) pointed out that the difference between (136a) and (136a') is that in (136a), the overall message (136a') is divided into two separate pieces of information in order to give increased prominence to *only briefly*. In other words, the speaker's purpose of choosing (136a) over (136a') is to focus *only briefly*. Note that the second conjunct adds a focused piece of information as an afterthought to the event depicted by the first conjunct, which lacks a phrase XP that is contrastively focused with XP in the second conjunct. Note also that *reading* in (136c) is an intransitive verb (Chapter 4 (37a)), the access to which activates the corresponding transitive verb (Chapter 4 (37b)), which is a natural extension (Chapter 4 (36e)) of the former and is used for constructing the inferred syntax.

Chapter 7

An Automodular View of Right Node Raising

> In this chapter, we will examine various properties of Right Node Raising (RNR) and analyze them from our multi-modular perspective. We will extend to RNR the constructional view that we employed in Chapter 6. It will emerge that the procedure involved in RNR comprehension is quite similar to the comprehension procedures for the other ellipsis types discussed in previous chapters.

7.1 Preliminary Description of Right Node Raising

According to McCawley's (1998: 282) transformational description, Right Node Raising (RNR) applies to conjoined Ss ending in identical constituents, replacing the separate copies of that constituent in each conjunct with a single copy of it at the end of the whole constituent structure. In (1a), RNR is applied to a three-term S-coordinate structure (i.e., [$_S$ S, S, *and* S]), in which the "raised constituent" at the end of the coordinate structure is an NP. As shown in (1a, a'), a constituent can be raised out of a deeply embedded clause in any of the conjuncts. Various syntactic categories can be raised by RNR: an NP is raised in (1a) and a PP in (1a', b). More data are given in (3). In (1c), a sequence of two phrases (NP PP), which does not make up a single constituent, is raised by RNR, resulting in unacceptability to some speakers. However, many speakers do accept this type of RNR, as will be discussed in relation to (30) and (31). (1d, e) show that RNR is restricted to coordinate structures. Notable exceptions are (1f, f', g, h) and (3d, e).

(1) a. Ted is interested in, Alice has done some research on, and you are probably aware that Jenny is a recognized authority on, [_NP_ the circulatory system of flatworms]. (McCawley 1998: 282)
 a'. Alice thinks that Bill put the money, and Fred is convinced that Geraldine hid the jewels, [_PP_ inside the mattress]. (McCawley 1998: 282)
 b. Smith sells luxury cars, and Jones rents pickup trucks, [_PP_ to insurance executives]. (McCawley 1998: 61)
 c. *Smith sells, and Jones rents, [_NP_ luxury cars] [_PP_ to insurance executives]. (ibid.)
 d. *That Alice composes makes it likely that Fred enjoys listening to, organ fugues. (McCawley 1998: 282)
 cf. Alice composes, and that makes it likely that Fred enjoys listening to, organ fugues.
 e. *Although Fred puts up, his brother defaces, billboards advertising beer. (McCawley 1998: 282)
 f. Of the people questioned, those who liked outnumbered by two to one those who disliked [_NP_ the way in which the devaluation of the pound had been handled].
 (McCawley 1998: 308, note 10; from Hudson 1976: 550)
 f'. Those who voted against far outnumbered those who voted for [_NP_ my father's motion]. (Huddleston and Pullum 2002: 1344)
 g. Those graduate students who are studying are {as smart as | smarter than} those 20th century mathematicians who did fundamental research on—[_NP_ the theory of analytic functions of several complex variables].
 h. I think of those who study today as smarter than those who did research on ten years ago—[_NP_ the theory of analytic functions of several complex variables].

There is an obligatory intonation break before the raised constituent (Jerry Sadock (p.c.)). In addition, the acceptability diminishes as the raised constituent becomes shorter/lighter (Jerry Sadock (p.c.)), as is shown in (2a). These properties are shared by Heavy Constituent Shift (HCS) (Sadock 2012: 212, Ueno 2014: 170). In (2a), the symbol > in "A > B" indicates that expression A is more acceptable than expression B. (2b) and the last example in (2a) show that the RNR of a personal pronoun is unacceptable. However, the RNR of an interrogative pronoun is acceptable, as in (3f). A personal pronoun is very light not only phonologically but also informationally, since it carries old information. By contrast, an interrogative pronoun is phonologically heavy because it is stressed and informationally heavy, and also, because it serves as the focus in IS. Furthermore, recall that a *wh*-fragment is dominated by a CP[WH[Q]] node in syntax (4.2). Therefore, (3f) is of the same type as (3d').

(2) a. John bought and Mary sold, <u>diamonds mined in Arkansas</u>. >
John bought and Mary sold, <u>various things</u>. >
John bought and Mary sold, <u>things</u>. >
John bought and Mary sold, <u>them</u>.
  b. *He tried to persuade, but he couldn't convince, them.
(McCawley 1998: 282; from Bresnan 1974: 615)

A phrase (XP) of any category and a clause of any type (S, CP[{*that* | *for*}], CP[WH[Q]]) can be raised by RNR, except for S[*to*], which cannot be raised by RNR. (See Ueno (2014: 180) for details.)

(3) a. Smith sells luxury cars, and Jones rents pickup trucks, to insurance executives. (PP; = (1b))
  b. Ted already is, and Alice expects soon to be, working for IBM. (VP[PRP]; McCawley 1998: 282)
  b'. I know that Tom, and I suspect that Dick, admires Reagan. (VP[FIN]; McCawley 1998: 285)
  b". He wants her to but is afraid to ask her to—go to the prom. (VP[BSE]; Postal 1998: 106)
  b"'. Will Jordan, will the U.A.E., will Egypt, will Saudi Arabia, provide other peace keepers to look at those areas? (VP[BSE]; MSNBC *Morning Joe*, February 19, 2015)
  c. Bob always has been, and Carol recently has become, afraid of flying. (AP; McCawley 1998: 282)
  d. It would seem likely to me, though it seemed unlikely to everyone else, that he would be impeached. (CP[*that*]; McCawley 1998: 282; from Bresnan 1974)
  d'. I know and I'm sure you want to hear, when and where Amanda met Steve. (CP[WH[Q]])
  d". Tom bought a can-opener and Alice bought a dictionary that were once owned by Leonard Bloomfield. (restrictive relative clause CP[*that*] with split antecedents; McCawley 1982: 100)
  d"'. A man came in the front door and a woman came in the side door who had met in Vienna. (restrictive relative clause CP[WH[R]] with split antecedents; McCawley 1993a: 240, Ueno 2014: 242)

e. I wouldn't even wonder whether, let alone suggest that, John was contributing too little. (S[FIN]; McCawley 1998: 62; from Bresnan 1974)
e'. I know when but I don't know where—Amanda met Steve. (S[FIN] immediately dominated by CP[WH[Q]]; Postal 1998: 106)
e". They know when but they don't know where—he abused the dog. (S[FIN]; Postal 1998: 97)
f. *The Chicago Tribune* reported that a senator committed adultery. I happen to know and I'm sure you want to find out, which (senator). (CP[WH[Q]])

Although an NP[DET] can be raised by RNR as in (1a), an NP cannot be raised with its determiner and adjective left behind. This is shown in (4a, b). When an XP is adjoined by a modifier ([$_{XP}$ modifier XP]), RNR cannot strand its modifier in any conjunct, as shown in (4c). In other words, RNR must raise the maximal XP.

(4) a. ??John wants just any, but I want the very best, portrait of Elvis. (McCawley 1998: 282)
b. *Ted has always wanted a, so I've given him my, coffee grinder. (ibid.)
c. *Tony is slightly and Fred is greatly—upset. (Postal 1998: 107)

A raised constituent does not have to be a major constituent, a constituent that is directly dominated by S, VP, or AP (cf. Chapter 6 (4)). The raised constituent is the NP object of a PP[*to*] in (5a), the complement PP of a noun in (5b), and the NP object of a PP[*of*] that is the complement of a noun in (5c). These raised constituents are not major constituents.

(5) a. I first offered apples to and then sold peaches to—the immigrant from Paraguay. (Postal 1998: 123)
b. Glen was looking for photos, but only found sketches—of Ted and Alice. (Postal 1998: 125)
c. Glen was looking for photos of, but only found sketches of—Ted and Alice. (ibid.)

McCawley's description given at the beginning of this section is too narrow in two respects. First, although he described the raised constituent of RNR as being the final constituent in each conjunct, some non-final identical constituents can be raised by RNR, as in (6a, b). These examples are often explained by the application of HCS to each conjunct before the application of RNR. However, the RNR in (6c) cannot be explained in the same way, because HCS cannot be applied to an NP complement of a PP. This restriction was first observed by Ross (1967/1986: 139) and is shown in (6d, e).

(6) HCS and RNR
    a. Tom sells to Chicagoans, and John buys from Londoners, luxury cars made in Germany.
    b. Eloise peeled and Frank ate raw—the large Spanish onion. (Postal 1998: 97)
    c. Mike may have talked to __ about love and certainly talked to __ about marriage—the tall woman in the black dress. (Postal 1998: 195, note 18)
    d. *I talked to __ about love—the tall woman in the black dress. (HCS applied to an NP object of a PP; Postal 1998: 195, note 18)
    e. *Mary talked with __ yesterday someone she hadn't seen in years. (Culicover and Rochemont 1990: 35)
    cf. Mary talked with someone yesterday *(who) she hadn't seen in years.

The contrast between (6c) and (6d, e) shows that although RNR can target (non-final) PP objects, HCS cannot.

The other respect in which McCawley's description of RNR is too narrow is that a coordinate structure that allows RNR does not have to be S-coordination. The following examples are instances of RNR out of VP-coordination (VP-level RNR), AP-coordination (AP-level RNR), and NP-coordination (NP-level RNR).

(7) a. She [knew of but never mentioned] my other work.
      (VP-level RNR; Huddleston and Pullum 2002: 1343)
    a'. He had [either telephoned or written a letter to] his son's boss.
      (VP-level RNR; Huddleston and Pullum 2002: 1344)
    b. I'm [interested in but rather appreciative about] their new proposal.
      (AP-level RNR; Huddleston and Pullum 2002: 1344)
    b'. She [was then, is now, and always will be], devoted to the cause of peace.
      (VP-level RNR; Huddleston and Pullum 2002: 1344)
    c. [Anyone who likes, or anyone who thinks their family would like], a vacation is welcome to this club.
      (NP-level RNR; Chae 1991: 56)

A constituent raised by RNR is outside the entire coordinate structure. This is confirmed by three pieces of evidence. First, RNR interacts with the gapping construction, as we discussed in relation to Chapter 6 (76), repeated here as (8). (8a) is a gapping construction unacceptable to many speakers, because three NPs are retained in the second conjunct (Kuno and Takami 2007: 156). However, if we raise the last NP to the end of the coordinate structure by RNR as in (8b), the sentence becomes acceptable to these speakers. Jackendoff's example in (8c) shows the same point.

(8) a. *[Fred] sent [the President] [a nasty letter], and [Bernice] [the governor] [a bomb]. (gapping) (McCawley 1998: 280)
   b. [Fred] sent [the President], and [Bernice] [the Vice President], a nasty letter about the CIA. (gapping + RNR of the last NP)
   c. [Harry] told [Sue], and [Tom] [Sally], [$_{CP[that]}$ that Albania is a lovely place for a vacation]. (Jackendoff 1971: 25; gapping + RNR of CP[*that*])
      cf. ??Harry told Sue that he wanted to visit China, and Tom Sally that he wanted to visit Japan.
   d. the syntax of (8b)

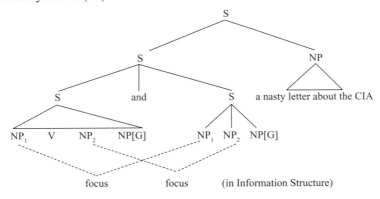

The acceptability of (8b, c) shows that their second conjunct consists of two phrases that are each contrastively focused with their corresponding phrase in the first conjunct, thus meeting the gapping construction (Chapter 6 (33)). The gaps (NP[G] in (8b) and CP[*that*, G] in (8c)) in both conjuncts are phonologically null and are not contrastively focused with each other.

The second piece of evidence that the constituent raised by RNR is outside the coordinate structure is that the focus bearing elements such as *too* and *also* can be placed immediately before the raised constituent. As McCawley (1998: 70) observed, "if *too* with the verb as focus can appear between the NP and the P', then that position must be the end of [V NP] constituent and the P' must be outside that constituent." In (9a), *sent* is interpreted as focus and is implicitly contrasted with showing a copy of his book to me, for example. In (9b), *recited* is interpreted as focus and is implicitly contrasted with writing a poem for me, for example.

(9) a. *He <u>sent</u> a copy of his book too to me. (McCawley 1998: 70)
    b. He <u>recited</u> the poem too for me. (ibid.)
    c. Mary sent me and <u>showed</u> me too, a copy of her latest novel.
    d. Mary wrote a poem and <u>read</u> it too, to that group of her friends.

In the acceptable (9c, d), the appearance of *too* shows that the constituent (i.e., the second conjunct) ends there.

The third piece of evidence is that the *that*-trace effect is almost suspended by RNR, as shown in (10a). Note that (10a) is syntactically ambiguous between the RNR of the whole S[FIN], as in (10b), and the RNR of the VP[FIN] *could well be cancelled*, as in (10c). (Recall that RNR of S[FIN] and that of VP[FIN] are both permitted, as shown in (3e, e'), (3b').) In (10b), the adjacency between *that* and the subject gap (NP[G]) is avoided by the presence of a phonologically null S[FIN, G] (a sentential gap) at the end of each conjunct. By contrast, the adjacency between the complementizer and the NP[G] persists in (10c). The acceptability of (10a) shows that (10b) must be the right syntactic structure, in which the raised S[FIN] is outside the coordinate structure.

(10) a. ?That's the meeting which I've been thinking that, and Jim's been saying that, could well be cancelled. (Merchant 2001: 184 (66a); from de Chene 1995: 3)
    b. That's the meeting which I've been thinking that S[FIN, G], and Jim's been saying that S[FIN, G], [$_{S[FIN]}$ NP[G] could well be cancelled].
    c. *That's the meeting which I've been thinking that NP[G] VP[FIN, G], and Jim's been saying that NP[G] VP[FIN, G], [$_{VP[FIN]}$ could well be cancelled].

d. Who does Mary buy and Bill sell—picture of? (Postal 1998: 145)
   e. Which official did they say Bob suspected and Frank proved—that Sally bribed? (Postal 1998: 146)

In (10b), the *wh*-phrase is extracted out of a raised constituent, which is generally permitted, as in (10d, e).

According to McCawley's (1998: 284) analysis of RNR, RNR was formulated as a "fusion" transformation, a transformation that "fuses the identical final constituents" with all the constituency relations being retained and only the linear order being altered. His "fusion" RNR transformation produces a discontinuous surface structure in which the raised constituent "has more than one mother." However, Postal (1998) claimed that the raised constituent of RNR is "extracted" out of the coordinate structure. Postal provided twenty-seven arguments for his claim that RNR is an extraction. Here are eight of his arguments that show extraction-like properties of RNR. First, RNR obeys the Coordinate Structure Constraint (CSC) (both the conjunct and the element subcases). (Regarding the CSC, see Ueno 2014: 269, 303 for its AMG treatment.)

(11) a. the conjunct subcase
       *Tom is writing an article on Aristotle and __ and Elaine has just published a monograph on Mesmer and __—Freud. (McCawley 1982: 101, note 11)
   b. the element subcase
       *Tom may have bought sketches of Gail and photos of __, and Bob saw __—Louise. (Postal 1998: 122)

Second, it has been observed that the extraction of an indirect object (i.e., the first NP of the ditransitive construction [$_{VP}$ V NP NP] (cf. Chapter 1 (63))) is quite unacceptable, if not impossible, for some speakers (Huddleston and Pullum 2002: 248–249, 2005: 72). The same is true for the RNR of an indirect object.

(12) extraction and RNR of an indirect object
   a. *Which hostess did Ernest sell __ drugs? (Postal 1998: 122)
       cf. Which hostess did Ernest sell drugs to __?
   b. *I first offered __ apples and then sold __ peaches—the immigrant from Paraguay. (Postal 1998: 123)
       cf. I first offered apples __ and then sold peaches __—to the immigrant from Paraguay. (ibid.)

cf. I first offered apples to __ and then sold peaches to __—the immigrant from Paraguay. (ibid.)

Third, it has been observed that the extraction of a genitive NP is impossible, as in (13a–c), as is the RNR of a genitive NP, as shown in (13d).

(13) a. She saw several children of Ted('s). (Postal 1998: 124)
  b. *It was Ted's that she saw several children of.
    cf. It was Ted that she saw several children of.
  c. *Kim's, I read a book of. (Gazdar et al. 1985: 148)
  d. *Glen was looking for nieces of, but only found cousins of—Ted and Alice's. (Postal 1998: 125)

Fourth, certain verbs take as their complement an "inherent" (or "fake") reflexive, a reflexive pronoun that does not carry any semantic role. It is impossible to extract an inherent reflexive such as the one in *perjure oneself*. This is also true for RNR.

(14) a. Lois perjured herself. cf. Lois criticized herself.
  b. *Herself, Lois perjured. cf. Herself, Lois criticized. (Postal 1998: 126)
  c. *Lois may have perjured and should have perjured—herself. (Postal 1998: 126)
    cf. Lois may have criticized and should have criticized—herself.

Fifth, it has been observed (Postal 1998: 127) that there are three types of PP in terms of how it behaves under extraction: preposition stranding is (i) required, such as *scoff at* NP as in (15a, a'), (ii) blocked, such as *in the way* as in (15b, b'), or (iii) optional, such as *under* NP as in (15c, c').

(15) Postal 1998: 127–128
  a. Who(m) did they scoff at?
  a'. *At whom did they scoff?
  b. *What way did Jerome tickle Marsha in?
  b'. In what way did Jerome tickle Marsha?
  c. What bridge did he discover the troll under?
  c'. Under what bridge did he discover the troll?

The same distinction holds for RNR.

(16) Postal 1998: 128
   a. *Jane could have scoffed and should have scoffed—at that idea.
   a'. Jane could have scoffed at and should have scoffed at—that idea.
   b. Jerome may have tickled Marsha and certainly should have tickled her—in the way that I told you.
   b'. *Jerome may have tickled Marsha in and certainly should have tickled her in—the way that I told you.
   c. They might have discovered the troll and should have discovered it—under the bridge near the falls.
   c'. They might have discovered the troll under and should have discovered it under—the bridge near the falls.

Sixth, an NP or PP that is contained in an NP quantified by *all* or *none* cannot be extracted. The same is true for RNR.

(17) Postal 1998: 132
   a. *Which victims did they interrogate none of?
   b. *Of which victims did they interrogate none?
   c. *the perpetrators who they interrogated all (of)
   d. *the perpetrators of whom they interrogated all

(18) Postal 1998: 132
   a. *He should have interrogated all and did interrogate all—(of) the victims of the terrorist attack.
   b. *I told him not to interrogate any of and he didn't interrogate any of—the perpetrators of the bloody bomb attack.

Seventh, both extraction and RNR allow interwoven coordination, a coordinate structure with *respectively*, as in (19b) for extraction and (19c, d) for RNR.

(19) Postal 1998: 134
   a. [Which woman] did Fred date __ and Bob marry __?
   b. [Which nurse] and [which hostess] did Fred date __ and Bob marry __, respectively?
   c. John loves __ and Mary hates __ —[oysters] and [clams], respectively.

d. Marsha argued for __ on Tuesday and Louise argued against __ on Thursday—[communism] and [fascism], respectively.

Finally, Postal pointed out that the gaps left by RNR license parasitic gaps, just like regular gaps created by "*wh*-movement."

(20) Postal 1998: 133
   a. Jerome fired after finding drunk and Bill hired after finding sober—the tall young woman standing over there.
   b. The boss warned that he would fire and the police informed that they would arrest—all those who were involved in the embezzling.
   c. Greg decided to buy after reading about and Gail agreed to lease before test driving—that new model electric car which actually doesn't work.

On a related note, McCawley (1998: 540) observed that the gaps left by the HCS license parasitic gaps. Taking this into account, we might want to say that RNR examples with parasitic gaps such as (20) and (21b) involve the HCS in each conjunct. (However, the issue pointed out in relation to (6) remains.)

(21) a. John threw in the wastebasket without even showing to his assistant any reports that were full of statistics. (HCS; McCawley 1998: 540)
   b. John filed without reading and his secretary threw without showing to him, many of the reports that were full of statistics. (RNR)

We accept Postal's conclusion that RNR is extraction and conclude that it is not a double-mother discontinuous structure created by a "fusion" RNR transformation, as claimed by McCawley (1982, 1998).

7.2 RNR as a Construction

We will register RNR in the lexicon as a construction, according to our view of constructions (1.5, Ueno 2014: 43–44). (22) is the lexical entry for the RNR construction. The reasons why we need to formulate it as a construction will be discussed at the end of this section.

(22) lexical entry for RNR construction

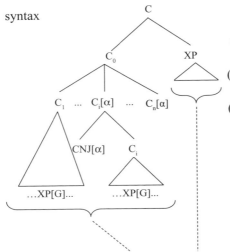

(i) The raised constituent XP can be a clause.
(ii) XP is adjoined to the coordinate structure C_0.
(iii) XP[G] is at or near the end of each conjunct.
(iv) CNJ[α] is a coordinating conjunction with its form feature value α, where α ∈ {*and, or, but*}.

Information Structure [$_U$ *rest* ≺ new/focused]

"A ≺ B" in the IS of (22) indicates that A precedes B. C_0 is required to precede the raised constituent XP, which is due to the ordering requirement specified in IS, but does not have to immediately precede it, because a parenthetical expression can appear between the two.

(23) parenthetical between C_0 and XP
Smith sells luxury cars, and Jones rents pickup trucks, {probably | I suppose | if I'm not mistaken}, only to insurance executives. (cf. (1b))

In each conjunct in (22), the presence of a phonologically null XP[G] in syntax is required to meet the subcategorization requirement if the raised constituent is a complement. For example, in (23), the lexical entries for the verb in the first conjunct *sell* and that in the second conjunct *rent* are V in [$_{VP}$ __, NP, PP[*to*]] in their syntactic field. Therefore, each conjunct S must have a phonologically null PP[*to*, G] at the end.

The category identity between the gapped XP[G] and the raised XP is required in (22), and is confirmed by a class of verbs that take an NP complement but not a CP[*that*] complement (namely, V in [$_{VP}$ __, {NP | *CP[*that*]}]). This class of verbs includes *capture*, *express*, and *reflect*. (See Ueno 2014: 117–8.)

(24) a. This theory {captures | expresses | reflects} *(the fact) [that verbs exist]. (Postal 1998: 109)
   b. A good theory should capture and would express—*(the fact) [that verbs exist]. (RNR; Postal 1998: 109)

In this respect, RNR is different from topicalization and passivization.

(25) a. [That verbs exist], this theory fails to {capture | express | reflect}. (Postal 1998: 109)
   b. [That verbs exist] is {captured | expressed | reflected} by this theory. (ibid.)

The category identity between XP[G] and XP is also confirmed by the object-raising construction, whose object position is limited to an NP. (See Ueno 2014: 165 (8d).)

(26) a. *Mary considers [that three and three are seven] to be definitely false. ([$_{VP}$ V$_{OR}$ {NP | *CP[*that*]} VP[*to*]] for object raising verbs V$_{OR}$; Postal 1998: 107)
   b. *John considers [that two and two are five] and Mary considers [that three and three are seven]—to be definitely false. (RNR of VP[*to*]; ibid.)
   c. *Ted considers to be unimportant and Frank considers to be crucial—[that three and three are seven]. (RNR of CP[*that*]; Postal 1998: 114)
      cf. Ted considers it to be unimportant and Frank considers it to be crucial—[that three and three are seven]. (RNR of an extraposed CP[*that*]; Postal 1998: 114)

The same point is also confirmed by adjectives that take as their complement a PP or CP[*that*]. (27a) shows that CP[*that*] cannot be a complement of the preposition *of*. The same restriction holds in RNR between the gap in the conjuncts and the raised CP[*that*] as in (27b).

(27) a. I am no longer certain (*of) [that Nancy is an extraterrestrial]. (Postal 1998: 114)
   b. Frank may be certain (*of) and should be certain (*of)—[that Nancy is an extraterrestrial]. (RNR; ibid.)
      cf. [That Nancy is an extraterrestrial], Frank is certain *(of). (topicalization)

354   7 AN AUTOMODULAR VIEW OF RIGHT NODE RAISING

The raised constituent XP in (22) can still contain another RNR construction, as in (28a). Furthermore, the final part of the raised constituent can be targeted by another RNR construction, as in (28b). Both possibilities are allowed by (22). In (28a), the raised constituent is a CP[*that*], within which another RNR construction appears. In (28b), the overall structure is a layered two-term S-coordination ($[_S [_{S4} S_1$ and $S_2]$ and $S_3]$), in which RNR is applied to S_1 and S_2 and to S_4 and S_3.

(28) a. Mary suspects and his husband believes, [that Smith sells luxury cars and his brother rents pickup trucks, [to insurance executives]].
   b. [$_{S1}$ John gave silver] and [$_{S2}$ Harry gave gold]—to the mother, and [$_{S3}$ I gave platinum to the father]—of the famous quintuplets. (Postal 1998: 155)
   c. the syntax of (28b)

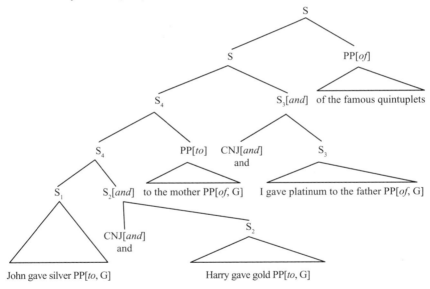

However, the formulation in (22) of RNR as a construction, which is registered in the lexicon, does not allow its recursive application, because it cannot apply to the same domain twice, if it has applied to it once and its lexical properties are projected into syntax and IS. If it were possible, the syntax after the second application of RNR would produce a syntactic structure (29b) or (29c). Note the reverse order of XP and YP in (29c). If (29b) is described in derivational terms, the non-final YP (i.e., NP) first undergoes RNR, and then the final XP (i.e., PP[*to*]) undergoes RNR. On the other hand, the order of two applications of RNR is reversed in (29c).

(29) a. first application of RNR
[$_S$ [$_S$ [$_S$ .... XP[G]] and [$_S$ .... XP[G]]] < XP]
Smith sells luxury cars, and Jones rents pickup trucks, [to insurance executives]. (= (1b)) or
Smith sells to New Yorkers, and Jones rents to Chicagoans, [luxury Italian cars].
b. second application of RNR
*[$_S$ [$_S$ [$_S$ [$_S$ .... YP[G] XP[G]] and [$_S$ .... YP[G] XP[G]]] < YP] < XP]
(*)Smith sells, and Jones rents, [luxury cars] [to insurance executives]. (= (1c))
c. the other second application of RNR
*[$_S$ [$_S$ [$_S$ [$_S$ .... YP[G] XP[G]] and [$_S$ .... YP[G] XP[G]]] < XP] < YP]
*Smith sells, and Jones rents, [to insurance executives] [luxury cars].
d. ?Smith sells, and Jones rents, [to executives] [luxury cars made in European countries].

As was pointed out in (1c), (29b) is acceptable to many speakers. As for (29c) with the reverse order PP[*to*] NP, this is less acceptable than (29b), probably because this order violates the default order in VP: NP precedes PP (Chapter 1 (59b), Ueno 2014: 39). We expect that (29c) will be improved by the HCS if the NP is heavy enough. This expectation is borne out, as shown in (29d). However, the syntactic structures (29b, c) violate (22). On the one hand, two separate phrases are adjoined to the coordinate structure C_0 and two separate phrases are focused, on the other.

As noted above concerning (29b), there are speakers who allow a sequence of two constituents to be raised by RNR, though the sequence does not make up a single constituent.

(30) (Abbott 1976: 639–640, cf. (1c))
a. Smith loaned, and his widow later donated, [a valuable collection of manuscripts] [to the library].
b. I borrowed, and my sisters stole, [large sums of money] [from the Chase Manhattan Bank].

c. Joan offered, and Mary actually gave, [a gold Cadillac] [to Billy Schwartz].
d. ?John tried to persuade, but failed to convince, [his skeptical examiners] [that he knew the right answers].
e. *John offered, and Harry gave, Sally a Cadillac.

The sequence of raised constituents in (30a-c) is NP+PP. That of (30d) is NP+CP[*that*]. In the unacceptable (30e), the sequence of raised constituents is NP+NP. There seem to be two factors involved in the unacceptability of (30e). The first factor concerns processing load. In general, processing a sequence of the same category without any distinguishing mark requires more effort than processing a sequence of different categories. Second, raising an indirect object NP in RNR is impossible to many speakers, as was shown in (12).

Those speakers who accept (30a-d) have in their mental lexicon the lexical entry (31) for the extended RNR construction, in which a sequence of two constituents is adjoined to the coordinate structure.

(31) lexical entry for extended RNR construction

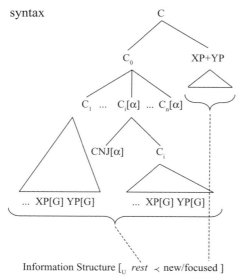

(i) the sequence XP+YP is the last two phrases of each conjunct.
(ii) CNJ[α] is a coordinating conjunction

In the above, XP+YP is a sequence (juxtaposition) of two constituents XP and YP in this order, and is treated as a nonce constituent. Each conjunct contains a sequence of two gaps XP[G] YP[G] in the same order.

When an entire RNR construction is not embedded and constitutes a single utterance, the topmost S corresponds to a speech act (SA) with its illocutionary force (IF) #assert# in E/R, if it is a declarative, as in Chapter 2 (36a), whereas it corresponds to an SA with its IF #inquire# in E/R, if it is a yes/no interrogative, as in Chapter 2 (36b). The falling and rising intonations arise at the end, namely, on the raised constituent.

(32) a. [$_{S[FIN]}$ Smith sells luxury cars PP[*to*, G]], and [$_{S[FIN]}$ Jones rents pickup trucks PP[*to*, G]], [$_{PP[to]}$ to insurance executives]. ↘ (= (1b))
    a'. [$_{S[FIN]}$ Smith sells NP[G] PP[*to*, G]], and [$_{S[FIN]}$ Jones rents NP[G] PP[*to*, G]], [$_{NP}$ luxury cars] [$_{PP[to]}$ to insurance executives]. ↘ (= (1c))
    b. Does [$_{S[BSE]}$ Smith sell luxury cars PP[*to*, G]], and [$_{S[BSE]}$ Jones rent pickup trucks PP[*to*, G]], [$_{PP[to]}$ to insurance executives]? ↗
    b'. Does [$_{S[BSE]}$ Smith sell NP[G] PP[*to*, G]], and [$_{S[BSE]}$ Jones rent NP[G] PP[*to*, G]], [$_{NP}$ luxury cars] [$_{PP[to]}$ to insurance executives]? ↗

When the S-final complement XP in each conjunct is raised by RNR, a subcategorization violation between the raised XP and the head of the second (or last) conjunct results in greater unacceptability than one between XP and the head of the first (or an earlier) conjunct. Subject-verb agreement works in the same way, as in (33e). This is probably because, in processing an RNR construction, a subcategorization or agreement violation between the raised XP and the last conjunct is more conspicuous than one between XP and an earlier conjunct, due to the proximity of the raised constituent XP to the last conjunct.

(33) (a to c from Chae 1991)
    a. (*count on CP[*that*])
        ?I count on, but Mary does not believe, that you are trustworthy.
        ?? Mary does not believe, but I am willing to count on, that you are trustworthy.
    b. (*capture CP[*that*])
        ?My theory captures, and your theory proves, that language is innate.
        ?? My theory proves, but your theory can only capture, that language is innate.

c. (*dislike VP[*to*])
   I dislike, but most people like, to win at poker.
   ?I like, but most people dislike, to lose at poker.
d. (*will VP[PSP]; *have VP[BSE])
   ?I always have and always will, value her advice.
   *I always have and always will, valued her advice. (Huddleston and Pullum 2002: 1343, note 66)
e. I know that Tom, and I suspect that his brothers, *admires/?admire Reagan. (McCawley 1998: 285)

For example, in (33a), the raised constituent CP[*that*] violates the subcategorization requirement of *depend on* but meets that of *believe*. The shorter the distance between the verb and the raised complement, the more strongly the subcategorization violation between them is felt.

So far, we have provided two lexical entries for RNR, (22) and (31). The former is a basic RNR construction and the latter is an extended RNR construction. In (31), the basic RNR construction is extended to cases where the raised constituent consists of a sequence of two phrases. In other words, the restriction on the basic RNR (22) that the raised constituent must be a single constituent is dropped in (31). There is another way of extending RNR, namely, by dropping the restriction in (22) that RNR requires a coordinate structure. This type of RNR was illustrated in (1f, f', g, h), repeated here as (34). The lexical entry for this extended RNR is given in (35).

(34) second type of extended RNR
   a. Of the people questioned, [those who liked] outnumbered by two to one [those who disliked] the way in which the devaluation of the pound had been handled.
   b. [Those who voted against] far outnumbered [those who voted for] my father's motion.
   c. [Those graduate students who are studying] are smarter than [those 20th-century mathematicians who did fundamental research on]—the theory of analytic functions of several complex variables.
   d. I think of [those who are studying now] as smarter than [those who did research on ten years ago]—the theory of analytic functions of several complex variables.

(35) lexical entry for extended RNR construction (second type)

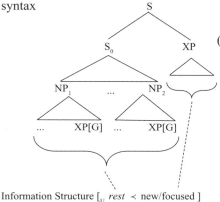

(i) XP[G] is at or near the end of each NP.

(ii) The F/A correspondent of NP_1 c-commands the F/A correspondent of NP_2.

Information Structure [$_U$ rest ≺ new/focused]

The reason why (35ii) is stated in F/A terms and not in syntactic terms (e.g., NP_1 c-commands NP_2) is that we need to cover cases such as (34d), in which [$_{NP}$ *those who are studying now*] does not c-command [$_{NP}$ *those who did research on ten years ago*] in syntax but the F/A correspondent (ARG) of the former c-commands the F/A correspondent (ARG) of the latter in F/A.

Before closing this section, we need to discuss why we chose to formulate RNR as a construction. This is partly because there are phenomena involving RNR (to be enumerated below) that are difficult to account for in derivational terms, and partly because this is probably the only way to deal with RNR in non-derivational multi-modular approaches such as AMG, in which there is no transformational rule (no movement rule and no deletion rule). This formulation of RNR as a construction (i.e., (22), (31), and (35)) is in the same spirit as the formulation of gapping (Chapter 6 (33)) and stripping (Chapter 6 (119)) as constructions.

The first reason for formulating RNR as a construction is that there are cases of RNR, such as the RNR examples in (36), in which what looks like a raised constituent, when put back in each conjunct, does not result in an acceptable sentence with the intended meaning. This set of data means that if we took a derivational approach to RNR, we could not posit a well-formed underlying structure in which full clauses without any gap are coordinated. (36a) is interpreted in such a way that the sum of the amount John borrowed and the amount Mary won was $30,000. (36b-c') are interpreted in the same way. (36d) can be interpreted as describing the situation in which the book John bought and the book Mary borrowed looked remarkably similar. The interpretation of (36e) is that the tune John hummed and the tune Mary sang were the same. (36f) is interpreted in the same way.

(36) a. John borrowed and Mary won, [a total of $30,000]. (based on Abbott 1976: 642, note 3 (i))
b. Greg captured and Lucille trained—312 frogs between them. (Postal 1998: 137)
c. Speaking of your new draft, I noticed on the first page, Jane pointed out on the second page, and Tom corrected on the third page, a total of 20 mistakes. (S-coordination)
c'. Speaking of your new draft, I noticed on the first page, pointed out on the second page, and corrected on the third page, a total of 20 mistakes. (VP-coordination)
d. John bought and Mary borrowed, [books that looked remarkably similar]. (based on Abbott 1976: 642, note 3 (i))
e. John hummed and Mary sang—the same tune. (Postal 1998: 137)
f. John hummed and Mary sang—different tunes.

In addition to (36), the following cases of split antecedents also present RNR with the same problem that there is no well-formed underlying structure from which the RNR construction in question must have been derived transformationally. *Their* in (37c) and *themselves* in (37d) both refer to *John* and *Mary*.

(37) split antecedents
a. Tom bought a can-opener and Alice bought a dictionary [that were once owned by Leonard Bloomfield]. (= (3d")) (restrictive relative clause CP[*that*] with split antecedents; McCawley 1982: 100)
b. A man came in the front door and a woman came in the side door [who had met in Vienna]. (= (3d'")) (restrictive relative clause CP[WH[R]] with split antecedents; McCawley 1993a: 240)
c. John likes very much and Mary dislikes strongly, [their uncle in Chicago].
d. John likes very much and Mary dislikes strongly, [that old picture of themselves].

Third, as we discussed in relation to (10a), repeated here as (38a), the *that*-trace effect is suspended in RNR, because the adjacency between *that* and the trace is broken by RNR. If we took derivational approaches, there would be no grammatical underlying structure for (38a), as shown in (38b).

(38) *that*-trace effect
  a. ?That's the meeting which I've been thinking that, and Jim's been saying that, could well be cancelled.
  b. *That's the meeting which I've been thinking that could well be cancelled, and Jim's been saying that could well be cancelled.

Fourth, in (39a), *respectively* signifies that the first NP-conjunct *oysters* is to be associated with the first S-conjunct *John loves* and the second NP-conjunct *clams* with the second S-conjunct *Mary hates*, exactly as in the *wh*-question with *respectively* in (39b). If we took derivational approaches and tried to set up a semantically well-formed underlying structure for (39a), the only candidate would be *John loves oysters and Mary hates clams*. However, *respectively* cannot be added to this structure: **John loves oysters and Mary hates clams, respectively*, because this violates the syntax field of the lexical entry for *respectively*, which, roughly speaking, requires two instances of n-term coordinate structure in which *respectively* must be adjoined to the second coordinate structure (cf. McCawley 1998: 296).

(39) interwoven coordination with *respectively*
  a. [John loves __] and [Mary hates __], [[oysters] and [clams], respectively]. (= (19c))
  b. [Which oysters] and [which clams] does [[John love __] and [Mary hate __], respectively]? (cf. (19b))
  c. [John] and [Mary] love [[oysters] and [clams], respectively].

Recall that we followed Postal (1998) and concluded in 7.1 that RNR is an extraction, which obeys the Coordinate Structure Constraint (CSC). Therefore, it is impossible in (39a) to extract *oysters* and *clams* from an underlying structure such as *John loves oysters and Mary hates clams* without violating the CSC.

7.3 Inferentially Interpreting the RNR Construction

In order to interpret the RNR construction properly, the hearer/interpreter needs to follow the Relevance-guided Comprehension Heuristic (Chapter 2 (8)) and a procedure similar to the Procedure for fragment comprehension (Chapter 3 (5c)), the latter of which is reformulated specifically for RNR, as in (40).

(40) Procedure for RNR comprehension
The hearer follows the Relevance-guided comprehension heuristic (Chapter 2 (8)) and executes the following steps.
  (i) The LM computes the decoded four-tuple of an utterance U of the RNR construction (i.e., its gapped conjuncts and raised constituent).
  (ii) By non-demonstrative inference, the ICM constructs the inferred syntactic structure of U by filling the gaps with a copy of the raised constituent on the basis of the decoded syntax obtained in (i) and the contextual information.
  (iii) The ICM constructs the inferred four-tuple of U on the basis of the inferred syntax obtained in (ii) and the contextual information.
  (iv) The ICM develops the inferred four-tuple of U obtained in (iii) on the basis of the contextual information.
  (v) The ICM constructs the explicatures and implicatures of U on the basis of the developed four-tuple obtained in (iv) and the contextual information.

(41) is an example of the procedure for RNR comprehension. Note that in the inferred syntax of step ii, the raised NP is put back to the NP gap in each conjunct.

(41) A: Which do you think is richer, John or Bill?
    B: John owns but Bill rents, a big Mercedes.
      (i) decoded four-tuple of *John owns NP[G], but Bill rents NP[G], a big Mercedes*
      (ii) inferred syntax: John owns [a big Mercedes] but Bill rents [a big Mercedes].
      (iii) inferred four-tuple of *John owns a big Mercedes but Bill rents a big Mercedes*
      (iv) higher-level explicature: 'B believes that John owns a big Mercedes and Bill rents a big Mercedes.'
          implicature: 'B thinks that John is richer than Bill.'

When the NP raised by RNR refers to a single entity, as in (1a), repeated here as (42a), the interpretation of such an RNR construction is so constructed that each gap is replaced with a copy of the raised NP and these copies share the same referential index. This is shown in (42).

(42) a. Ted is interested in, Alice has done some research on, and you are probably aware that Jenny is a recognized authority on, the circulatory system of flatworms.
   b. decoded syntax of (42a)
      [$_S$ [$_S$ Ted is interested in NP[G]], [$_S$ Alice has done some research on NP[G]], and [$_S$ you are probably aware that Jenny is a recognized authority on NP[G]]], [$_{NP}$ the circulatory system of flatworms].
   c. inferred syntax (step ii of (40))
      Ted is interested in [$_{NP}$ the circulatory system of flatworms], Alice has done some research on [$_{NP}$ the circulatory system of flatworms], and you are probably aware that Jenny is a recognized authority on [$_{NP}$ the circulatory system of flatworms]

In such cases of RNR as (42a), the hearer/interpreter infers by step ii of (40) a coordinated S structure in which the gap in each conjunct is filled by a copy of the raised constituent. This is illustrated in (43).

(43)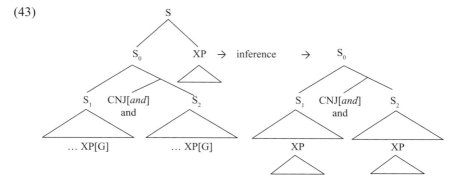

In the five-step RNR comprehension procedure (40), step ii of inferring the syntactic structure of an RNR construction precedes step iii of computing the corresponding F/A and E/R. This ordering is needed to account for the following cases. First, it is quite possible for the raised NP of RNR to have a different referent in each conjunct. This was shown in (41). More examples are provided in (44). In (44a), the set of washing machines sold by Joan this month and the set of washing machines repaired by Fred's acquaintance last month are different. In (44b), the raised NP is a definite NP but it requires a different referent in each conjunct, because each conjunct provides a different situation and the definite NP is interpreted with respect to that situation in which it appears. If we assume in (44a, b) that the ICM fills the gap position of each conjunct with a separate copy of the raised NP (as step ii of (40)) before computing their corresponding F/A and E/R, the F/A correspondent (ARG) of each copied NP can carry a different referential index in step iv of (40), as shown in (44a, b). Recall that a referential index is contained in the index (IND) feature together with the agreement (AGR) feature and is carried by an argument (ARG) in F/A, as in ARG[IND[j, AGR]] (Chapter 1 (32), Ueno 2014: 25 (6)).

(44) a. Joan sold this month, and Fred knows a man who repaired last month, 100 washing machines. (cf. McCawley 1998: 284)
→ Joan sold [100 washing machines]$_i$ this month, and Fred knows a man who repaired [100 washing machines]$_j$ last month.
b. Chicagoans voted for, and New Yorkers voted against, the incumbent mayor who was in his third term.
→ Chicagoans voted for [the incumbent mayor who was in his third term]$_i$ and New Yorkers voted against [the incumbent mayor who was in his third term]$_j$.

Second, (45a) is an example of RNR in which a quantified NP (QNP) is raised. This is interpreted ambiguously. In one interpretation, the QNP *most students in the department* has both S-conjuncts in its scope, which corresponds to the F/A in (45b). In the other interpretation, the set of students John greeted and the set of students Mary smiled at are different, just as in (44). That is, it is interpreted as if there are two instances of the QNP *most students* and each binds a different variable in each conjunct. This is shown in (45c). To arrive at the F/A structure (45c), the hearer/interpreter first needs to arrive at the inferred syntactic structure *John greeted most students in the department and Mary smiled at most students in the department* by applying step ii of (40), before computing the F/A structure.

(45) a. John greeted and Mary smiled at, most students in the department. (ambiguous)
→ John greeted most students in the department and Mary smiled at most students in the department.
b. [$_{QPx}$ MOST STUDENTS] [(PAST(JOHN GREET x)) AND (PAST(MARY SMILE AT x))]
c. [[$_{QPx}$ MOST STUDENTS] (PAST(JOHN GREET x))] AND [[$_{QPy}$ MOST STUDENTS] (PAST(MARY SMILE AT y))]

Third, if we assume that step ii of (40) is at work in interpreting a raised constituent, the ungrammaticality of (46) is attributed to the fact that *she* precedes and c-commands its antecedent *Mary* in the inferred syntactic structure.

(46) *She$_i$ said, and I happen to agree, that Mary$_i$ needs a new car. (McCawley 1998: 284)
→ *She$_i$ said that Mary$_i$ needs a new car, and I happen to agree that Mary$_i$ needs a new car.

Fourth, to the extent that (47a) is acceptable with its idiomatic interpretation, the hearer/interpreter needs to infer that *yours* represents *your leg* and that the first and second conjuncts represent *John's leg seems to be being pulled by Mary* and *I'm sure that your leg is being pulled by Mary*, respectively. Without arriving at this inferred syntactic structure, the idiomatic interpretation of (47a) cannot be recovered. (47b) illustrates the same point with the idiom *cook someone's goose*.

(47) a. John's leg seems to be and I'm sure that yours is too, being pulled by Mary.
→ John's leg seems to be being pulled by Mary and I'm sure that your leg is being pulled by Mary too.
b. John's goose was and Mary said hers might have been too, cooked not by accident but by design.
→ John's goose was cooked not by accident but by design and Mary said her goose might have been cooked not by accident but by design too.

Fifth, a pro-VP form can have a raised constituent of RNR within its antecedent. Furthermore, a pro-VP form can appear in a raised constituent and is interpreted differently in each conjunct.

(48) RNR and VP ellipsis
a. Tom admires and is sure that everyone else admires—Adolf Hitler, but of course you and I don't. (McCawley 1982: 100)
→ Tom admires Adolf Hitler and is sure that everyone else admires Adolf Hitler.
b. Every employee who can't speak Japanese is required, and every executive who can't read Korean is advised, to be able to by the end of this year.

→ Every employee who can't speak Japanese is required to be able to speak Japanese by the end of this year, and every executive who can't read Korean is advised to be able to read Korean by the end of this year.

In (48a), RNR must be undone by step (ii) of the comprehension process (40) before the antecedent *admire Adolf Hitler* of the pro-VP form *don't* is determined. In (48b), the raised constituent *to be able to by the end of this year* contains the pro-VP form *to*, which is interpreted differently in each conjunct: the antecedent in the first conjunct is *speak Japanese* and the antecedent in the second conjunct is *read Korean*. This again shows the need for step (ii), which constructs an inferred S by replacing the gap in each conjunct with the raised constituent.

Sixth, raising an NP by RNR out of a complex NP is possible as in (44a) and (49a), because the raised NP is within the complex NP in the inferred syntax after step ii of the comprehension process (40). However, "*wh*-movement" out of a raised constituent is impossible if the gap corresponding to the raised constituent is already contained in a complex NP in one of the conjuncts, as in (49b, d), because the "*wh*-movement" is from within the complex NP after step ii. By contrast, "*wh*-movement" is possible out of a raised constituent if there is no island involved in any of the conjuncts. This is shown in (49c). Note that the dominance path conditions on "*wh*-movement" (Chapter 1 (100)) need to be applied to the inferred syntactic structure. This shows again that the inferred structure constructed by step ii of (40) is syntactic, because the syntactic dominance path conditions are applied to it.

(49) a. Mary owned, and John knew a man who wanted to buy, a portrait of Elvis Presley. (McCawley 1998: 284)
→ Mary owned a portrait of Elvis Presley, and John knew a man who wanted to buy a portrait of Elvis Presley.
b. *Which pop singer did [Mary own, and John know a man who wanted to buy], a portrait of? (McCawley 1998: 284)
→ *Which pop singer did Mary own a portrait of, and John know a man who wanted to buy a portrait of?
c. I don't know which company [Ted already is, and Mary says she expects soon to be], working for. (cf. (3b))

→ I don't know which company Ted already is working for, and Mary says she expects soon to be working for.
d. *I don't know which company [Ted already is, and he knows a woman who expects soon to be], working for.
→ *I don't know which company Ted already is working for, and he knows a woman who expects soon to be working for.

Seventh, a controlled VP[*to*] can be raised by RNR, as in (50a). The coreference requirement stated in the E/R field of the lexical entries for subject-control *promise* and object-control *order* will be met when the inferred syntax of (50a) is constructed.

(50) a. John promised his son and Mary ordered her husband—to buy a new laser printer.
b. decoded syntax of (50a)
John promised his son VP[*to*, G] and Mary ordered her husband VP[*to*, G]—[$_{VP[to]}$ to buy a new laser printer.
c. inferred syntax of (50a) (by step ii of (40))
John promised his son to buy a new laser printer and Mary ordered her husband to buy a new laser printer.

In conclusion, step ii of the Procedure for RNR comprehension (40) of constructing the inferred syntactic structure of an utterance U is necessary and must precede step iii of constructing the inferred four-tuple (syntax, F/A, RS, IS) of U. Step ii is applied in the above examples in such a way that a copy of the raised constituent replaces the gap in each conjunct.

However, there is another way of applying step ii to the RNR construction. As we discussed in relation to (45), the raised constituent in (45a) is interpreted in two ways, of which the second interpretation (45c) was accounted for by the application of step ii as described above. On the other hand, to account for the first interpretation (45b) of (45a), repeated here as (51a, b), we need to assume that step ii applies vacuously to (51a) in such a way that the gap in each conjunct is kept as such and interpreted as representing the same variable in F/A.

(51) a. John greeted NP[G] and Mary smiled at NP[G], [$_{NP}$ most students in the department].

→ 'For most students in the department, John greeted them and Mary smiled at them'

b. [$_{QPx}$ MOST STUDENTS] [(PAST(JOHN GREET x)) AND (PAST(MARY SMILE AT x))]

In (51a), the QNP *most students in the department* has wide scope and takes both conjuncts in its scope. Note that the decoded syntactic structure (51a) and the F/A structure (51b) are isomorphic, which explains the high accessibility of this interpretation.

In fact, (49a), repeated here as (52a), is ambiguous in exactly the same way as (51a), namely, in the way the QNP *a portrait of Elvis Presley* is interpreted. (52d) is the interpretation in which step ii is applied vacuously and the two gaps are taken as representing the same variable.

(52) a. Mary owned, and John knew a man who wanted to buy, a portrait of Elvis Presley.
  b. decoded syntax of (52a)
   [Mary owned NP[G], and John knew a man who wanted to buy NP[G]], [$_{NP}$ a portrait of Elvis Presley].
  c. → (step ii) inferred syntax
     Mary owned a portrait of Elvis Presley, and John knew a man who wanted to buy a portrait of Elvis Presley.
   (step iii) inferred four-tuple
     F/A: [[$_{QPx}$ A x=PORTRAIT.OF.EP] PAST(MARY OWN x)]
       AND [[$_{QPy}$ A y=PORTRAIT.OF.EP] ... (RHO BUY y)]
  d. → (step ii) applied vacuously
     Mary owned NP[G], and John knew a man who wanted to buy NP[G], a portrait of Elvis Presley.
   (step iii) inferred four-tuple
     F/A: [[$_{QPx}$ A x=PORTRAIT.OF.EP] [PAST(MARY OWN x)]
       AND [PAST ... (RHO BUY x)]]

Note again that the inferred F/A in (52d) is isomorphic to the decoded syntax of (52a). Regarding the quantifier use of the indefinite article, see Chapter 1 (41) for its lexical entry.

7.3 INFERENTIALLY INTERPRETING THE RNR CONSTRUCTION   369

There is another way of applying step ii vacuously to the RNR construction. This time, the NP gaps are taken as representing different variables. (36e, f), repeated here as (53a) and (54a), are such examples.

(53) a. John hummed and Mary sang—the same tune.
   b. John hummed NP[G] and Mary sang NP[G]—[$_{NP}$ the same tune].
      → (step ii) applied vacuously
         John hummed NP[G] and Mary sang NP[G]—[$_{NP}$ the same tune].
      → (step iii) constructing the inferred four-tuple

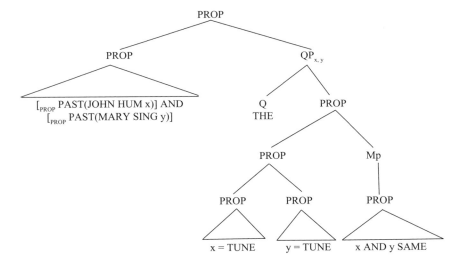

Regarding the quantifier use of the definite article, see Chapter 1 (44) for its lexical entry. The quantifier in (53b) and (54b) is a polyadic quantifier (McCawley 1993a: 240) and binds two variables x and y.

(54) a. John hummed and Mary sang—different tunes.
   b. John hummed NP[G] and Mary sang NP[G]—[$_{NP}$ different tunes].
      → (step ii) applied vacuously
         John hummed NP[G] and Mary sang NP[G]—[$_{NP}$ different tunes].
      → (step iii) constructing the inferred four-tuple

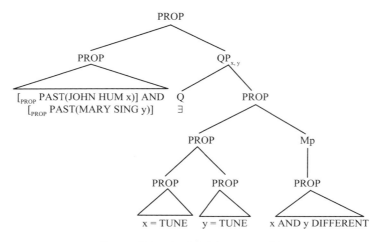

The same account applies to (36a, c). (36a) is repeated here as (55).

(55) a. John borrowed and Mary won, a total of $30,000. (= (36a))
  b. John borrowed NP[G] and Mary won NP[G], [$_{NP}$ a total of $30,000].
    → (step ii) applied vacuously
        John borrowed NP[G] and Mary won NP[G], [$_{NP}$ a total of $30,000].
    → (step iii) constructing the inferred four-tuple

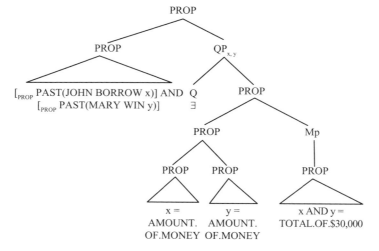

The availability of this type of interpretation is another example of the autonomy of the F/A module.

Chapter 8
Conclusion

> In the preceding chapters, we investigated six major types of ellipsis in English, namely, fragments, sluicing, VP ellipsis, gapping, stripping, and Right Node Raising, paying special attention to their properties and how they are interpreted in discourse. Here in the final chapter, I would like to review the main points of each chapter and add a few closing remarks.

8.1 Summary of Chapter 1

Chapter 1 provided an overview of the version of Automodular Grammar (AMG) that is assumed in this book and presented a brief sketch of the modules that were required in the subsequent chapters, namely, Syntax, Function Argument (F/A) Structure, Event Role (E/R) Structure, and Information Structure (IS). The content of this chapter was based on Sadock (2012) and Ueno (2014) with some minor revisions.

AMG is a non-derivational approach to the grammar of natural languages and hence does not employ "transformation," which includes movement, insertion, and deletion. Each of the autonomous modules is generative in its own way and formulated in context-free phrase structure grammar (CFPSG). Each module only does its own work with its own primitives and rules. All the modules are connected by the interface, including intermodular default correspondences. Because of this multi-modular architecture, lexical entries and lexical rules are stated module by module, which forms the basis of the interface.

It has been agreed across all theoretical persuasions that lexical entries consist of, at least, syntactic, semantic, and phonological information. This is a standard and traditional view. Each type of information of a lexical item can be diachronically affected independently of the other types of information (e.g., a new meaning is added to a lexical item) and can be learned separately from the other types of information in language acquisition (e.g., only the pronunciation of a new lexical item is learned without learning its syntactic category or meaning). AMG is a natural extension of this traditional view in that there is a set of generative rules behind each type of lexical information.

As readers may have noticed by now, lexical entries play a very important role in AMG. This is an advantage from a cognitive scientific point of view. The late Giyoo Hatano (1987: 194, 196, 197) emphasized repeatedly that when cognitive scientists propose a theory to explain a certain phenomenon, they must also make clear how the relevant knowledge is accessed in real time. Otherwise, it is impossible to discuss its psychological reality. In other words, theoretical explanation and how to access the relevant knowledge that is used in that explanation must go hand in hand. There is no doubt that the hearer accesses each lexical entry in the mental lexicon in the brain when he receives a phonological input that meets the information contained in its (morpho)phonological field. We claimed that even constructions are registered in the mental lexicon. The syntactic, semantic, and pragmatic properties of every construction are encoded as part of its lexical entry. Therefore, when he receives an appropriate phonological input, the hearer accesses the lexical entry for a particular construction, in which its various properties are stated. For example, a "moved" *wh*-phrase (a clause-initial XP[WH[Q]]) is registered in the mental lexicon together with its dominance path conditions, as in Chapter 1 (100), repeated here as (1).

(1) lexical entry for clause-initial interrogative *wh*-phrase XP[WH[Q], α]
 syntax: XP[WH[Q], α] in $[_{CP[WH[Q]]} \_\_ S[\{FIN|INV\}]]$,
  where α is a PFORM value if X = P
 • syntactic dominance path conditions
  a. subject gap: CP[WH[Q]] $\mathcal{A}$* S[FIN] NP[G]
  b. non-subject gap: CP[WH[Q]] $\mathcal{A}$* VP $\mathcal{B}$* XP[G, α],
   where $\mathcal{A}$ = {S, VP, AP, CP[{*that* | *for*}]} and $\mathcal{B}$ = {NP, PP}
 • F/A dominance path condition
  PROP {PROP, Fa, Faa, Fpa}* {ARG, POS}* $[_{ARG} x]$

When the hearer encounters a "moved" *wh*-phrase in discourse and recognizes it as such, he accesses this lexical entry and checks if these dominance path conditions are met in this instance of "*wh*-movement." Every island violation shows up as a *wh*-question that does not meet the dominance path conditions. Furthermore, this lexical entry correctly predicts that only "moved" *wh*-phrases are sensitive to islands. In other words, *wh*-phrases *in situ* that are found in quiz questions and multiple *wh*-questions do not exhibit any effect of island violation (Ueno 2014: 286, 297).

8.2 Summary of Chapter 2

In Chapter 2, we considered the inferential nature of utterance comprehension in general and ellipsis comprehension in particular, based on AMG and Relevance Theory (RT).

As has been claimed in RT, the hearer's process of utterance interpretation is largely inferential. An utterance produced by the speaker and directed to the hearer only provides him with a piece of "evidence" of her intended meaning (what the speaker intended to communicate) in the sense that the meaning that is linguistically encoded by the speaker and then linguistically decoded by the hearer vastly underdetermines its explicit content (i.e., explicatures) and implicit content (i.e., implicatures). The hearer, therefore, needs to infer the speaker's intended meaning on the basis of the "evidence" (i.e., the utterance) provided to him, the linguistic and non-linguistic context in which it is uttered, and the set of assumptions the hearer can access at that time. The following was the exchange Wilson and Sperber (2012: 14) used to illustrate this point.

(2) (= Chapter 2 (1))
 [context: The following exchange takes place when Lisa drops by her neighbor Alan one evening as he and his family are sitting down to supper.]
 Alan: Do you want to join us for supper?
 Lisa: No, thanks. I've eaten.

Lisa does not interpret Alan's interrogative sentence as a request for information about whether she desires to join them for supper but rather inferentially interprets it as an invitation to supper, probably based on a script that a family invites to supper a friend of theirs who happens to visit them at supper time. Lisa replies "No, thanks" based on this invitation interpretation. Alan inferentially interprets Lisa's "I've eaten" as 'Lisa has already eaten supper this evening.' Note the inferential enrichments indicated by the underlines. Enrichment of this type is usually performed automatically and unconsciously during the on-line processing of utterances. Furthermore, Alan inferentially interprets this as Lisa's providing a reason for declining his invitation, probably based on the encyclopedic information about the concept of supper: (a) people don't normally want to eat supper twice in one evening and (b) the fact that one has already eaten supper on a given evening is a good reason for refusing an invitation to supper that evening.

We claimed, regarding human inferential ability, that humans are extremely good at inferring another person's feelings, thoughts, and intentions. This inferential ability seems to have antedated linguistic ability both phylogenetically and ontogenetically. For one thing, not only humans but also other primates possess inferential ability. For another, very young children are able to infer what is in another person's mind even before learning their first language. In fact, infants are engaged in inferential communication, for example, at the one-word stage of language acquisition. They communicate with their parents and other infants by producing one-word utterances (i.e., fragments). The communication at this stage is largely based on inference. Human inferential ability seems to come with a substantial innate endowment, just as human linguistic ability does. Therefore, we followed RT and assumed the existence of the Inferential Comprehension Module (ICM), a dedicated module for inferential comprehension, in addition to the Language Module (LM).

We proposed the following utterance comprehension process.

(3) Utterance comprehension process (= Chapter 2 (3))
utterance (U) → $\boxed{\text{LM (AMG)}}$ → decoded four-tuple (syntax, F/A, E/R, IS) of U → $\boxed{\text{ICM}}$ → developed four-tuple of U → explicatures and implicatures of U

We assumed that the LM is an input system that automatically and unconsciously decodes every utterance U and that the LM is equipped with the current version of AMG that was reviewed in Chapter 1. The LM computes the decoded four-tuple (syntax, F/A, E/R, IS) of U on the basis of the information from the lexical items in U, the phrase structure rules in each module of AMG, and the default correspondences between the syntax, F/A, and E/R modules. The decoded four-tuple of U, namely the output of the LM, is then input to the ICM. The ICM integrates information coming from various input systems, including the LM, vision, smell, and memory, performs non-demonstrative inference, develops the decoded four-tuple, and constructs the explicatures and implicatures of U. The non-demonstrative inference carried out by the ICM is guided by the Relevance-guided comprehension heuristic (4). The explicatures of U are obtained through

8.2 SUMMARY OF CHAPTER 2

development of the decoded four-tuple of U, as defined in (5). The final output of the ICM is the explicatures and implicatures of U expressed in Mentalese.

(4) Relevance-guided comprehension heuristic (Wilson and Sperber 2012: 7, 276) (= Chapter 2 (8))
   a. The hearer follows a path of least effort (in order of accessibility) in constructing the explicatures and implicatures of an utterance U.
   b. The hearer stops constructing the explicatures and implicatures of U when his expectations of relevance are satisfied.

(5) definition of *development of decoded/inferred four-tuple of an utterance* (= Chapter 2 (9))
   The development of the decoded/inferred four-tuple (syntax, F/A, E/R, IS) of an utterance U is a process of constructing a semantically complete, truth-evaluable (i.e., fully propositional) interpretive hypothesis from the syntactically and semantically incomplete decoded/inferred four-tuple of U on the basis of the contextual assumptions, the information accessible from memory, the background knowledge shared by the speaker and the hearer, etc., through such inferential tasks as disambiguation, reference assignment, enrichment, and assumption schema embedding.

The following was the example we used to illustrate the comprehension process of a sentential utterance, which was described in (3).

(6) a. (utterance) "It will get cold." (= Chapter 2 (17a))
   STEP 1: computing the decoded four-tuple of "It will get cold"
   STEP 2: developing the decoded four-tuple
   reference assignment: *It* refers to *the soup on the table*
   disambiguation: *cold* is used in a cold-inducing sense
   enrichment: the future *will* refers to immediate future 'will very soon'
   assumption schema embedding: embedding the basic explicature into 'The speaker has said that,' 'The speaker believes that,' etc.
   STEP 3: basic explicature: 'The soup on the table will get cold very soon.'
   higher-level explicatures: 'The speaker has said that the soup on the table will get cold very soon.' 'The speaker believes that the soup on the table will get cold very soon.'
   implicature: 'The speaker tells the hearer to come and eat the soup on the table before it gets cold very soon.'

8.3 Summary of Chapter 3

In Chapter 3, we considered various properties of fragments and how fragments are interpreted. We pointed out that the ability to use fragments (e.g., one-word utterances) is acquired very early in children's language acquisition, and is enabled by human inferential ability. The learning of other forms of ellipsis such as sluicing, VP ellipsis, gapping, and RNR comes later. Therefore, we reasoned that it would be surprising if humans, when comprehending other types of ellipsis, did not use their inferential ability, which has been at their disposal since birth. We concluded that when these elliptic forms are interpreted, the same type of inference that is involved in fragment interpretation is also involved. In fact, fragments provided a strong motivation to assume extra-grammatical pragmatic inference processes, without which they will not be accounted for adequately. We observed that fragments are curious in two ways: that children learn to use them very early before the acquisition of syntax and that non-demonstrative inference plays a much larger role in fragment interpretation than in the interpretation of any other ellipsis type.

We examined various properties of fragments in Chapter 3 and accounted for not only acceptable but also unacceptable examples. Readers might have supposed that because the ICM is very powerful, such an ellipsis comprehension process as (7) or (11) accepts too many utterances (i.e., the danger of overgeneration) including those that are excluded as ungrammatical in other approaches. However, we showed that most of those utterances that are excluded as ungrammatical are also excluded as such in our approach, by reducing them to the ungrammaticality of their decoded and/or inferred four-tuple representations. Furthermore, our approach will correctly predict that there are utterances in real verbal communication that are grammatically ill-formed (e.g., due to slips of the tongue) but have clear intended meaning (i.e., explicatures and implicatures). In our terms, these utterances have ill-formed decoded and/or inferred four-tuple representations but the ICM still constructs their explicatures and implicatures.

When the hearer interprets a fragment utterance U, he basically follows the same process as described in (3), but he needs to infer the missing parts in the decoded syntax, F/A, E/R, and IS of U, because U is not an utterance of a full sentence. We proposed the following on the basis of (3).

(7) Fragment utterance comprehension process (= Chapter 3 (5b))
fragment utterance (U) → LM (AMG) → decoded four-tuple of U → ICM
→ inferred four-tuple of U → developed four-tuple of U → explicatures and implicatures of U (in Mentalese)

The following was the example we used to illustrate (7).

(8) (= Chapter 2 (18))
[context: The following exchange takes place in a cafeteria, where Mary has almost finished eating breakfast, when John comes in and talks to her.]
John: What did you have?
Mary [happily]: A steak.

When Mary interprets John's *wh*-question, she needs to construct its explicatures and implicatures by determining the referent of *you*, disambiguating the verb *have*, and enriching the interpretation with 'for breakfast' and 'this morning.'

(9) Mary's interpretation process of John's "What did you have?"
STEP 1: computing the decoded four-tuple of "What did you have?"
STEP 2: developing the decoded four-tuple by
reference assignment: *you* refers to *Mary*.
disambiguation: *have* means 'eat.'
enrichment: narrowing the past tense to 'this morning' and adding 'for breakfast'
STEP 3: basic explicature: 'What did Mary eat for breakfast this morning?'
higher-level explicatures: 'John asks Mary what she ate for breakfast this morning.'
'John does not know what Mary ate for breakfast this morning.'
'John wants to know what Mary ate for breakfast this morning.'

We claimed that the fragment "A steak" uttered by Mary in (8), or any other fragment for that matter, is not ignored as ungrammatical or gibberish by John or by the other audience because it is directed by the speaker to the hearer as part of ostensive-inferential communication, which conveys to the hearer a presumption of its own optimal relevance (Chapter 2 (7)), due to the Communicative Principle of Relevance (Chapter 2 (6)), and therefore the hearer expects that it is relevant enough to be worth processing. This triggers on the part of the hearer an inferential comprehension process, which in turn supplies the fragment with its missing elements based on their accessibility. The whole interpretive process of Mary's NP fragment "A steak" in (8) is shown in (10).

(10) interpretive process of Mary's NP fragment "A steak" in (8) (= Chapter 3 (7))

STEP 1: The LM computes the decoded four-tuple of the fragment utterance "A steak" from the lexical entries of *a* and *steak*, from the default correspondences between syntax, F/A, and E/R (NP ↔ ARG ↔ ROLE), and from the fact that the NP fragment is intended as an answer to a *wh*-question (i.e., FOC in IS): ($[_{NP[DET]}$ $[_{DET}$ a$]$ $[_{NP}$ steak$]]$, $[_{ARG}$ STEAK$]$, ROLE, $[_U$ $[_{FOC}$ "a steak"$]]$).

STEP 2: Because of the default correspondences (S ↔ PROP ↔ EV ↔ $[_U$ FOC, BI$]$) and the facts that the NP must be an NP of some S, that the ARG must be an argument of some proposition (PROP) and that the ROLE must be a role of some event (EV), the ICM computes the skeletal four-tuple (8b).

STEP 3: The LM sends this skeletal four-tuple to the ICM. The ICM, following the Relevance-guided comprehension heuristic, accesses the most accessible information, namely, the four-tuple of the preceding *wh*-question and its explicatures and implicatures.

STEP 4: The ICM first constructs the inferred four-tuple of the NP fragment, namely, the four-tuple of *I had a steak*, develops it, and then constructs its explicatures
(e.g., 'Mary is happy that she ate a steak for breakfast this morning.')
and implicatures (e.g., 'Mary is full.') by referring to the contextual information and the explicatures and implicatures of the *wh*-question.

We presented in 3.2 seven pieces of evidence that fragments are inferentially interpreted as contextually appropriate S in syntax, PROP in F/A, and SA in E/R, as is shown in this example.

We proposed the following Procedure for fragment comprehension on the basis of (7).

(11) Procedure for fragment comprehension (= Chapter 3 (5c))
The hearer follows the Relevance-guided comprehension heuristic and executes the following steps.
 (i) The LM computes the decoded four-tuple of a fragment utterance U and its skeletal four-tuple.
 (ii) By non-demonstrative inference, the ICM constructs the inferred syntactic structure of U on the basis of the skeletal syntax obtained in (i) and the contextual information.

8.3 SUMMARY OF CHAPTER 3

(iii) The ICM constructs the inferred four-tuple of U on the basis of the skeletal four-tuple obtained in (i), the inferred syntax obtained in (ii), and the contextual information.

(iv) The ICM develops the inferred four-tuple of U obtained in (iii) on the basis of the contextual information.

(v) The ICM constructs the explicatures and implicatures of U on the basis of the developed four-tuple obtained in (iv) and the contextual information.

One reason why in (11) constructing the inferred syntax (step ii) precedes constructing the inferred F/A, E/R, and IS (step iii) was that we needed to deal with idiom chunk fragments. To properly interpret the fragment *Mary's* in (12) as part of the idiom *pull X's leg*, we need to infer that *Mary's* represents *Mary's leg* in syntax and that this is intended as the syntactic structure of *John pulled Mary's leg at the party* in (12a) and *Mary's leg was pulled at the party* in (12b). Without these inferred syntactic structures, we would not be able to recover the idiomatic interpretation of this fragment. Note that we need the syntactic structures [$_{VP}$ [$_V$ pull] [$_{NP}$ NP's leg]] in the active and [$_{NP}$ NP's leg] [$_{VP[PAS]}$ pulled] in the passive in order to recover their idiomatic interpretation. See the lexical entry for this idiom in Chapter 2 (28) and (29).

(12) (= Chapter 3 (18))
    a. A: Whose leg did John pull at the party?
       B: Mary's.
          inferred syntax of the fragment: [$_{S[PAST]}$ John pulled Mary's leg at the party]
          basic explicature: 'John teased Mary at the party.'
    b. A: Whose leg was pulled at the party?
       B: Mary's.
          inferred syntax of the fragment: [$_{S[PAST]}$ Mary's leg was pulled at the party]
          basic explicature: 'Mary was teased at the party.'

We pointed out two factors that trigger the inferential comprehension process of a fragment. The first factor was the Communicative Principle of Relevance (Chapter 2 (6)). This was described above. The second factor was the multi-modularity of AMG. Because AMG is organized in a multi-modular fashion, default correspondences between the modules create a situation in which a fragment leads to a skeletal four-tuple such as ([$_S$ ... NP ...], [$_{PROP}$ ... ARG ...], [$_{EV}$ ...

ROLE ...], [$_U$ ... FOC ...]) for an NP fragment, ([$_S$ ... PP ...], [$_{PROP}$ ... Mp ...], [$_{EV}$ ... TIME-MOD ...], [$_U$ ... FOC ...]) for a temporal PP fragment, and ([$_{CP[WH[Q]]}$ XP[WH[Q]] ...], [$_{PROP}$ QP ...], [$_{EV}$ ... ROLE ...], [$_U$ ... FOC ...]) for a *wh*-fragment. For example, when an NP fragment such as "A steak" in (8) is uttered, its decoded four-tuple is computed automatically by the default categorial correspondences (NP ↔ ARG ↔ ROLE ↔ FOC). These correspondences imply that an NP in syntax, which must be part of some S, corresponds to an ARG in F/A that must be part of some PROP, to a ROLE in E/R that must be part of some event (EV), and to a focus (FOC) in IS that must carry new information against the phonologically unrealized old information (i.e., background information (BI), as in [$_U$ FOC, BI]). This in turn induces the default modular correspondences S ↔ PROP ↔ EV ↔ U. Therefore, every time an NP fragment is uttered, there is a skeletal four-tuple ([$_S$ ... NP ...], [$_{PROP}$ ... ARG ...], [$_{EV}$ ... ROLE ...], [$_U$ ... FOC ...]) available to the hearer.

(13) (= Chapter 3 (8))
    a. decoded four-tuple of the NP fragment "A steak"

    b. skeletal four-tuple of "A steak"

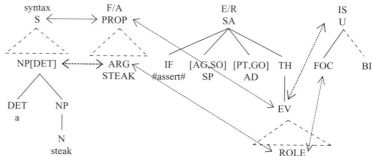

    c. inferred four-tuple of "A steak"
       the syntax, F/A, E/R, and IS of *I had a steak*

The skeletal four-tuple triggers non-demonstrative inference that leads to identifying the S, PROP, and EV in which the NP, ARG, and ROLE are properly located, respectively.

We pointed out that there are three types of inferred syntax constructed from an NP fragment. In (14), B's NP fragment "Japanese" is understood in three ways depending on what inferred syntax is constructed from the NP fragment. We claimed that its inferred syntax can be constructed either from the global domain (15a), from the local domain (15b), or by directly referring to the antecedent NP (15c).

(14) (= Chapter 3 (43))
[context: A and B share the knowledge that Japanese is a foreign language.]
A: Mary said John is learning a foreign language.
B: Yes. Japanese.

(15) the interpretations of the NP fragment "Japanese" in (14B)
   a. syntax inferred from global domain: Mary said John is learning Japanese.
   b. syntax inferred from local domain: John is learning Japanese.
   c. syntax inferred by direct reference: It is Japanese. (*it* refers to *a foreign language* in (14A).)

Because of the availability of multiple inferred syntactic structures, fragments are not sensitive to island effects, as we discussed in 3.3.10.

8.4 Summary of Chapter 4

In Chapter 4, we discussed various properties of sluicing including the island insensitivity that it exhibits and explained them from our AMG and RT perspectives. We called sluiced *wh*-phrases *wh*-fragments and treated them exactly the same way as fragments, which were discussed in Chapter 3.

We confirmed by presenting seven pieces of evidence that a *wh*-fragment (XP[WH[Q]]) behaves syntactically as a *wh*-interrogative clause (CP[WH[Q]]) and claimed that a *wh*-fragment is directly dominated by a CP[WH[Q]] node in syntax. This is due to the lexical entry for a *wh*-phrase (1). When the hearer encounters a *wh*-phrase, he accesses this lexical entry, in which the syntactic rule

[$_{\text{CP[WH[Q]]}}$ XP[WH[Q]] S] is stated. Furthermore, the hearer's LM decodes the *wh*-fragment into the four-tuple (XP[WH[Q]], QP, ROLE, [$_\text{U}$ FOC]), according to the Procedure for fragment comprehension (11). Because the hearer knows the syntactic rule [$_{\text{CP[WH[Q]]}}$ XP[WH[Q]] S], the F/A rule [$_{\text{PROP}}$ QP, PROP], the E/R rule [$_{\text{EV}}$ TYPE ROLE^n], and the IS rule [$_\text{U}$ FOC, BI], this much knowledge leads to the skeletal four-tuple (16), which triggers non-demonstrative inference in the hearer's ICM, resulting in a suitable S in syntax, a suitable PROP in F/A, a suitable EV in E/R, and a suitable BI in IS that properly situate the *wh*-fragment in question.

(16) skeletal four-tuple of *wh*-fragment (= Chapter 4 (11))

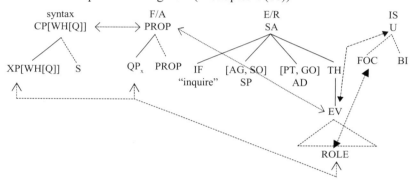

Wh-fragments are insensitive to islands, just as fragments. This is because they have three types of inferred syntax: inferred from the global domain, inferred from the local domain, and inferred by direct reference. Although the syntax of each *wh*-fragment in (17) that is inferred from the global domain is ungrammatical due to an island violation, the syntactic structure inferred either from the local domain or by direct reference does not involve any island violation. This explains the island insensitivity of *wh*-fragments. This is exactly the same reason why fragments are island insensitive.

(17) (= Chapter 4 (43))
    a. Bob found a plumber who fixed the sink, but I'm not sure with what. [CNPC; sprouting]
        syntax inferred from global domain: *but I'm not sure with what [Bob found a plumber who fixed the sink]

syntax inferred from local domain: but I'm not sure with what [he fixed the sink]
he refers to *a plumber who fixed the sink*

b. That Tony is eating right now is conceivable, but I'm having a hard time imagining what. [Sentential Subject Constraint; sprouting]
syntax inferred from global domain: *but I'm having a hard time imagining what [that Tony is eating right now is conceivable]
syntax inferred from local domain: but I'm having a hard time imagining what [Tony might be eating right now] (*might*: modal subordination (Merchant 2001: 218))

c. A: Harriet drinks scotch that comes from a very special part of Scotland.
B: Where? [CNPC; matching]
syntax inferred from global domain: *Where [does Harriet drink scotch that comes from]?
syntax inferred from local domain: Where [does it come from]?
it refers to *scotch that comes from a very special part of Scotland*

d. A: John met a guy who speaks a very unusual language.
B: Which language? [CNPC; matching]
syntax inferred from global domain: *Which language did [John meet a guy who speaks]?
syntax inferred from local domain: Which language does he speak?
he refers to *a guy who speaks a very unusual language*
syntax inferred by direct reference: Which language is it?
it refers to *a very unusual language*

8.5 Summary of Chapter 5

In Chapter 5, we discussed various phenomena related to "VP ellipsis" and claimed that they are best explained by categorizing auxiliary verbs left behind by "VP deletion" as pro-VP forms. In fact, we showed that just like pronouns (i.e., pro-NP forms), pro-VP forms obey the well-known syntactic condition on anaphoric device (AD) that "an AD must not precede and c-command its antecedent" (McCawley 1998: 359). In addition, just like pronouns, pro-VP forms allow deictic use, the use of AD in which its antecedent is found not in the prior linguistic context but in the non-linguistic context.

384   8 CONCLUSION

(18) (= Chapter 5 (39))
    a. [context: John tries to kiss Mary.] "John, you mustn't."
    b. [context: John hands Mary the expensive present he has bought for her.] "Oh, John, you shouldn't have."
    c. "Will she or won't she? Clinton sidesteps the 2016 question." (MSNBC *Morning Joe*, January 28, 2013)

We proposed the following based on (7) and (11).

(19) Procedure for pro-VP form comprehension (= Chapter 5 (13))
The hearer follows the Relevance-guided comprehension heuristic and executes the following steps.
    (i) The LM computes the decoded four-tuple of an utterance U that contains pro-VP forms.
    (ii) By non-demonstrative inference, the ICM (iia) finds potential antecedents of the pro-VP forms in the linguistic and/or non-linguistic context and (iib) constructs the inferred syntactic structure of U that includes inferred VPs on the basis of the decoded syntax obtained in (i) and the contextual information.
    (iii) The ICM constructs the inferred four-tuple of U on the basis of the decoded four-tuple obtained in (i), the inferred syntax obtained in (ii), and the contextual information.
    (iv) The ICM develops the inferred four-tuple of U obtained in (iii) on the basis of the contextual information.
    (v) The ICM constructs the explicatures and implicatures of U on the basis of the developed four-tuple obtained in (iv) and the contextual information.

(20b) shows how (19) works to derive the explicatures and implicatures of (20a). If (20a) is uttered as an answer to "Which is better qualified as manager of our Tokyo office, Mary or John?," one of its implicatures is that this speaker believes that Mary is better qualified for the job' (Chapter 5 (8)).

(20) a. John can't speak Japanese but Mary can. (= Chapter 5 (1b))
      b. (= Chapter 5 (14b))
          Mary [$_{\text{VP[PRES, AUX]}}$ *can*] →
            (i) decoded four-tuple of *Mary can*
            (iia) potential antecedent: *speak Japanese*

8.5 SUMMARY OF CHAPTER 5

(iib) inferred VP: [$_{VP[PRES, AUX]}$ *can speak Japanese*]

(iii) inferred four-tuple of *Mary can*: *Mary can speak Japanese*

(iv) development: enrichment (*fluently*) and assumption schema embedding (*this speaker knows that*)

(v) explicature: 'This speaker knows that John cannot speak Japanese but Mary can speak Japanese fluently.'

implicature: 'This speaker thinks that Mary knows a lot more about Japan than John does.'

c. syntax and F/A of *Mary can*

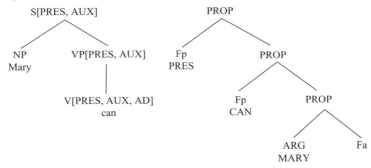

Although the syntax of *Mary can* in (20a) is complete, as shown in (20c), its F/A is incomplete because the Fa is not filled. However, this utterance is not treated as ungrammatical or gibberish, because it is part of ostensive-inferential communication and is guaranteed to be worth processing by the Communicative Principle of Relevance. Therefore, non-demonstrative inference is triggered by this principle, on the one hand, and by the unfilled Fa, on the other. The hearer seeks the most accessible VP that is contextually appropriate, serves as the antecedent of the pro-VP form *can*, and provides a value of the unfilled Fa. As a result, the inferred syntax of *can* turns out to be [$_{VP[PRES]}$ *can speak Japanese*].

We claimed that all pro-VP forms and all auxiliary verbs are registered in the lexicon and that the lexical entry for an auxiliary verb and that for its corresponding pro-VP form are related by the Pro-VP Form Lexical Rule (Chapter 5 (43)).

We provided several reasons why the step of constructing in syntax an inferred VP of a pro-VP form (Step (iib) in (19)) must precede the step of constructing the other parts of the inferred four-tuple (Step (iii) in (19)). One of them concerns idiom interpretation of VP ellipsis.

(21) a. My goose is cooked, but yours isn't. (= Chapter 5 (16a))
  b. *yours* → inferred syntax of *yours*: *your goose*
       inferred syntax of *isn't*: *isn't cooked* (by (19))
       inferred syntax of *yours isn't*: *your goose isn't cooked*

To interpret the second conjunct *yours isn't* of (21a) as an idiom, we first need to determine in syntax that *yours* represents *your goose* and the pro-VP form *isn't* represents *isn't cooked*, and therefore that the inferred syntax of the second conjunct is *your goose isn't cooked*, namely, the passive form of the VP idiom *cook NP's goose*. Without inferring this syntactic structure first, the intended idiomatic interpretation is not recoverable, because [$_{NP}$ *your goose*] and [$_{VP}$ *isn't cooked*] are both needed to qualify as the passive form of the VP idiom in question.

On the basis of (19), we accounted for, among other things, the Missing Antecedent Phenomenon (5.5), Antecedent Contained Deletion (ACD) (5.7), the sloppy identity reading of VP ellipsis (5.9), and the two intriguing restrictions on VP ellipsis (5.10). We also pointed out that Bach-Peters sentences are possible with VP ellipsis (Chapter 5 (40b)) and showed that (19) is sufficient to recover their interpretation. We provided in 5.6 seven pieces of evidence that inferred VPs are real SYNTACTIC entities and do not exist in the abstract.

The following was the example we used to illustrate how the ACD construction is interpreted.

(22) Children may not even be learning what they ought to. (ambiguous) (= Chapter 5 (77a))
    decoded four-tuple of *what they ought to*
    potential antecedents: {*learning what they ought to*, *be learning what they ought to*}
    inferred VPs: {[$_{VP[to, AUX]}$ *to learn* NP[G]], [$_{VP[to, AUX]}$ *to be learning* NP[G]]}
    inferred four-tuples of *what they ought to learn* and *what they ought to be learning*

The antecedent of the pro-VP form in the ACD construction is found locally, as in (22). We noted that the potential antecedents of the pro-VP form *to* in (22) contain the pro-VP form *to* itself. This is what happens with pronouns, as in [*The man next to* [*his*] *dog*] *is smiling* and [*The boy with a collar that suits* [*him*]] *is a designer* (Imanishi and Asano 1990: 120), in which an NP contains a coreferential pronoun within itself. We also noted that the NP gap (NP[G]) in each inferred VP in (22) is required by two factors: (i) through access to the lexical entry for the verb in the inferred VP, namely, *learn*, which contains the syntactic requirement V in [__, NP], and, more importantly, (ii) by the dominance path conditions (1) triggered by the free relative *what*, which require that there be a gap (XP[G]) in the inferred VP headed by *to*. Because of these factors, an inferred VP in the ACD construction must contain an NP[G]. Our claim here is that when a pro-VP form is dominated by a node that triggers the dominance path conditions (e.g., CP[WH[Q]] for interrogative *wh*-clauses or CP[WH[R]] for *wh*-relative clauses), its inferred VP must meet the dominance path conditions. This is a natural consequence of the fact that inferred VPs are syntactic entities, as was shown in 5.6. In addition, we pointed out that ACD constructions can only be apparent and that the pro-VP forms in them can find their antecedent outside the constructions, which was illustrated in Chapter 5 (77b), (82c), and (85c, d).

8.6 Summary of Chapter 6

In Chapter 6, we examined various properties of gapping and claimed that they are best explained by formulating it as a construction that involves a coordinate structure. We proposed the lexical entry for the gapping construction (23) and the Procedure for gapping comprehension (25).

(23) lexical entry for gapping (as a construction) (= Chapter 6 (33))
The gapping construction is a coordinate structure of conjuncts with the syntactic category C, where C is clausal (<BAR, 2>, cf. Chapter 1 (2)) or VP (cf. 6.4).

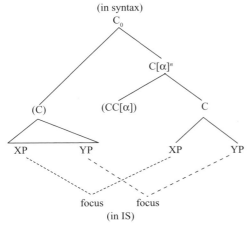

(i) Each gapped conjunct consists of two remnant phrases XP and YP.
(ii) The antecedent of the gapped conjuncts is the first conjunct if it is not gapped. Otherwise, it is in the prior discourse.
(iii) XP and YP in the antecedent must be major constituents.
(iv) The antecedent is the smallest CP[WH[Q]], S, or VP that dominates both XP and YP.
(v) XP and YP of the gapped conjuncts are contrastively focused with XP and YP in the antecedent, respectively.

One of the reasons we formulated gapping as a construction is that there are cases of gapping in which there is no well-formed "underlying structure" with coordinated full sentences. For example, (24) does not mean 'Kim didn't play bingo or Sandy didn't sit at home all evening.' Rather, it means 'Kim didn't play bingo and Sandy didn't sit at home all evening.'

(24) [Kim] didn't [play bingo] or [Sandy] [sit at home all evening]. (= Chapter 6 (29a))

We pointed out that this interpretation follows the de Morgan Law: $\neg(P \vee Q)$ is deductively equivalent to $(\neg P) \wedge (\neg Q)$. This is because *didn't* in (24) is shared between the first conjunct and the second conjunct, that is, it has both propositions in its scope.

(25) Procedure for gapping comprehension (= Chapter 6 (24))
　　　The hearer follows the Relevance-guided comprehension heuristic (Chapter 2 (8)) and executes the following steps.
　　(i) The LM computes the decoded four-tuple of the gapped conjunct.
　　(ii) By non-demonstrative inference, the ICM constructs the inferred syntactic structure of the gapped conjunct on the basis of the decoded syntax obtained in (i), the developed four-tuple of the first conjunct, and the contextual information.
　　(iii) The ICM constructs the inferred four-tuple of the gapped conjunct on the basis of its inferred syntax obtained in (ii), the developed four-tuple of the first conjunct, and the contextual information.
　　(iv) The ICM develops the inferred four-tuple of the gapped conjunct obtained in (iii) on the basis of the contextual information.
　　(v) The ICM constructs the explicatures and implicatures of the whole gapping construction on the basis of the developed four-tuple obtained in (iv) and the contextual information including the developed four-tuple of the first conjunct.

The following was the example we used to illustrate the interpretation process of a gapping construction.

(26) [context: at a party] (= Chapter 6 (25))
　　　Hostess: Come to the table and help yourself.
　　　Host: The food will get cold and the beer lukewarm.
　　　　　and the beer lukewarm →

(i) decoded four-tuple of *and the beer lukewarm*:
   ([$_{S[and]}$ and [$_S$ [$_{NP[DET]}$ the beer] [$_{AP}$ lukewarm]]], [$_{PROP}$ ARG Fa],
   [$_{EV}$ ROLE TYPE], [$_U$ FOC FOC])
(ii) inferred syntax: *and the beer will get lukewarm*
(iii) inferred four-tuple of *and the beer will get lukewarm*
(iv) development of inferred four-tuple:
   enrichment of *will*: immediate future 'will very soon'
   reference assignment: *the beer* refers to 'the beer on the table where the food is put'
(v) explicature and implicatures
   explicature: 'The host believes that the food on the table will get cold very soon and the beer on the table will get lukewarm very soon.'
   implicature: 'The host tells the guests to come to the table and have the food and beer before the food gets cold and the beer gets lukewarm.'

In (25), as in the other comprehension procedures, the construction of an inferred syntax (step ii) precedes the construction of the other inferred structures (step iii). One of the reasons is that inferred syntactic structures are required to interpret idiom chunks.

(27) [John's goose] was cooked [by accident] and [Mary's] [by design]. (= Chapter 6 (20a))

To properly interpret the second conjunct *Mary's by design* of (27) as the idiom *cook* NP*'s goose*, the hearer needs to determine its inferred syntax by referring to the first conjunct. The first remnant phrase *Mary's* of the gapped conjunct represents *Mary's goose* and therefore the inferred syntax of the gapped conjunct is *Mary's goose was cooked by design*. Once the hearer has determined its inferred syntax, he can interpret the gapped conjunct as the passive of the VP idiom *cook someone's goose*. Without determining its inferred syntax, the hearer cannot recover the idiomatic interpretation of the second conjunct, because he needs both *Mary's goose* and *was cooked (by design)* to interpret the second conjunct as the idiom.

We also discussed the difference between S-level gapping and VP-level gapping. The latter type of gapping is illustrated below.

(28) Sandy [$_{VP}$ gave books to Lee] [$_{VP}$ and pictures to Kim], and Mary did too.
(= Chapter 6 (65a))

Note that the pro-VP form *did* in the second conjunct takes as its antecedent the coordinated VP in the first conjunct *gave books to Lee and pictures to Kim*.

To determine the most accessible interpretation of the gapping construction, we adopted Kuno and Takami's two principles. The following were the restatements of their principles in our terms.

(29) Minimal Distance Principle (MDP) (= Chapter 6 (81))
The most accessible association in (33) of XP and YP of the gapped conjunct with XP and YP of the first conjunct is when XP and YP of the first conjunct are its rightmost phrases.

(30) Semantic Relatedness Principle (SRP) (= Chapter 6 (90))
The most accessible association in (33) of XP and YP of the gapped conjunct with XP and YP of the first conjunct is when XP of the first conjunct is s-related to its YP.

(31) definition of *semantic relatedness* (*s-relatedness*) (= Chapter 6 (91))
Of two phrases XP and YP of a sentence, XP is <u>s-related to</u> YP if and only if
 (i) The F/A correspondent of XP is PROP-mates with the F/A correspondent of YP, or
 (ii) The F/A correspondent of XP is coreferential with an ARG that is PROP-mates with the F/A correspondent of YP.

As McCawley (1993b) pointed out, the sharing of *didn't* observed in (24) is in fact quite general. We discussed the interpretation process of the gapping construction with such shared operators.

(32) Kim didn't play bingo or Sandy sit at home all evening. (=(24), Chapter 6 (106))
or Sandy sit at home all evening →
 (i) decoded four-tuple of *or Sandy sit at home all evening*
 (ii) inferred syntax of gapped conjunct: *or Sandy sit at home all evening* (= decoded syntax of (i))
 (iii) inferred four-tuple of gapping construction

1. computing decoded F/A of first conjunct
   [$_{Fp}$ PAST]∘[$_{Fp}$ NOT] ([$_{PROP}$ (KIM(PLAY(BINGO)))])
2. computing decoded F/A of gapped conjunct
   [$_{PROP}$ (SANDY(SIT.AT.HOME.ALL.EVENING))]
3. coordinating this F/A with inner PROP of first conjunct
   [$_{PROP}$ (KIM(PLAY(BINGO)))] OR
   [$_{PROP}$ (SANDY(SIT.AT.HOME.ALL.EVENING))]
4. embedding coordinated PROP under shared operators
   [$_{Fp}$ PAST]∘[$_{Fp}$ NOT] ([$_{PROP}$ (KIM(PLAY(BINGO)))] OR
   [$_{PROP}$ (SANDY(SIT.AT.HOME.ALL.EVENING))])
(iv) explicatures and implicatures
   higher-level explicature: 'The speaker knows that Kim didn't play bingo and Sandy didn't sit at home all evening.'
   implicature: 'The speaker wonders what Kim and Sandy did all evening.'

We pointed out that the comprehension step in (32iii) of constructing the inferred F/A of the gapping construction demonstrates that the F/A module is autonomous in and of itself and is separate from the syntax module.

In the last section of Chapter 6, we discussed stripping, which we formulated as another construction, taking into account the fact that there are many commonalities between gapping and stripping.

(33) lexical entry for stripping construction (= Chapter 6 (119))
   (in syntax)

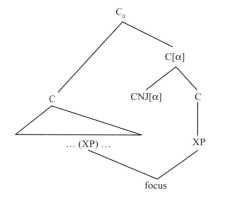
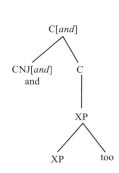

(in syntax)
  (i) C_0 is a nonce coordinate structure of the syntactic category C with a coordinate conjunction (CNJ) $\alpha \in \{and, or, but\}$.
  (ii) The left conjunct C is the smallest CP[WH[Q]], S, or VP that contains XP.
  (iii) The right conjunct consists of a single constituent XP.
  (iv) XP of the first conjunct, if present, is a major constituent.
(in Information Structure)
  (v) XP of the left conjunct and XP of the right conjunct are contrastively focused.
  (vi) XP of the right conjunct is often added as an afterthought.

(34) Procedure for stripping comprehension (= Chapter 6 (120))
The hearer follows the Relevance-guided comprehension heuristic (Chapter 2 (8)) and executes the following steps.
  (i) The LM computes the decoded four-tuple of the stripped conjunct.
  (ii) By non-demonstrative inference, the ICM constructs the inferred syntactic structure of the stripped conjunct on the basis of the decoded syntax of the stripped conjunct obtained in (i), the developed four-tuple of the first conjunct, and the contextual information.
  (iii) The ICM constructs the inferred four-tuple of the stripped conjunct on the basis of the inferred syntax obtained in (ii), the developed four-tuple of the first conjunct, and the contextual information.
  (iv) The ICM develops the inferred four-tuple of the stripped conjunct obtained in (iii) on the basis of the contextual information.
  (v) The ICM constructs the explicatures and implicatures of the whole stripping construction on the basis of the developed four-tuple obtained in (iv) and the contextual information including the developed four-tuple of the first conjunct.

8.7 Summary of Chapter 7

In Chapter 7, we examined various properties of Right Node Raising (RNR) and analyzed them from our multi-modular perspective. We extended the constructional analyses of gapping and stripping to RNR. The lexical entry for the basic type of RNR is repeated below. We also discussed two extended types of RNR (Chapter 7 (31) and (35)).

8.7 SUMMARY OF CHAPTER 7

(35) lexical entry for RNR construction (basic type) (= Chapter 7 (22))

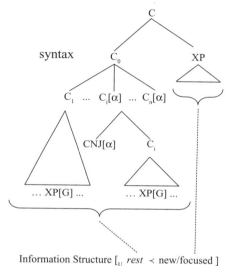

(i) The raised constituent XP can be a clause.

(ii) XP is adjoined to the coordinate structure C_0.

(iii) XP[G] is at or near the end of each conjunct.

(iv) CNJ[α] is a coordinating conjunction with its form feature value α, where α ∈ {*and, or, but*}.

Information Structure [$_U$ *rest* ≺ new/focused]

We reviewed some of Postal's (1998) arguments and concluded that the raised constituent XP is "extracted" from the coordinate structure and not "fused" (pace McCawley 1982, 1998). We proposed (36) and claimed that the RNR construction is interpreted in the same way as the other elliptic expressions.

(36) Procedure for RNR comprehension (= Chapter 7 (40))

The hearer follows the Relevance-guided comprehension heuristic (Chapter 2 (8)) and executes the following steps.

  (i) The LM computes the decoded four-tuple of an utterance U of the RNR construction (i.e., its gapped conjuncts and raised constituent).

  (ii) By non-demonstrative inference, the ICM constructs the inferred syntactic structure of U by filling the gaps with a copy of the raised constituent on the basis of the decoded syntax obtained in (i) and the contextual information.

  (iii) The ICM constructs the inferred four-tuple of U on the basis of the inferred syntax obtained in (ii) and the contextual information.

  (iv) The ICM develops the inferred four-tuple of U obtained in (iii) on the basis of the contextual information.

  (v) The ICM constructs the explicatures and implicatures of U on the basis of the developed four-tuple obtained in (iv) and the contextual information.

The following was the example we used to illustrate (36). Note that in the inferred syntax of step ii, the raised NP is put back to the NP gap in each conjunct.

(37) (= Chapter 7 (41))
   A: Which do you think is richer, John or Bill?
   B: John owns but Bill rents, a big Mercedes.
   (i) decoded four-tuple of *John owns NP[G], but Bill rents NP[G], a big Mercedes*
   (ii) inferred syntax: John owns [a big Mercedes] but Bill rents [a big Mercedes].
   (iii) inferred four-tuple of *John owns a big Mercedes but Bill rents a big Mercedes*
   (iv) higher-level explicature: 'B believes that John owns a big Mercedes and Bill rents a big Mercedes.'
   implicature: 'B thinks that John is richer than Bill.'

Note that the raised constituent *a big Mercedes* in (37B) has a different referent in each conjunct.

We gave seven reasons why the step of constructing the inferred syntax must precede that of constructing the inferred F/A and E/R. One of these reasons concerned idiom chunks. To the extent that (38) is acceptable with its idiomatic interpretation, the hearer needs to infer that *yours* represents *your leg* and that the first and second conjuncts represent *John's leg seems to be being pulled by Mary* and *I'm sure that your leg is being pulled by Mary*, respectively. Without arriving at this inferred syntactic structure, the idiomatic interpretation of (38) cannot be recovered.

(38) John's leg seems to be and I'm sure that yours is too, being pulled by Mary.
    (= Chapter (47a))
    → John's leg seems to be being pulled by Mary and I'm sure that your leg is being pulled by Mary too.

We pointed out that when a quantified NP is raised by RNR, the RNR construction exhibits ambiguity. This was illustrated by the following example.

(39) a. John greeted and Mary smiled at, most students in the department.
    (= Chapter 7 (45a))
       decoded syntax: [John greeted NP[G] and Mary smiled at NP[G]], [$_{NP}$ most students in the department].

8.7 SUMMARY OF CHAPTER 7   395

inferred syntax: John greeted [most students in the department] and Mary smiled at [most students in the department].
inferred F/A: [[$_{QP_x}$ MOST STUDENTS] (PAST(JOHN GREET x))] AND [[$_{QP_y}$ MOST STUDENTS] (PAST(MARY SMILE AT y))]

b. John greeted and Mary smiled at, most students in the department. (= Chapter 7 (51))
decoded syntax: [John greeted NP[G] and Mary smiled at NP[G]], [$_{NP}$ most students in the department].
inferred syntax: Step ii of (36) skipped
inferred F/A: [$_{QP_x}$ MOST STUDENTS] [(PAST(JOHN GREET x)) AND (PAST(MARY SMILE AT x))]

As for (39b), we noted that step ii of (36) is skipped and that the two NP gaps are taken as representing the same variable. As a result, the decoded syntax and the inferred F/A are isomorphic. The other example of skipping Step ii of (36) was the following, in which we adopted McCawley's (1993a: 240) polyactic quantifier. In (40) and (41), the NP gaps are taken as corresponding to different variables in F/A.

(40) (= Chapter 7 (54))
a. John hummed and Mary sang—different tunes. (= Chapter 7 (36f))
b. decoded syntax: John hummed NP[G] and Mary sang NP[G]—[$_{NP}$ different tunes].
inferred syntax: Step ii of (36) skipped
[John hummed NP[G] and Mary sang NP[G]]—[$_{NP}$ different tunes].

computing the inferred F/A

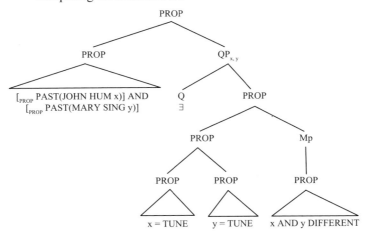

396   8 CONCLUSION

We extended the same account to (41a).

(41) (= Chapter 7 (55))
   a. John borrowed and Mary won, a total of $30,000. (= Chapter 7 (36a))
   b. decoded syntax: [John borrowed NP[G] and Mary won NP[G]], [$_{NP}$ a total of $30,000].
      inferred syntax: Step ii of (36) skipped
      [John borrowed NP[G] and Mary won NP[G]], [$_{NP}$ a total of $30,000].

      computing the inferred F/A

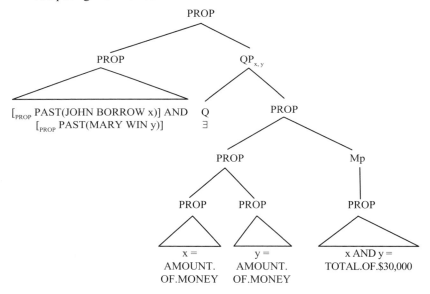

8.8 Epilogue

Through the close examination of the comprehension processes of fragments (7), (11), sluicing, VP ellipsis (19), gapping (25), stripping (34), and RNR (36), the following picture of ellipsis comprehension has emerged.

(42) Elliptic utterance comprehension process
   elliptic utterance U → LM (AMG) → decoded four-tuple of U → ICM → inferred syntax of U → inferred four-tuple of U → developed four-tuple of U → explicatures and implicatures of U (in Mentalese)

Recall that the Language Module (LM) is equipped with the current version of AMG, which consists of four autonomous submodules: syntax, F/A, E/R, and IS. It has become clear by now that the LM is purely representational and static in that it only computes the four-tuple representations of an utterance, whereas the Inferential Comprehension Module (ICM) is fully derivational and dynamic in that the ICM constructs the explicatures and implicatures of an utterance with maximal relevance. We have also noted that the on-line inferential discourse comprehension proceeds successively, cumulatively, and incrementally.

Since the Elliptic utterance comprehension process (42) is applied, for example, to one-word utterances at a very early stage of language acquisition, the decoded and inferred four-tuple representations of an elliptic utterance U have to depend on how much syntactic, F/A, E/R, and IS structures the hearer has learned in terms of their phrase structure rules as well as the lexical entries for the words in U. This implies that the explicatures and implicatures of U depend in part on the stage of language acquisition of the hearer.

The next stage of our future research is to investigate the nature of the ICM in general and its non-demonstrative inference in particular (What does the ICM do to decoded four-tuple representations to construct the most relevant explicatures and implicatures?) and determine the two as narrowly and precisely as possible.

Appendix

Definitions, Rules, and Principles

definition of *directly dominate* (Ch1 (17))

For two nodes X and Y in a given tree, X *directly dominates* Y iff there is a branch in the tree that connects X and Y with X immediately above Y.

definition of *dominate* (Ch1 (18))

For two nodes X and Y in a given tree, X *dominates* Y iff there is a series of nodes in the tree $X = X_1, \ldots, X_n = Y$, such that for each pair of X_i and X_{i+1}, X_i directly dominates X_{i+1}.

definition of *x-command* (Ch1 (19))

For two nodes X and Y in a given tree, X *x-commands* Y iff (i) the first (lowest) non-adjoined node that dominates X and is a member of $\phi(x)$, the set of bounding nodes for x, also dominates Y, and (ii) X does not dominate Y.

definition of *non-adjoined node* (Ch1 (20))

The *non-adjoined node* in an adjunction structure is the node that dominates all the adjoined nodes.

Elsewhere Principle (McCawley 1998: 163, Ueno 2014: 11)

When the conditions of application for one rule are a special case of those for another rule, the more general rule is inapplicable in those cases in which the conditions for the more specific rule are met, that is, specific rules preempt the application of general rules.

Economy of Language Use (Ueno 2014: 61)

When two grammatical expressions express the same information and compete for the same syntactic environment, the simpler one must be chosen over the more complex one unless there is a special reason for choosing the latter.

Feature Osmosis (Sadock 2012: 154, Ueno 2014: 25)

In unmarked situations, there will be a correspondence of features between modules.

default correspondences (Ch1 (57))

a. default categorial correspondences (Sadock 2012: 78)

syntax		F/A		E/R
S	<---------->	PROP	<---------->	EV
NP	<---------->	ARG	<---------->	ROLE
VP	<---------->	Fa		

b. default geometrical correspondences (Sadock 2012: 35)
  i. Dominance relations should be preserved between corresponding nodes in each module.
  ii. C-command relations should be preserved between corresponding nodes in syntax and F/A.
  iii. C-command relations in syntax and F/A and outrank relations in E/R should be harmonic.

Raising Principle (Ch1 (80))

The subject ARG of the complement PROP of a raising predicate X_R (X = V or A) is allowed to correspond to a matrix NP position in syntax.

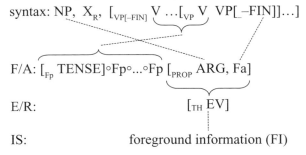

syntax: NP, X_R, [$_{VP[-FIN]}$ V ...[$_{VP}$ V VP[-FIN]]...]

F/A: [$_{Fp}$ TENSE]∘Fp∘...∘Fp [$_{PROP}$ ARG, Fa]

E/R: [$_{TH}$ EV]

IS: foreground information (FI)

Coordinate Structure Convention in Dominance Paths (Ueno 2014: 305)

When a coordinate structure occurs in the middle part of a dominance path, the mother node and each of its daughter conjunct nodes constitute a single node with the daughter's category label for the purposes of the dominance path conditions.

Syntax Module

definition of *well-formed* syntactic structure (Ch1 (25))

a. A local syntactic structure is *well formed* iff it is either (ia) an instantiation of one of the PS rules for syntax admitted by the language in question or (ib) an instantiation of the syntactic field of one of the lexical entries of the language in question, and (ii) it meets all the relevant syntactic constraints on syntactic structures.
b. A syntactic structure is *well formed* iff all the local syntactic structures that it contains are well formed.

definition of *c-command* in syntax (Ch1 (21))

For two nodes X and Y in a given syntactic structure, X *c-commands* Y iff X x-commands Y, where $\phi(x)$ = {all nodes in the syntactic structure}.

definition of *asymmetric c-command* in syntax (Ch1 (22))

For two nodes X and Y in a given syntactic structure, X *asymmetrically c-commands* Y iff X c-commands Y and Y does not c-command X.

definition of *S-command* in syntax (Ch1 (23))

For two nodes X and Y in a given syntactic structure, X *S-commands* Y iff X x-commands Y, where $\phi(x) = \{S\}$.

definition of *S-mates* in syntax (Ch1 (24))

For two nodes X and Y in a given syntactic structure, X and Y are *S-mates* iff X and Y S-command each other.

PS rules for syntax (Ch1 (1))

$[_S \text{NP, VP}]$ $[_{\text{NP[DET]}} \text{NP[POS], NP}]$ $[_{\text{NP}} \{A \mid RRC\}, \text{NP}]$
$[_{\text{HP}} \{PP \mid ADVP\}, HP]$, where $H \in \{A, V, P\}$
$[_{\text{HS}} \{PP \mid ADVP\}, HS]$, where $H \in \{A, V, P\}$

BAR values in syntax (Ch1 (2))

category	N	V	A	P	ADV	C
<BAR, 0>	N	V	A	P	ADV	C
<BAR, 1>	NP	VP	AP	PP	ADVP	
<BAR, 2>	NS	VS(=S)	AS	PS		CP

subject-verb agreement (Ch1 (11))

$[_{S[FIN,\ AGR[3SGN]]}$ NP[AGR[α, β]], VP[FIN, AGR[α, β]]], where α is a PER value and $\alpha \in \{1, 2, 3\}$, and β is a NUM value and $\beta \in \{SG, PL\}$

default linear order between sisters based on complexity (Ch1 (59))

A less complex sister precedes a more complex sister by default.
a. pronoun < word < phrase < clause
b. NP < PP
c. syntactic correspondent of ARG < syntactic correspondent of Fa or PROP

head-initial language (Ch1 (60))

In head-complement structures in a head-initial language, where a lexical head (H[0]) takes one or more complements within its phrase (H[1]), the head must precede all the complements.

Head Feature Convention (HFC) (Ch1 (3))

In each headed local tree, the mother and its head daughter must meet conditions (i) and (ii), unless specified otherwise.
(i) The set of head features on the mother is identical to that on its head daughter.
(ii) For each head feature in (i), its value on the mother is identical to that on the daughter.

list of head features (Ch1 (4))

BAR, form features (NFORM, PFORM, VFORM, and CFORM),
POSP (part of speech feature), AUX, INV,
AGR, which subsumes PER, NUM, and GEN

list of VFORM values (Ch1 (5))

BSE (base form), PRP (present participial form), PSP (past participial form), PAS (passive participial form), *to*, FIN (finite, covering PRES (present tense) and PAST (past tense))

INV Feature Co-occurrence Restriction (Ch1 (13))

INV → {AUX, <VFORM, FIN>, <POSP, V>}

F/A Module

definition of *well-formed* F/A structure (Ch1 (30))

a. A local F/A structure is *well formed* iff it is an instantiation of (a) or (b) of the PS rules for F/A, and its terminal nodes, if any, are instantiations of the F/A field of one of the lexical entries of the language in question.
b. An F/A structure is *well formed* iff all the local F/A structures that it contains are well formed.

definition of *c-command* in F/A (Ch1 (45))

For two nodes X and Y in a given F/A structure, X *c-commands* Y iff X x-commands Y, where $\phi(x) = $ {all nodes in the F/A structure}.

definition of *PROP-command* (Ch6 (92c))

For two nodes X and Y in a given F/A structure, X *PROP-commands* Y iff X x-commands Y, where $\phi(x) = $ {PROP}.

definition of *PROP-mates* (Ch6 (92d))

For two nodes X and Y in a given F/A structure, X and Y are *PROP-mates* iff X and Y PROP-command each other.

PS rules for F/A (Ch1 (26))

a. $[_{F\varphi} Fx\varphi, x]$, where x is either *a* or *p*, and φ is a finite string of *a*'s and *p*'s, and Fe = PROP for the empty string e. (Sadock 2012: 16)
b. $[_{\alpha} M\alpha, \alpha]$, where $M\alpha$ is a modifier of an F/A category α. (Sadock 2012: 17–18)

feature structure of INDEX (Ch1 (32))

$$\text{IND} \begin{pmatrix} \text{ref} & i \\ \text{AGR} & \begin{pmatrix} \text{PER} & \{1\mid 2\mid 3\} \\ \text{NUM} & \{\text{SG}\mid\text{PL}\} \\ \text{GEN} & \{\text{M}\mid\text{F}\mid\text{N}\} \end{pmatrix} \end{pmatrix}$$

well-formedness conditions on QPs (Ch1 (36), cf. Sadock 2012: 61)

a. $[_{\text{PROP}}\, \text{QP}_x, \text{PROP}]$, where the matrix PROP must contain x.
b. $[_{\text{QPx}}\, \text{Q}, \text{PROP}]$, where the domain expression PROP must contain x.
c. All the instances of a variable x must be either dominated or c-commanded by a single QP_x.

E/R Module

definition of *well-formed* E/R structure (Ch1 (48))

a. A local E/R structure is *well formed* iff it is an instantiation of (a), (b), or (c) of the PS rules for E/R, and is matched by the E/R field of one of the lexical entries of the language in question.
b. An E/R structure is *well formed* iff all the local E/Rs that it contains are well formed.

definition of *outrank* (Ch1 (56))

i. *Outrank* (" > ") is determined by the action tier specifications of roles. Otherwise, it is determined by their thematic tier specifications.
ii. If A *outranks* B and B dominates C in E/R, then A *outranks* C.
iii. If A *outranks* B and B *outranks* C, then A *outranks* C. (transitive relation)

Role Hierarchy (Ch1 (55))

action tier: AG > PT > ø
thematic tier: SO > GO > TH > LO > MOD

APPENDIX

Event Hierarchy (Ch1 (50))

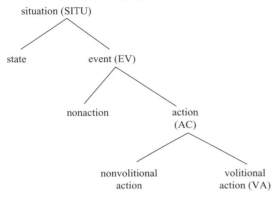

PS rules for E/R (Ch1 (47))

a. [$_{EV}$ TYPE ROLE^m MOD^n] b. [$_{ROLE}$ EV] c. [$_{MOD}$ EV]

Lexical Entries

definition of *natural extension* of lexical entry (Ch4 (36e))

Of two lexical entries L_1 and L_2, L_2 is a *natural extension* of L_1, iff (i) the E/R of L_1 and that of L_2 have the same set of roles (and, therefore, the same outrank relations), and (ii) the role lowest in outranking is suppressed/unassociable in the E/R of L_1 but overt/associable in the E/R of L_2.

lexical entry for default transitive construction (Ch1 (62))

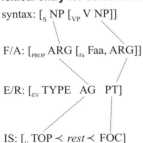

syntax: [$_S$ NP [$_{VP}$ V NP]]

F/A: [$_{PROP}$ ARG [$_{Fa}$ Faa, ARG]]

E/R: [$_{EV}$ TYPE AG PT]

IS: [$_U$ TOP ≺ *rest* ≺ FOC]

lexical entry for RHO (revised) (Ch1 (85))

syntax: nil
F/A: ARG[IND[j, AGR(j)]] in [$_{PROP}$ __, Fa], where the PROP corresponds to a VP[−FIN] in syntax.
E/R: ROLE
morph: nil
mphon: nil

bi-partite lexical entry for idiom *pull strings* (Ch1 (95))

syntax: [$_{VP}$ [$_V$ pull] [$_{NP[3PL]}$ strings]]
F/A: [$_{Fa}$ [$_{Faa}$ EXPLOIT],
    [$_{ARG}$ PERSONAL.CONNECTIONS]]
E/R: [$_{EV}$ [$_{TYPE}$ "exploit"] AG
    [$_{PT}$ "personal connections"]]

syntax: V in [__, NP]
F/A: Faa
E/R: TYPE in [$_{EV}$ __ AG PT]
morph: V[0]

lexical entry for clause-initial interrogative *wh*-phrase XP[WH[Q], α] (Ch1 (100))

syntax: XP[WH[Q], α] in [$_{CP[WH[Q]]}$ __ S[{FIN|INV}]], where α is a PFORM value if X = P

- syntactic dominance path conditions
  a. subject gap: CP[WH[Q]] 𝓐* S[FIN] NP[G]
  b. non-subject gap: CP[WH[Q]] 𝓐* VP 𝓑* XP[G, α],
     where 𝓐 ={S, VP, AP, CP[{*that* | *for*}]} and 𝓑 ={NP, PP}
- F/A dominance path condition
  PROP {PROP, Fa, Faa, Fpa} * {ARG, POS} * [$_{ARG}$ x]

lexical entry for SA superstructure (Ch2 (34b))

syntax: nil
F/A: nil
E/R: [$_{SA}$ IF [$_{[AG, SO]}$ SP] [$_{[PT, GO]}$ AD] [$_{TH}$ EV]]
phonology: nil

APPENDIX   407

default lexical entry for declaratives (as a construction) (Ch2 (36a))

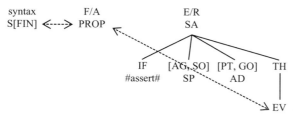

phonology: falling intonation

default lexical entry for yes/no interrogatives with inversion (as a construction) (Ch2 (36b))

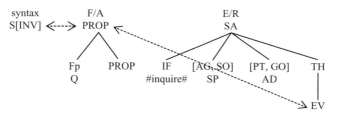

phonology: raising intonation

default lexical entry for imperatives (as a construction) (Ch2 (36c))

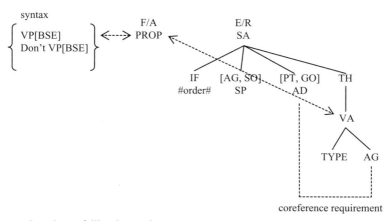

phonology: falling intonation

lexical entry for LA superstructure (Ch2 (37d))

syntax: nil
F/A: nil
E/R: [$_{LA}$ [$_{TYPE}$ #direct#] [$_{[AG, SO]}$ SP] [$_{[PT, GO]}$ AD] [$_{TH}$ SA] (MANNER)]
phonology: nil

Lexical Rules

Inversion Lexical Rule (Ch1 (14))

input lexical entry	output lexical entry
syntax: V[AUX, FIN] in [$_{VP}$ __, VP[α]] →	V[INV] in [$_{S[INV]}$ __, S[α]], where [$_{S[INV]}$ V[INV] ⩽ NP…]

Passive Lexical Rule for transitive verbs (Ch1 (88))

input: active lexical entry → output: passive lexical entry
syntax: V in [__, NP, ψ] → V[PAS] in [__, ψ]
F/A: Fφa → Fφ
E/R: TYPE in [$_{EV}$ __ AG PT χ] → TYPE in [$_{EV}$ __ <AG> PT χ]
morph: V[0] → V[1, PSP]

Pro-VP Form Lexical Rule (Ch5 (43))

input: lexical entry for auxiliary verb → output: lexical entry for corresponding pro-VP form

syntax: V[AUX, Ψ] in [__, XP] → syntax: V[AUX, Ψ, AD] in [__]
morph: Word → morph: Word

Definitions and Rules from Relevance Theory

definition of *relevance* (Ch2 (4)) (Wilson and Sperber 2012: 6, 63)

a. *Relevance* is a property of inputs to cognitive processes that makes them worth processing (whether external stimuli, which can be perceived and attended to, or internal representations, which can be stored, recalled, or used as premises in inference).
b. An input is *relevant* to an individual when it connects with available contextual assumptions to yield positive cognitive effects: for example, true contextual implications, or warranted strengthenings or revisions of existing assumptions.
c. Everything else being equal, the greater the positive cognitive effects achieved, and the smaller the mental effort required (to represent the input, access a context, and

derive these cognitive effects), the greater the *relevance* of the input to the individual at that time.

Cognitive Principle of Relevance (Ch2 (5)) (Wilson and Sperber 2012: 6, 38, 64, 103, 272)

Human cognition tends to be geared to the maximization of relevance.

Communicative Principle of Relevance (Ch2 (6)) (Wilson and Sperber 2012: 6, 38, 65, 104, 275)

Every act of ostensive-inferential communication (i.e., every utterance) by the speaker conveys to the hearer a presumption of its own optimal relevance.

definition of *presumption of optimal relevance* (Ch2 (7)) (cf. Wilson and Sperber 2012: 7, 65, 276)

a. The hearer presumes that the utterance directed to him is so relevant to him that he expects it to be worth processing.
b. The hearer presumes that the utterance directed to him is the most relevant one compatible with the speaker's abilities and preferences.

Relevance-guided comprehension heuristic (Ch2 (8), Ch8 (4)) (Wilson and Sperber 2012: 7, 276)

a. The hearer follows a path of least effort (in order of accessibility) in constructing interpretative hypotheses about the utterance (and in particular in resolving ambiguities and referential indeterminacies, in going beyond linguistic meaning, in supplying contextual assumptions, constructing implicatures, etc.).
b. The hearer stops constructing interpretive hypotheses when his expectations of relevance are satisfied.

definition of *development of decoded/inferred four-tuple representations of utterance* (Ch2 (9), Ch8 (5))

(cf. Sperber and Wilson 1995: 181, Wilson and Sperber 2012: 12)
The development of the decoded/inferred four-tuple (syntax, F/A, E/R, IS) of an utterance U is a process of constructing a semantically complete, truth-evaluable (i.e., fully propositional) interpretive hypothesis from the syntactically and semantically incomplete decoded/inferred four-tuple of U on the basis of the contextual assumptions, the information assessable from memory, the background knowledge shared by the speaker

and hearer, etc., through such inferential tasks as disambiguation, reference assignment, enrichment, and assumption schema embedding.

definition of *explicitness* (Ch2 (10)) (cf. Sperber and Wilson 1995: 182)

An interpretive hypothesis constructed by the hearer from an utterance U is *explicit* iff it is a development of the decoded linguistic four-tuple representations (syntax, F/A, E/R, IS) of U.

definition of *implicitness* (Ch2 (11)) (cf. Sperber and Wilson 1995: 182)

An interpretive hypothesis constructed by the hearer from an utterance U is *implicit* iff it is not explicit.

definition of *explicature* (Ch2 (12)) (cf. Sperber and Wilson 1995: 182, Wilson and Sperber 2012: 12)

An *explicature* of an utterance U is a fully propositional interpretive hypothesis (expressed in Mentalese) that is explicit (i.e., a development of the decoded four-tuple representations of U).

definition of *implicature* (Ch2 (13)) (cf. Sperber and Wilson 1995: 182, Wilson and Sperber 2012: 12)

An *implicature* of an utterance U is a fully propositional interpretive hypothesis (expressed in Mentalese) that is implicit (i.e., not a development of the decoded four-tuple representations of U).

definitions of *basic* and *higher-level explicatures* (Ch2 (14))

(cf. Carston 2002: 119, Wilson and Sperber 2012: 23, 153)
a. The *basic explicature* of an utterance U is the explicature of U that determines the explicit truth-conditional content of U. It is also called the proposition expressed.
b. The *higher-level explicatures* of U are those explicatures that the hearer constructs by embedding the basic explicature P into higher-level descriptions such as X (= the speaker of U) *says that P* and *X asks whether P* (speech-act descriptions), and *X believes that P*, *X regrets that P*, and *X is surprised that P* (propositional-attitude descriptions).

Utterance comprehension process (Ch2 (3), Ch3 (5a, b), Ch5 (11), (12), Ch6 (23a), Ch8 (3))

utterance (U) → $\boxed{\text{LM (AMG)}}$ → decoded four-tuple (syntax, F/A, E/R, IS) of U → $\boxed{\text{ICM}}$ → developed four-tuple of U → explicatures and implicatures of U (in Mentalese)

Elliptic utterance comprehension process (Ch8 (42))

elliptic utterance (U) → |LM (AMG)| → decoded four-tuple of U → |ICM| → inferred syntax of U → inferred four-tuple of U → developed four-tuple of U → explicatures and implicatures of U (in Mentalese)

Fragments

Fragment utterance comprehension process (Ch3 (5b), Ch8 (7))

fragment utterance (U) → |LM (AMG)| → decoded four-tuple of U → |ICM| → inferred four-tuple of U → developed four-tuple of U → explicatures and implicatures of U (in Mentalese)

Procedure for fragment comprehension (Ch3 (5c), Ch8 (11))

The hearer follows the Relevance-guided comprehension heuristic and executes the following steps.

(i) The LM computes the decoded four-tuple of a fragment utterance U and its skeletal four-tuple.
(ii) By non-demonstrative inference, the ICM constructs the inferred syntactic structure of U on the basis of the skeletal syntax obtained in (i) and the contextual information.
(iii) The ICM constructs the inferred four-tuple of U on the basis of the skeletal four-tuple obtained in (i), the inferred syntax obtained in (ii), and the contextual information.
(iv) The ICM develops the inferred four-tuple of U obtained in (iii) on the basis of the contextual information.
(v) The ICM constructs the explicatures and implicatures of U on the basis of the developed four-tuple obtained in (iv) and the contextual information.

skeletal four-tuple of NP fragment "A steak" (Ch3 (8b), Ch8 (13b))

skeletal four-tuple of embedded fragment "Bush imagines poached" (Ch3 (11))

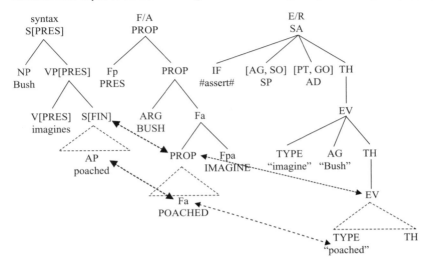

Sluicing

skeletal four-tuple of *wh*-fragment (Ch4 (11), Ch8 (16))

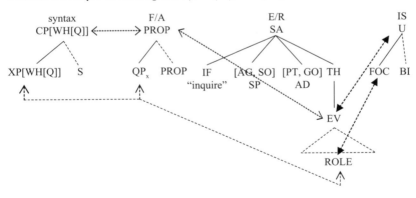

VP ellipsis

Procedure for pro-VP form comprehension (Ch5 (13), Ch8 (19))

The hearer follows the Relevance-guided comprehension heuristic and executes the following steps.

(i) The LM computes the decoded four-tuple of an utterance U that contains pro-VP forms.
(ii) By non-demonstrative inference, the ICM (iia) finds potential antecedents of the pro-VP forms in the linguistic and/or non-linguistic context and (iib) constructs the inferred syntactic structure of U that includes inferred VPs on the basis of the decoded syntax obtained in (i) and the contextual information.
(iii) The ICM constructs the inferred four-tuple of U on the basis of the decoded four-tuple obtained in (i), the inferred syntax obtained in (ii), and the contextual information.
(iv) The ICM develops the inferred four-tuple of U obtained in (iii) on the basis of the contextual information.
(v) The ICM constructs the explicatures and implicatures of U on the basis of the developed four-tuple obtained in (iv) and the contextual information.

Gapping

Procedure for gapping comprehension (Ch6 (24), Ch8 (25))

The hearer follows the Relevance-guided comprehension heuristic and executes the following steps.
(i) The LM computes the decoded four-tuple of the gapped conjunct.
(ii) By non-demonstrative inference, the ICM constructs the inferred syntactic structure of the gapped conjunct on the basis of the decoded syntax obtained in (i), the developed four-tuple of the first conjunct, and the contextual information.
(iii) The ICM constructs the inferred four-tuple of the gapped conjunct on the basis of its inferred syntax obtained in (ii), the developed four-tuple of the first conjunct, and the contextual information.
(iv) The ICM develops the inferred four-tuple of the gapped conjunct obtained in (iii) on the basis of the contextual information.
(v) The ICM constructs the explicatures and implicatures of the whole gapping construction on the basis of the developed four-tuple obtained in (iv) and the contextual information including the developed four-tuple of the first conjunct.

lexical entry for gapping construction (Ch6 (33), Ch8 (23))

The gapping construction is a coordinate structure of conjuncts with the syntactic category C, where C is clausal (<BAR, 2>, cf. Chapter 1 (2)) or VP (cf. 6.4).

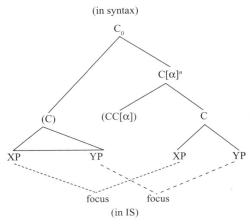

(i) Each gapped conjunct consists of two remnant phrases XP and YP.
(ii) The antecedent of the gapped conjuncts is the first conjunct if it is not gapped. Otherwise, it is in the prior discourse.
(iii) XP and YP in the antecedent must be major constituents.
(iv) The antecedent is the smallest CP[WH[Q]], S, or VP that dominates both XP and YP.
(v) XP and YP of the gapped conjuncts are contrastively focused with XP and YP in the antecedent, respectively.

Minimal Distance Principle (MDP) (Ch6 (81), Ch8 (29))

The most accessible association in (33) of XP and YP of the gapped conjunct with XP and YP of the first conjunct is when XP and YP of the first conjunct are its rightmost phrases.

Semantic Relatedness Principle (SRP) (Ch6 (90), Ch8 (30))

The most accessible association in (33) of XP and YP of the gapped conjunct with XP and YP of the first conjunct is when XP of the first conjunct is s-related to its YP.

definition of *semantic relatedness* (*s-relatedness*) (Ch6 (91), Ch8 (31))

Of two phrases XP and YP of a sentence, XP is s-related to YP if and only if
(i) The F/A correspondent of XP is PROP-mates with the F/A correspondent of YP, or
(ii) The F/A correspondent of XP is coreferential with an ARG that is PROP-mates with the F/A correspondent of YP.

/ APPENDIX 415

lexical entry for stripping construction (Ch6 (119), Ch8 (33))

(in syntax)

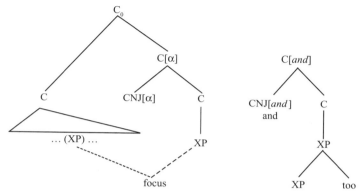

in syntax

(i) C_0 is a nonce coordinate structure of the syntactic category C with a coordinate conjunction (CNJ) $\alpha \in \{and, or, but\}$.
(ii) The left conjunct C is the smallest CP[WH[Q]], S, or VP that contains XP.
(iii) The right conjunct consists of a single constituent XP.
(iv) XP of the first conjunct, if present, is a major constituent.

in Information Structure

(v) XP of the left conjunct and XP of the right conjunct are contrastively focused.
(vi) XP of the right conjunct is often added as an afterthought.

Procedure for stripping comprehension (Ch6 (120), Ch8 (34))

The hearer follows the Relevance-guided comprehension heuristic and executes the following steps.

(i) The LM computes the decoded four-tuple of the stripped conjunct.
(ii) By non-demonstrative inference, the ICM constructs the inferred syntactic structure of the stripped conjunct on the basis of the decoded syntax of the stripped conjunct

obtained in (i), the developed four-tuple of the first conjunct, and the contextual information.
(iii) The ICM constructs the inferred four-tuple of the stripped conjunct on the basis of the inferred syntax obtained in (ii), the developed four-tuple of the first conjunct, and the contextual information.
(iv) The ICM develops the inferred four-tuple of the stripped conjunct obtained in (iii) on the basis of the contextual information.
(v) The ICM constructs the explicatures and implicatures of the whole stripping construction on the basis of the developed four-tuple obtained in (iv) and the contextual information including the developed four-tuple of the first conjunct.

Right Node Raising (RNR)

lexical entry for RNR construction (Ch7 (22), Ch8 (35))

syntax

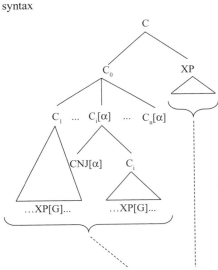

(i) The raised constituent XP can be a clause.
(ii) XP is adjoined to the coordinate structure C_0.
(iii) XP[G] is at or near the end of each conjunct.
(iv) CNJ[α] is a coordinating conjunction with its form feature value α, where α ∈ {*and, or, but*}.

Information Structure [$_U$ *rest* ≺ new/focused]

APPENDIX 417

lexical entry for extended RNR construction (Ch7 (31))

syntax

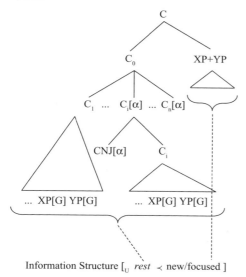

(i) the sequence XP+YP is the last two phrases of each conjunct.
(ii) CNJ[α] is a coordinating conjunction.

Information Structure [$_U$ *rest* ≺ new/focused]

lexical entry for extended RNR construction (second type) (Ch7 (35))

syntax

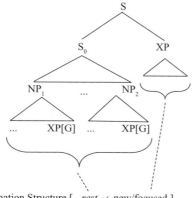

(i) XP[G] is at or near the end of each NP.
(ii) The F/A correspondent of NP_1 c-commands the F/A correspondent of NP_2.

Information Structure [$_U$ *rest* ≺ new/focused]

Procedure for RNR comprehension (Ch7 (40), Ch8 (36))

The hearer follows the Relevance-guided comprehension heuristic and executes the following steps.
 (i) The LM computes the decoded four-tuple of an utterance U of the RNR construction (i.e., its gapped conjuncts and raised constituent).
 (ii) By non-demonstrative inference, the ICM constructs the inferred syntactic structure of U by filling the gaps with a copy of the raised constituent on the basis of the decoded syntax obtained in (i) and the contextual information.
 (iii) The ICM constructs the inferred four-tuple of U on the basis of the inferred syntax obtained in (ii) and the contextual information.
 (iv) The ICM develops the inferred four-tuple of U obtained in (iii) on the basis of the contextual information.
 (v) The ICM constructs the explicatures and implicatures of U on the basis of the developed four-tuple obtained in (iv) and the contextual information.

References

Abbott, Barbara. 1976. Right Node Raising as a test for constituenthood. *Linguistic Inquiry* 4: 639–642.
Akmajian, Adrian and Tom Wasow. 1975. The constituent structure of VP and AUX and the position of the verb *be*. *Linguistic Analysis* 1: 205–245.
Anderson, John R. 2010. *Cognitive Psychology and Its Implications*. Seventh edition. Worth Publishers.
安西祐一郎 (Anzai, Yuichiro). 2011. 『心と脳 (*Mind and Brain*)』岩波書店 (Iwanami).
Baltin, Mark. 1995. Floating quantifiers, PRO, and predication. *Linguistic Inquiry* 26: 199–248.
Bloom, Paul. 2002. *How Children Learn the Meanings of Words*. MIT Press.
Borsley, Robert. 1999. *Syntactic Theory: A Unified Approach*. Second edition. Arnold.
Bresnan, Joan. 1971. A note on the notion of "identity of sense anaphora." *Linguistic Inquiry* 2: 589–597.
Bresnan, Joan. 1974. The position of certain clause particles in phrase structure. *Linguistic Inquiry* 5: 614–619.
Bresnan, Joan. 1976. On the form and functioning of transformations. *Linguistic Inquiry* 7: 3–40.
Carston, Robyn. 2002. *Thoughts and Utterances*. Blackwell.
Chae, Hee-Rahk. 1991. Right node raising and a licensor feature. *CLS* 27/1: 46–59.
Chomsky, Noam. 1995. *The Minimalist Program*. MIT Press.
Chung, Sandra, William A. Ladusaw and James McClosky. 1995. Sluicing and logical form. *Natural Language Semantics* 3: 239–282.
Clark, Billy. 2013. *Relevance Theory*. Cambridge University Press.
Collins, Allan M. and Elizabeth F. Loftus (1975) A spreading-activation theory of semantic processing. *Psychological Review* 82: 407–428.
Cruse, Alan. 2011. *Meaning in Language*. Third edition. Oxford University Press.
Culicover, Peter W. 2009. *Natural Language Syntax*. Oxford University Press.
Culicover, Peter W. and Ray Jackendoff. 2005. *Simpler Syntax*. Oxford University Press.
Culicover, Peter W. and Michael S. Rochemont. 1990. Extraposition and the complement principle. *Linguistic Inquiry* 21: 23–47. MIT Press.
de Chene, Brent. 1995. Complementizer-trace effects and the ECP. *Geneva Generative Papers* 3: 1–4.
Durrell, Martin. 2011. *Hammer's German Grammar and Usage*. Fifth edition. Hodder Education.
Evans, Gareth. 1980. Pronouns. *Linguistic Inquiry* 11: 337–362.

Eysenck, Michael W. and Mark T. Keane. 2010. *Cognitive Psychology*. Sixth edition. Psychology Press.
Fiengo, Robert and Robert May. 1994. *Indices and Identity*. MIT Press.
Fillmore, Charles. 1986. Pragmatically controlled zero anaphora. *BLS* 12: 95–107.
Fillmore, Charles, Paul Kay, and Mary Catherine O'Connor. 1988. Regularity and idiomaticity in grammatical constructions: The case of *let alone*. *Language* 64: 501–538.
Fodor, Jerry A. 1983. *The Modularity of Mind*. MIT Press.
Gazdar, Gerald, Ewan Klein, Geoffrey Pullum, and Ivan Sag. 1985. *Generalized Phrase Structure Grammar*. Blackwell.
Goffman, Erving. 1981. *Forms of Talk*. University of Pennsylvania Press.
Gray, Peter. 2011. *Psychology*. Sixth edition. Worth Publishers.
Grinder, John. 1970. Super equi NP deletion. *CLS* 6: 297–317.
Grinder, John and Paul M. Postal. 1971. Missing antecedents. *Linguistic Inquiry* 2: 269–312.
Grosu, Alexander. 1976. A note on Subject Raising to Object and Right Node Raising. *Linguistic Inquiry* 4: 642–645.
Grosu, Alexander. 1981. *Approaches to Island Phenomena*. North-Holland.
Grosu, Alexander. 1985. Subcategorization and parallelism. *Theoretical Linguistics* 12: 231–239.
Grosu, Alexander. 1987. On acceptable violations of parallelism constraints. In Dirven, R and V. Fried (eds), *Functionalism in Linguistics*, John Benjamins, pp. 425–457.
箱田裕司・都築誉史・川畑秀明・萩原滋 (Hakoda, Yuji et al.) 2010. 『認知心理学 (*Cognitive Psychology*)』有斐閣 (Yuhikaku).
Hankamer, Jorge. 1973. Unacceptable ambiguity. *Linguistic Inquiry* 4:17–68.
Hankamer, Jorge. 1979. *Deletion in Coordinate Structures*. Garland. (PhD dissertation, Yale University, 1971.)
Hankamer, Jorge and Ivan Sag. 1976. Deep and surface anaphora. *Linguistic Inquiry*: 391–428.
Hardt, Daniel. 1993. *Verb Phrase Ellipsis: Form, Meaning and Processing*. PhD dissertation, University of Pennsylvania.
Hardt, Daniel. 1999. Dynamic interpretation of verb phrase ellipsis. *Linguistics and Philosophy* 22: 185–291.
波多野誼余夫(Hatano, Giyoo). 1987. 「ナイーヴな認知科学者の視点から (From a naïve cognitive scientist's point of view)」大津由紀夫編 (Otsu, Yukio ed.)『ことばからみた心 (Mind viewed from language)』東京大学出版会 (University of Tokyo Press), pp. 191–203.
Hawkins, Roger and Richard Towell. 2010. *French Grammar and Usage*. Third edition. Hodder Education.
Horn, Laurence R. 1981. A pragmatic approach to certain ambiguities. *Linguistics and Philosophy* 4: 321–358.
Horn, Laurence R. and Gregory Ward. (eds.) 2004. *The Handbook of Pragmatics*. Blackwell.

Hornstein, Norbert. 1984. *Logic as Grammar*. MIT Press.
Hornstein, Norbert. 1995. *Logical Form*. Blackwell.
Huddleston, Rodney and Geoffrey K. Pullum. 2002. *The Cambridge Grammar of the English Language*. Cambridge University Press.
Huddleston, Rodney and Geoffrey K. Pullum. 2005. *A Student's Introduction to English Grammar*. Cambridge University Press.
Hudson, Richard A. 1976. Conjunction reduction, gapping and right-node raising. *Language* 52: 535–562.
Hudson, Richard A. 1982. Incomplete conjuncts. *Linguistic Inquiry* 13: 547–550.
Hudson, Richard A. 1989. Gapping and grammatical relations. *Journal of Linguistics* 25: 57–94.
今西典子 (Imanishi, Noriko) and 浅野一郎 (Asano, Ichiro). 1990. 『照応と削除 (*Anaphora and Deletion*)』大修館 (Taishukan).
Jackendoff, Ray. 1971. Gapping and related rules. *Linguistic Inquiry* 2: 21–36.
Jackendoff, Ray. 1972. *Semantic Interpretation in Generative Grammar*. MIT Press.
Jackendoff, Ray. 1977. *X̄ Syntax: A Study of Phrase Structure*. MIT Press.
Jackendoff, Ray. 2002. *Foundations of Language*. Oxford University Press.
Jackendoff, Ray. 2010. *Meaning and the Lexicon*. Oxford University Press.
Jacobson, Paul and P. Neubauer. 1976. Rule cyclicity. *Linguistic Inquiry* 7: 429–62.
Johnson, Kyle. 2001. What VP ellipsis can do, and what it can't, but not why. In Mark Baltin and Chris Collins eds, *The Handbook of Contemporary Syntactic Theory*, Blackwell, pp. 439–479.
梶田優(Kajita, Masaru). 1974. 「変形文法 (Transformational Grammar)」In 太田朗 (Ota, Akira) and 梶田優 (Masaru Kajita),『文法論 (Grammatical Theory) II』大修館 (Taishukan).
鹿取廣人・杉本敏夫・鳥居修晃 (Katori, Hiroto et al.) 2011.『心理学 (*Psychology*)』Fourth edition. 東京大学 出版会 (University of Tokyo Press).
Kiparsky, Paul and Carol Kiparsky. 1971. Fact. In Danny D. Steinberg and Leon A. Jakobovits (eds.), *Semantics*, Cambridge University Press, pp. 345–369.
Klima, Edward S. 1964. Negation in English. In Fodor, Jerry A. and Jerrold J. Katz, (eds.), *The Structure of Language: Readings in the Philosophy of Language*, Prentice-Hall, pp. 246–323.
Kuno, Susumu. 1976. Gapping: a functional analysis. *Linguistic Inquiry* 7: 300–318.
Kuno, Susumu. 1987. *Functional Syntax*. University of Chicago Press.
久野暲 (Kuno, Susumu) and 高見健一 (Takami, Ken-ich). 2007.『英語の構文とその意味 (*Constructions and their Meanings in English*)』開拓社 (Kaitakusha).
Landau, Idan. 2000. *Elements of Control*. Kluwer.
Levin, Nancy S. 1986. *Main-Verb Ellipsis in Spoken English*. Garland.
Marantz, Alec. 1984. *On the Nature of Grammatical Relations*. MIT Press.
May, Robert. 1985. *Logical Form*. MIT Press.
McCawley, James D. 1973. *Grammar and Meaning*. Taishukan.
McCawley, James D. 1982. Parentheticals and discontinuous constituent structure. *Linguistic Inquiry* 13: 91–106.

McCawley, James D. 1983. What's with *with*? *Language* 59: 271–287.
McCawley, James D. 1984. Anaphora and notions of command. *BLS* 10: 220–232.
McCawley, James D. 1985. What price the performative hypothesis? *University of Chicago Working Papers in Linguistics* 1: 43–64.
McCawley, James D. 1993a. *Everything that Linguists Have Always Wanted to Know about Logic* *but Were Ashamed to Ask*. Second edition. University of Chicago Press.
McCawley, James D. 1993b. Gapping with shared operators. *BLS* 10: 245–253.
McCawley, James D. 1998. *The Syntactic Phenomena of English*. Second edition. University of Chicago Press.
McCawley, James D. 1999. Participant roles, frames, and speech acts. *Linguistics and Philosophy* 22: 595–616.
Merchant, Jason. 2001. *The Syntax of Silence*. Oxford University Press.
Merchant, Jason. 2004. Fragments and ellipsis. *Linguistics and Philosophy* 27: 661–738.
道又爾・北﨑充晃・大久保街亜・今井久登・山川恵子・黒沢学 (Michimata, Chikashi et al.) 2011. 『認知心理学 (*Cognitive Psychology*)』Second edition. 有斐閣 (Yuhikaku).
Morgan, Jerry. 1973. Sentence fragments and the notion of "sentence". In Kachru, Braj, et al. (eds.) 1973. *Issues on Linguistics: Papers in Honor of Henry and Renée Kahane*, University of Illinois Press, pp. 719–751.
Napoli, Donna Jo. 1985. Verb phrase deletion in English: a base-generated analysis. *Journal of Linguistics* 21: 281–319.
Neijt, Anneke. 1979. *Gapping: A contribution to sentence grammar*. Foris.
Nunberg, Geoffrey, Ivan. A. Sag, and Thomas Wasow. 1994. Idioms. *Language* 70: 491–538.
Pollard, Carl and Ivan A. Sag. 1994. *Head-Driven Phrase Structure Grammar*. CSLI.
Postal, Paul M. 1974. *On Raising*. MIT Press.
Postal, Paul M. 1998. *Three Investigations of Extraction*. MIT Press.
Quirk, Randolph, Sidney Greenbaum, Geoffrey Leech, and Jan Svartvik. 1972. *A Grammar of Contemporary English*. Longman.
Quirk, Randolph, Sidney Greenbaum, Geoffrey Leech, and Jan Svartvik. 1985. *A Comprehensive Grammar of the English Language*. Longman.
Reinhart, Tanya. 1983. *Anaphora and Semantic Interpretation*. University of Chicago Press.
Rosen, Carol. 1976. Guess what about? *NELS* 6: 205–211.
Rosenbaum, Peter S. 1967. *The Grammar of English Predicate Complement Constructions*. MIT Press.
Ross, John Robert. 1967/1986. *Infinite Syntax!* (published version of his 1967 MIT dissertation *Constraints on variables in syntax*) Ablex Publishing.
Ross, John Robert. 1969. Guess who. *CLS* 5: 252–286. Reprinted in Jason Merchant and Andrew Simpson (eds.), *Sluicing: Cross-Linguistic Perspectives*, Oxford University Press, 2012, pp. 14–39.
Ross, John Robert. 1970. Gapping and the order of constituents. In M. Bierwisch and K. E. Heidolph (eds.), *Progress in Linguistics*, Mouton, pp. 249–259.

Sadock, Jerrold M. 1974. *Toward a Linguistic Theory of Speech Acts*. Academic Press.
Sadock, Jerrold M. 1984. The polyredundant lexicon. *CLS* 20, *Parasession*, pp. 250–269.
Sadock, Jerrold M. 1991. *Autolexical Syntax*. University of Chicago Press.
Sadock, Jerrold M. 1996. The lexicon as bridge between phrase structure components. In J. Rooryck and L. Zaring (eds.), *Phrase Structure and the Lexicon*, Kluwer, pp. 173–185.
Sadock, Jerrold M. 2012. *The Modular Architecture of Grammar*. Cambridge University Press.
Sag, Ivan Andrew. 1976. *Deletion and Logical Form*. Reproduced by the Indiana University Linguistics Club, 1977.
Sag, Ivan A., Gerald Gazdar, Thomas Wasow, and Steven Weisler. 1985. Coordination and how to distinguish categories. *Natural Language and Linguistic Theory* 3:117–171.
Sag, Ivan A., Thomas Wasow, Emily M. Bender. 2003. *Syntactic Theory*. Second edition. CSLI.
Schachter, Paul. 1977. Does she or doesn't she? *Linguistic Inquiry* 8: 763–767.
Schachter, Paul. 1978. English propredicates. *Linguistic Analysis* 4: 187–224.
Schachter, Paul and Susan Mordechay. 1983. A phrase structure account of "non-constituent" conjunctions. *WCCFL* 2: 260–274.
Schank, Roger and Robert Abelson. 1977. *Scripts, plans, goals, and understanding*. Lawrence Erlbaum.
Sells, Peter. 1985. *Lectures on Contemporary Syntactic Theories*. CSLI.
Sobin, Nicholas. 1981. On ADV/PP-first reduction. *Linguistic Inquiry* 12: 488–491.
Sperber, Dan and Deirdre Wilson. 1995. *Relevance*. Second edition. Blackwell.
Stainton, Robert, J. 2004. The pragmatics of non-sentences. In Laurence R. Horn and Gregory Ward (eds.), *The Handbook of Pragmatics*, Blackwell, pp. 266–287.
Tomasello, Michael. 2003. *Constructing a Language*. Harvard University Press.
上野義雄 (Ueno, Yoshio). 1997.「Antecedent-Contained Deletion 構文を巡る諸問題 (Issues on the antecedent-contained deletion construction)」『大妻レヴュー (*Otsuma Review*)』30: 99–121.
Ueno, Yoshio. 2005. A Note on the Structure of Predicate Phrase + *be* + *that*-CP, *Linguistic Inquiry* 36: 155–160, MIT Press.
Ueno, Yoshio. 2014. *An Automodular View of English Grammar*. Waseda University Press.
Webber, Bonnie. 1978. *A Formal Approach to Discourse Anaphora*. PhD dissertation, Harvard University.
Wilson, Deirdre and Dan Sperber. 2002. Relevance theory. In Horn and Ward (eds.), pp. 607–32.
Wilson, Deirdre and Dan Sperber. 2012. *Meaning and Relevance*. Cambridge University Press.
山梨正明 (Yamanashi, Masaaki). 1992.『推論と照応 (*Inference and Anaphora*)』くろしお出版 (Kuroshio).
Zwicky, Arnold M. 1981. Stranded *to* and phonological phrasing. *Linguistics* 20: 3–58.
Zwicky, Arnold M. and Jerrold M. Sadock. 1975. Ambiguity tests and how to fail them. In John P. Kimball (ed.), *Syntax and Semantics* 4, Academic Press, pp. 1–36.

Index

a (indefinite article) 20, 22, 23[entry], 368
a certain 170, 182, 183
agreement
　subject-verb agreement 8, 14, 145, 357
anaphoric device (AD) 54, 122, 124, 200, 219, 220, 224, 383
Antecedent Contained Deletion (ACD) 243, 386
Automodular Grammar (AMG) 1, 5, 63

Bach-Peters sentence 220, 222, 386
baby (common noun) 19[entry]
bathe 164, 165[entry], 166
be (progressive) 227[entry]
　be (pro-VP form) 227[entry]
believe (object raising verb) 39, 40, 51, 52[entry], 303

careful (attributive and predicative adjective) 15[entry]
clause-initial *wh*-phrase 55, 56[entry], 57, 138, 219
coercion 42, 81
　coerced material 40, 80, 81
command
　c-command 18, 13[def], 28, 29, 35,
　asymmetric c-command 13[def]
　c-command in F/A 24[def]
　S-command 23[def]
　x-command 13[def]
Complex NP Constraint (CNPC) (→ island)
comprehension process
　ellipsis comprehension process 4, 376

elliptic utterance comprehension process 396
　fragment utterance comprehension process 376
　utterance comprehension process 64, 96, 201, 275, 374
COMP-trace effect (→ *that*-trace effect) 179
Conjunct Constraint (→ island)
control 44
　controlled VP 46, 114, 367
　controllee 44
　controller 44
　free control 45
　object control 44, 51, 314, 367
　subject control 39, 44, 52, 123, 258, 314, 367
　unique control verb 44, 316
Coordinate Structure Constraint (CSC) (→ island)
coordinating connective (CC) 282, 300
coreference relation 17
count on 333[entry], 357

declaratives 81[entry], 87
default
　default correspondences 29
　default linear order 59
de Morgan laws 280, 388
depend on 298[entry]
dependency
　referential dependency 223
　semantic dependency 223

unbounded dependencies 54, 127, 168, 219
de re and *de dicto* 302
development of decoded four-tuple 65[def]
didn't 231[entry]
  didn't (pro-VP form) 231[entry]
discontinuous structure 351
ditransitive construction 33[entry], 162, 287, 348
does (dummy) 224[entry]
  does (pro-VP form) 224[entry]
dominance path conditions 56, 139, 156, 168
dominate 13[def]
  directly dominate 12[def]
do so 132, 236, 238[entry], 246, 338,
drink 129[entry], 161
drunk (predicative adjective) 15[entry]
drunken (attributive adjective) 15[entry]

economy of language use 199, 206, 399[def]
Element Constraint (→ island)
empathy 256, 309, 310, 311, 312
enrichment 62
entailment 181, 210, 211, 221, 242
Event Hierarchy 26
Event Role (E/R) Structure 24
  PS rules for E/R module 25
  well-formed E/R structure 25[def]
every 21[entry]
Exceptional Case Marking (ECM) 39
explain 25[entry]
explicature 66[def]
  basic explicature 67[def]
  higher-level explicature 67[def]

factive verb 32, 43
feature
  agreement (AGR) feature 8, 9, 17, 237, 364
  BAR feature 6, 7
  feature co-occurrence restriction (FCR) for inversion 11
  Feature Osmosis 17, 237, 255
  form feature 7, 283
  head feature 7
  Head Feature Convention (HFC) 7, 32, 230
  index (IND) feature 17, 237
  part-of-speech (POSP) feature 6
  unary feature 6
focus (FOC) 31, 32, 72, 73, 78, 97, 98, 113, 142, 147, 282
  contrastive tocus 289, 308
  focus of negation 111, 334, 335
for (complementizer) 10[entry]
four-tuple
  decoded four-tuple 63, 64, 66, 67, 68
  inferred four-tuple 72, 73, 95, 96, 97
  skeletal four-tuple 72, 73, 74, 78, 96, 97, 98
fragment 2, 63, 70
  answer fragment 93, 94, 95
  clarification fragment 93, 94
  discourse-initial fragment 93, 94
  exclamative *wh*-fragment 144
  fragment utterance comprehension process 376
  idiom chunk fragment 75, 107, 379
  procedure for fragment comprehension 96, 143, 201, 361, 378
  quantifier fragment 120
  wh-fragment 74, 141, 145, 147, 149
fürchten (reflexive verb) 298[entry]
Function Argument (F/A) Structure 14
  PS rules for F/A module 14
  well-formed F/A structure 16[def]
functor 14
  type-identity functor 19, 20, 23[entry]
fusion (transformation) 348, 351

gapping 77, 104, 265
  gapping construction 282[entry]

procedure for gapping comprehension 276, 299, 301, 321, 324
pseudo-gapping 241
S-level gapping 294, 295, 300, 320
VP-level gapping 288, 293, 294, 295, 296, 300, 320
give 28[entry]

hasn't 230[entry]
  hasn't (pro-VP form) 230[entry]
have (perfect auxiliary) 227[entry]
Heavy Constituent Shift (HCS) 335, 342, 345, 351, 355
how 185[entry]

idiom chunk 75, 102, 107, 273, 333, 334
idiomatically combining expression (ICE) 53, 204
illocutionary force (IF) 56, 67, 79, 80, 83, 86, 89, 148, 317, 357
imperatives 82[entry]
implicature 64, 66[def], 67, 89
inferential ability 2, 62, 63
Inferential Comprehension Module (ICM) 4, 63, 64, 87, 95, 107, 122, 133, 143, 152, 169
information
  background information (BI) 31, 43, 72, 98, 147
  foreground information (FI) 31, 43, 113, 154
  Information Structure (IS) 17, 31, 104, 113, 142
island 58
  adjunct island 178, 271
  anaphoric island 240
  Complex NP Constraint (CNPC) 58, 125, 127, 153, 167, 168, 169, 245, 270
  Conjunct Constraint 171
  Coordinate Structure Constraint (CSC) 126, 127, 171, 172, 266, 270, 348, 361

  Element Constraint 172, 173
  island insensitivity 125, 166, 169
  Left Branch Constraint (LBC) 156, 183
  Sentential Subject Constraint (SSC) 178
  Subject Condition 127, 175
  weak (selective) island 180
  wh-island 271
isn't 231[entry]
  isn't (pro-VP form) 231[entry]

kick 50[entry]

language acquisition 1, 2, 33, 34, 45, 63, 133, 134
Language Module (LM) 3, 4, 63, 64, 87, 95, 107, 122, 133, 152, 201
LA superstructure 78, 84[entry], 317
Left Branch Constraint (LBC) (→ island)
lexical item 1, 9, 32, 45
lexical rule 12
  Intransitivization Lexical Rule 129
  Inversion Lexical Rule 11
  Passive Lexical Rule for transitive verbs 49
  Pro-VP Form Lexical Rule 224

Mainstream Generative Grammar (MGG) 3, 222
major constituent 266[def]
march 165[entry]
mates
  PROP-mates 314[def]
  S-mates 13[def]
Minimal Distance Principle (in control) 45
  Minimal Distance Principle (MDP) (in gapping) 307
mismatch 17, 35, 38, 40
  innocuous mismatch 17, 18, 36, 37, 38, 40, 42, 43, 46
Missing Antecedent Phenomenon 234, 272, 334

natural extension (of a lexical entry) 163[def], 180, 339
non-adjoined node 13[def]
non-demonstrative inference 2, 3, 63, 64[def], 87, 88, 90, 91, 92, 95, 96, 99, 100, 101, 104, 107, 108, 122, 133, 134, 142, 143, 147, 152, 161, 169, 198, 201, 209, 243, 271, 331, 362
non-factive 43
not 229[entry]
   not (pro-XP form) 229[entry]

object
   in F/A 15
   in syntax 6
   object raising verb 40[entry]
only (focus particle) 101
operator sharing 280, 319
order (object control verb) 44[entry]
outrank 28[def]
   outrank condition (on NPs) 124, 223

parallelism constraint 327
parasitic gap 351
parenthetical 102, 109, 111, 284, 300, 328, 352
passivization 47, 51, 52, 353
performative verb (PV) 78, 81, 86, 87, 89
perjure 332[entry]
preposition (P)
   P-dropping property 137, 139
   P-repeating property 135, 136, 137, 138, 139, 298
   preposition language 134, 135, 138, 139
   preposition pied-piping 134, 135, 138, 139
   preposition stranding 130, 134, 135, 137, 138, 139, 349
present tense (PRES) 35[entry]
   nonfinite PRES 41[entry]
presumption of optimal relevance 65[def]
priming 189, 299

promise (subject control verb) 44[entry]
pro-VP form 2, 169, 195, 197, 216, 224, 252,
   procedure for pro-VP form comprehension 202, 384
psychological reality 121, 147, 372
pull strings 53[entry]
pull X's leg 76[entry]

quantifier 20
   polyadic quantifier 325, 369
   quantified NP (QNP) 120, 180, 181, 188, 193, 222, 239, 252, 303, 324, 364
   quantifier phrase (QP) 20
   well-formedness conditions on QPs 20
question
   existential presupposition of *wh*-question 94, 99, 193, 194
   multiple *wh*-question 57, 159, 277, 300, 316
   quiz question 57, 127
   wh-question 54, 139, 193

raising
   object raising 39, 40, 42, 51,
   Raising Principle 43
   subject raising 17, 34, 35, 42
read 164[entry]
ready 258[entry]
reconstruction 222
redundancy 33, 34
reference transfer 299
relevance 64[def]
   Cognitive Principle of Relevance 65[def]
   Communicative Principle of Relevance 65[def]
   Relevance-guided comprehension heuristic 65[def]
respectively 102, 350, 361
restrictive relative clause (RRC) 5, 6, 326
RHO (controllee) 46[entry]
Right Node Raising (RNR) 304, 305, 341

Procedure for RNR comprehension 362
RNR construction 351, 356[entry], 359[entry]
role 24
  associable role 48
  highest associable role (HAR) 44, 50, 123
  Role Hierarchy 28
  role sharing 169, 304
  unassociable role 48, 128, 129, 162, 163

script 62, 69, 70, 109, 152
seem (subject raising verb) 38[entry]
selectional restriction 129, 130, 299, 303, 304
semantic relatedness (s-relatedness) 313[def]
  Semantic Relatedness Principle (SRP) 313
Sentential Subject Constraint (SSC) (→ island)
set-membership 23[entry]
sloppy identity 199, 200, 211, 241, 242, 243, 255, 262
sluicing (→ *wh*-fragment) 141
sneeze 9[entry]
speech act (SA) 55, 79, 80, 83, 86, 88, 89
  gapping and speech acts 317
  indirect speech act 80, 89
  separate speech act 111, 284, 300, 328
  speech act (SA) superstructure 80[entry]
split antecedents 206, 217, 218, 236, 343, 360
spreading activation 128, 161, 214, 215, 228
sprouting 128, 130, 136, 137, 161, 162, 164, 166, 167
strict identity 200, 211, 242, 243, 255, 256, 257, 262, 263
stripping 3, 77, 206, 300, 327
  procedure for stripping comprehension 331
  stripping construction 330[entry]

subject
  in F/A 15
  in syntax 6
Subject Condition (→ island)
syntax 5
  inferred syntax 95, 117
  PS rules for syntax module 5
  syntax inferred by direct reference 117, 153
  syntax inferred from global domain 117
  syntax inferred from local domain 117
  syntax module 3, 5, 195
  well-formed syntactic structure 14[def]

take 9[entry]
tend (subject raising verb) 115[entry]
tense 14, 17, 18, 35
  habitual present tense (h-PRES) 85, 87
  instantaneous present tense (i-PRES) 78, 81, 85
  present tense (PRES) 35[entry]
that (complementizer) 10[entry]
  that-trace effect 271, 347, 360, 361
the (definite article) 23[entry]
tier
  action tier 26, 27, 28
  thematic tier 26, 27, 28
  two-tiered roles 26, 27
to 10[entry], 228[entry]
  to (pro-VP form) 228[entry]
transitive construction 33[entry]
try (subject control) 124[entry]
type-identity Faa functor 23[entry]

vehicle change 204, 211, 253, 254, 255, 274, 275
VP ellipsis (→ pro-VP form) 195

want 115[entry]
working memory 293, 298, 299, 332

yes/no interrogatives 82[entry]

著者紹介

上野 義雄（うえの　よしお）

Ph.D.（言語学；シカゴ大学）
福島県立喜多方高等学校卒業
早稲田大学理工学部数学科卒業
早稲田大学大学院文学研究科修士課程修了
シカゴ大学大学院言語学科博士課程修了（フルブライト奨学生）
シカゴ大学大学院言語学科客員研究員
現在、早稲田大学理工学術院英語教育センター教授

著書　*An Automodular View of English Grammar*（早稲田大学学術叢書 35）
　　　早稲田大学出版部
論文　"A note on the structure of predicate phrase + *be* + *that*-CP" *Linguistic Inquiry* 36: 155-160, MIT Press など
辞書　大修館『ジーニアス英和大辞典』校閲、『ジーニアス英和辞典　第 4 版』、
　　　三省堂『英語語義語源辞典』などの執筆

早稲田大学学術叢書 42

An Automodular View of Ellipsis

2015 年 5 月 30 日　　初版第 1 刷発行

著　者 ……………… 上 野　義 雄
発行者 ……………… 島 田　陽 一
発行所 ……………… 株式会社　早稲田大学出版部
　　　　　　　　　　169-0051 東京都新宿区西早稲田 1-9-12
　　　　　　　　　　電話 03-3203-1551　　http://www.waseda-up.co.jp/
校正協力・DTP ……… Cactus Communications K. K.
装　丁 ……………… 笠 井　亞 子
印刷・製本 ………… 株式会社　平文社

Ⓒ 2015, Yoshio Ueno. Printed in Japan　　ISBN978-4-657-15706-5
無断転載を禁じます。落丁・乱丁本はお取替えいたします。

刊行のことば

　早稲田大学は、2007年、創立125周年を迎えた。創立者である大隈重信が唱えた「人生125歳」の節目に当たるこの年をもって、早稲田大学は「早稲田第2世紀」、すなわち次の125年に向けて新たなスタートを切ったのである。それは、研究・教育いずれの面においても、日本の「早稲田」から世界の「WASEDA」への強い志向を持つものである。特に「研究の早稲田」を発信するために、出版活動の重要性に改めて注目することとなった。

　出版とは人間の叡智と情操の結実を世界に広め、また後世に残す事業である。大学は、研究活動とその教授を通して社会に寄与することを使命としてきた。したがって、大学の行う出版事業とは大学の存在意義の表出であるといっても過言ではない。そこで早稲田大学では、「早稲田大学モノグラフ」、「早稲田大学学術叢書」の2種類の学術研究書シリーズを刊行し、研究の成果を広く世に問うこととした。

　このうち、「早稲田大学学術叢書」は、研究成果の公開を目的としながらも、学術研究書としての質の高さを担保するために厳しい審査を行い、採択されたもののみを刊行するものである。

　近年の学問の進歩はその速度を速め、専門領域が狭く囲い込まれる傾向にある。専門性の深化に意義があることは言うまでもないが、一方で、時代を画するような研究成果が出現するのは、複数の学問領域の研究成果や手法が横断的にかつ有機的に手を組んだときであろう。こうした意味においても質の高い学術研究書を世に送り出すことは、総合大学である早稲田大学に課せられた大きな使命である。

　「早稲田大学学術叢書」が、わが国のみならず、世界においても学問の発展に大きく貢献するものとなることを願ってやまない。

2008年10月

早稲田大学

「研究の早稲田」 早稲田大学学術叢書シリーズ

濱川 栄 著 **中国古代の社会と黄河** ¥5,500	五十嵐 誠一 著 **民主化と市民社会の新地平** フィリピン政治のダイナミズム ¥8,600
真辺 将之 著 **東京専門学校の研究** 「学問の独立」の具体相と「早稲田憲法草案」 ¥5,400	内田 悦生 著　下田 一太（コラム執筆） **石が語るアンコール遺跡** 岩石学からみた世界遺産 ¥6,100
中垣 啓 著 **命題的推論の理論** 論理的推論の一般理論に向けて ¥6,800	青木 雅浩 著 **モンゴル近現代史研究** **：1921～1924年** 外モンゴルとソヴィエト，コミンテルン　¥8,200
堀 真清 著 **一亡命者の記録** 池明観のこと ¥4,600	飯山 知保 著 **金元時代の華北社会と科挙制度** もう一つの「士人層」 ¥8,900
藤井 千春 著 **ジョン・デューイの経験主義哲学における思考論** 知性的な思考の構造的解明　¥5,800	上野 和昭 著 **平曲譜本による近世京都アクセントの史的研究** ¥9,800
鳥越 皓之 編著 **霞ヶ浦の環境と水辺の暮らし** パートナーシップ的発展論の可能性 ¥6,500	YOSHINO, Ayako 著 **Pageant Fever** Local History and Consumerism in Edwardian England　¥6,500
山内 晴子 著 **朝河貫一論** その学問形成と実践 ¥8,900	河西 宏祐 著 **全契約社員の正社員化** 私鉄広電支部・混迷から再生へ (1993年～2009年)　¥6,100
金 孝淑 著 **源氏物語の言葉と異国** ¥4,900	市川 熹 著 **対話のことばの科学** プロソディが支えるコミュニケーション ¥5,600
鈴木 勘一郎 著 **経営変革と組織ダイナミズム** 組織アライメントの研究 ¥5,500	伊藤 りさ 著 **人形浄瑠璃のドラマツルギー** 近松以降の浄瑠璃作者と平家物語 ¥7,400
佐藤 洋一 著 **帝政期のウラジオストク** 市街地形成の歴史的研究 ¥9,300	石濱 裕美子 著 **清朝とチベット仏教** 菩薩王となった乾隆帝 ¥7,000

黒崎 剛 著 **ヘーゲル・未完の弁証法** 「意識の経験の学」としての『精神現象学』の批判的研究　　　　¥12,000	渡邉 将智 著 **後漢政治制度の研究** 　　　　¥8,400
片木 淳 著 **日独比較研究 市町村合併** 平成の大合併はなぜ進展したか？　　　　¥6,500	石井 裕晶 著 **制度変革の政治経済過程** 戦前期日本における営業税廃税運動の研究　　　　¥8,500
SUZUKI, Rieko 著 **Negotiating History** From Romanticism to Victorianism　　　　¥5,900	森 佳子 著 **オッフェンバックと大衆芸術** パリジャンが愛した夢幻オペレッタ　　　　¥8,200
杵渕 博樹 著 **人類は原子力で滅亡した** ギュンター・グラスと『女ねずみ』　　　　¥6,600	北山 夕華 著 **英国のシティズンシップ教育** 社会的包摂の試み　　　　¥5,400
奥野 武志 著 **兵式体操成立史の研究** 　　　　¥7,900	UENO, Yoshio 著 **An Automodular View of English Grammar** 　　　　¥8,400
井黒 忍 著 **分水と支配** 金・モンゴル時代華北の水利と農業　　　　¥8,400	森 祐司 著 **地域銀行の経営行動** 変革期の対応　　　　¥6,800
岩佐 壯四郎 著 **島村抱月の文藝批評と美学理論** 　　　　¥10,000	竹中 晃二 著 **アクティブ・ライフスタイルの構築** 身体活動・運動の行動変容研究　　　　¥7,600
高橋 弘幸 著 **企業競争力と人材技能** 三井物産創業半世紀の経営分析　　　　¥8,200	岩田 圭一 著 **アリストテレスの存在論** 〈実体〉とは何か　　　　¥8,300
高橋 勝幸 著 **アジア冷戦に挑んだ平和運動** タイ共産党の統一戦線活動と大衆参加　　　　¥7,900	渡邉 詞男 著 **格差社会の住宅政策** ミックスト・インカム住宅の可能性　　　　¥4,600
小松 志朗 著 **人道的介入** 秩序と正義，武力と外交　　　　¥4,900	藤岡 典夫 著 **環境リスク管理の法原則** 予防原則と比例原則を中心に　　　　¥6,200

すべて A5 判・価格は税別